THE WONDER YEARS

ISSUES #11-16
WRITER: Jeff Parker
ARTISTS: Nick Dragotta with Colleen Coover
Roger Cruz
Karl Kesel
Patrick Scherberger & Craig Yeung
COLORIST: Val Staples
LETTERER: Blambot's Nate Piekos
COVER ARTISTS: Carlo Pagulayan with Christina Strain
Roger Cruz with Guru eFX & Val Staples
Patrick Scherberger with Val Staples
ASSISTANT EDITOR: Nathan Cosby
EDITOR: Mark Paniccia

GIANT-SIZE SPECIAL #1
WRITERS: Jeff Parker with Roger Langridge
ARTISTS: Jeff Parker & Kevin Nowlan
Dean Haspiel
David Williams & Tim Townsend
Nick Kilislian
Roger Langridge
Michael Cho
COLORISTS: Brad Anderson, Michael Cavallaro, Val Staples & Michael Cho
LETTERER: Blambot's Nate Piekos
COVER ARTISTS: Jeff Parker with Kevin Nowlan & Brad Anderson
CONSULTING EDITORS: Mark Paniccia & Ralph Macchio
EDITOR: Nathan Cosby

COLLECTION EDITOR: Cory Levine
EDITORIAL ASSISTANT: Alex Starbuck
ASSISTANT EDITOR: John Denning
EDITORS, SPECIAL PROJECTS: Jennifer Grünwald & Mark D. Beazley
SENIOR EDITOR, SPECIAL PROJECTS: Jeff Youngquist
SENIOR VICE PRESIDENT OF SALES: David Gabriel
PRODUCTION: Carrie Beadle & Jerry Kalinowski

EDITOR IN CHIEF: Joe Quesada
PUBLISHER: Dan Buckley

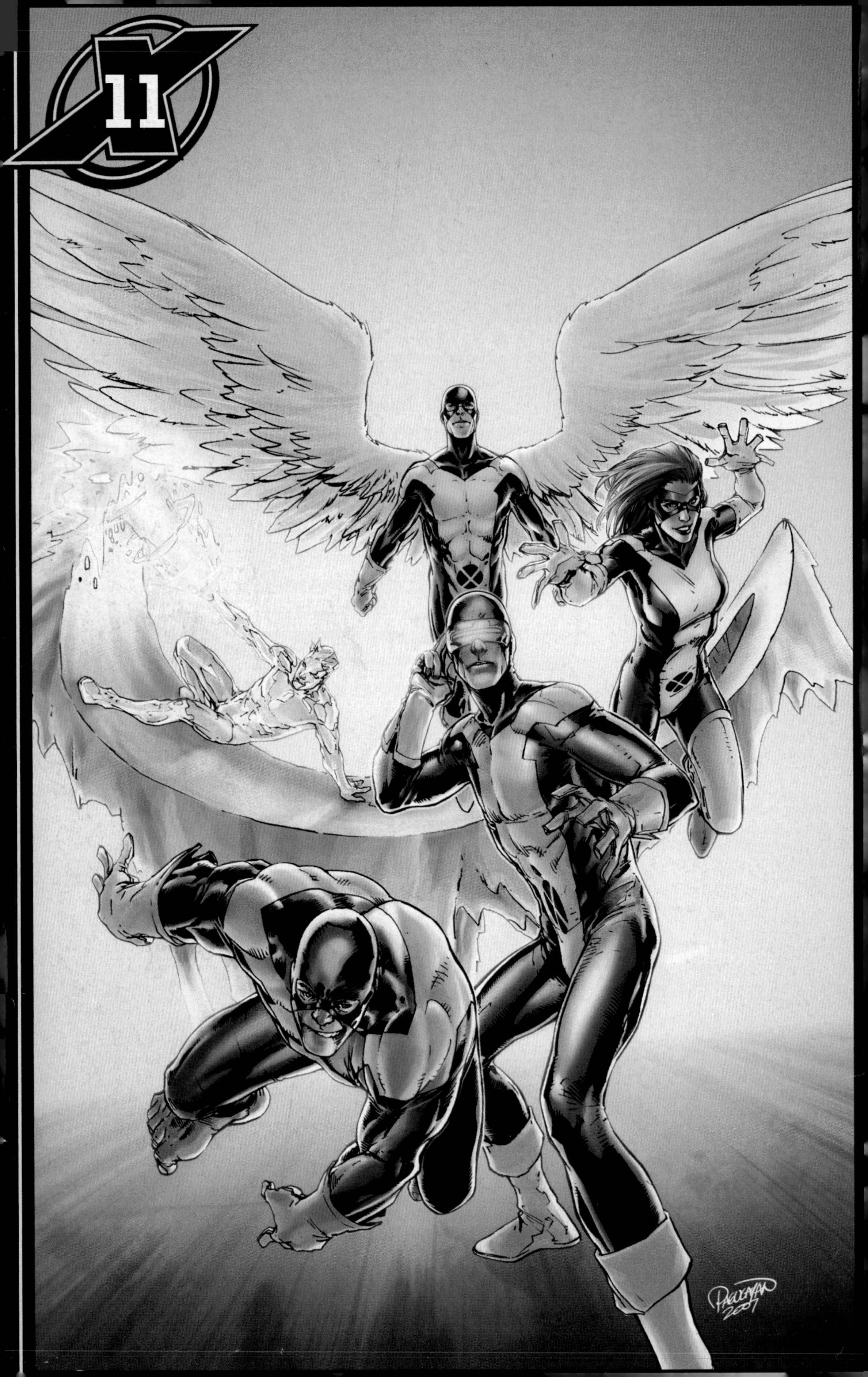
11

G.O.O.M.

GUARDIANS OF OLD MARVEL

Senior Editor Doyle Cubbins
Editorial Treasurer Marin Stevens
Editorial Producer Kell Pabst

The APA for Serious Comics Readers

KELL'S LONGBOX

ITEM! Big news here at Continuity Castle—it's our ONE YEAR ANNIVERSARY of publishing the official Continuiteen 'Zine! (Co-Editor Note: the term APA is preferred, but we'll relax the standards this once for Kell's understandable enthusiasm—Doyle) An **EGO THE LIVING PLANET**-sized **thanks** to all of you who have joined our circulation in record numbers over the past few months! We promise to keep bringing you all the senses-shattering content and insider news you've come to expect!

HEARD AROUND TOWN: Our favorite web-slinger might be going for a new, **darker** look this Fall! * Any gals going on dates with DAREDEVIL might want to wear an **adamantium blouse**—just sayin'! What would you true believers say to the notion of LADY HULK smashing around soon...?

ITEM! Budget-conscious comic lovers, do you feel your Spidey Sense tingling? That's because your favorite comics are about to go up to a DOLLAR in eight months! We here at the Continuity Castle are as concerned as you! Now sure, this will go along with some nice improvements in quality—Marin for one, can't wait to see the Heavenly Halls of Asgard in flexographic color on BAXTER PAPER!

ITEM! Ravenous ROGER CRUZ is rested up from his vacation and returning soon to draw more X-MEN FIRST CLASS! As you may know, The Continuiteens have some serious issues (and back issues!) with this book because it sometimes stretches the parameters of what was clearly established in the original series—nonetheless, if it must exist, we're glad to have the Brazilian Bomber back at the art desk!

CONTINUITY ABOVE ALL

MARIN'S MAILBAG

Okay gang—HOW do you do it? Do you sit in on the Mighty Marvel Meetings? You seem to know what's coming up in every comic—and even in the real lives of our fave heroes in tights! I thought your "item" about THE AVENGERS battling Ultron referred to an upcoming book, and then it happened last week in Central Park! C'mon, what gives..?!

THE MAD MAPLE
Ontario, Canada

Just lucky, I guess!- M

Sayyy... you three said that Iron Man would be adding jet-skates to his next model of armor, yet as of press time, he ALREADY had been using the jet-skates. By Odin's Errant Eye, I think I've finally caught you in a slip-up! Do I get a No Prize?

Kurtis Busiek
Boston, MA

*Check again, young Busiek. We said REMOVING the jet-skates. So you don't get a No Prize, but we will say this: All your comics knowledge is going to serve you **very well** in your future work!-M*

Hey Warriors Three, I finally got my driver's license! What's the best car for super fan like me to head to the LCS on Wednesdays with?

Dusty Abel
Los Angeles, CA

Dusty, we highly recommend a 1975 AMC Gremlin. You'll get excellent gas mileage, which will leave more of your budget to pursue our favorite hobby. But the real attraction is the rear hatchback area, which can hold SIX longboxes and ONE shortbox. I think Reed Richards based his designs for the Fantasticar on this incredible auto! -M

Marin! I found one of these little booklets over at my Mother's house, and it has your name in it! I thought you were cutting back on this funny book thing to make more time for ME. I'll let it slide this time, but if you want to make a serious commitment to me, something is going to have to go!

Jenn D.
Yonkers, NY

Okay Doyle, now come on. We cannot run this, this has nothing to do with comics. Don't overrule me on this.-M

—Sorry Marin, the letter falls under our print policy, and... she made me promise to run it. I hear girls like kittens, why don't you smooth things over with a purring present?- Doyle

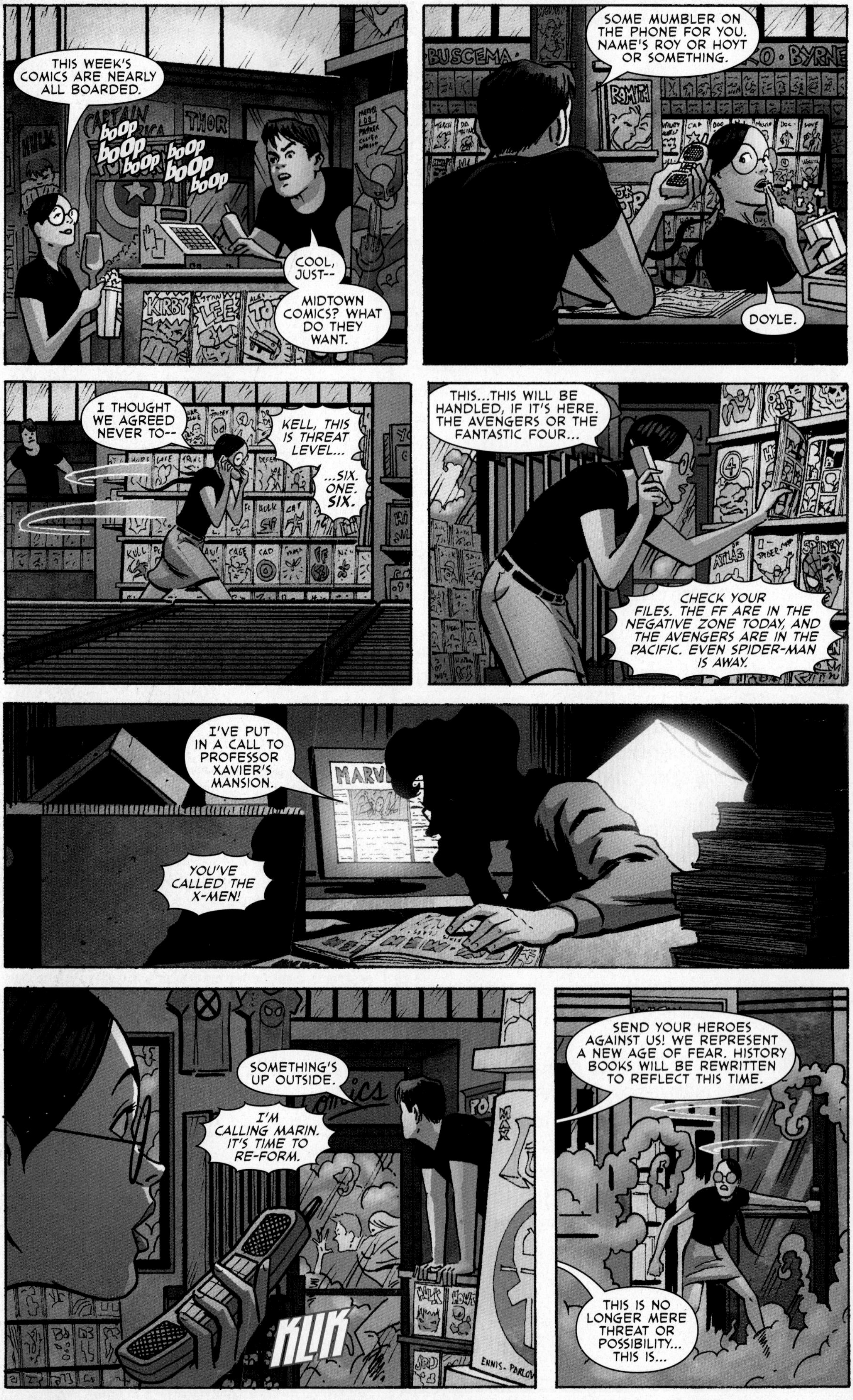
THIS WEEK'S COMICS ARE NEARLY ALL BOARDED.
boop boop boop boop boop boop
COOL, JUST--
MIDTOWN COMICS? WHAT DO THEY WANT.
SOME MUMBLER ON THE PHONE FOR YOU. NAME'S ROY OR HOYT OR SOMETHING.
DOYLE.
I THOUGHT WE AGREED NEVER TO--
KELL, THIS IS THREAT LEVEL...
...SIX. ONE. SIX.
THIS...THIS WILL BE HANDLED, IF IT'S HERE. THE AVENGERS OR THE FANTASTIC FOUR...
CHECK YOUR FILES. THE FF ARE IN THE NEGATIVE ZONE TODAY, AND THE AVENGERS ARE IN THE PACIFIC. EVEN SPIDER-MAN IS AWAY.
I'VE PUT IN A CALL TO PROFESSOR XAVIER'S MANSION.
YOU'VE CALLED THE X-MEN!
SOMETHING'S UP OUTSIDE.
I'M CALLING MARIN. IT'S TIME TO RE-FORM.
KLIK
SEND YOUR HEROES AGAINST US! WE REPRESENT A NEW AGE OF FEAR. HISTORY BOOKS WILL BE REWRITTEN TO REFLECT THIS TIME.
THIS IS NO LONGER MERE THREAT OR POSSIBILITY... THIS IS...

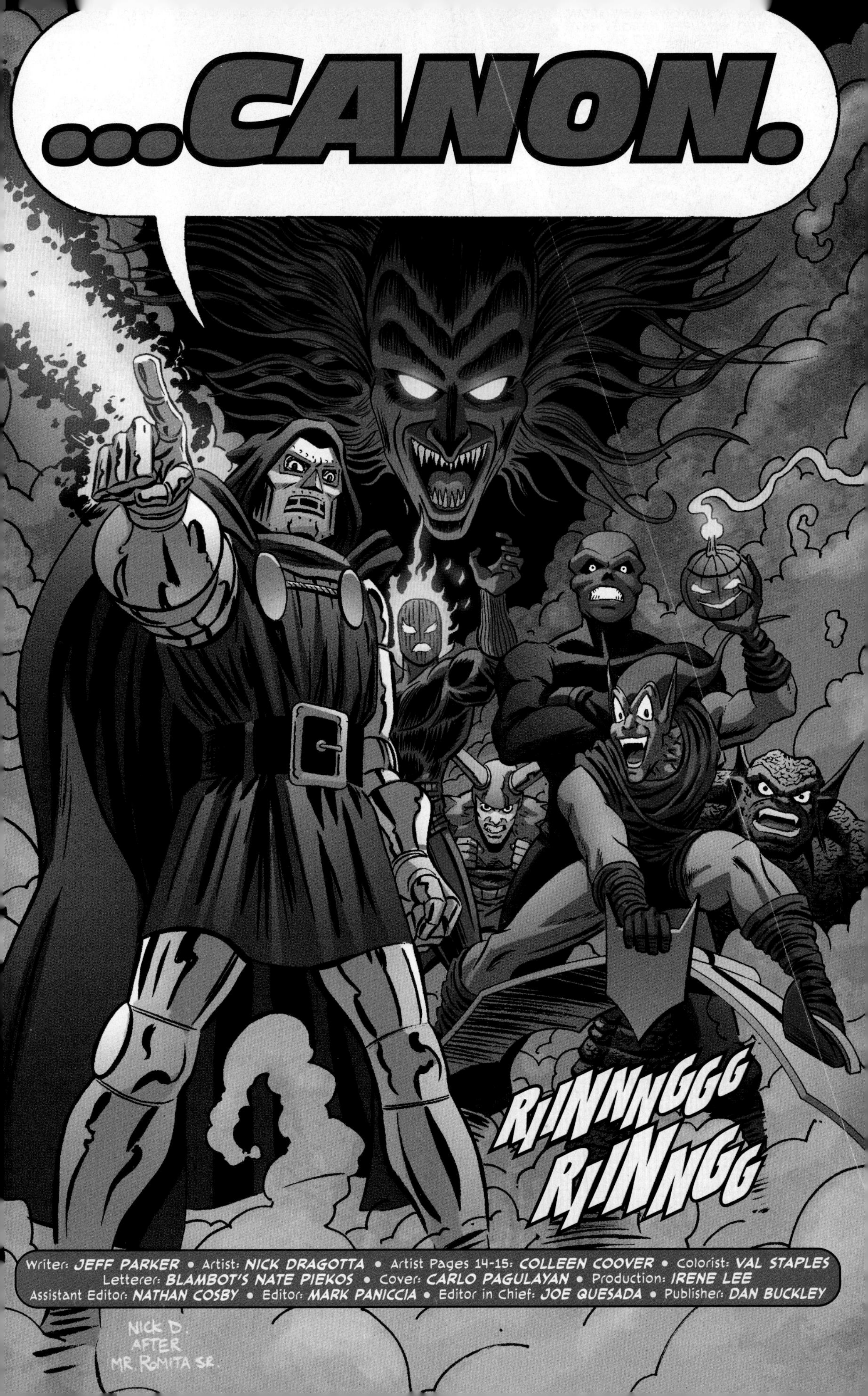
...CANON.
RINNNGGG
RINNGG
Writer: JEFF PARKER • Artist: NICK DRAGOTTA • Artist Pages 14-15: COLLEEN COOVER • Colorist: VAL STAPLES
Letterer: BLAMBOT'S NATE PIEKOS • Cover: CARLO PAGULAYAN • Production: IRENE LEE
Assistant Editor: NATHAN COSBY • Editor: MARK PANICCIA • Editor in Chief: JOE QUESADA • Publisher: DAN BUCKLEY
NICK D. AFTER MR. ROMITA SR.

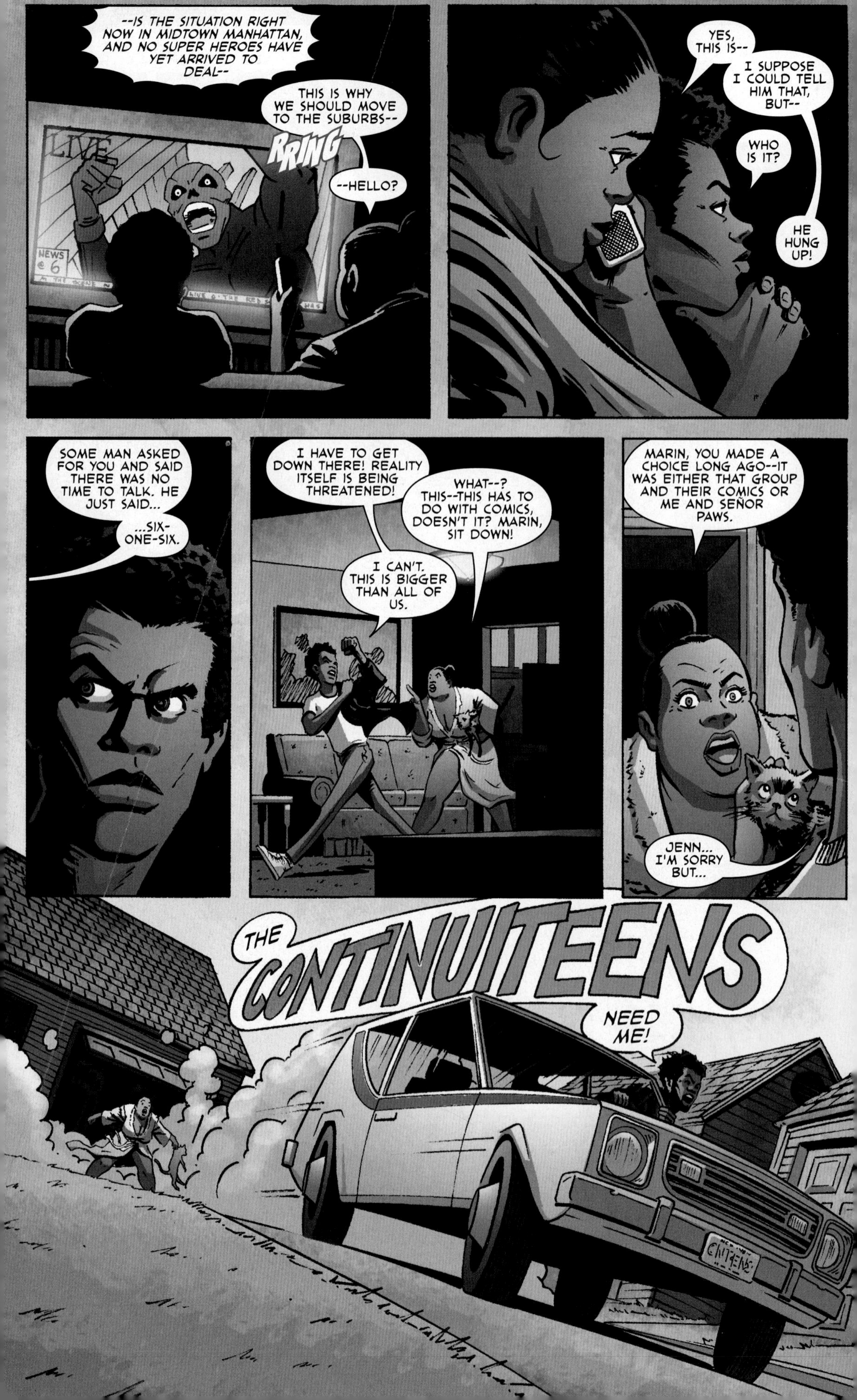

--IS THE SITUATION RIGHT NOW IN MIDTOWN MANHATTAN, AND NO SUPER HEROES HAVE YET ARRIVED TO DEAL--
LIVE
NEWS @ 6
THIS IS WHY WE SHOULD MOVE TO THE SUBURBS--
RRING
--HELLO?
YES, THIS IS--
I SUPPOSE I COULD TELL HIM THAT, BUT--
WHO IS IT?
HE HUNG UP!
SOME MAN ASKED FOR YOU AND SAID THERE WAS NO TIME TO TALK. HE JUST SAID...
...SIX-ONE-SIX.
I HAVE TO GET DOWN THERE! REALITY ITSELF IS BEING THREATENED!
WHAT--? THIS--THIS HAS TO DO WITH COMICS, DOESN'T IT? MARIN, SIT DOWN!
I CAN'T. THIS IS BIGGER THAN ALL OF US.
MARIN, YOU MADE A CHOICE LONG AGO--IT WAS EITHER THAT GROUP AND THEIR COMICS OR ME AND SEÑOR PAWS.
JENN... I'M SORRY BUT...
THE CONTINUITEENS
NEED ME!

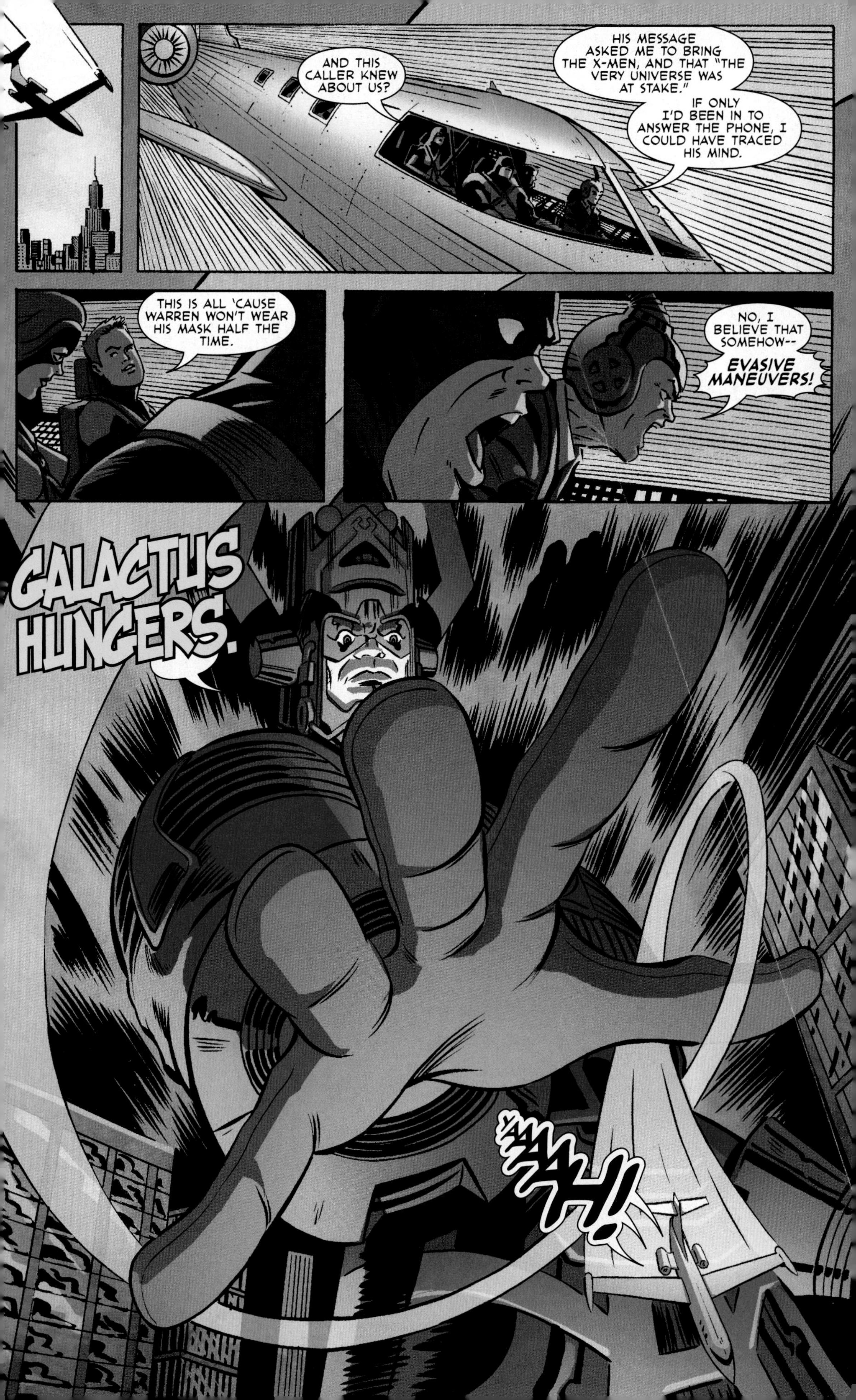
AND THIS CALLER KNEW ABOUT US?
HIS MESSAGE ASKED ME TO BRING THE X-MEN, AND THAT "THE VERY UNIVERSE WAS AT STAKE."
IF ONLY I'D BEEN IN TO ANSWER THE PHONE, I COULD HAVE TRACED HIS MIND.
THIS IS ALL 'CAUSE WARREN WON'T WEAR HIS MASK HALF THE TIME.
NO, I BELIEVE THAT SOMEHOW-- *EVASIVE MANEUVERS!*
GALACTUS HUNGERS.
YAAAAAAH!

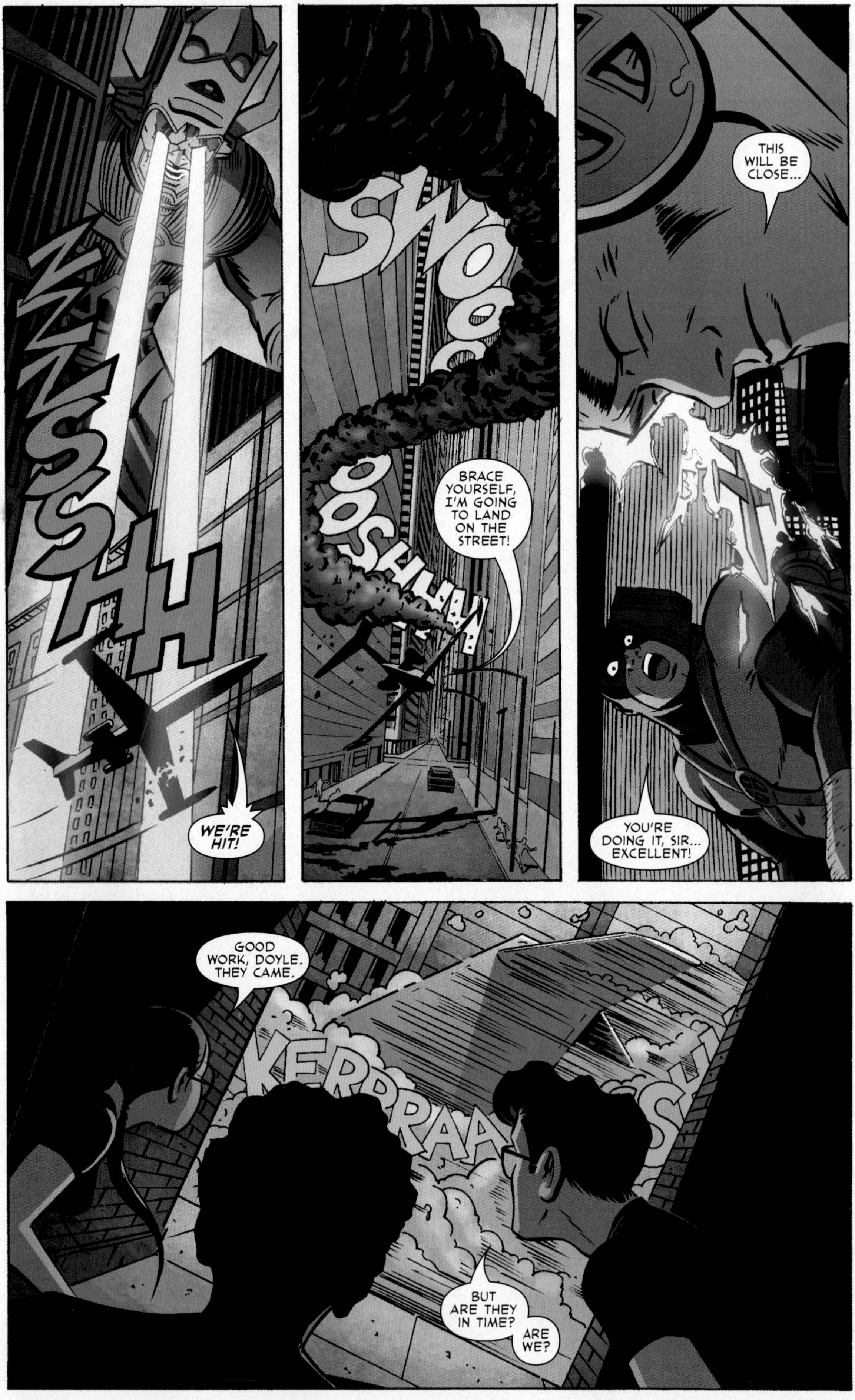

NNNSSHH
WE'RE HIT!
SWOOSHHH
BRACE YOURSELF, I'M GOING TO LAND ON THE STREET!
THIS WILL BE CLOSE...
YOU'RE DOING IT, SIR... EXCELLENT!
GOOD WORK, DOYLE. THEY CAME.
KERRAA
BUT ARE THEY IN TIME?
ARE WE?

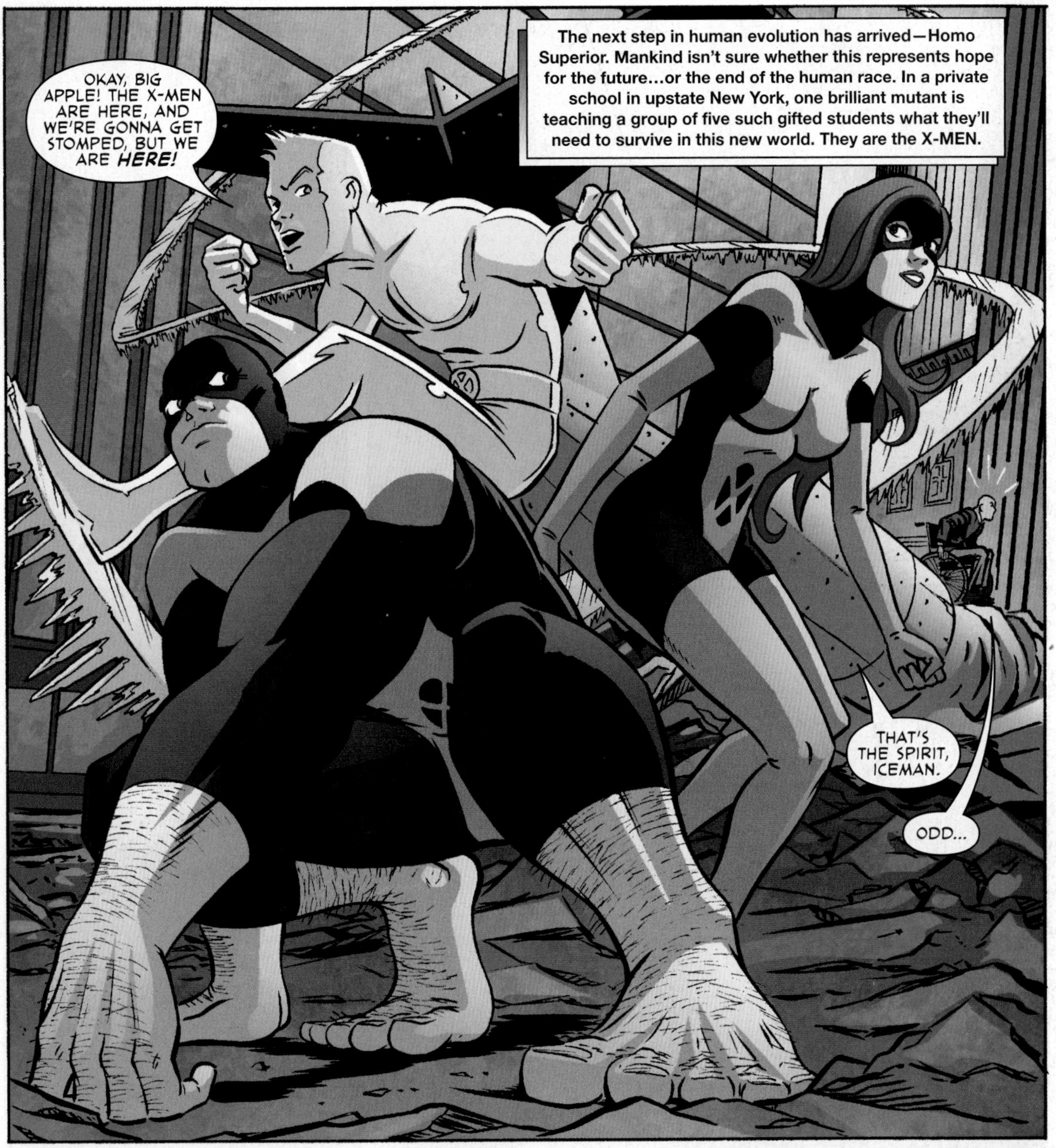
The next step in human evolution has arrived—Homo Superior. Mankind isn't sure whether this represents hope for the future…or the end of the human race. In a private school in upstate New York, one brilliant mutant is teaching a group of five such gifted students what they'll need to survive in this new world. They are the X-MEN.
OKAY, BIG APPLE! THE X-MEN ARE HERE, AND WE'RE GONNA GET STOMPED, BUT WE ARE *HERE!*
THAT'S THE SPIRIT, ICEMAN.
ODD...

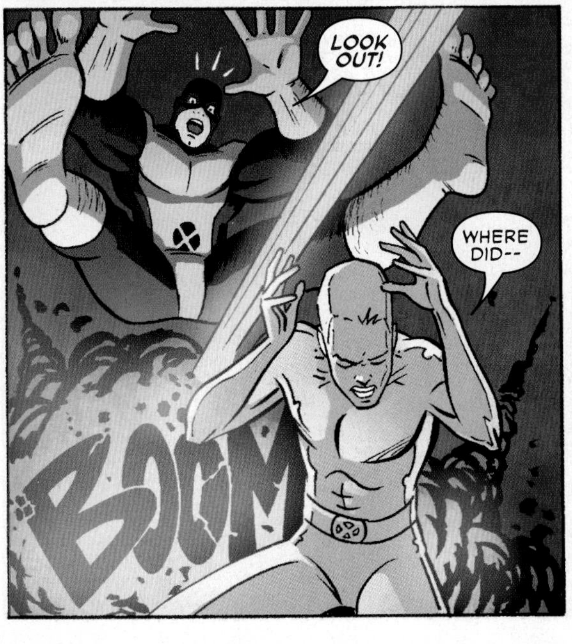
LOOK OUT!
WHERE DID--
BOOM

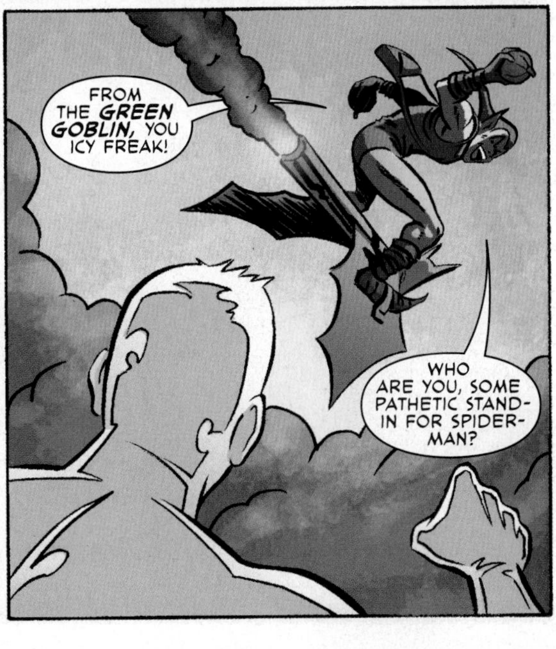
FROM THE *GREEN GOBLIN,* YOU ICY FREAK!
WHO ARE YOU, SOME PATHETIC STAND-IN FOR SPIDER-MAN?

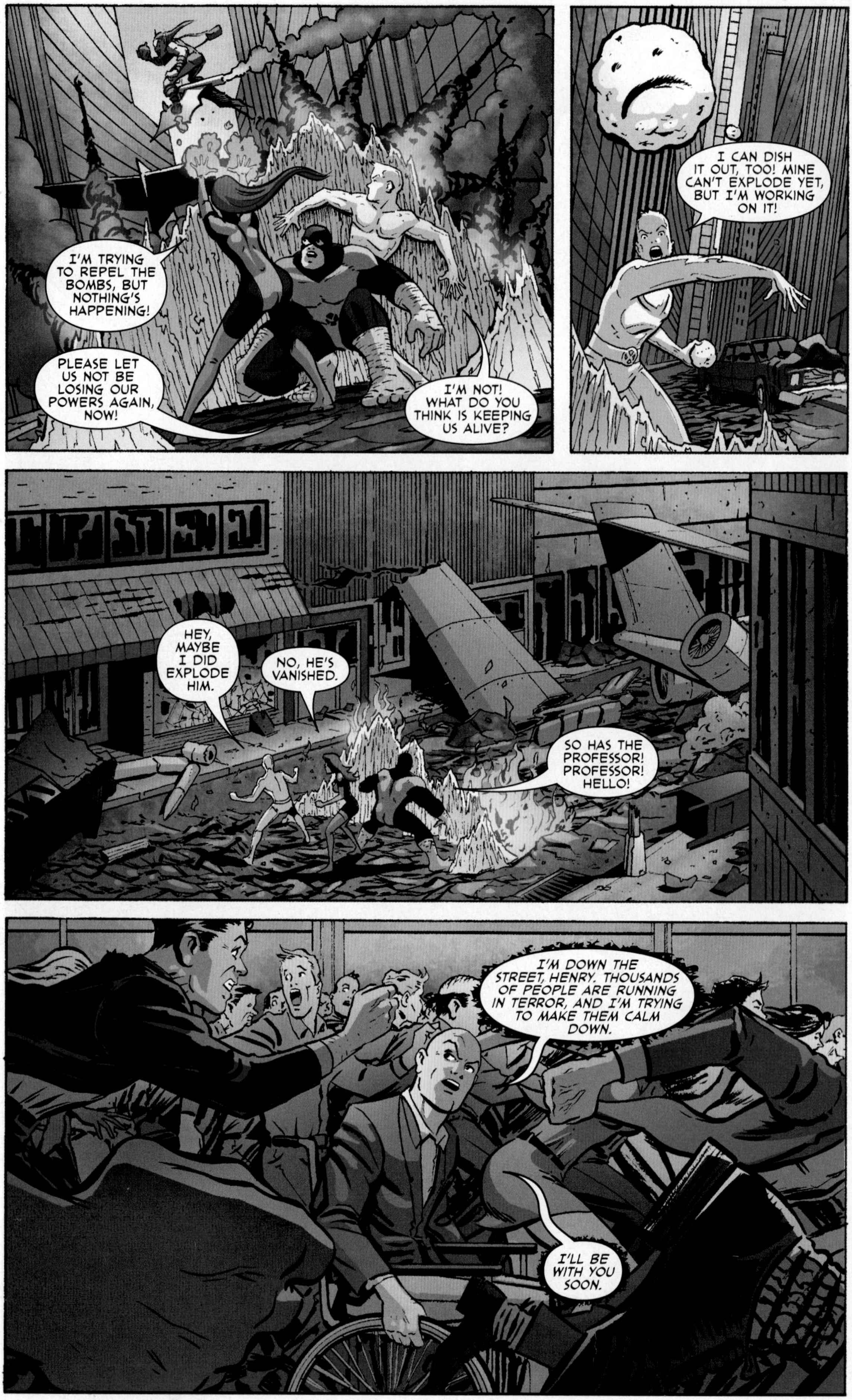
I'M TRYING TO REPEL THE BOMBS, BUT NOTHING'S HAPPENING!
PLEASE LET US NOT BE LOSING OUR POWERS AGAIN, NOW!
I'M NOT! WHAT DO YOU THINK IS KEEPING US ALIVE?
I CAN DISH IT OUT, TOO! MINE CAN'T EXPLODE YET, BUT I'M WORKING ON IT!
HEY, MAYBE I DID EXPLODE HIM.
NO, HE'S VANISHED.
SO HAS THE PROFESSOR! PROFESSOR! HELLO!
I'M DOWN THE STREET, HENRY. THOUSANDS OF PEOPLE ARE RUNNING IN TERROR, AND I'M TRYING TO MAKE THEM CALM DOWN.
I'LL BE WITH YOU SOON.

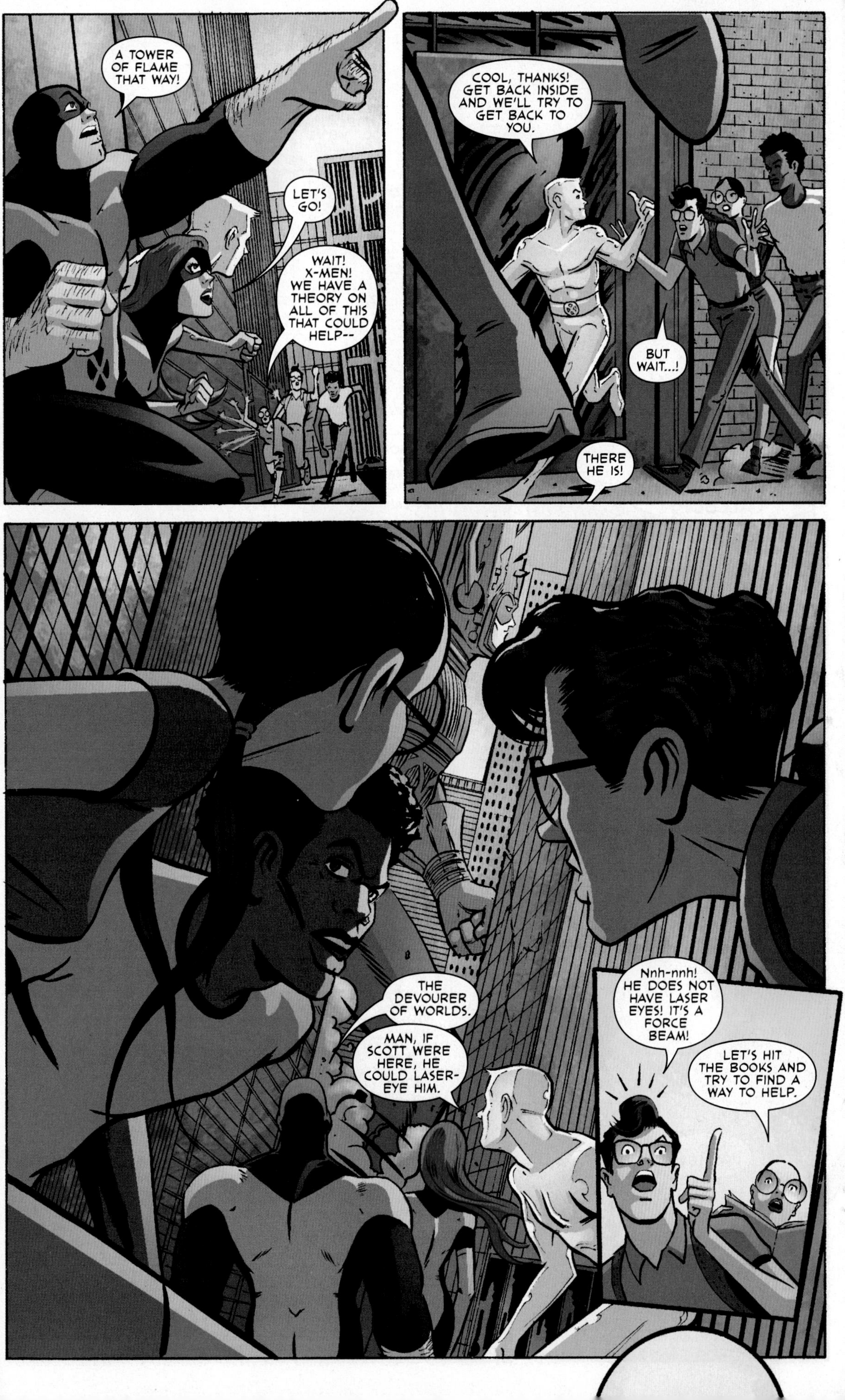
A TOWER OF FLAME THAT WAY!
LET'S GO!
WAIT! X-MEN! WE HAVE A THEORY ON ALL OF THIS THAT COULD HELP--
COOL, THANKS! GET BACK INSIDE AND WE'LL TRY TO GET BACK TO YOU.
BUT WAIT...!
THERE HE IS!
THE DEVOURER OF WORLDS.
MAN, IF SCOTT WERE HERE, HE COULD LASER-EYE HIM.
Nnh-nnh! HE DOES NOT HAVE LASER EYES! IT'S A FORCE BEAM!
LET'S HIT THE BOOKS AND TRY TO FIND A WAY TO HELP.

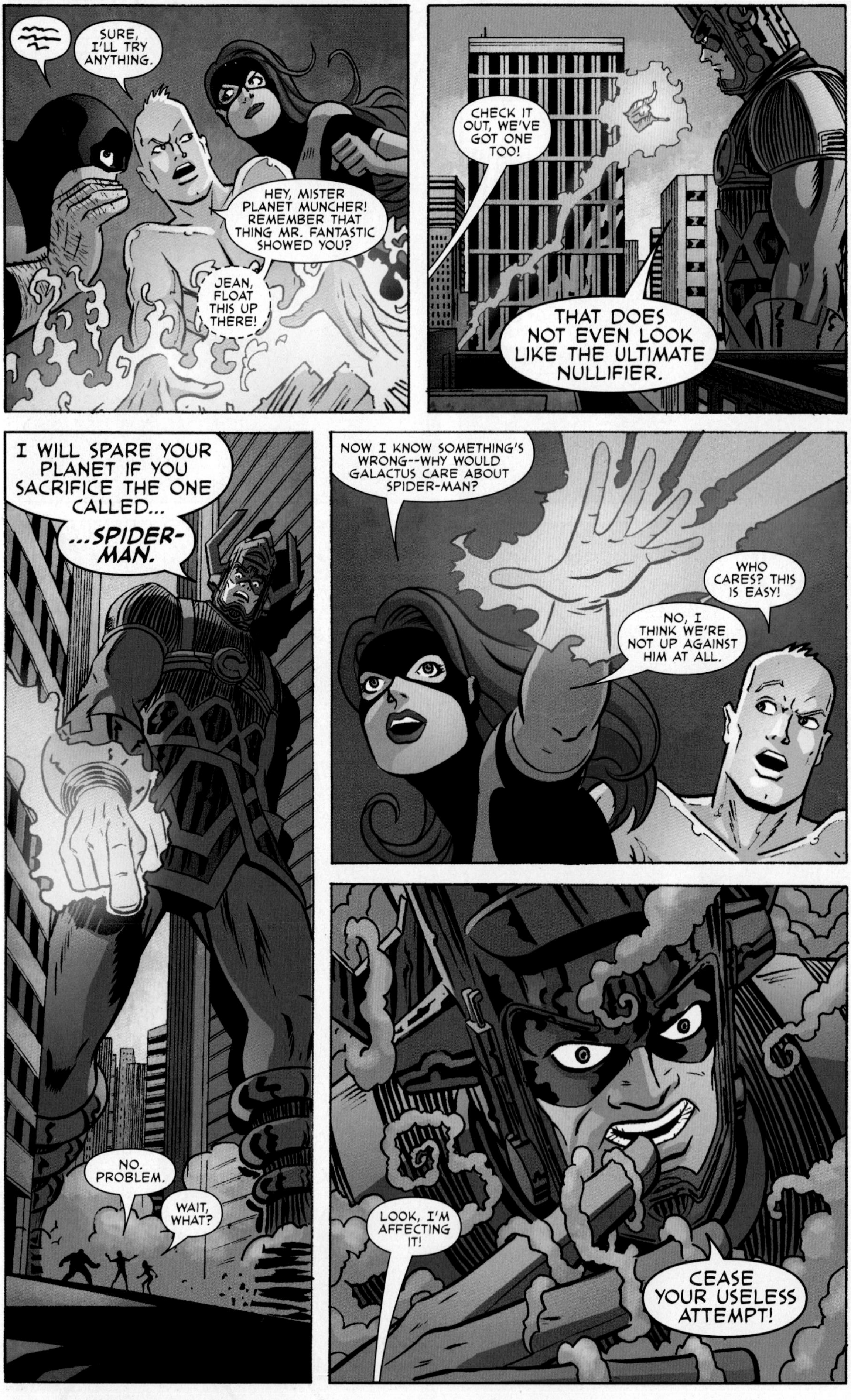
SURE, I'LL TRY ANYTHING.
HEY, MISTER PLANET MUNCHER! REMEMBER THAT THING MR. FANTASTIC SHOWED YOU?
JEAN, FLOAT THIS UP THERE!
CHECK IT OUT, WE'VE GOT ONE TOO!
THAT DOES NOT EVEN LOOK LIKE THE ULTIMATE NULLIFIER.
I WILL SPARE YOUR PLANET IF YOU SACRIFICE THE ONE CALLED...
...SPIDER-MAN.
NO. PROBLEM.
WAIT, WHAT?
NOW I KNOW SOMETHING'S WRONG--WHY WOULD GALACTUS CARE ABOUT SPIDER-MAN?
WHO CARES? THIS IS EASY!
NO, I THINK WE'RE NOT UP AGAINST HIM AT ALL.
LOOK, I'M AFFECTING IT!
CEASE YOUR USELESS ATTEMPT!

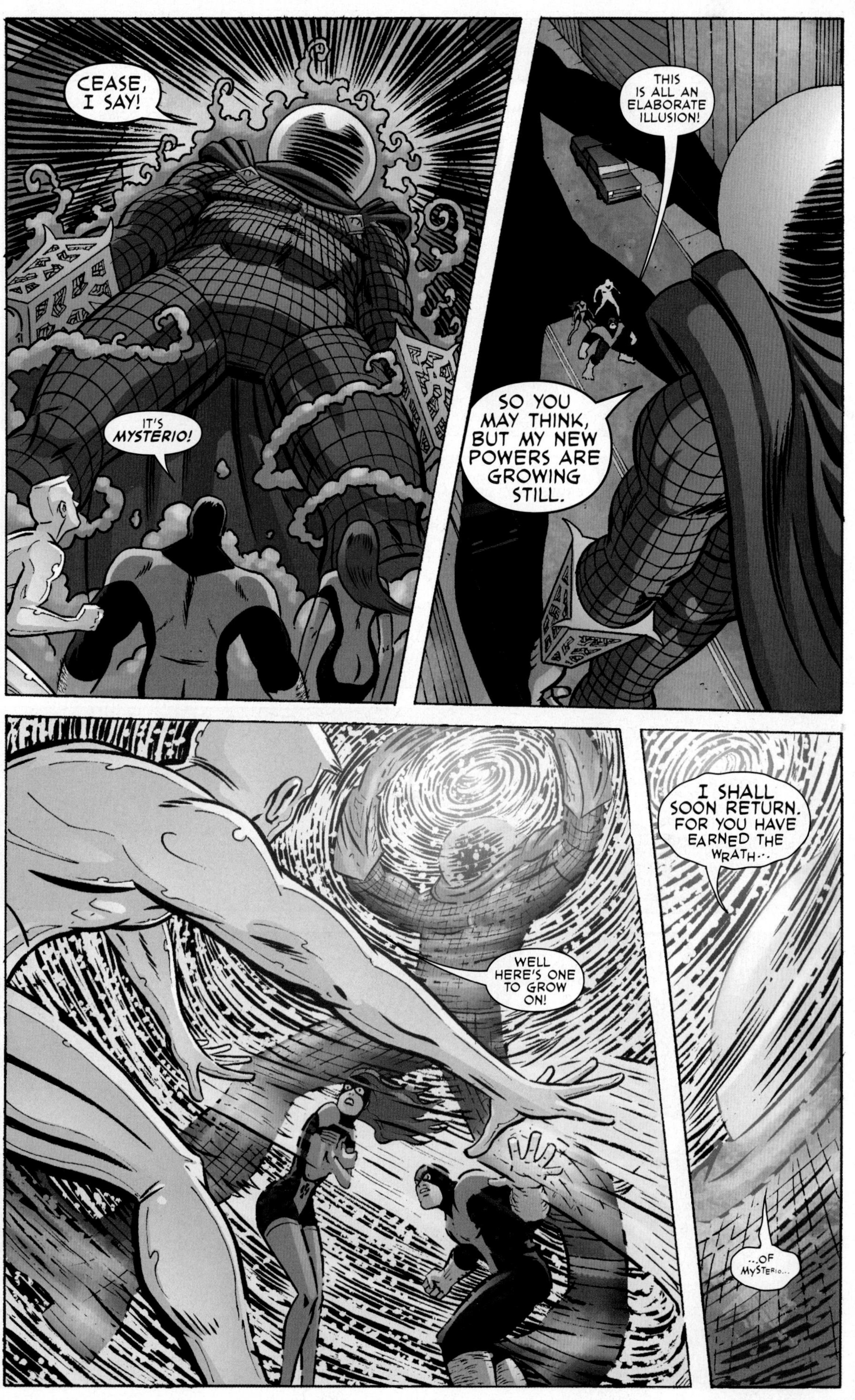
CEASE, I SAY!
IT'S MYSTERIO!
THIS IS ALL AN ELABORATE ILLUSION!
SO YOU MAY THINK, BUT MY NEW POWERS ARE GROWING STILL.
WELL HERE'S ONE TO GROW ON!
I SHALL SOON RETURN. FOR YOU HAVE EARNED THE WRATH...
...OF MYSTERIO...

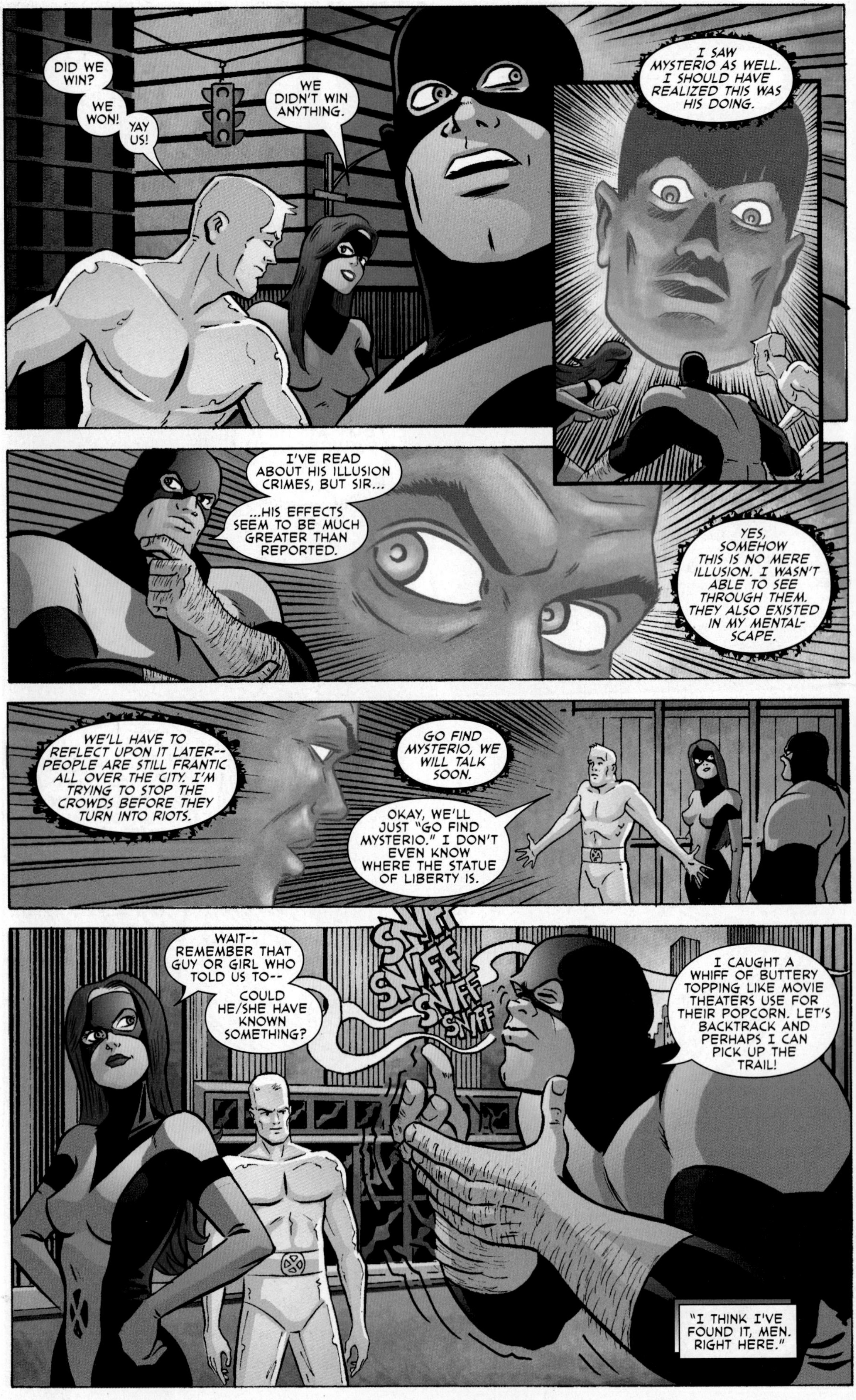

DID WE WIN?
WE WON!
YAY US!
WE DIDN'T WIN ANYTHING.
I SAW MYSTERIO AS WELL. I SHOULD HAVE REALIZED THIS WAS HIS DOING.
I'VE READ ABOUT HIS ILLUSION CRIMES, BUT SIR...
...HIS EFFECTS SEEM TO BE MUCH GREATER THAN REPORTED.
YES, SOMEHOW THIS IS NO MERE ILLUSION. I WASN'T ABLE TO SEE THROUGH THEM. THEY ALSO EXISTED IN MY MENTAL-SCAPE.
WE'LL HAVE TO REFLECT UPON IT LATER-- PEOPLE ARE STILL FRANTIC ALL OVER THE CITY. I'M TRYING TO STOP THE CROWDS BEFORE THEY TURN INTO RIOTS.
GO FIND MYSTERIO, WE WILL TALK SOON.
OKAY, WE'LL JUST "GO FIND MYSTERIO." I DON'T EVEN KNOW WHERE THE STATUE OF LIBERTY IS.
WAIT-- REMEMBER THAT GUY OR GIRL WHO TOLD US TO--
COULD HE/SHE HAVE KNOWN SOMETHING?
SNIFF SNIFF SNIFF SNIFF SNIFF
I CAUGHT A WHIFF OF BUTTERY TOPPING LIKE MOVIE THEATERS USE FOR THEIR POPCORN. LET'S BACKTRACK AND PERHAPS I CAN PICK UP THE TRAIL!
"I THINK I'VE FOUND IT, MEN. RIGHT HERE."

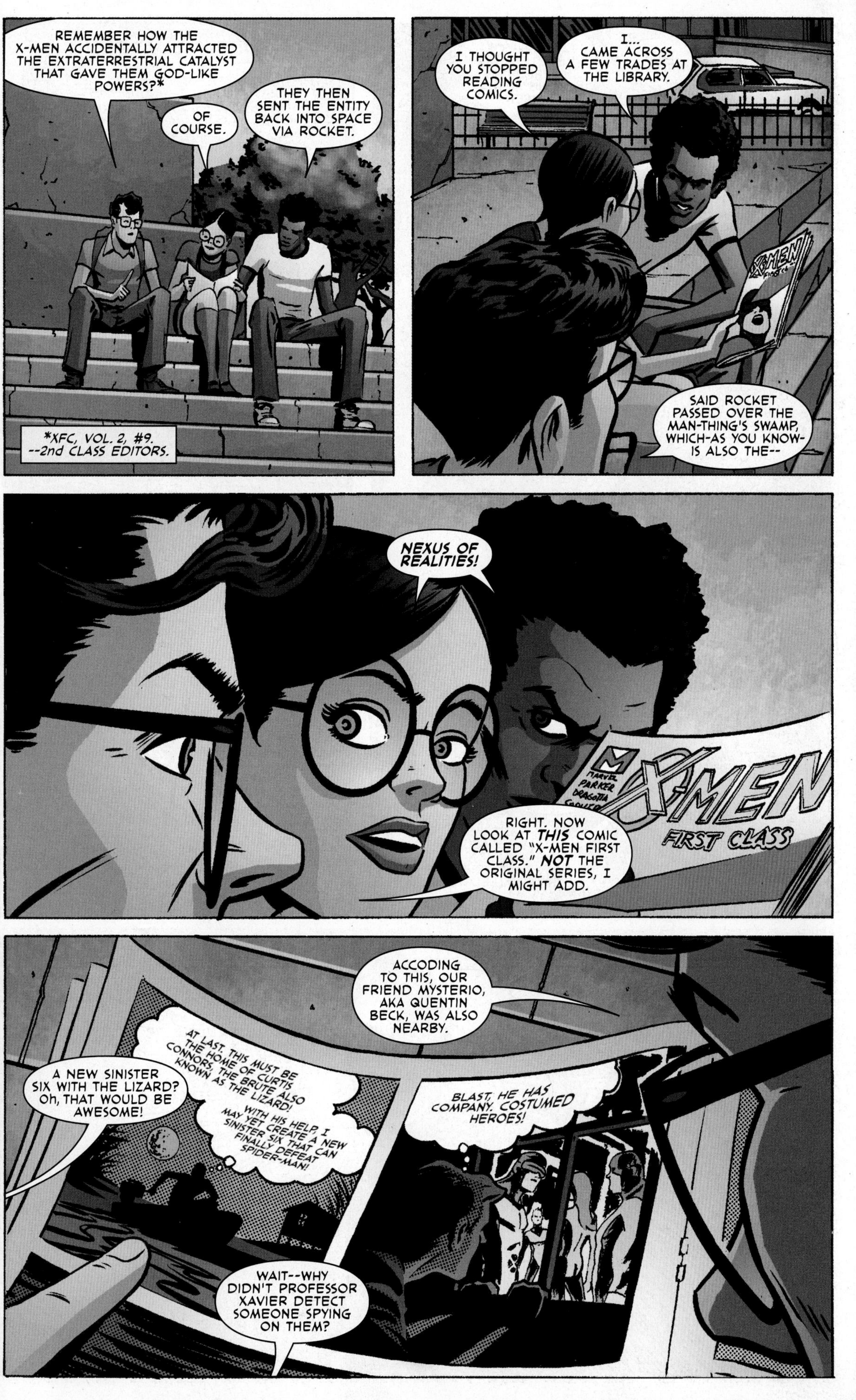
REMEMBER HOW THE X-MEN ACCIDENTALLY ATTRACTED THE EXTRATERRESTRIAL CATALYST THAT GAVE THEM GOD-LIKE POWERS?*
OF COURSE.
THEY THEN SENT THE ENTITY BACK INTO SPACE VIA ROCKET.
*XFC, VOL. 2, #9. --2nd CLASS EDITORS.
I THOUGHT YOU STOPPED READING COMICS.
I... CAME ACROSS A FEW TRADES AT THE LIBRARY.
SAID ROCKET PASSED OVER THE MAN-THING'S SWAMP, WHICH-AS YOU KNOW-IS ALSO THE--
NEXUS OF REALITIES!
X-MEN
FIRST CLASS
MARVEL
PARKER
DRAGOTTA
RIGHT. NOW LOOK AT THIS COMIC CALLED "X-MEN FIRST CLASS." NOT THE ORIGINAL SERIES, I MIGHT ADD.
ACCODING TO THIS, OUR FRIEND MYSTERIO, AKA QUENTIN BECK, WAS ALSO NEARBY.
A NEW SINISTER SIX WITH THE LIZARD? Oh, THAT WOULD BE AWESOME!
AT LAST, THIS MUST BE THE HOME OF CURTIS CONNORS, THE BRUTE ALSO KNOWN AS THE LIZARD!
WITH HIS HELP, I MAY YET CREATE A NEW SINISTER SIX THAT CAN FINALLY DEFEAT SPIDER-MAN!
BLAST, HE HAS COMPANY. COSTUMED HEROES!
WAIT--WHY DIDN'T PROFESSOR XAVIER DETECT SOMEONE SPYING ON THEM?

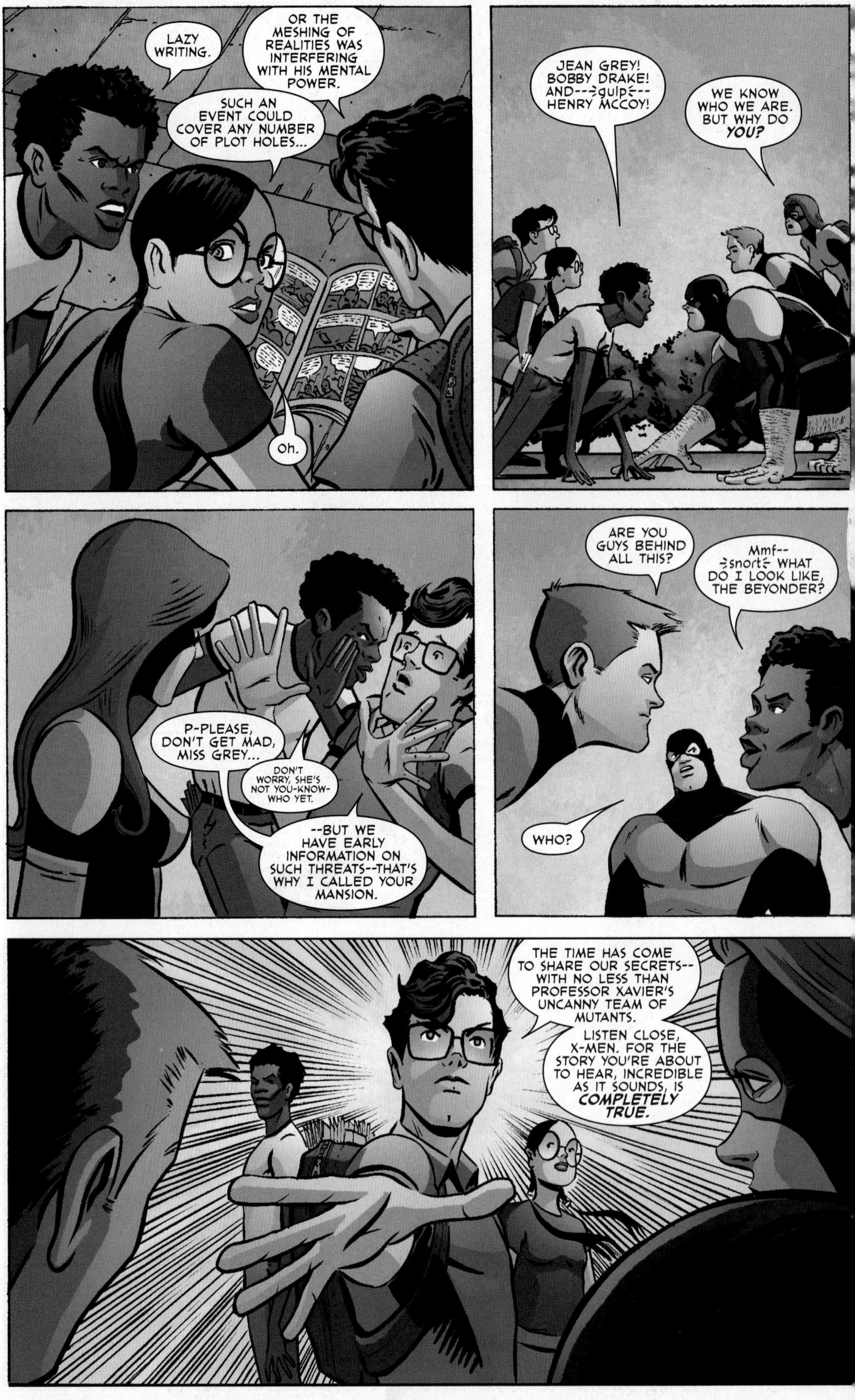
LAZY WRITING.
OR THE MESHING OF REALITIES WAS INTERFERING WITH HIS MENTAL POWER.
SUCH AN EVENT COULD COVER ANY NUMBER OF PLOT HOLES...
Oh.
JEAN GREY! BOBBY DRAKE! AND--⋟gulp⋞--HENRY McCOY!
WE KNOW WHO WE ARE. BUT WHY DO *YOU?*
P-PLEASE, DON'T GET MAD, MISS GREY...
DON'T WORRY, SHE'S NOT YOU-KNOW-WHO YET.
--BUT WE HAVE EARLY INFORMATION ON SUCH THREATS--THAT'S WHY I CALLED YOUR MANSION.
ARE YOU GUYS BEHIND ALL THIS?
Mmf--⋟snort⋞ WHAT DO I LOOK LIKE, THE BEYONDER?
WHO?
THE TIME HAS COME TO SHARE OUR SECRETS--WITH NO LESS THAN PROFESSOR XAVIER'S UNCANNY TEAM OF MUTANTS.
LISTEN CLOSE, X-MEN. FOR THE STORY YOU'RE ABOUT TO HEAR, INCREDIBLE AS IT SOUNDS, IS ***COMPLETELY TRUE.***

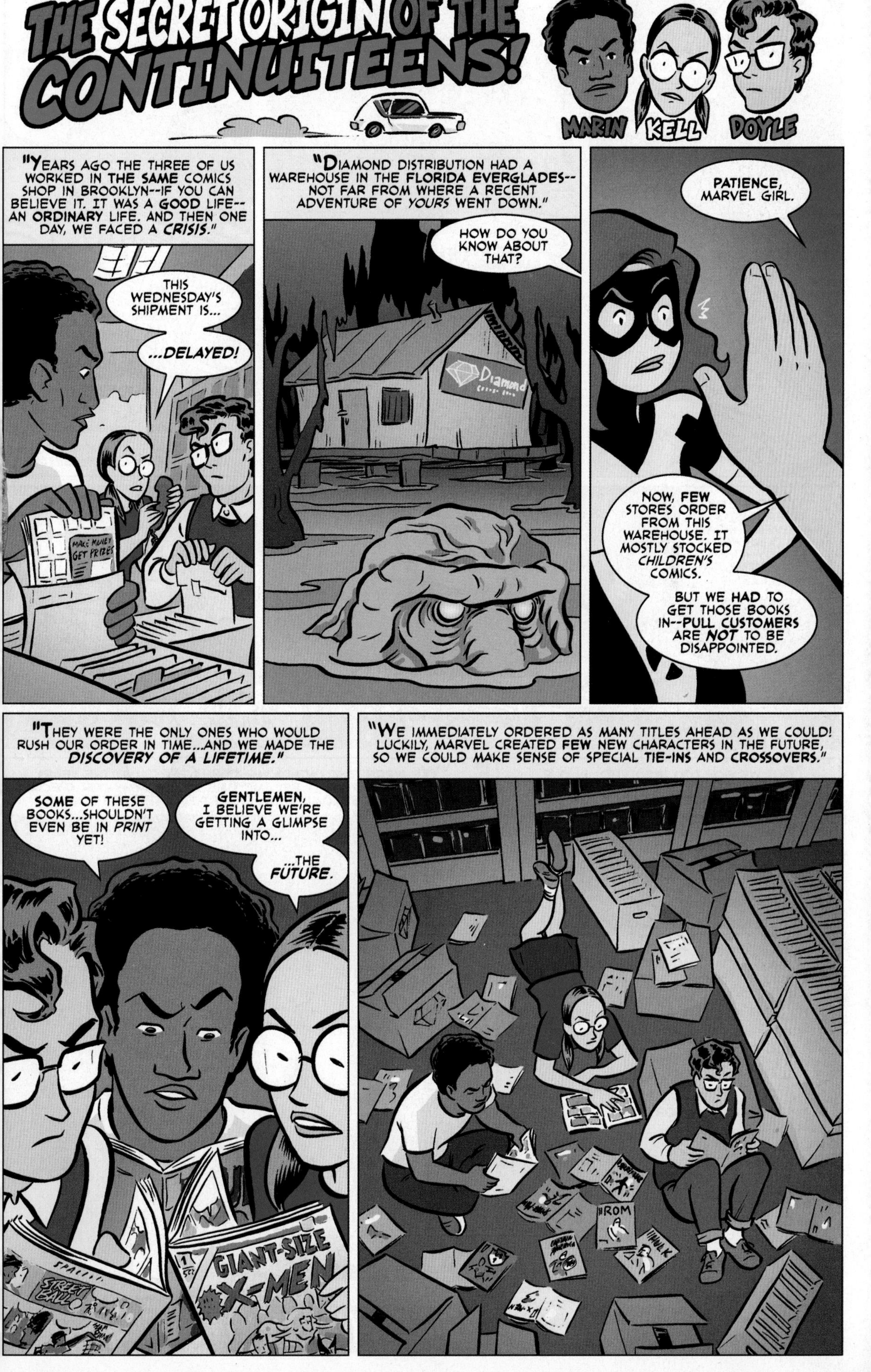
THE SECRET ORIGIN OF THE CONTINUITEENS!
MARIN
KELL
DOYLE
"YEARS AGO THE THREE OF US WORKED IN THE SAME COMICS SHOP IN BROOKLYN--IF YOU CAN BELIEVE IT. IT WAS A GOOD LIFE--AN ORDINARY LIFE. AND THEN ONE DAY, WE FACED A CRISIS."
THIS WEDNESDAY'S SHIPMENT IS...
...DELAYED!
MAKE MONEY GET PRIZES
"DIAMOND DISTRIBUTION HAD A WAREHOUSE IN THE FLORIDA EVERGLADES--NOT FAR FROM WHERE A RECENT ADVENTURE OF YOURS WENT DOWN."
HOW DO YOU KNOW ABOUT THAT?
Diamond
PATIENCE, MARVEL GIRL.
NOW, FEW STORES ORDER FROM THIS WAREHOUSE. IT MOSTLY STOCKED CHILDREN'S COMICS.
BUT WE HAD TO GET THOSE BOOKS IN--PULL CUSTOMERS ARE NOT TO BE DISAPPOINTED.
"THEY WERE THE ONLY ONES WHO WOULD RUSH OUR ORDER IN TIME...AND WE MADE THE DISCOVERY OF A LIFETIME."
SOME OF THESE BOOKS...SHOULDN'T EVEN BE IN PRINT YET!
GENTLEMEN, I BELIEVE WE'RE GETTING A GLIMPSE INTO...
...THE FUTURE.
STREET CALL
GIANT-SIZE X-MEN
"WE IMMEDIATELY ORDERED AS MANY TITLES AHEAD AS WE COULD! LUCKILY, MARVEL CREATED FEW NEW CHARACTERS IN THE FUTURE, SO WE COULD MAKE SENSE OF SPECIAL TIE-INS AND CROSSOVERS."
ROM
HULK

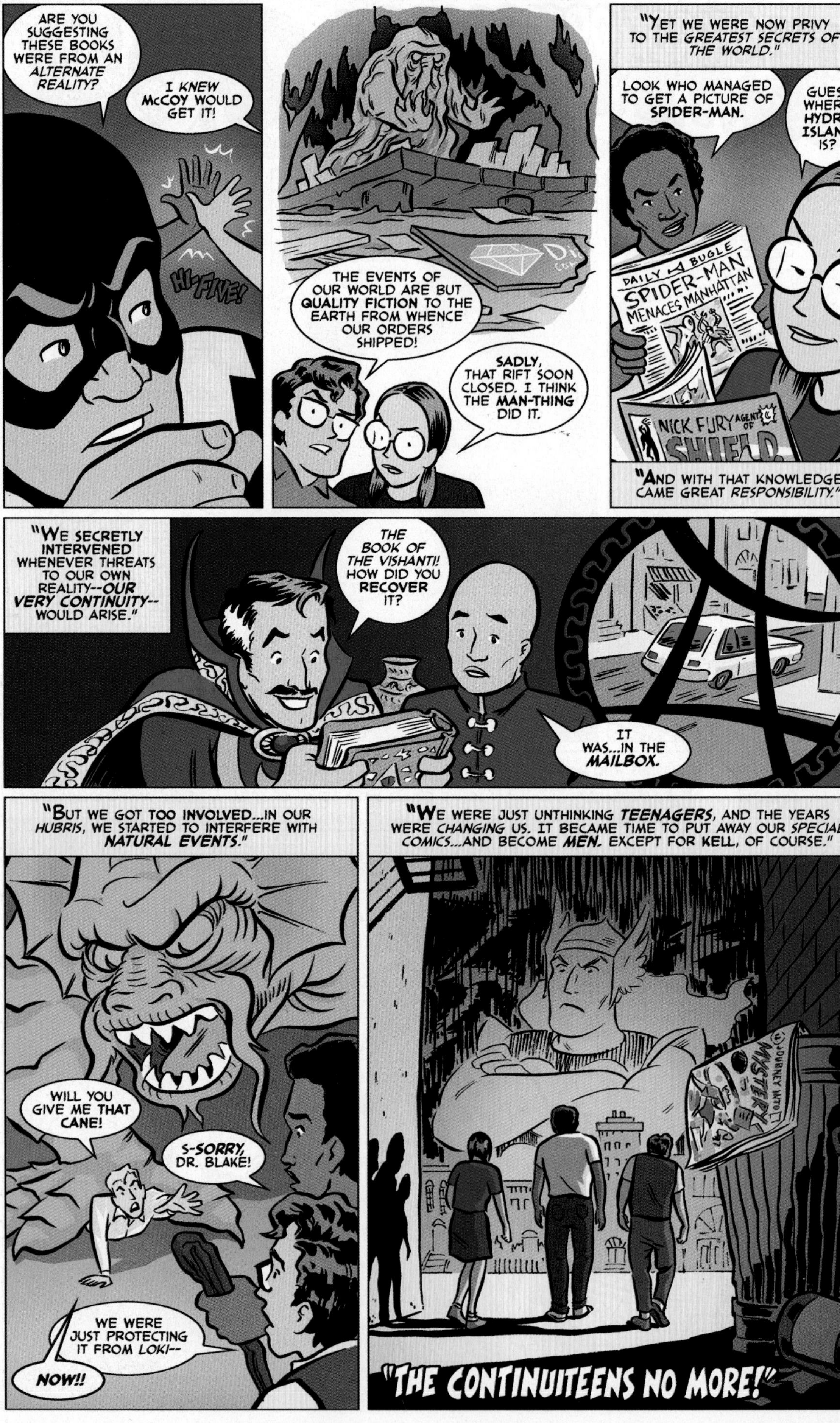

ARE YOU SUGGESTING THESE BOOKS WERE FROM AN ALTERNATE REALITY?
I KNEW McCOY WOULD GET IT!
HI-FIVE!
THE EVENTS OF OUR WORLD ARE BUT QUALITY FICTION TO THE EARTH FROM WHENCE OUR ORDERS SHIPPED!
SADLY, THAT RIFT SOON CLOSED. I THINK THE MAN-THING DID IT.
"YET WE WERE NOW PRIVY TO THE GREATEST SECRETS OF THE WORLD."
LOOK WHO MANAGED TO GET A PICTURE OF SPIDER-MAN.
GUESS WHERE HYDRA ISLAND IS?
DAILY BUGLE
SPIDER-MAN MENACES MANHATTAN
NICK FURY AGENT OF SHIELD
"AND WITH THAT KNOWLEDGE CAME GREAT RESPONSIBILITY."
"WE SECRETLY INTERVENED WHENEVER THREATS TO OUR OWN REALITY--OUR VERY CONTINUITY--WOULD ARISE."
THE BOOK OF THE VISHANTI! HOW DID YOU RECOVER IT?
IT WAS...IN THE MAILBOX.
"BUT WE GOT TOO INVOLVED...IN OUR HUBRIS, WE STARTED TO INTERFERE WITH NATURAL EVENTS."
WILL YOU GIVE ME THAT CANE!
S-SORRY, DR. BLAKE!
WE WERE JUST PROTECTING IT FROM LOKI--
NOW!!
"WE WERE JUST UNTHINKING TEENAGERS, AND THE YEARS WERE CHANGING US. IT BECAME TIME TO PUT AWAY OUR SPECIAL COMICS...AND BECOME MEN. EXCEPT FOR KELL, OF COURSE."
JOURNEY INTO MYSTERY
"THE CONTINUITEENS NO MORE!"

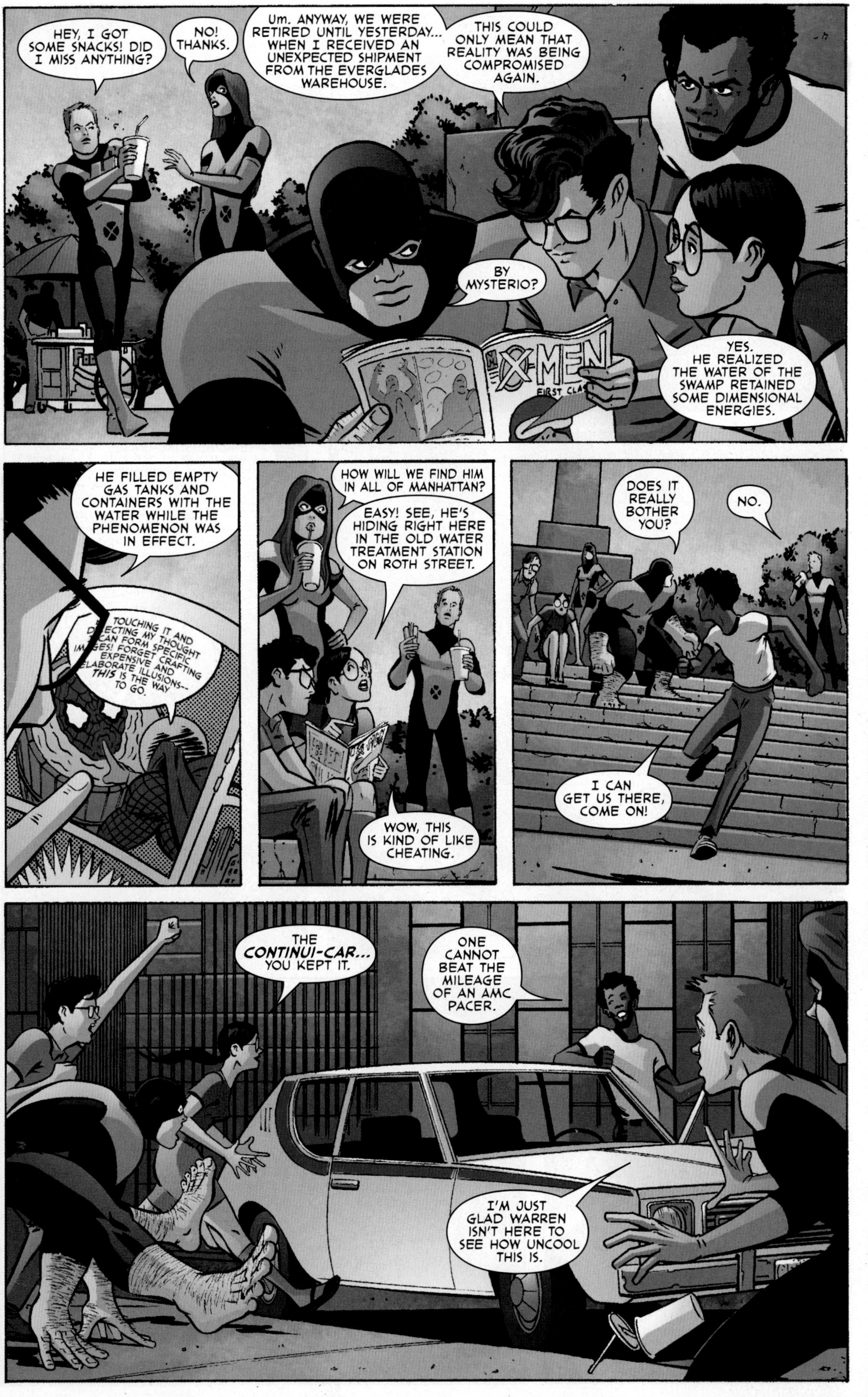

HEY, I GOT SOME SNACKS! DID I MISS ANYTHING?
NO! THANKS.
Um. ANYWAY, WE WERE RETIRED UNTIL YESTERDAY... WHEN I RECEIVED AN UNEXPECTED SHIPMENT FROM THE EVERGLADES WAREHOUSE.
THIS COULD ONLY MEAN THAT REALITY WAS BEING COMPROMISED AGAIN.
BY MYSTERIO?
X-MEN FIRST CLAS
YES. HE REALIZED THE WATER OF THE SWAMP RETAINED SOME DIMENSIONAL ENERGIES.
HE FILLED EMPTY GAS TANKS AND CONTAINERS WITH THE WATER WHILE THE PHENOMENON WAS IN EFFECT.
TOUCHING IT AND D ECTING MY THOUGHT CAN FORM SPECIFIC IM GES! FORGET CRAFTING EXPENSIVE AND ELABORATE ILLUSIONS-- THIS IS THE WAY TO GO.
HOW WILL WE FIND HIM IN ALL OF MANHATTAN?
EASY! SEE, HE'S HIDING RIGHT HERE IN THE OLD WATER TREATMENT STATION ON ROTH STREET.
WOW, THIS IS KIND OF LIKE CHEATING.
DOES IT REALLY BOTHER YOU?
NO.
I CAN GET US THERE, COME ON!
THE CONTINUI-CAR... YOU KEPT IT.
ONE CANNOT BEAT THE MILEAGE OF AN AMC PACER.
I'M JUST GLAD WARREN ISN'T HERE TO SEE HOW UNCOOL THIS IS.

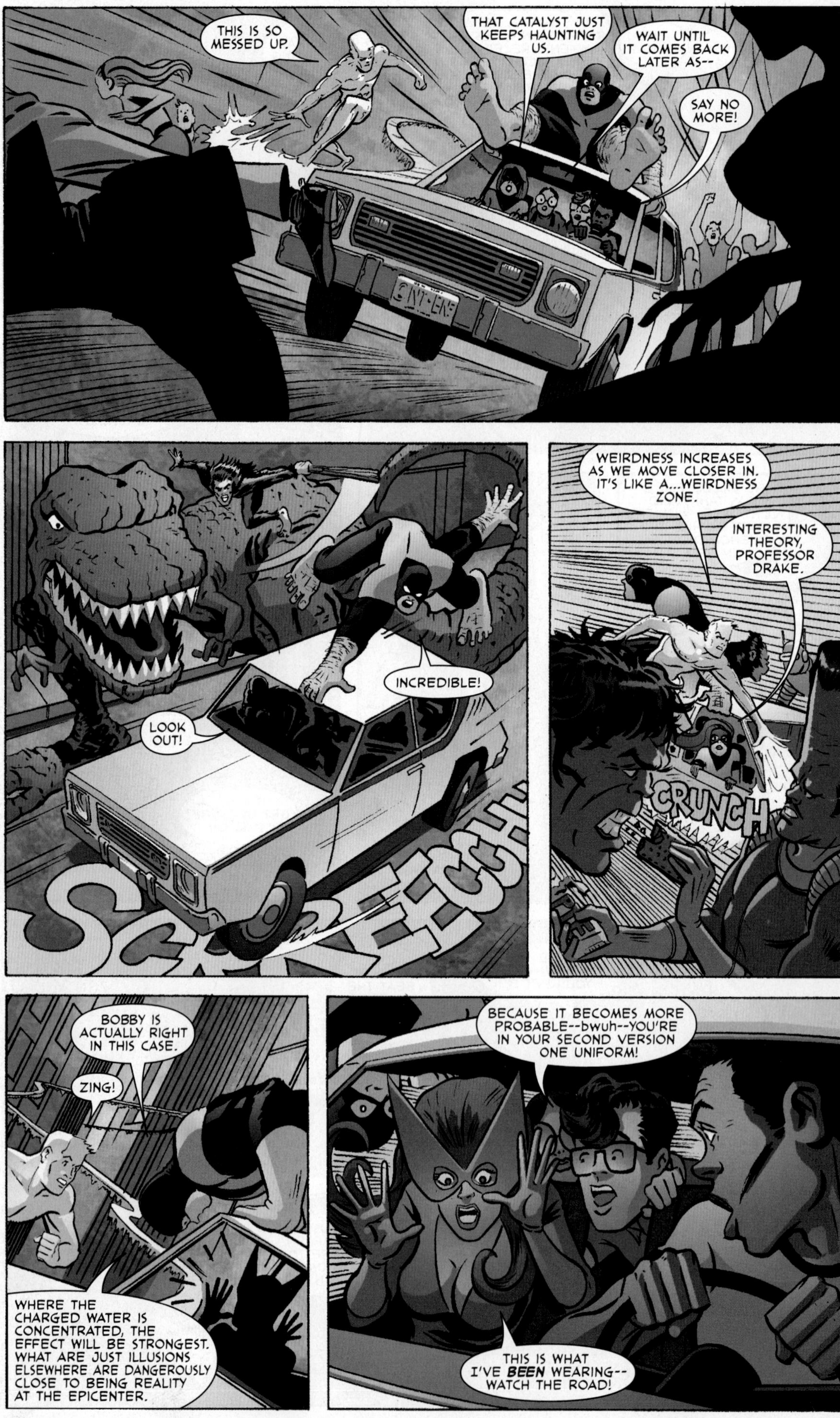

THIS IS SO MESSED UP.
THAT CATALYST JUST KEEPS HAUNTING US.
WAIT UNTIL IT COMES BACK LATER AS--
SAY NO MORE!
LOOK OUT!
INCREDIBLE!
SCREECH
WEIRDNESS INCREASES AS WE MOVE CLOSER IN. IT'S LIKE A...WEIRDNESS ZONE.
INTERESTING THEORY, PROFESSOR DRAKE.
CRUNCH
BOBBY IS ACTUALLY RIGHT IN THIS CASE.
ZING!
WHERE THE CHARGED WATER IS CONCENTRATED, THE EFFECT WILL BE STRONGEST. WHAT ARE JUST ILLUSIONS ELSEWHERE ARE DANGEROUSLY CLOSE TO BEING REALITY AT THE EPICENTER.
BECAUSE IT BECOMES MORE PROBABLE--bwuh--YOU'RE IN YOUR SECOND VERSION ONE UNIFORM!
THIS IS WHAT I'VE ***BEEN*** WEARING-- WATCH THE ROAD!

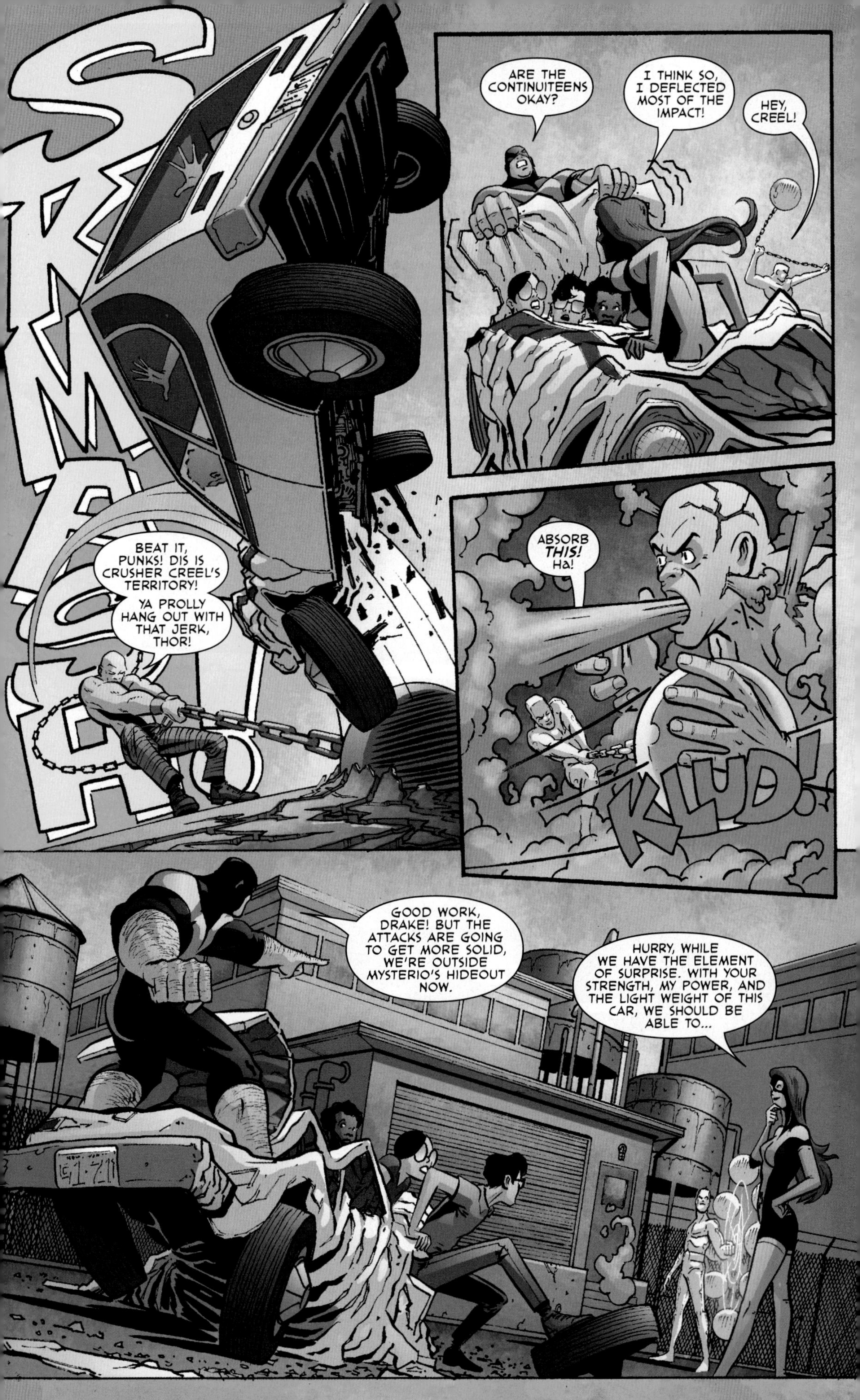
BEAT IT, PUNKS! DIS IS CRUSHER CREEL'S TERRITORY!
YA PROLLY HANG OUT WITH THAT JERK, THOR!
ARE THE CONTINUITEENS OKAY?
I THINK SO, I DEFLECTED MOST OF THE IMPACT!
HEY, CREEL!
ABSORB *THIS!* Ha!
KLUD!
GOOD WORK, DRAKE! BUT THE ATTACKS ARE GOING TO GET MORE SOLID, WE'RE OUTSIDE MYSTERIO'S HIDEOUT NOW.
HURRY, WHILE WE HAVE THE ELEMENT OF SURPRISE. WITH YOUR STRENGTH, MY POWER, AND THE LIGHT WEIGHT OF THIS CAR, WE SHOULD BE ABLE TO...

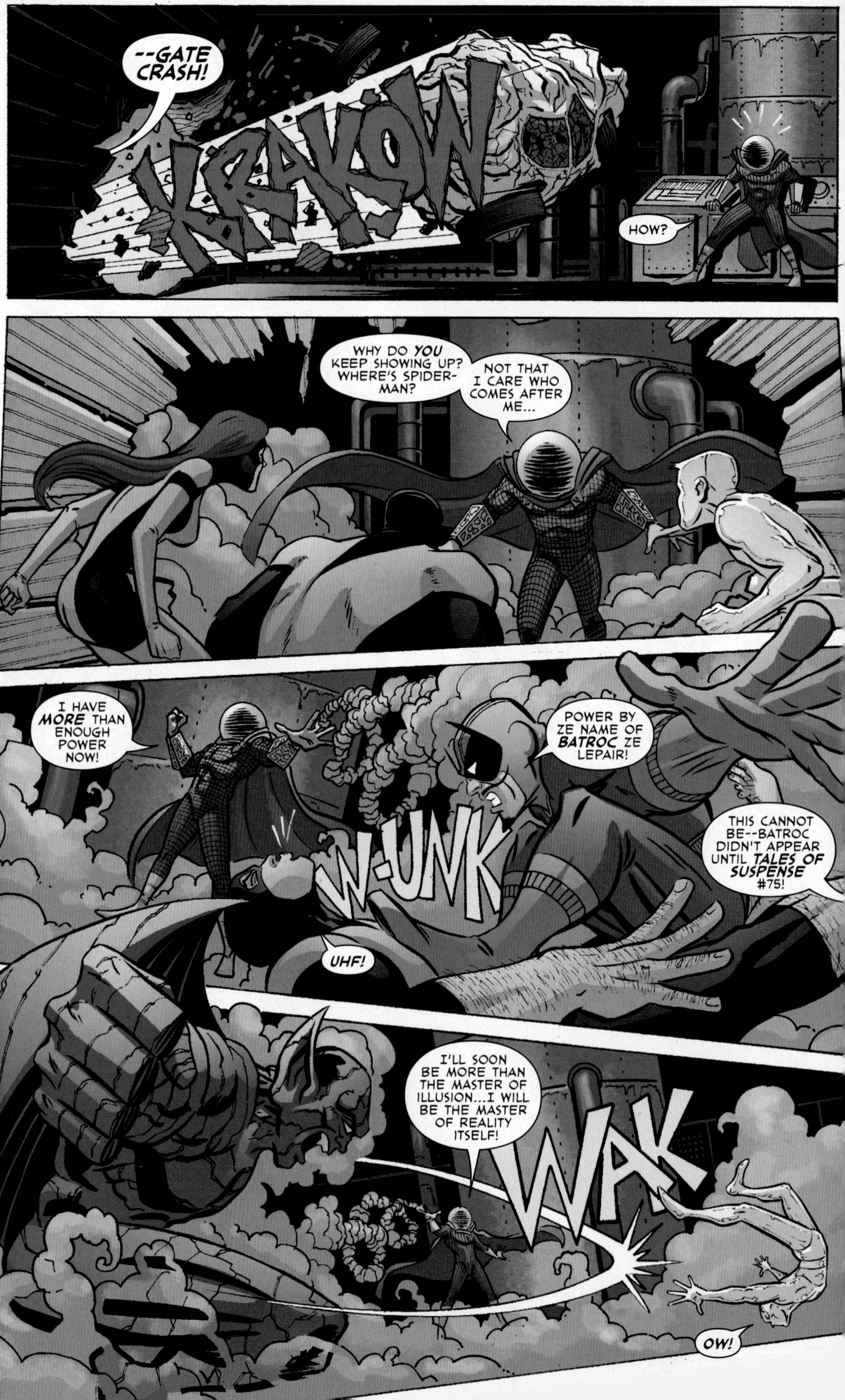
--GATE CRASH!
KRAKOW
HOW?
WHY DO YOU KEEP SHOWING UP? WHERE'S SPIDER-MAN?
NOT THAT I CARE WHO COMES AFTER ME...
I HAVE MORE THAN ENOUGH POWER NOW!
POWER BY ZE NAME OF BATROC ZE LEPAIR!
W-UNK
THIS CANNOT BE--BATROC DIDN'T APPEAR UNTIL TALES OF SUSPENSE #75!
UHF!
I'LL SOON BE MORE THAN THE MASTER OF ILLUSION...I WILL BE THE MASTER OF REALITY ITSELF!
WAK
OW!

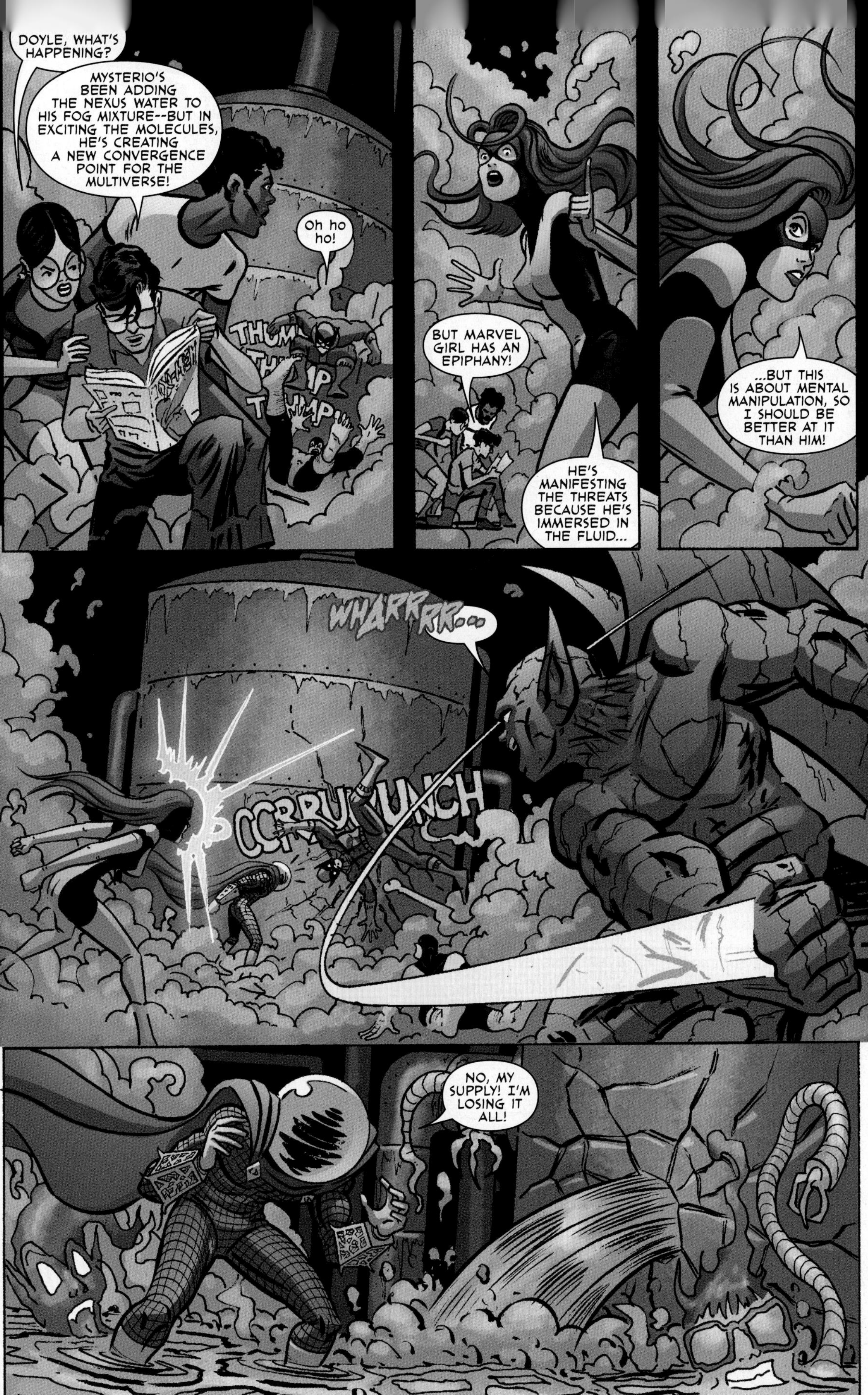
DOYLE, WHAT'S HAPPENING?
MYSTERIO'S BEEN ADDING THE NEXUS WATER TO HIS FOG MIXTURE--BUT IN EXCITING THE MOLECULES, HE'S CREATING A NEW CONVERGENCE POINT FOR THE MULTIVERSE!
Oh ho ho!
THUMP THUMP THUMP!
BUT MARVEL GIRL HAS AN EPIPHANY!
HE'S MANIFESTING THE THREATS BECAUSE HE'S IMMERSED IN THE FLUID...
...BUT THIS IS ABOUT MENTAL MANIPULATION, SO I SHOULD BE BETTER AT IT THAN HIM!
WHARRRRR...
CCRRUNCH
NO, MY SUPPLY! I'M LOSING IT ALL!

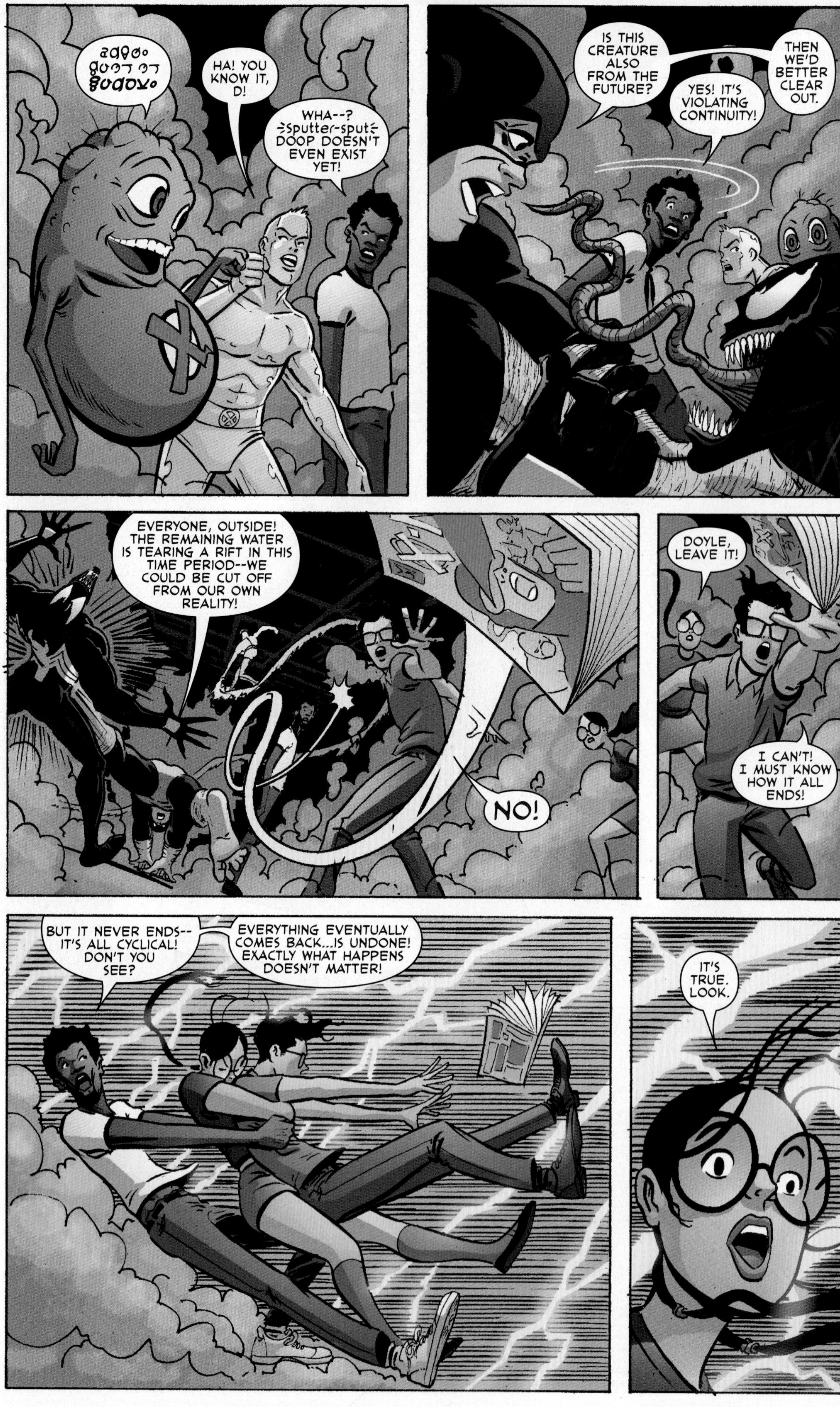
HA! YOU KNOW IT, D!
WHA--? ≈sputter-sput≈ DOOP DOESN'T EVEN EXIST YET!
IS THIS CREATURE ALSO FROM THE FUTURE?
YES! IT'S VIOLATING CONTINUITY!
THEN WE'D BETTER CLEAR OUT.
EVERYONE, OUTSIDE! THE REMAINING WATER IS TEARING A RIFT IN THIS TIME PERIOD--WE COULD BE CUT OFF FROM OUR OWN REALITY!
NO!
DOYLE, LEAVE IT!
I CAN'T! I MUST KNOW HOW IT ALL ENDS!
BUT IT NEVER ENDS-- IT'S ALL CYCLICAL! DON'T YOU SEE?
EVERYTHING EVENTUALLY COMES BACK...IS UNDONE! EXACTLY WHAT HAPPENS DOESN'T MATTER!
IT'S TRUE. LOOK.

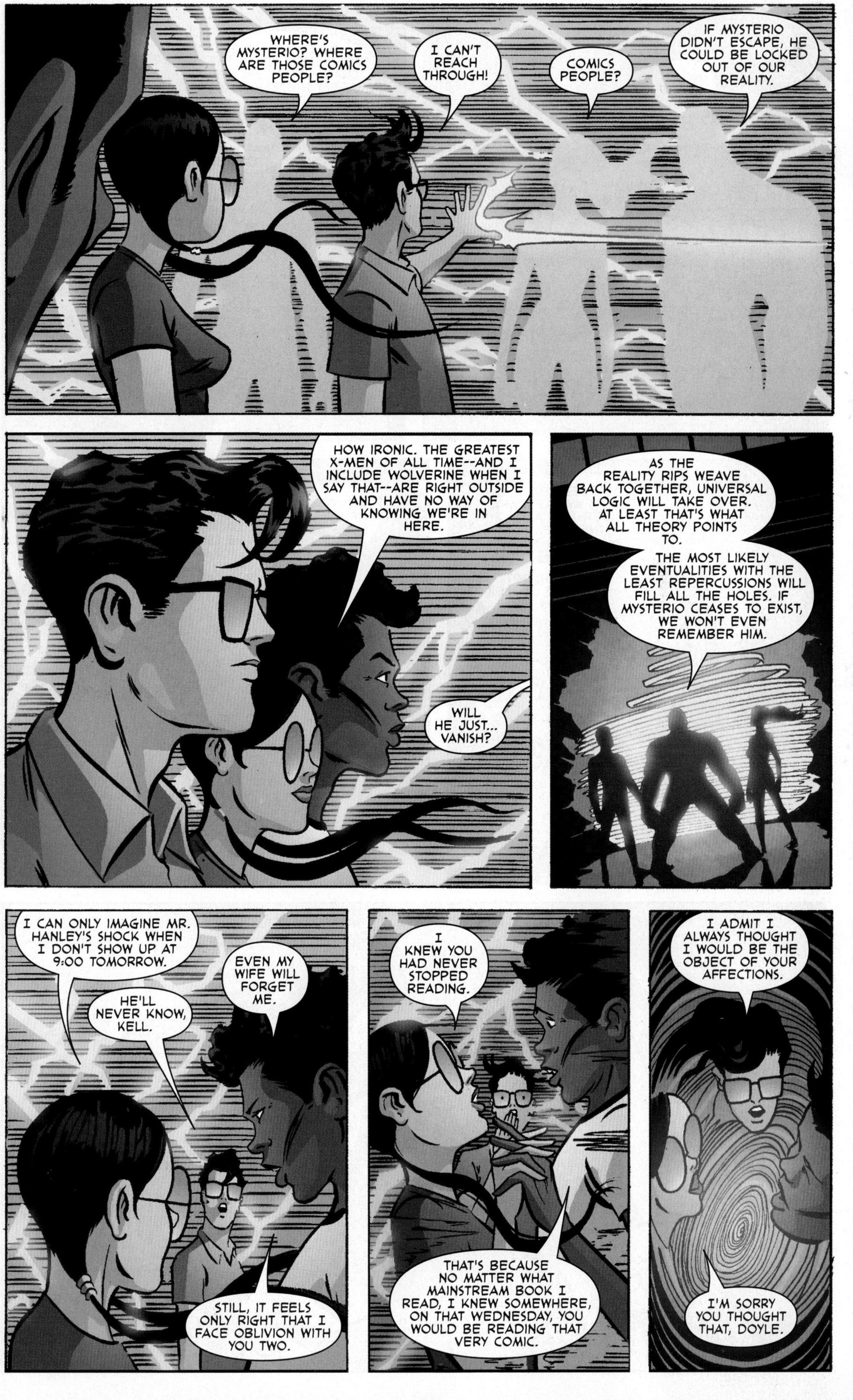
WHERE'S MYSTERIO? WHERE ARE THOSE COMICS PEOPLE?
I CAN'T REACH THROUGH!
COMICS PEOPLE?
IF MYSTERIO DIDN'T ESCAPE, HE COULD BE LOCKED OUT OF OUR REALITY.
HOW IRONIC. THE GREATEST X-MEN OF ALL TIME--AND I INCLUDE WOLVERINE WHEN I SAY THAT--ARE RIGHT OUTSIDE AND HAVE NO WAY OF KNOWING WE'RE IN HERE.
WILL HE JUST... VANISH?
AS THE REALITY RIPS WEAVE BACK TOGETHER, UNIVERSAL LOGIC WILL TAKE OVER. AT LEAST THAT'S WHAT ALL THEORY POINTS TO.
THE MOST LIKELY EVENTUALITIES WITH THE LEAST REPERCUSSIONS WILL FILL ALL THE HOLES. IF MYSTERIO CEASES TO EXIST, WE WON'T EVEN REMEMBER HIM.
I CAN ONLY IMAGINE MR. HANLEY'S SHOCK WHEN I DON'T SHOW UP AT 9:00 TOMORROW.
HE'LL NEVER KNOW, KELL.
EVEN MY WIFE WILL FORGET ME.
STILL, IT FEELS ONLY RIGHT THAT I FACE OBLIVION WITH YOU TWO.
I KNEW YOU HAD NEVER STOPPED READING.
THAT'S BECAUSE NO MATTER WHAT MAINSTREAM BOOK I READ, I KNEW SOMEWHERE, ON THAT WEDNESDAY, YOU WOULD BE READING THAT VERY COMIC.
I ADMIT I ALWAYS THOUGHT I WOULD BE THE OBJECT OF YOUR AFFECTIONS.
I'M SORRY YOU THOUGHT THAT, DOYLE.

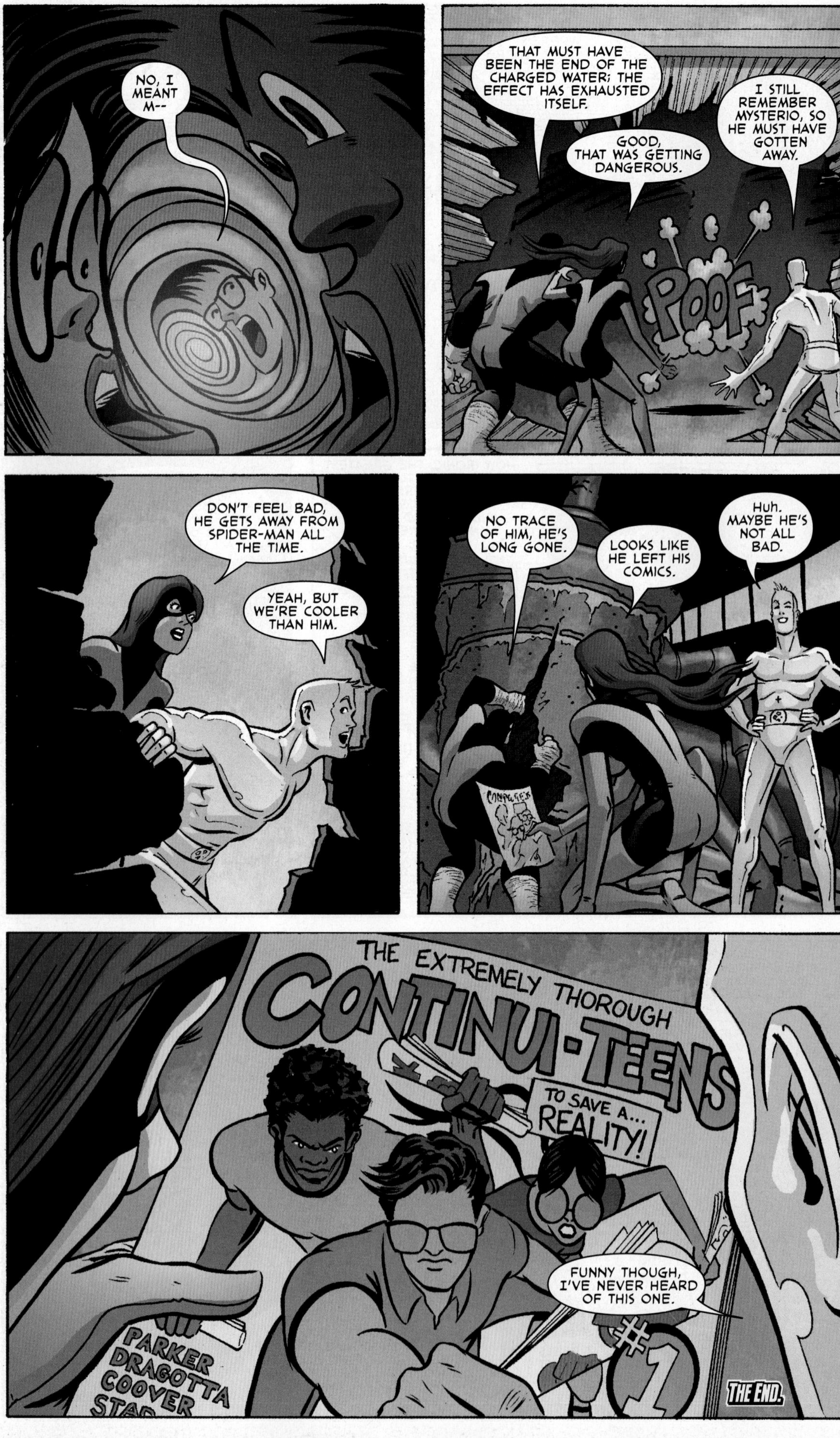
NO, I MEANT M--
THAT MUST HAVE BEEN THE END OF THE CHARGED WATER; THE EFFECT HAS EXHAUSTED ITSELF.
GOOD, THAT WAS GETTING DANGEROUS.
I STILL REMEMBER MYSTERIO, SO HE MUST HAVE GOTTEN AWAY.
POOF
DON'T FEEL BAD, HE GETS AWAY FROM SPIDER-MAN ALL THE TIME.
YEAH, BUT WE'RE COOLER THAN HIM.
NO TRACE OF HIM, HE'S LONG GONE.
LOOKS LIKE HE LEFT HIS COMICS.
Huh. MAYBE HE'S NOT ALL BAD.
THE EXTREMELY THOROUGH
CONTINUI-TEENS
TO SAVE A... REALITY!
#1
PARKER
DRAGOTTA
COOVER
FUNNY THOUGH, I'VE NEVER HEARD OF THIS ONE.
THE END.

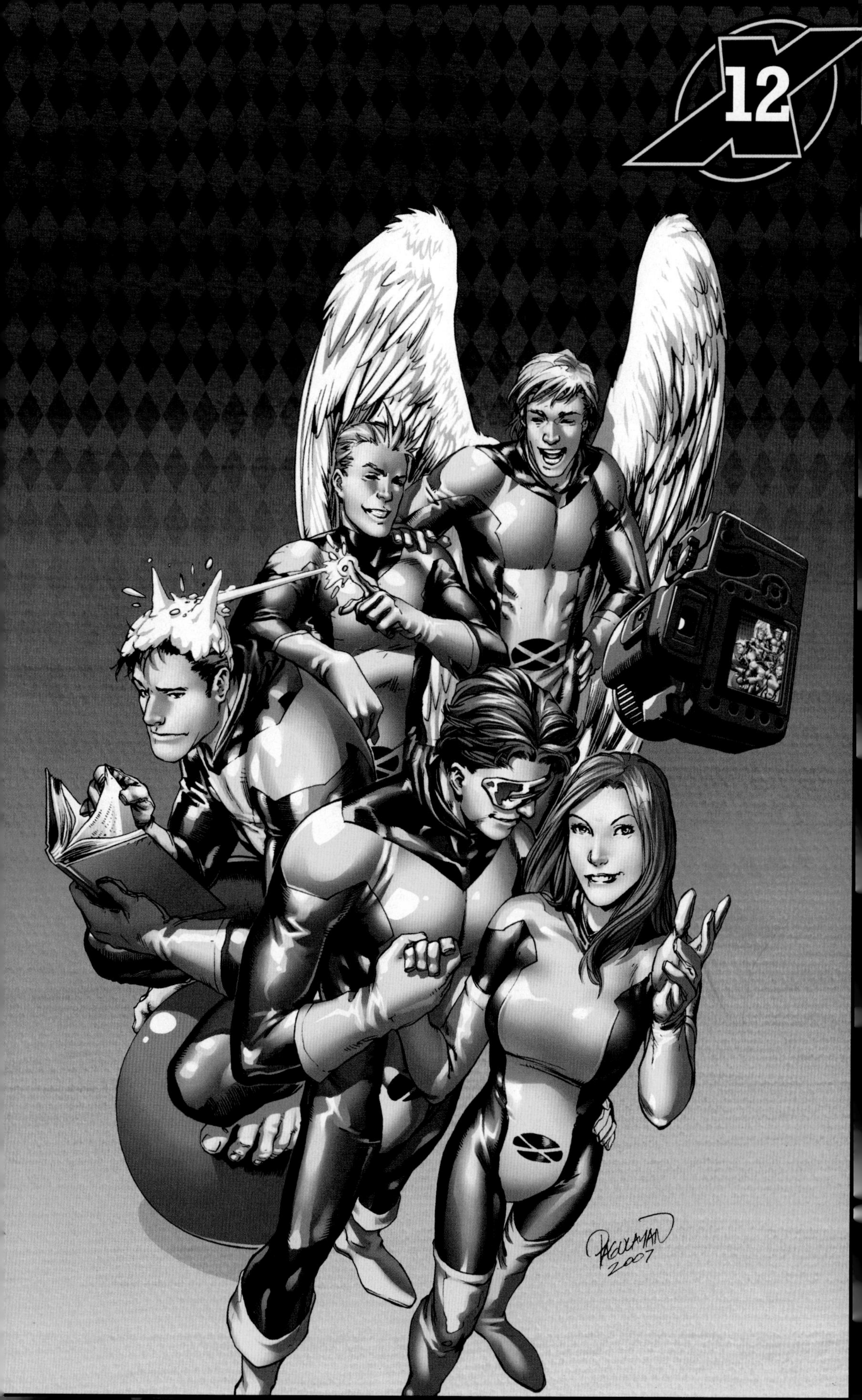
12
PAGULAYAN
2007

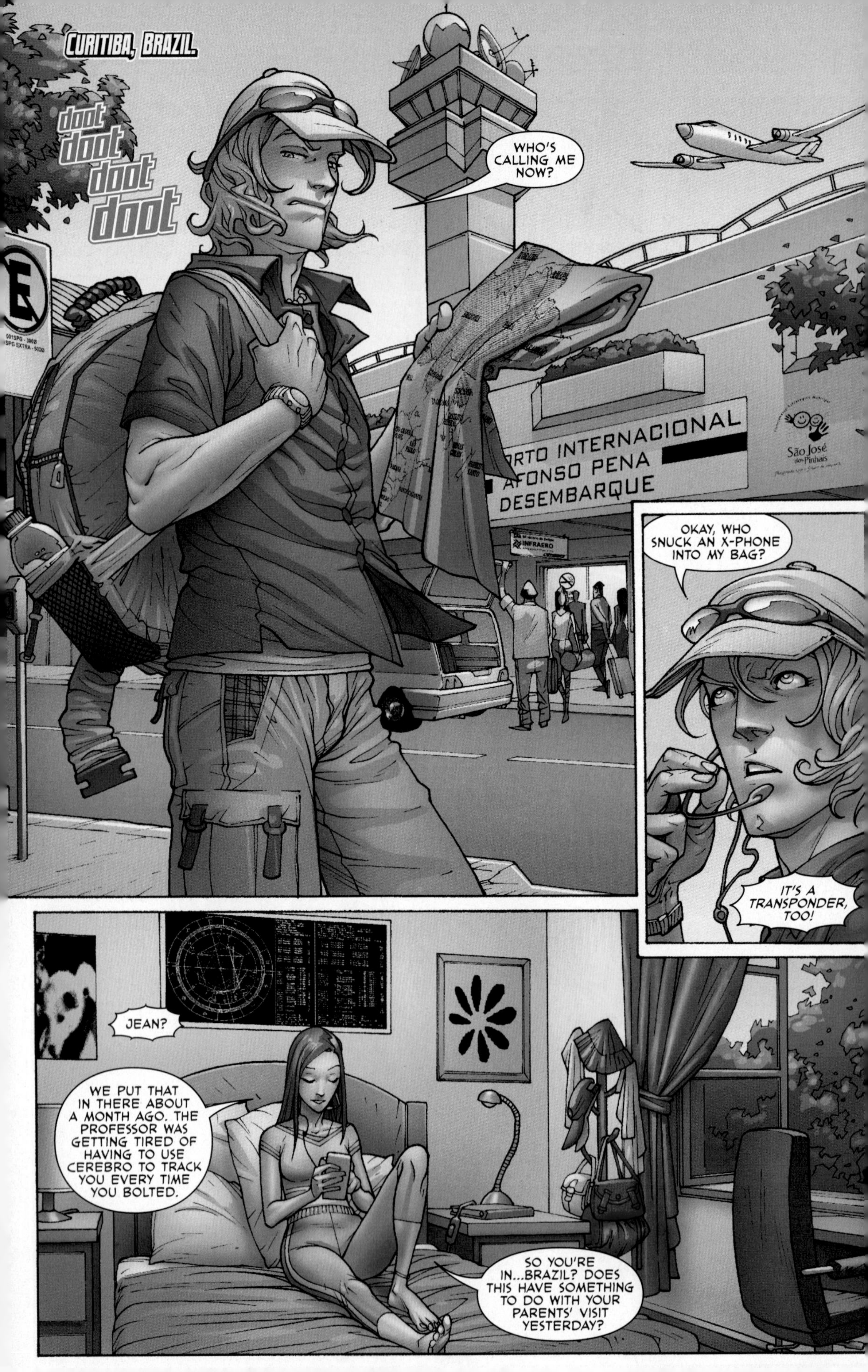

CURITIBA, BRAZIL.
doot doot doot doot
WHO'S CALLING ME NOW?
RTO INTERNACIONAL
AFONSO PENA
DESEMBARQUE
INFRAERO
São José dos Pinhais
OKAY, WHO SNUCK AN X-PHONE INTO MY BAG?
IT'S A TRANSPONDER, TOO!
JEAN?
WE PUT THAT IN THERE ABOUT A MONTH AGO. THE PROFESSOR WAS GETTING TIRED OF HAVING TO USE CEREBRO TO TRACK YOU EVERY TIME YOU BOLTED.
SO YOU'RE IN...BRAZIL? DOES THIS HAVE SOMETHING TO DO WITH YOUR PARENTS' VISIT YESTERDAY?

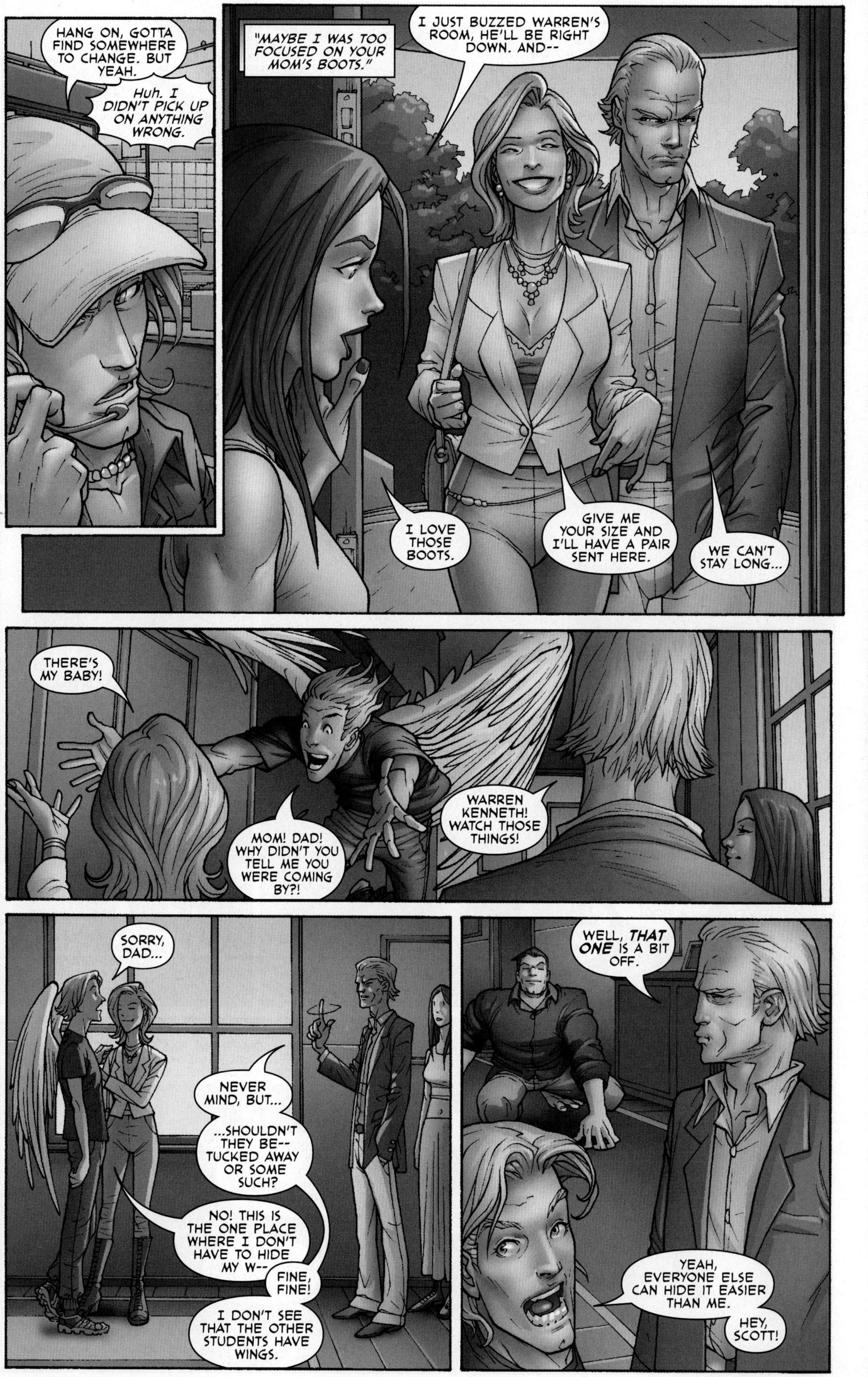
HANG ON, GOTTA FIND SOMEWHERE TO CHANGE. BUT YEAH.
Huh. I DIDN'T PICK UP ON ANYTHING WRONG.
"MAYBE I WAS TOO FOCUSED ON YOUR MOM'S BOOTS."
I JUST BUZZED WARREN'S ROOM, HE'LL BE RIGHT DOWN. AND--
I LOVE THOSE BOOTS.
GIVE ME YOUR SIZE AND I'LL HAVE A PAIR SENT HERE.
WE CAN'T STAY LONG...
THERE'S MY BABY!
MOM! DAD! WHY DIDN'T YOU TELL ME YOU WERE COMING BY?!
WARREN KENNETH! WATCH THOSE THINGS!
SORRY, DAD...
NEVER MIND, BUT...
...SHOULDN'T THEY BE-- TUCKED AWAY OR SOME SUCH?
NO! THIS IS THE ONE PLACE WHERE I DON'T HAVE TO HIDE MY W--
FINE, FINE!
I DON'T SEE THAT THE OTHER STUDENTS HAVE WINGS.
WELL, THAT ONE IS A BIT OFF.
YEAH, EVERYONE ELSE CAN HIDE IT EASIER THAN ME.
HEY, SCOTT!

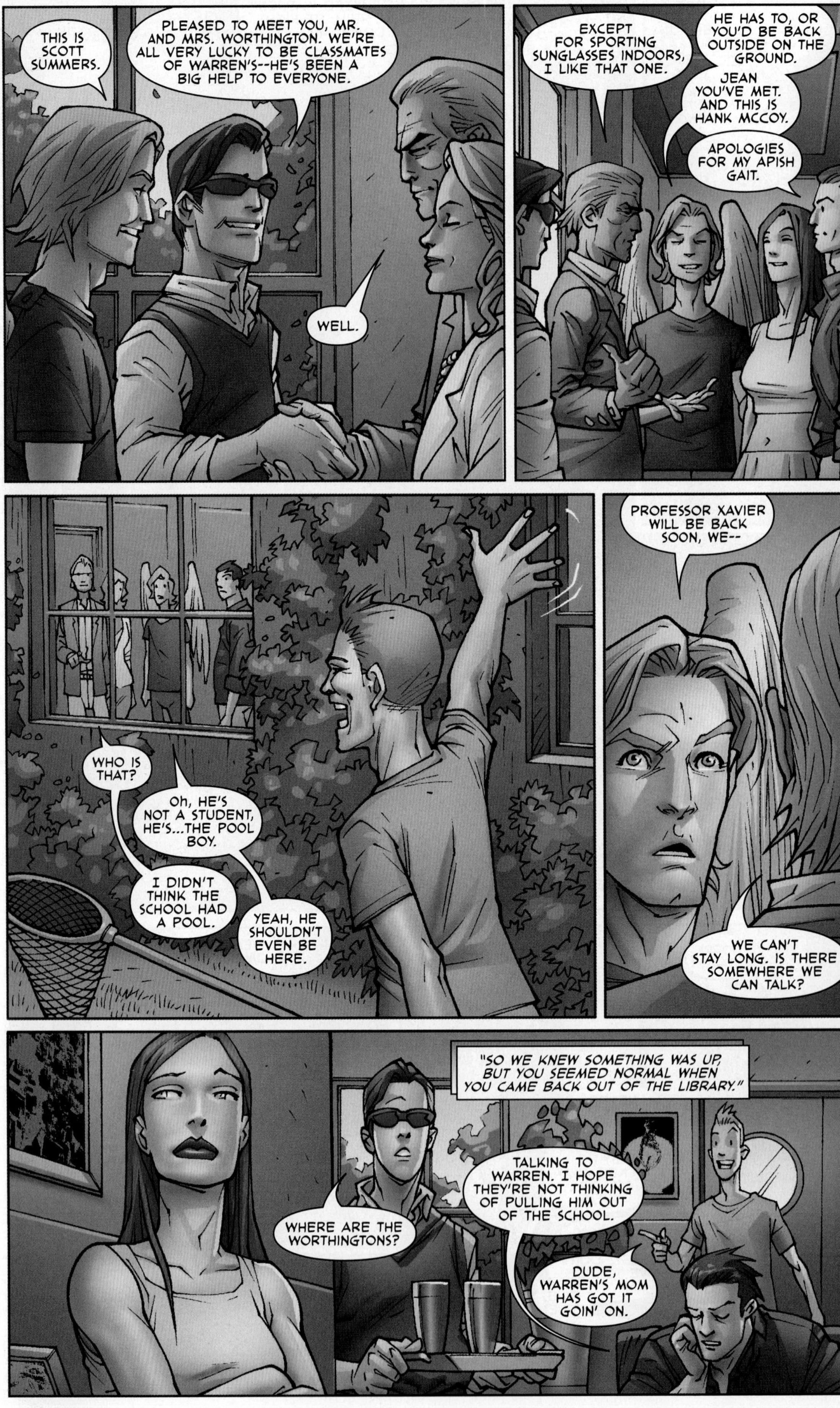
THIS IS SCOTT SUMMERS.
PLEASED TO MEET YOU, MR. AND MRS. WORTHINGTON. WE'RE ALL VERY LUCKY TO BE CLASSMATES OF WARREN'S--HE'S BEEN A BIG HELP TO EVERYONE.
WELL.
EXCEPT FOR SPORTING SUNGLASSES INDOORS, I LIKE THAT ONE.
HE HAS TO, OR YOU'D BE BACK OUTSIDE ON THE GROUND.
JEAN YOU'VE MET. AND THIS IS HANK MCCOY.
APOLOGIES FOR MY APISH GAIT.
WHO IS THAT?
Oh, HE'S NOT A STUDENT, HE'S...THE POOL BOY.
I DIDN'T THINK THE SCHOOL HAD A POOL.
YEAH, HE SHOULDN'T EVEN BE HERE.
PROFESSOR XAVIER WILL BE BACK SOON, WE--
WE CAN'T STAY LONG. IS THERE SOMEWHERE WE CAN TALK?
"SO WE KNEW SOMETHING WAS UP, BUT YOU SEEMED NORMAL WHEN YOU CAME BACK OUT OF THE LIBRARY."
WHERE ARE THE WORTHINGTONS?
TALKING TO WARREN. I HOPE THEY'RE NOT THINKING OF PULLING HIM OUT OF THE SCHOOL.
DUDE, WARREN'S MOM HAS GOT IT GOIN' ON.

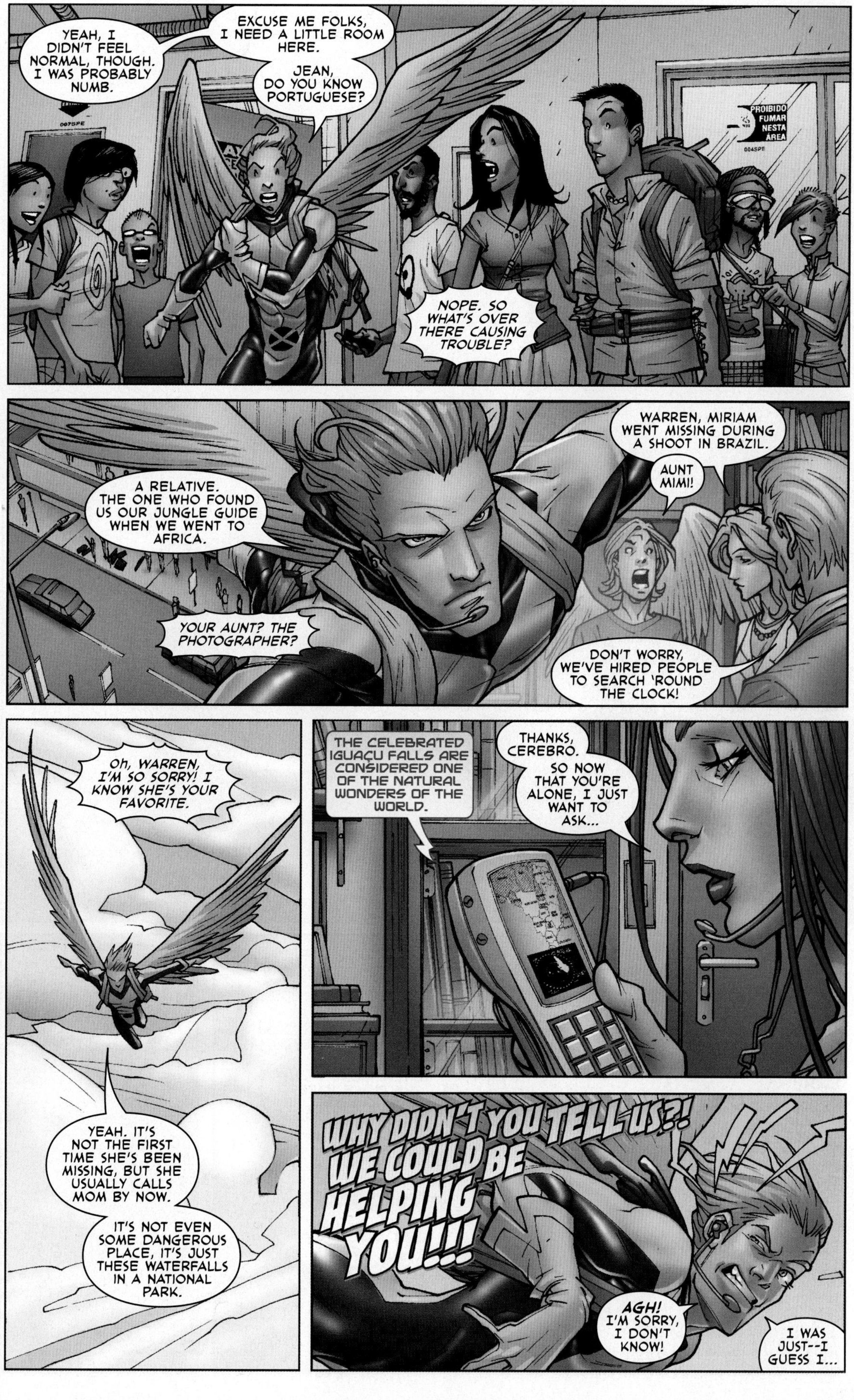
YEAH, I DIDN'T FEEL NORMAL, THOUGH. I WAS PROBABLY NUMB.
EXCUSE ME FOLKS, I NEED A LITTLE ROOM HERE.
JEAN, DO YOU KNOW PORTUGUESE?
PROIBIDO FUMAR NESTA ÁREA
NOPE. SO WHAT'S OVER THERE CAUSING TROUBLE?
A RELATIVE. THE ONE WHO FOUND US OUR JUNGLE GUIDE WHEN WE WENT TO AFRICA.
YOUR AUNT? THE PHOTOGRAPHER?
WARREN, MIRIAM WENT MISSING DURING A SHOOT IN BRAZIL.
AUNT MIMI!
DON'T WORRY, WE'VE HIRED PEOPLE TO SEARCH 'ROUND THE CLOCK!
Oh, WARREN, I'M SO SORRY! I KNOW SHE'S YOUR FAVORITE.
YEAH. IT'S NOT THE FIRST TIME SHE'S BEEN MISSING, BUT SHE USUALLY CALLS MOM BY NOW.
IT'S NOT EVEN SOME DANGEROUS PLACE, IT'S JUST THESE WATERFALLS IN A NATIONAL PARK.
THE CELEBRATED IGUAÇU FALLS ARE CONSIDERED ONE OF THE NATURAL WONDERS OF THE WORLD.
THANKS, CEREBRO.
SO NOW THAT YOU'RE ALONE, I JUST WANT TO ASK...
WHY DIDN'T YOU TELL US?! WE COULD BE HELPING YOU!!!
AGH! I'M SORRY, I DON'T KNOW!
I WAS JUST--I GUESS I...

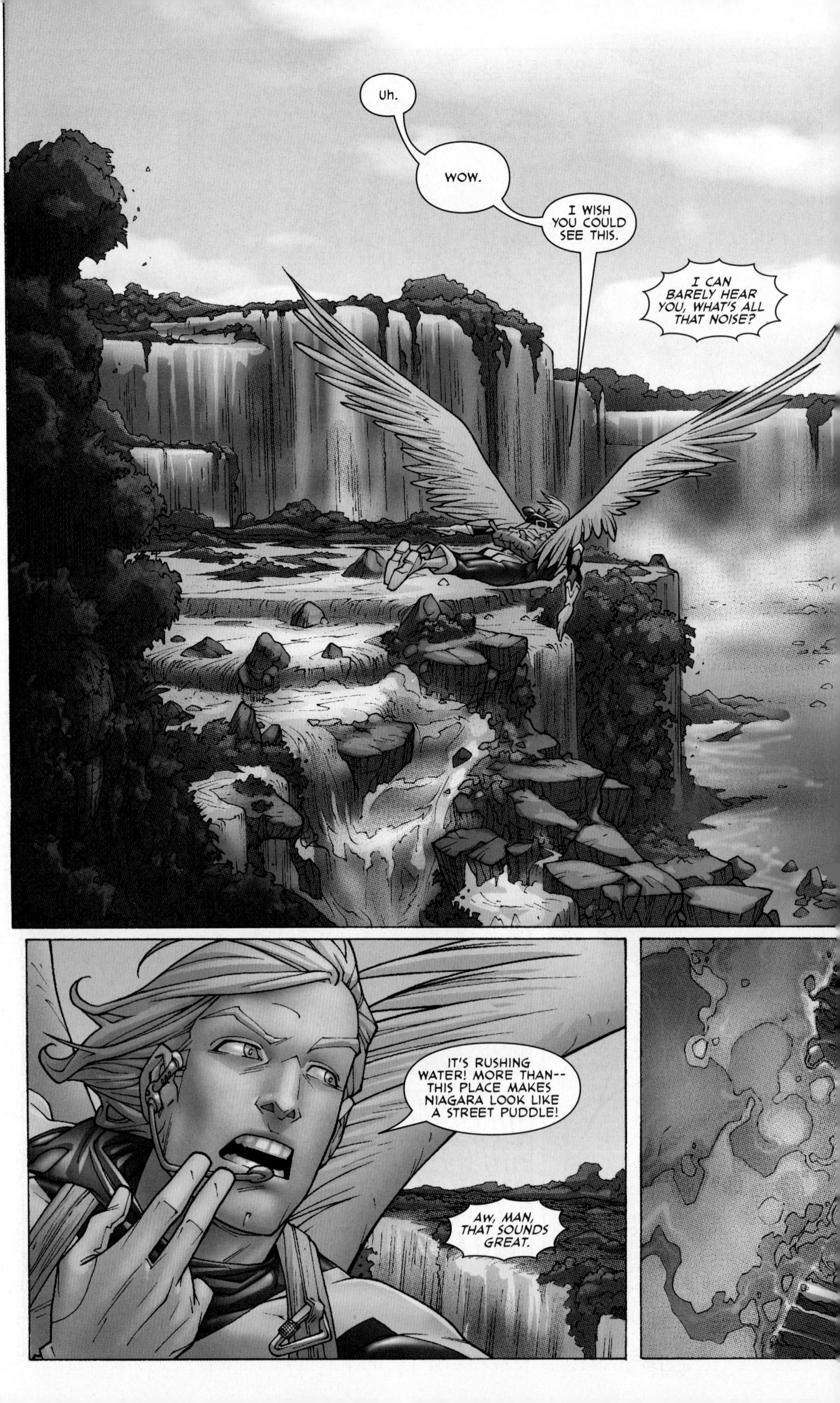
UH.
WOW.
I WISH YOU COULD SEE THIS.
I CAN BARELY HEAR YOU, WHAT'S ALL THAT NOISE?
IT'S RUSHING WATER! MORE THAN-- THIS PLACE MAKES NIAGARA LOOK LIKE A STREET PUDDLE!
AW, MAN, THAT SOUNDS GREAT.

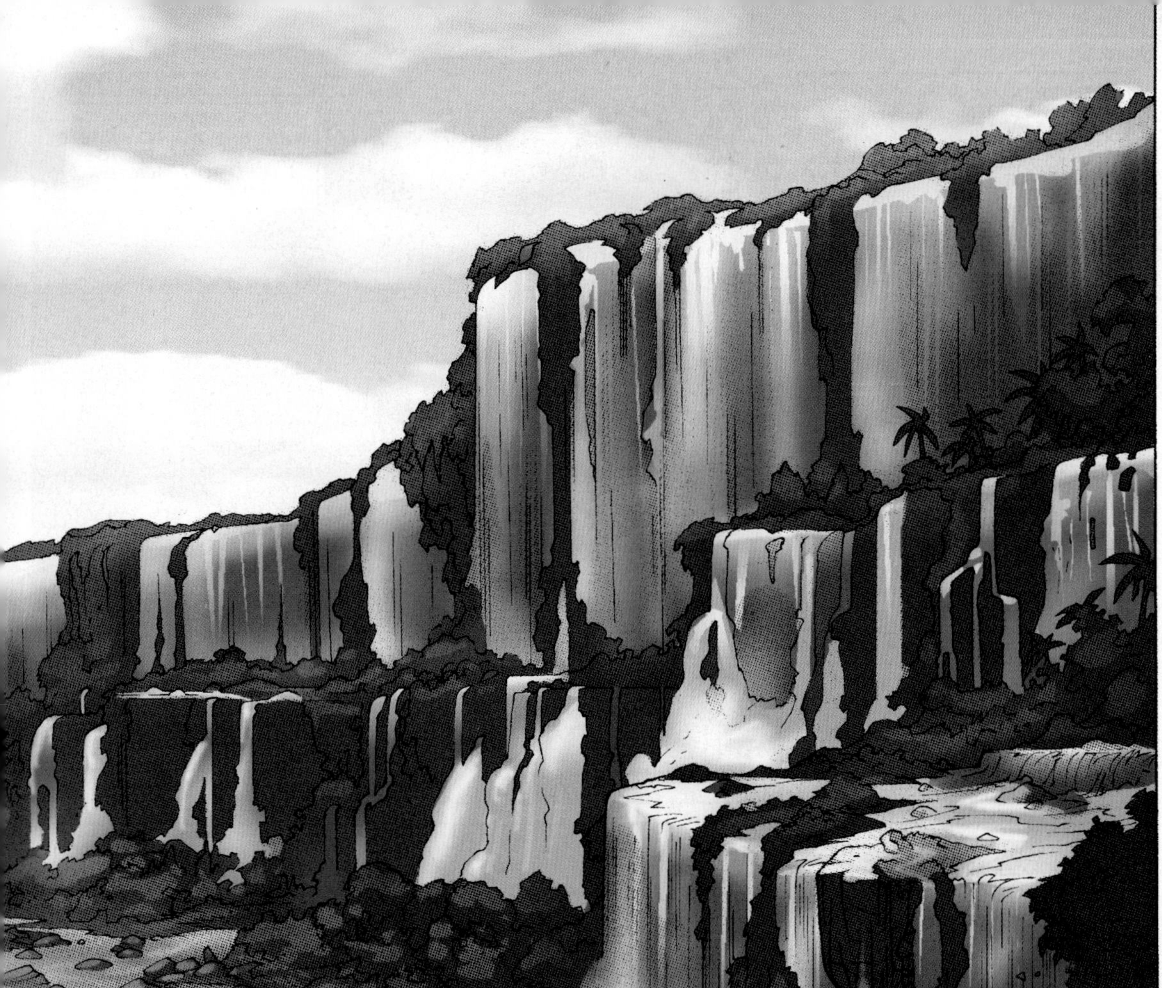

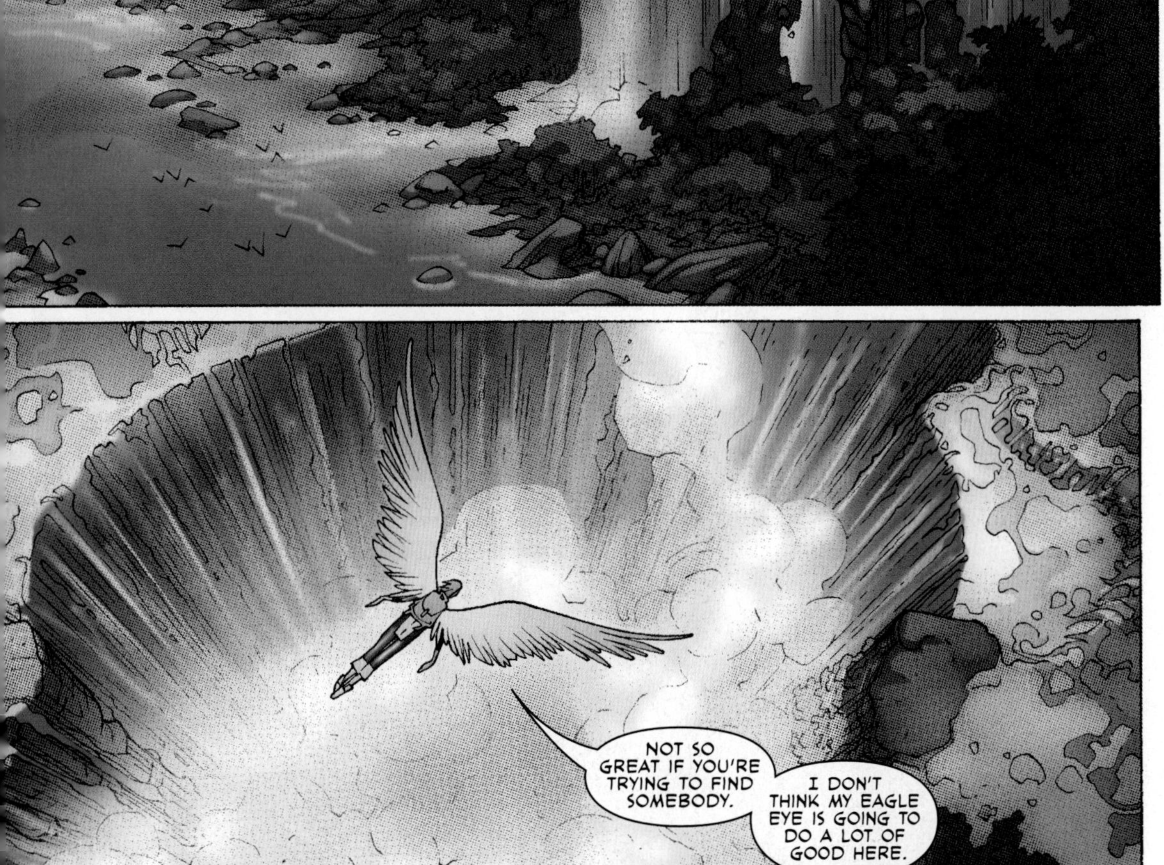
NOT SO GREAT IF YOU'RE TRYING TO FIND SOMEBODY.
I DON'T THINK MY EAGLE EYE IS GOING TO DO A LOT OF GOOD HERE.

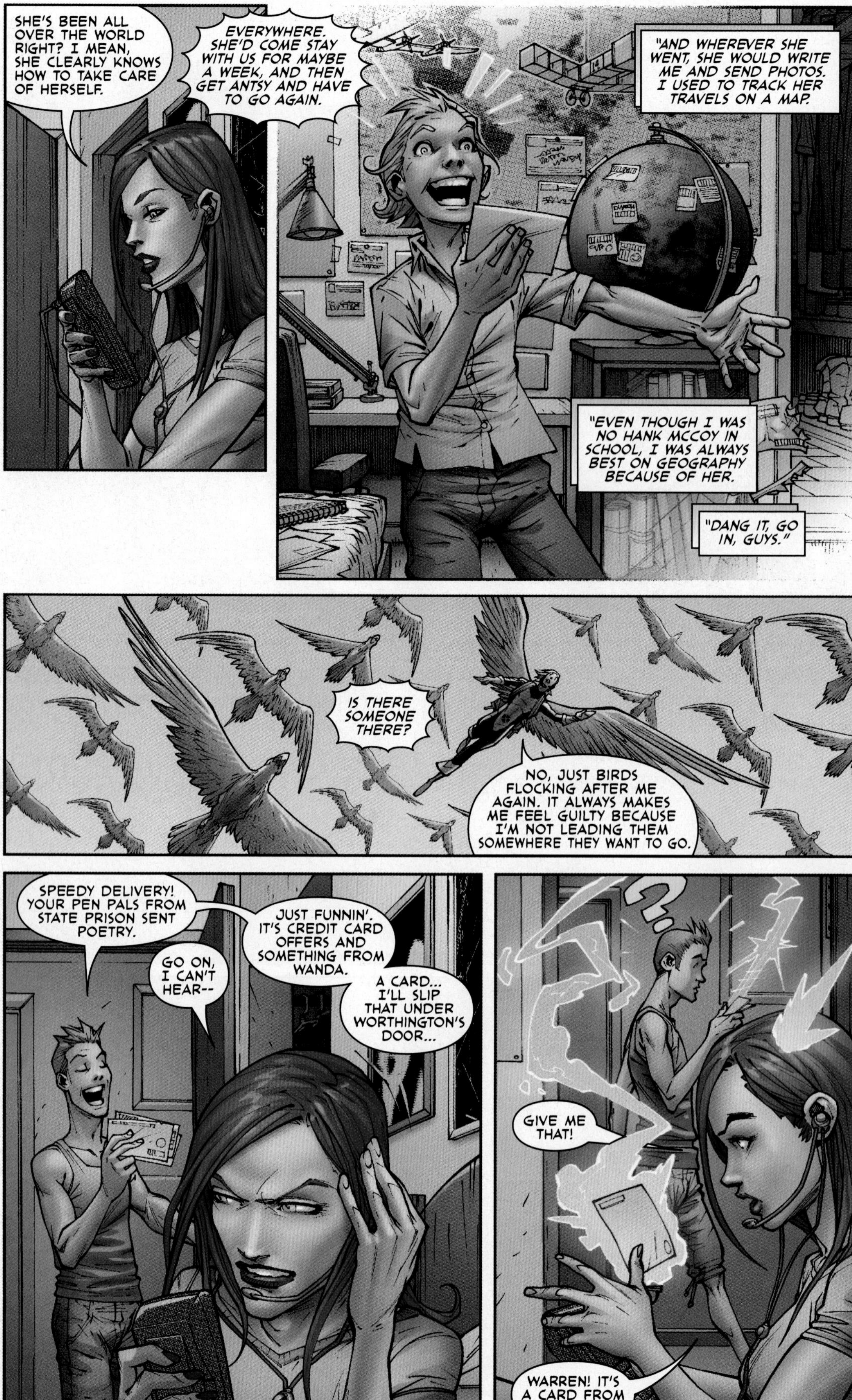
SHE'S BEEN ALL OVER THE WORLD RIGHT? I MEAN, SHE CLEARLY KNOWS HOW TO TAKE CARE OF HERSELF.
EVERYWHERE. SHE'D COME STAY WITH US FOR MAYBE A WEEK, AND THEN GET ANTSY AND HAVE TO GO AGAIN.
"AND WHEREVER SHE WENT, SHE WOULD WRITE ME AND SEND PHOTOS. I USED TO TRACK HER TRAVELS ON A MAP.
"EVEN THOUGH I WAS NO HANK MCCOY IN SCHOOL, I WAS ALWAYS BEST ON GEOGRAPHY BECAUSE OF HER.
"DANG IT, GO IN, GUYS."
IS THERE SOMEONE THERE?
NO, JUST BIRDS FLOCKING AFTER ME AGAIN. IT ALWAYS MAKES ME FEEL GUILTY BECAUSE I'M NOT LEADING THEM SOMEWHERE THEY WANT TO GO.
SPEEDY DELIVERY! YOUR PEN PALS FROM STATE PRISON SENT POETRY.
JUST FUNNIN'. IT'S CREDIT CARD OFFERS AND SOMETHING FROM WANDA.
GO ON, I CAN'T HEAR--
A CARD... I'LL SLIP THAT UNDER WORTHINGTON'S DOOR...
GIVE ME THAT!
WARREN! IT'S A CARD FROM YOUR AUNT!

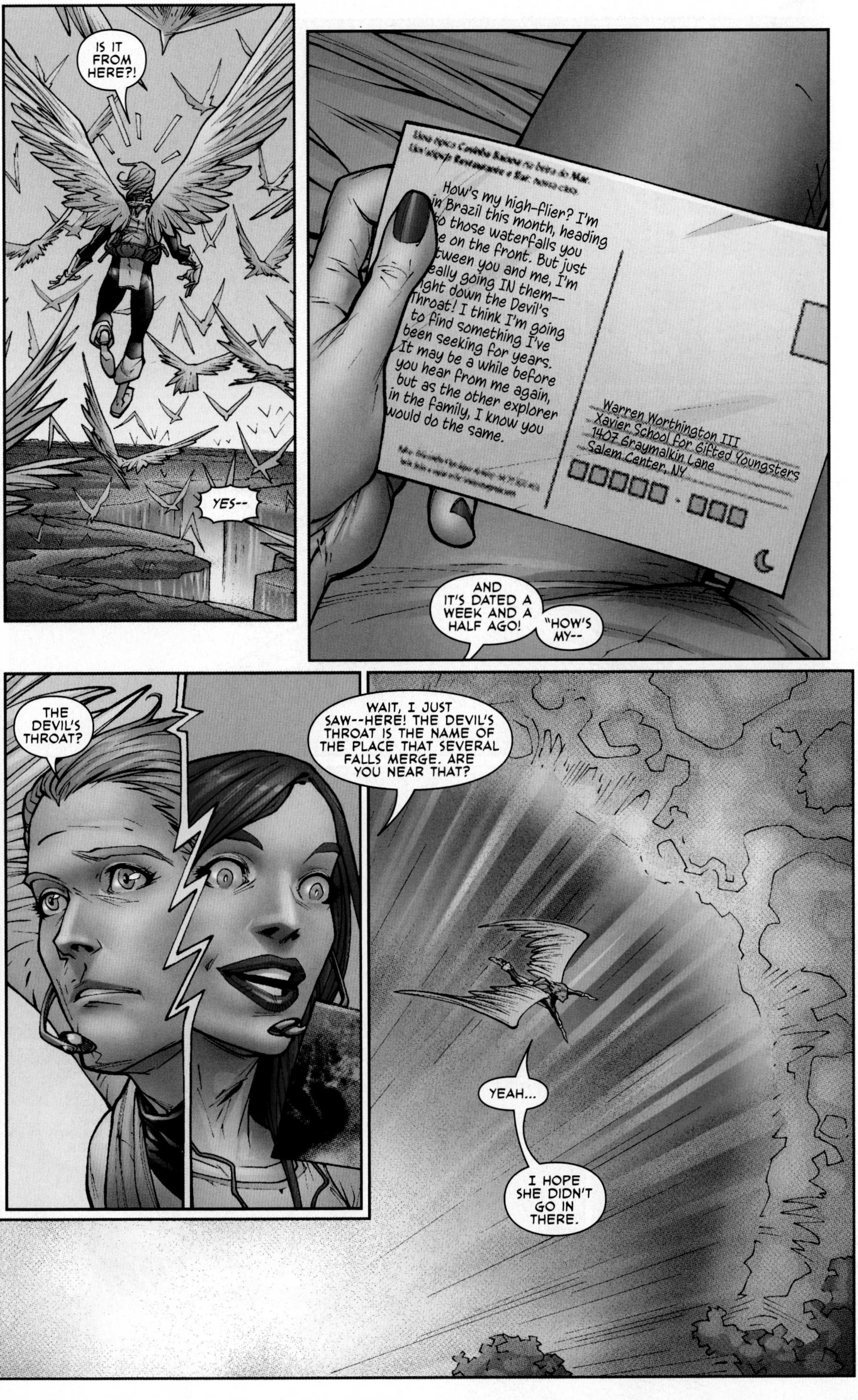
IS IT FROM HERE?!
YES--
How's my high-flier? I'm
in Brazil this month, heading
o those waterfalls you
e on the front. But just
tween you and me, I'm
eally going IN them--
ight down the Devil's
Throat! I think I'm going
to find something I've
been seeking for years.
It may be a while before
you hear from me again,
but as the other explorer
in the family, I know you
would do the same.
Warren Worthington III
Xavier School for Gifted Youngsters
1407 Graymalkin Lane
Salem Center, NY
"HOW'S MY--
AND IT'S DATED A WEEK AND A HALF AGO!
THE DEVIL'S THROAT?
WAIT, I JUST SAW--HERE! THE DEVIL'S THROAT IS THE NAME OF THE PLACE THAT SEVERAL FALLS MERGE. ARE YOU NEAR THAT?
YEAH...
I HOPE SHE DIDN'T GO IN THERE.

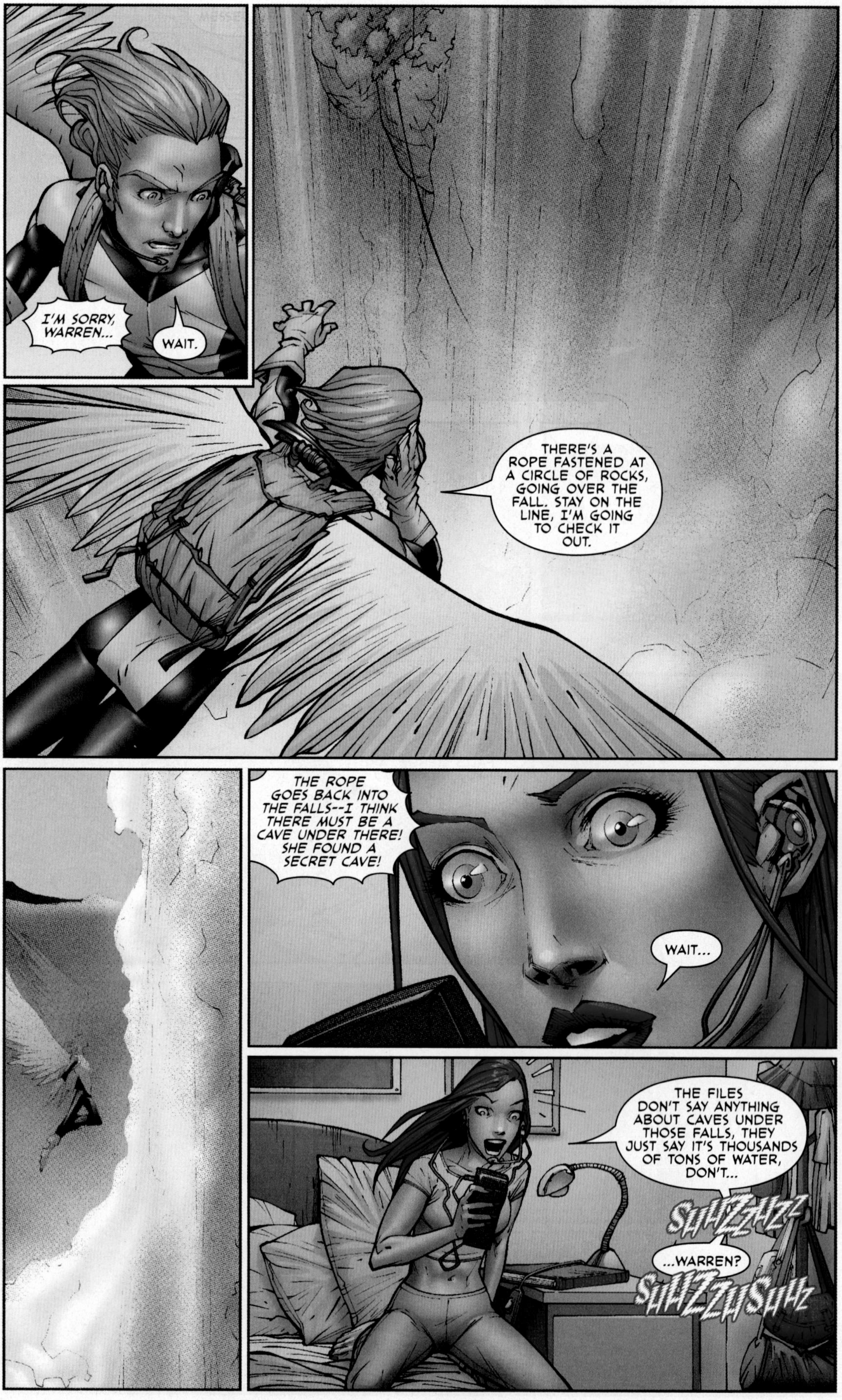
I'M SORRY, WARREN...
WAIT.
THERE'S A ROPE FASTENED AT A CIRCLE OF ROCKS, GOING OVER THE FALL. STAY ON THE LINE, I'M GOING TO CHECK IT OUT.
THE ROPE GOES BACK INTO THE FALLS--I THINK THERE MUST BE A CAVE UNDER THERE! SHE FOUND A SECRET CAVE!
WAIT...
THE FILES DON'T SAY ANYTHING ABOUT CAVES UNDER THOSE FALLS, THEY JUST SAY IT'S THOUSANDS OF TONS OF WATER, DON'T...
SKKZZKZ
...WARREN?
SKKZZKSKK

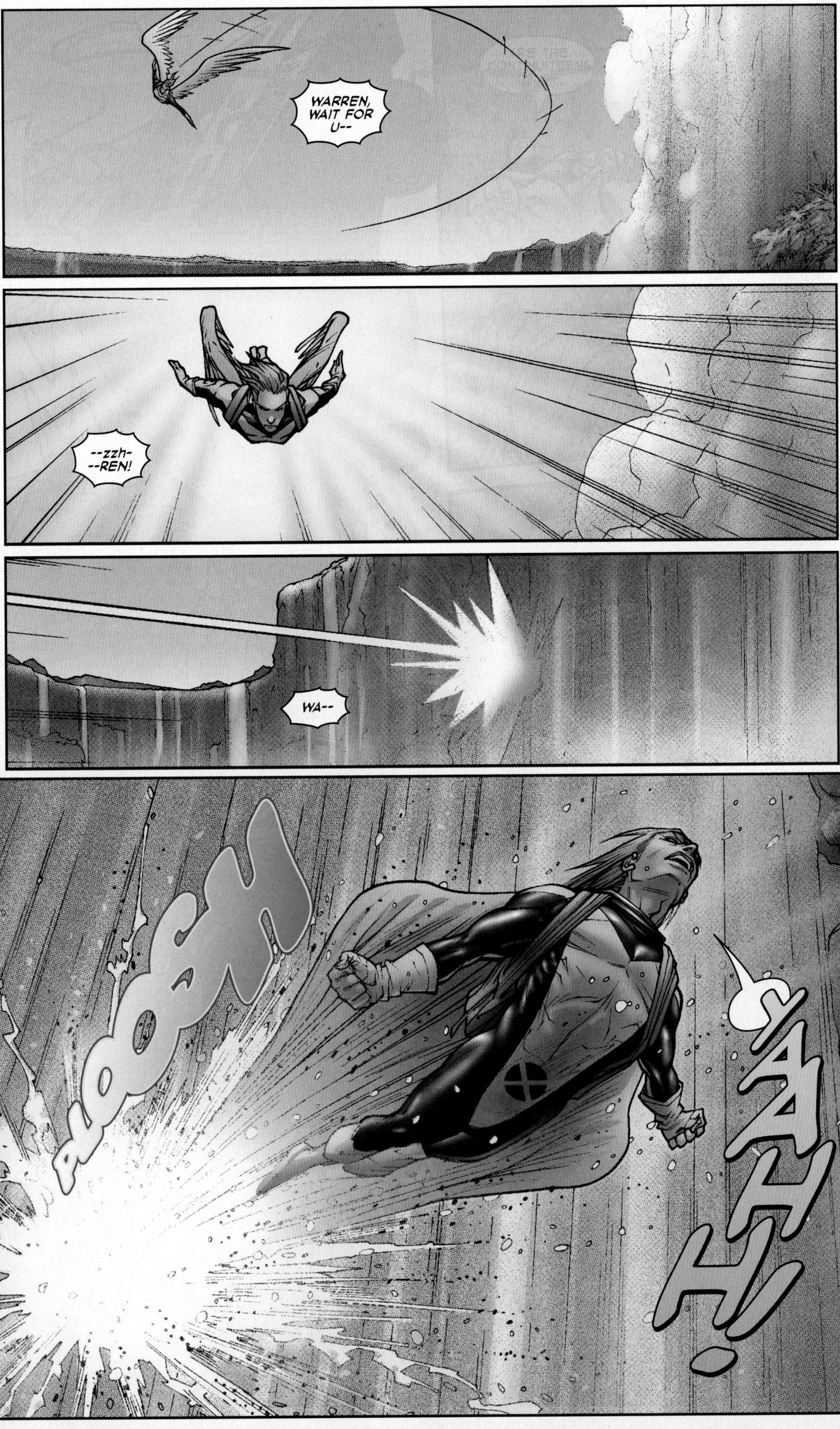
WARREN, WAIT FOR U--
--zzh- --REN!
WA--
PLOOSH
YAAHH!

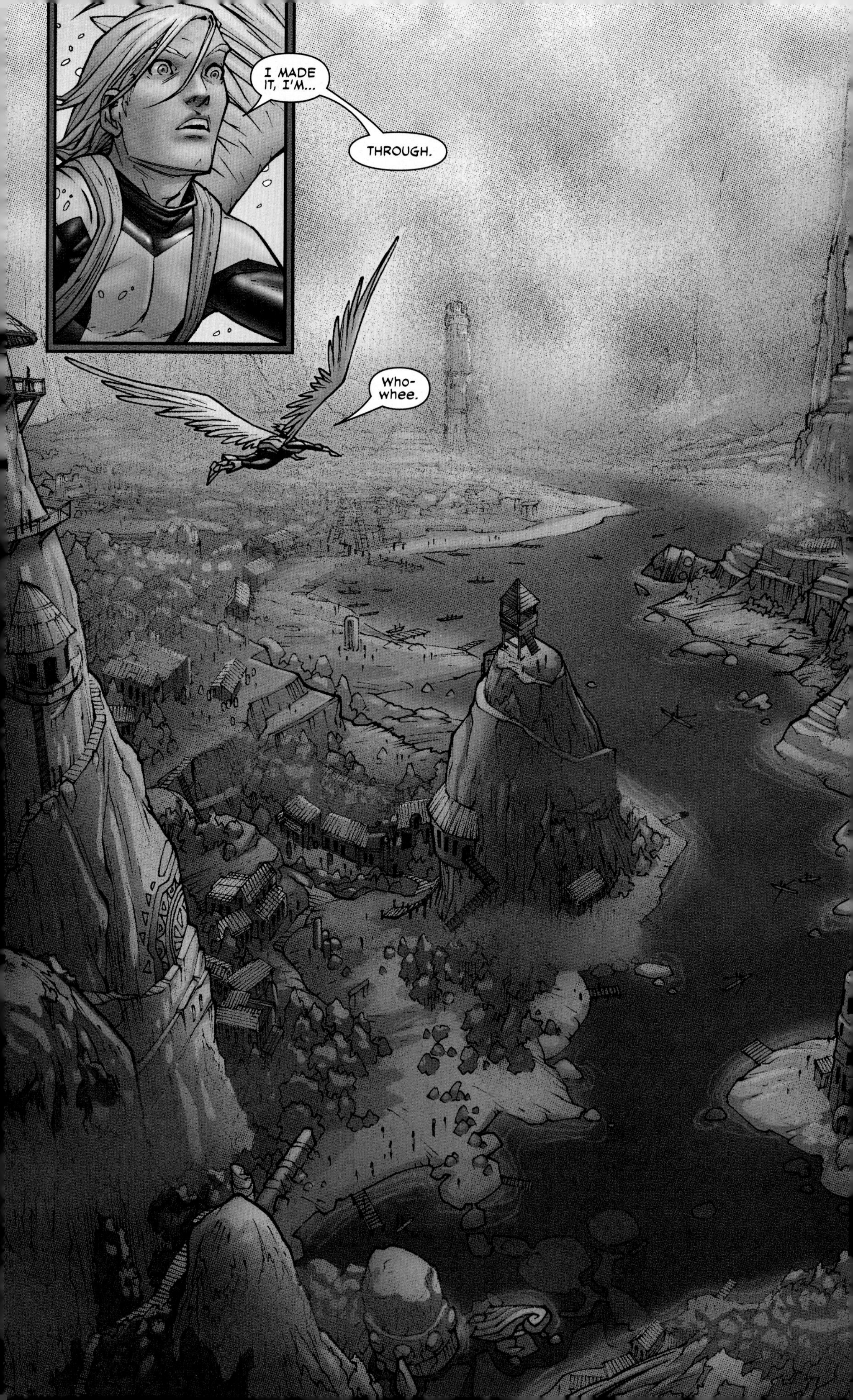
I MADE IT, I'M...
THROUGH.
Who-whee.

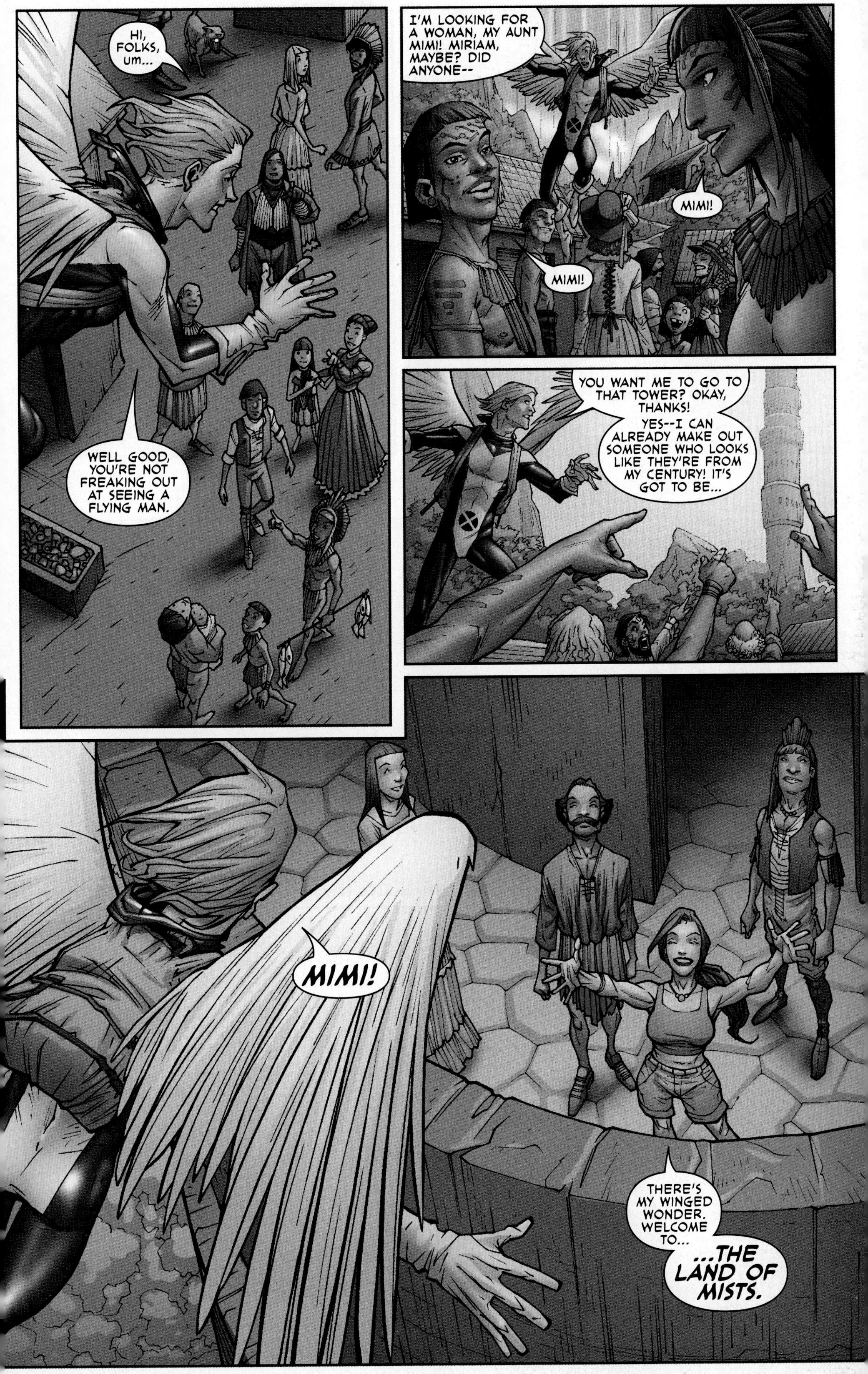
HI, FOLKS, UM...
WELL GOOD, YOU'RE NOT FREAKING OUT AT SEEING A FLYING MAN.
I'M LOOKING FOR A WOMAN, MY AUNT MIMI! MIRIAM, MAYBE? DID ANYONE--
MIMI!
MIMI!
YOU WANT ME TO GO TO THAT TOWER? OKAY, THANKS!
YES--I CAN ALREADY MAKE OUT SOMEONE WHO LOOKS LIKE THEY'RE FROM MY CENTURY! IT'S GOT TO BE...
MIMI!
THERE'S MY WINGED WONDER. WELCOME TO...
...THE LAND OF MISTS.

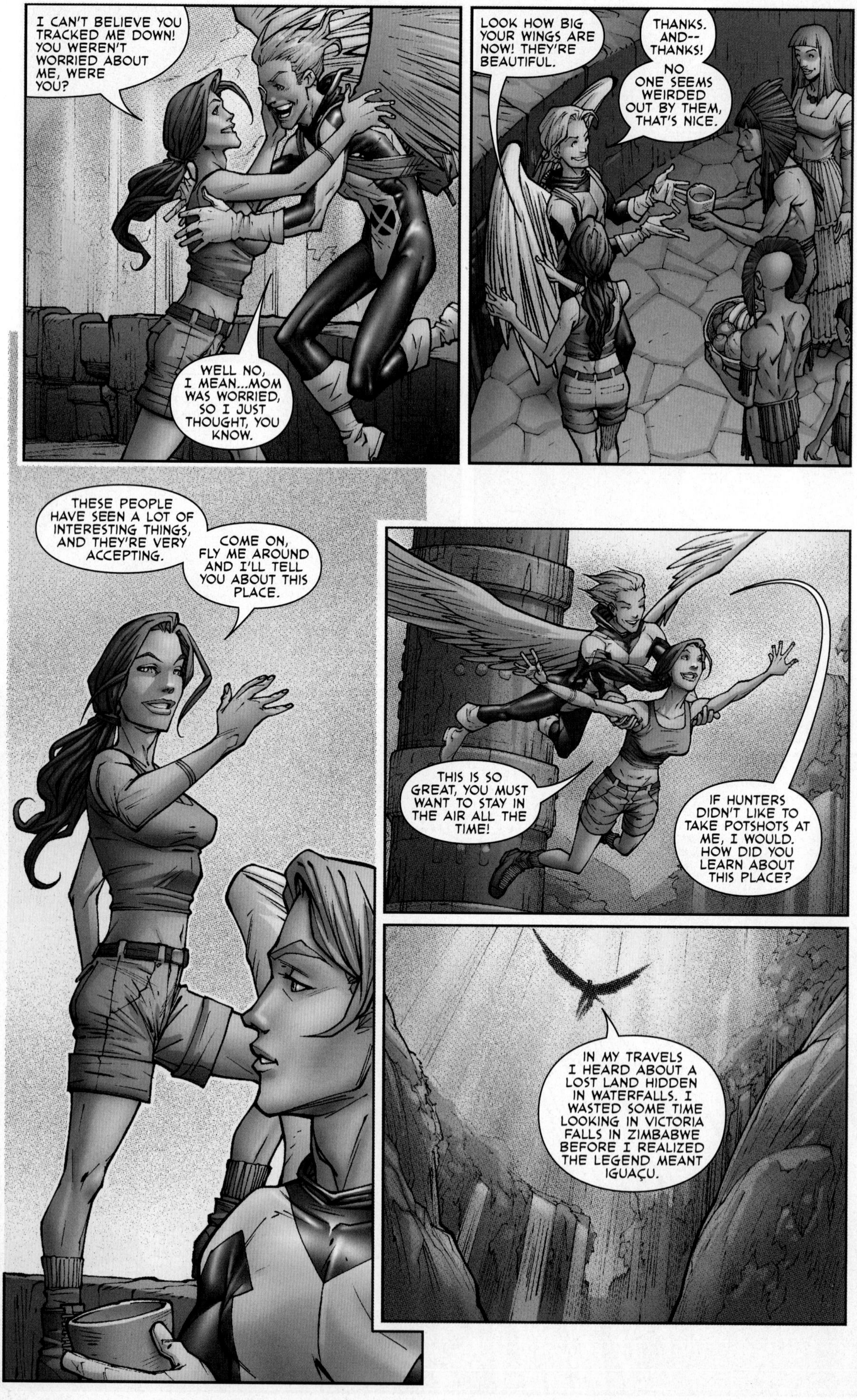
I CAN'T BELIEVE YOU TRACKED ME DOWN! YOU WEREN'T WORRIED ABOUT ME, WERE YOU?
WELL NO, I MEAN...MOM WAS WORRIED, SO I JUST THOUGHT, YOU KNOW.
LOOK HOW BIG YOUR WINGS ARE NOW! THEY'RE BEAUTIFUL.
THANKS. AND-- THANKS!
NO ONE SEEMS WEIRDED OUT BY THEM, THAT'S NICE.
THESE PEOPLE HAVE SEEN A LOT OF INTERESTING THINGS, AND THEY'RE VERY ACCEPTING.
COME ON, FLY ME AROUND AND I'LL TELL YOU ABOUT THIS PLACE.
THIS IS SO GREAT, YOU MUST WANT TO STAY IN THE AIR ALL THE TIME!
IF HUNTERS DIDN'T LIKE TO TAKE POTSHOTS AT ME, I WOULD. HOW DID YOU LEARN ABOUT THIS PLACE?
IN MY TRAVELS I HEARD ABOUT A LOST LAND HIDDEN IN WATERFALLS. I WASTED SOME TIME LOOKING IN VICTORIA FALLS IN ZIMBABWE BEFORE I REALIZED THE LEGEND MEANT IGUAÇU.

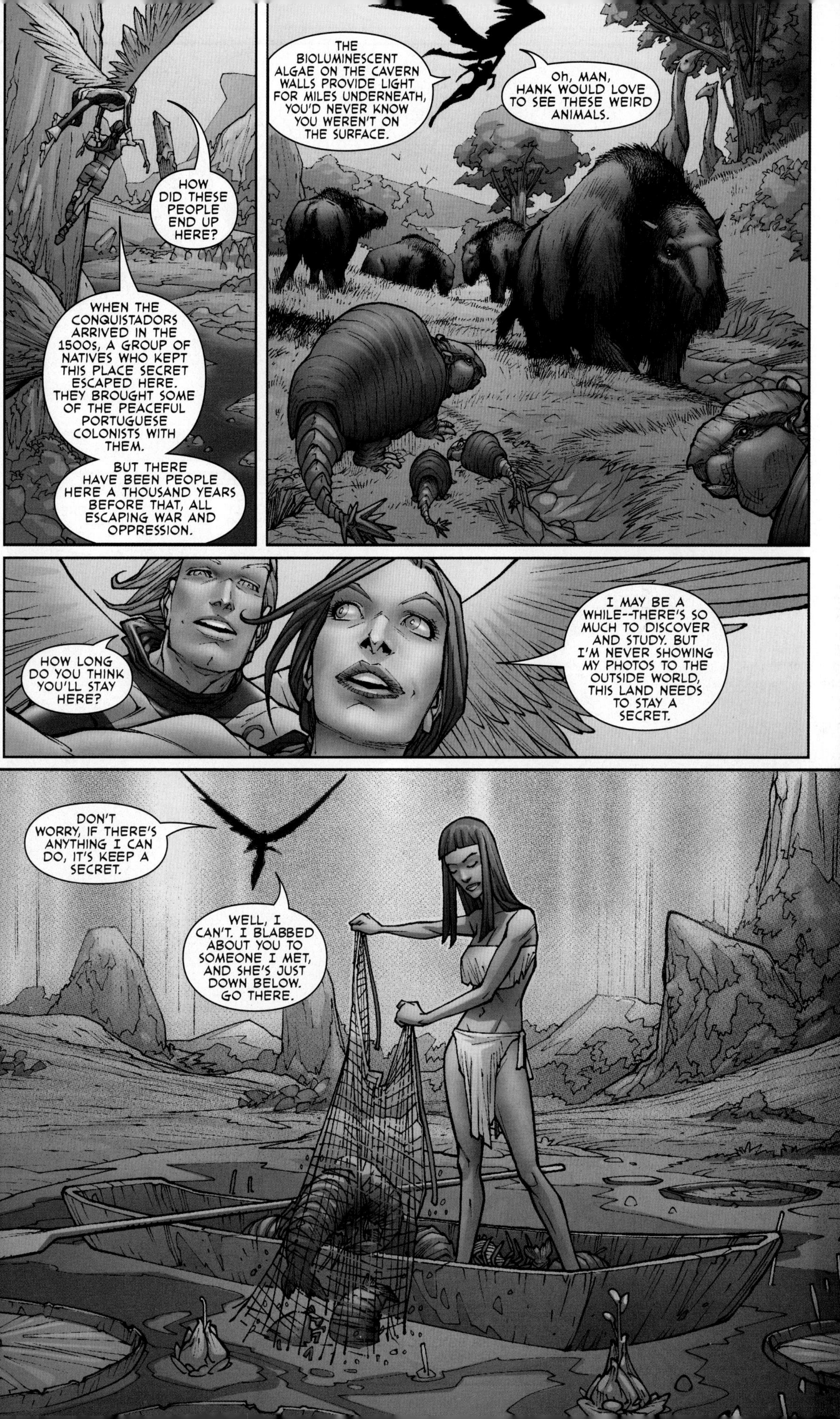
HOW DID THESE PEOPLE END UP HERE?
WHEN THE CONQUISTADORS ARRIVED IN THE 1500s, A GROUP OF NATIVES WHO KEPT THIS PLACE SECRET ESCAPED HERE. THEY BROUGHT SOME OF THE PEACEFUL PORTUGUESE COLONISTS WITH THEM.
BUT THERE HAVE BEEN PEOPLE HERE A THOUSAND YEARS BEFORE THAT, ALL ESCAPING WAR AND OPPRESSION.
THE BIOLUMINESCENT ALGAE ON THE CAVERN WALLS PROVIDE LIGHT FOR MILES UNDERNEATH, YOU'D NEVER KNOW YOU WEREN'T ON THE SURFACE.
Oh, MAN, HANK WOULD LOVE TO SEE THESE WEIRD ANIMALS.
HOW LONG DO YOU THINK YOU'LL STAY HERE?
I MAY BE A WHILE--THERE'S SO MUCH TO DISCOVER AND STUDY. BUT I'M NEVER SHOWING MY PHOTOS TO THE OUTSIDE WORLD, THIS LAND NEEDS TO STAY A SECRET.
DON'T WORRY, IF THERE'S ANYTHING I CAN DO, IT'S KEEP A SECRET.
WELL, I CAN'T. I BLABBED ABOUT YOU TO SOMEONE I MET, AND SHE'S JUST DOWN BELOW. GO THERE.

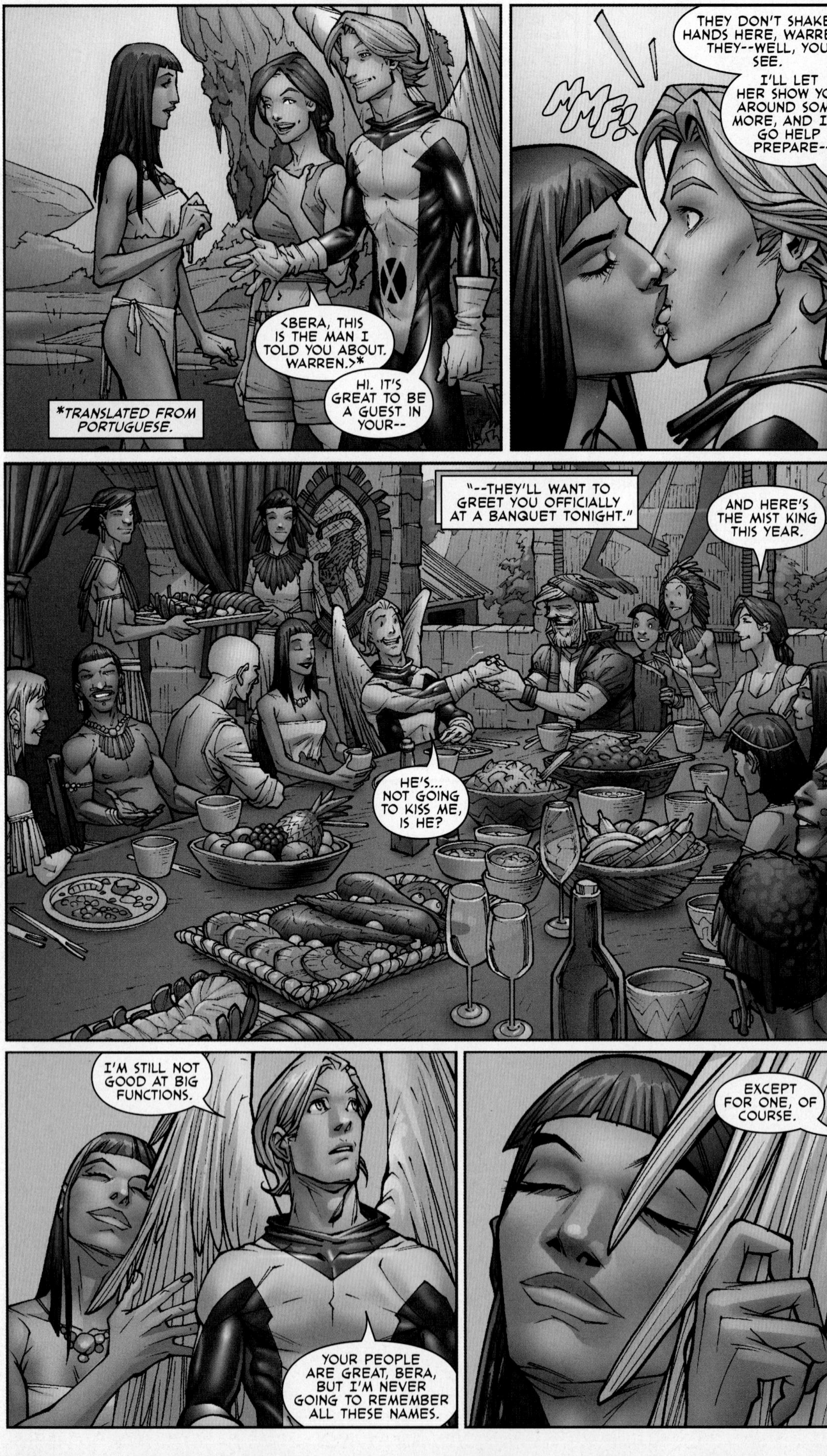

<BERA, THIS IS THE MAN I TOLD YOU ABOUT. WARREN.>*
HI. IT'S GREAT TO BE A GUEST IN YOUR--
*TRANSLATED FROM PORTUGUESE.
MMF!
THEY DON'T SHAKE HANDS HERE, WARREN, THEY--WELL, YOU SEE.
I'LL LET HER SHOW YOU AROUND SOME MORE, AND I'LL GO HELP PREPARE--
"--THEY'LL WANT TO GREET YOU OFFICIALLY AT A BANQUET TONIGHT."
AND HERE'S THE MIST KING THIS YEAR.
HE'S... NOT GOING TO KISS ME, IS HE?
I'M STILL NOT GOOD AT BIG FUNCTIONS.
YOUR PEOPLE ARE GREAT, BERA, BUT I'M NEVER GOING TO REMEMBER ALL THESE NAMES.
EXCEPT FOR ONE, OF COURSE.

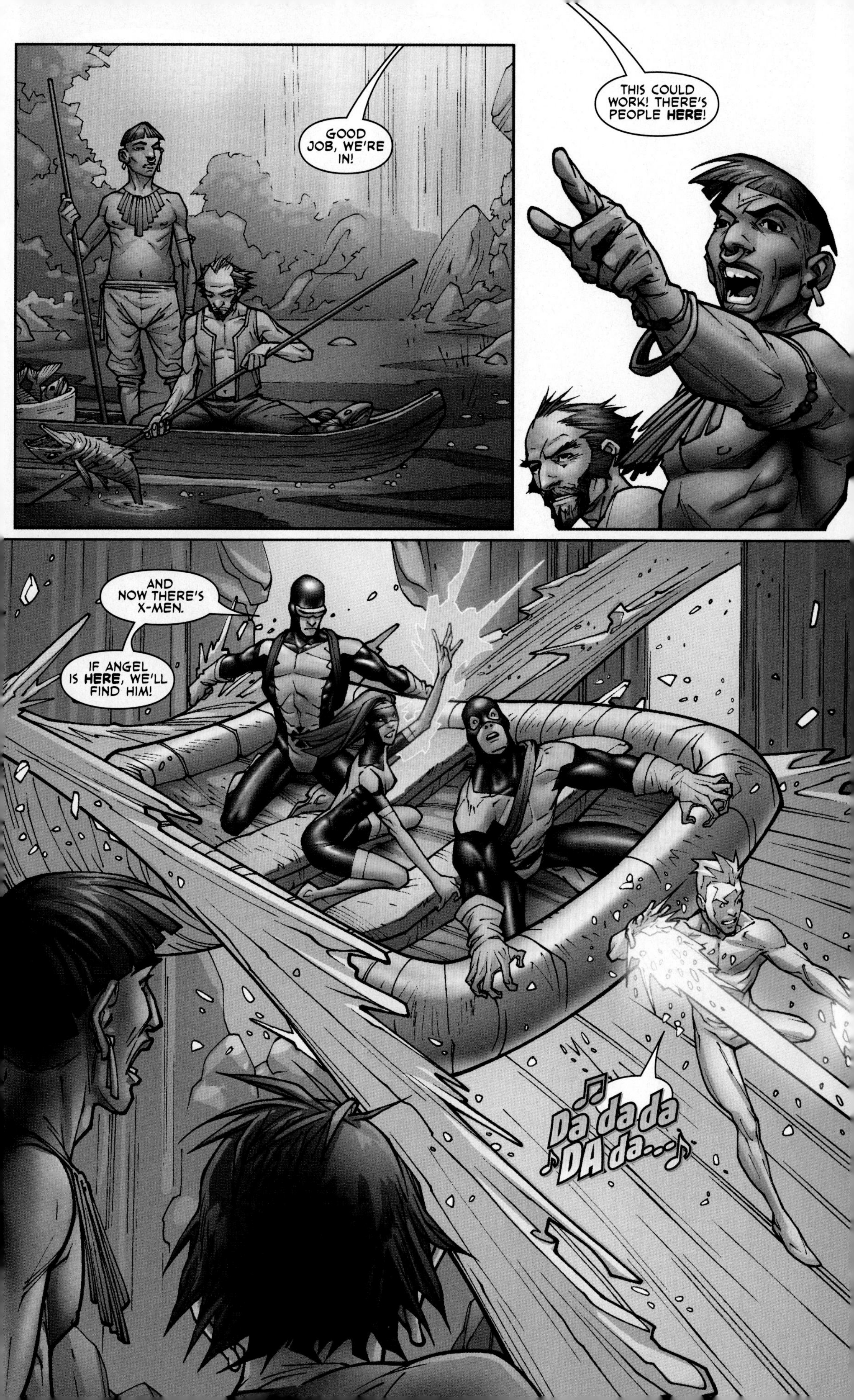
GOOD JOB, WE'RE IN!
THIS COULD WORK! THERE'S PEOPLE HERE!
AND NOW THERE'S X-MEN.
IF ANGEL IS HERE, WE'LL FIND HIM!
♪Da da da DA da...♪

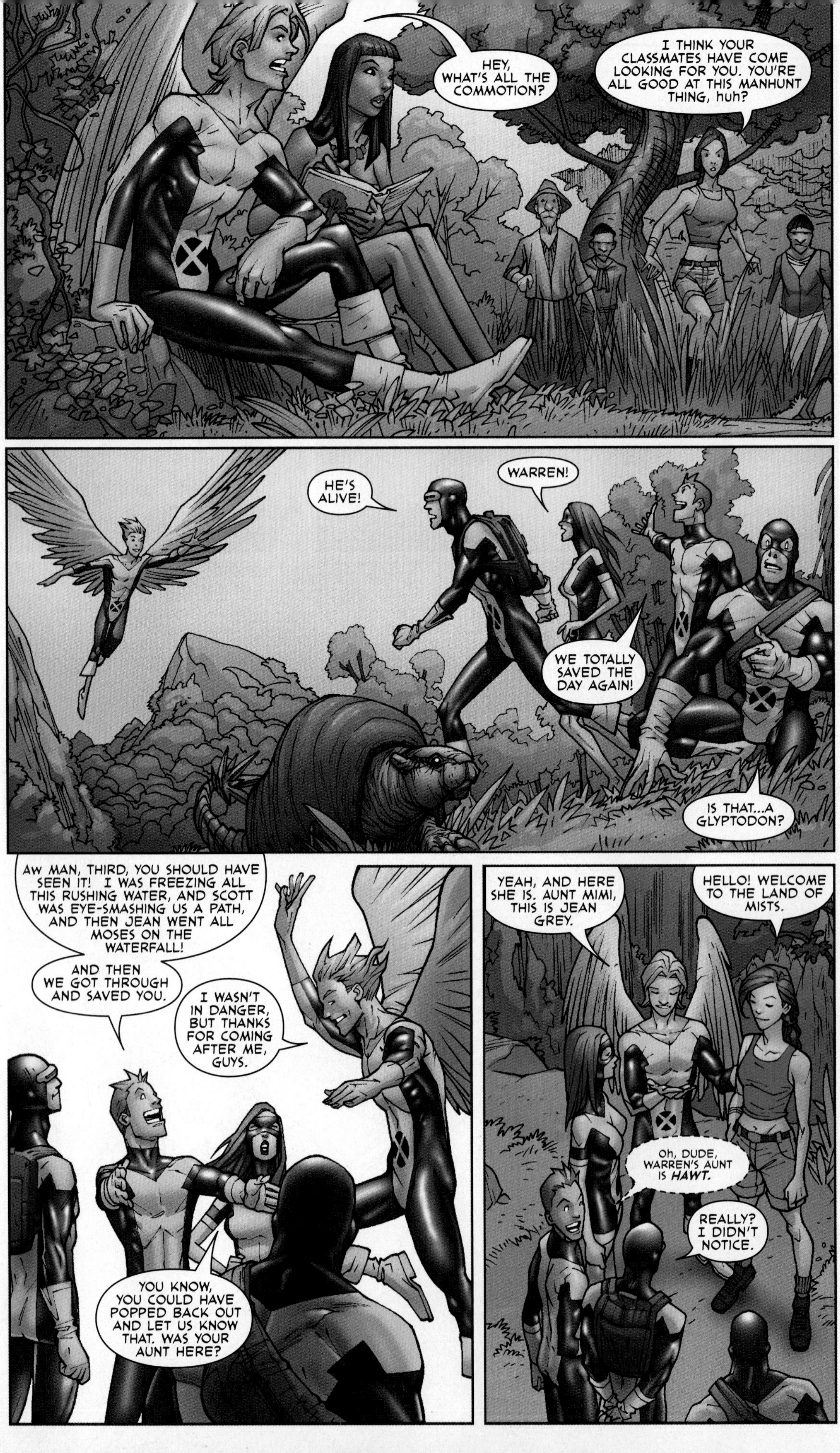
HEY, WHAT'S ALL THE COMMOTION?
I THINK YOUR CLASSMATES HAVE COME LOOKING FOR YOU. YOU'RE ALL GOOD AT THIS MANHUNT THING, huh?
HE'S ALIVE!
WARREN!
WE TOTALLY SAVED THE DAY AGAIN!
IS THAT...A GLYPTODON?
AW MAN, THIRD, YOU SHOULD HAVE SEEN IT! I WAS FREEZING ALL THIS RUSHING WATER, AND SCOTT WAS EYE-SMASHING US A PATH, AND THEN JEAN WENT ALL MOSES ON THE WATERFALL!
AND THEN WE GOT THROUGH AND SAVED YOU.
I WASN'T IN DANGER, BUT THANKS FOR COMING AFTER ME, GUYS.
YOU KNOW, YOU COULD HAVE POPPED BACK OUT AND LET US KNOW THAT. WAS YOUR AUNT HERE?
YEAH, AND HERE SHE IS. AUNT MIMI, THIS IS JEAN GREY.
HELLO! WELCOME TO THE LAND OF MISTS.
Oh, DUDE, WARREN'S AUNT IS *HAWT.*
REALLY? I DIDN'T NOTICE.

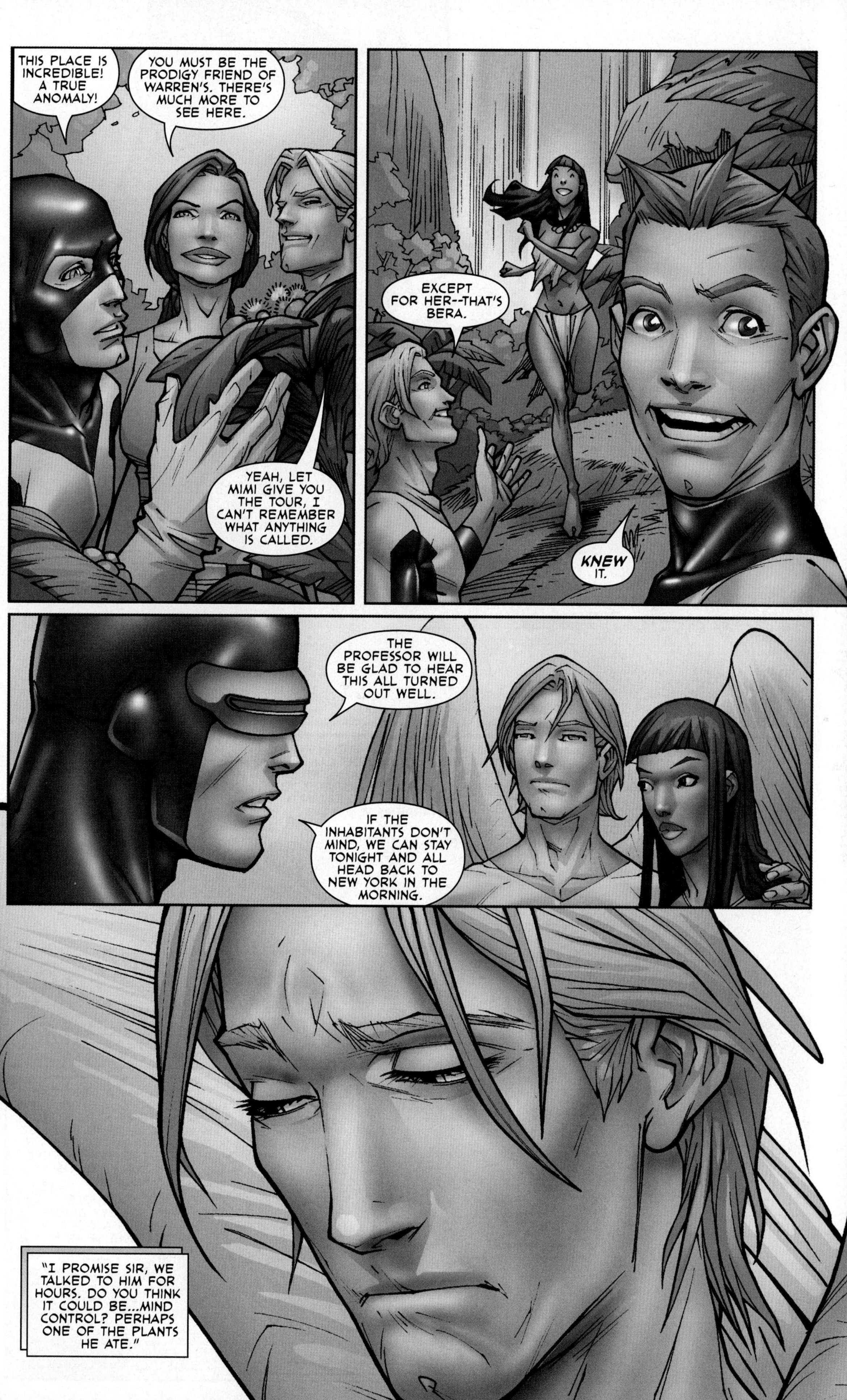
THIS PLACE IS INCREDIBLE! A TRUE ANOMALY!
YOU MUST BE THE PRODIGY FRIEND OF WARREN'S. THERE'S MUCH MORE TO SEE HERE.
YEAH, LET MIMI GIVE YOU THE TOUR, I CAN'T REMEMBER WHAT ANYTHING IS CALLED.
EXCEPT FOR HER--THAT'S BERA.
KNEW IT.
THE PROFESSOR WILL BE GLAD TO HEAR THIS ALL TURNED OUT WELL.
IF THE INHABITANTS DON'T MIND, WE CAN STAY TONIGHT AND ALL HEAD BACK TO NEW YORK IN THE MORNING.
"I PROMISE SIR, WE TALKED TO HIM FOR HOURS. DO YOU THINK IT COULD BE...MIND CONTROL? PERHAPS ONE OF THE PLANTS HE ATE."

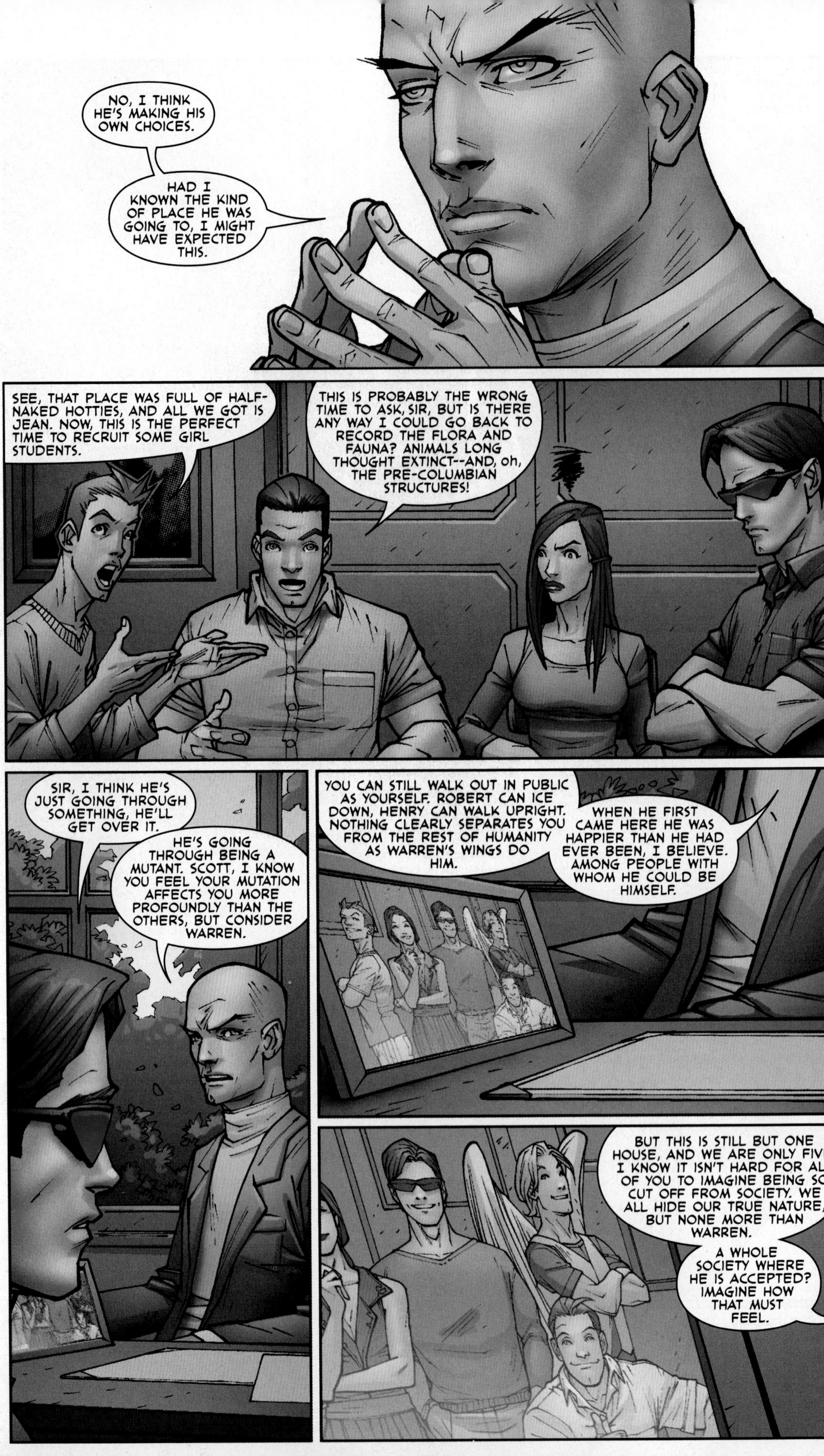
NO, I THINK HE'S MAKING HIS OWN CHOICES.
HAD I KNOWN THE KIND OF PLACE HE WAS GOING TO, I MIGHT HAVE EXPECTED THIS.
SEE, THAT PLACE WAS FULL OF HALF-NAKED HOTTIES, AND ALL WE GOT IS JEAN. NOW, THIS IS THE PERFECT TIME TO RECRUIT SOME GIRL STUDENTS.
THIS IS PROBABLY THE WRONG TIME TO ASK, SIR, BUT IS THERE ANY WAY I COULD GO BACK TO RECORD THE FLORA AND FAUNA? ANIMALS LONG THOUGHT EXTINCT--AND, oh, THE PRE-COLUMBIAN STRUCTURES!
SIR, I THINK HE'S JUST GOING THROUGH SOMETHING, HE'LL GET OVER IT.
HE'S GOING THROUGH BEING A MUTANT. SCOTT, I KNOW YOU FEEL YOUR MUTATION AFFECTS YOU MORE PROFOUNDLY THAN THE OTHERS, BUT CONSIDER WARREN.
YOU CAN STILL WALK OUT IN PUBLIC AS YOURSELF. ROBERT CAN ICE DOWN, HENRY CAN WALK UPRIGHT. NOTHING CLEARLY SEPARATES YOU FROM THE REST OF HUMANITY AS WARREN'S WINGS DO HIM.
WHEN HE FIRST CAME HERE HE WAS HAPPIER THAN HE HAD EVER BEEN, I BELIEVE. AMONG PEOPLE WITH WHOM HE COULD BE HIMSELF.
BUT THIS IS STILL BUT ONE HOUSE, AND WE ARE ONLY FIVE. I KNOW IT ISN'T HARD FOR ALL OF YOU TO IMAGINE BEING SO CUT OFF FROM SOCIETY. WE ALL HIDE OUR TRUE NATURE, BUT NONE MORE THAN WARREN.
A WHOLE SOCIETY WHERE HE IS ACCEPTED? IMAGINE HOW THAT MUST FEEL.

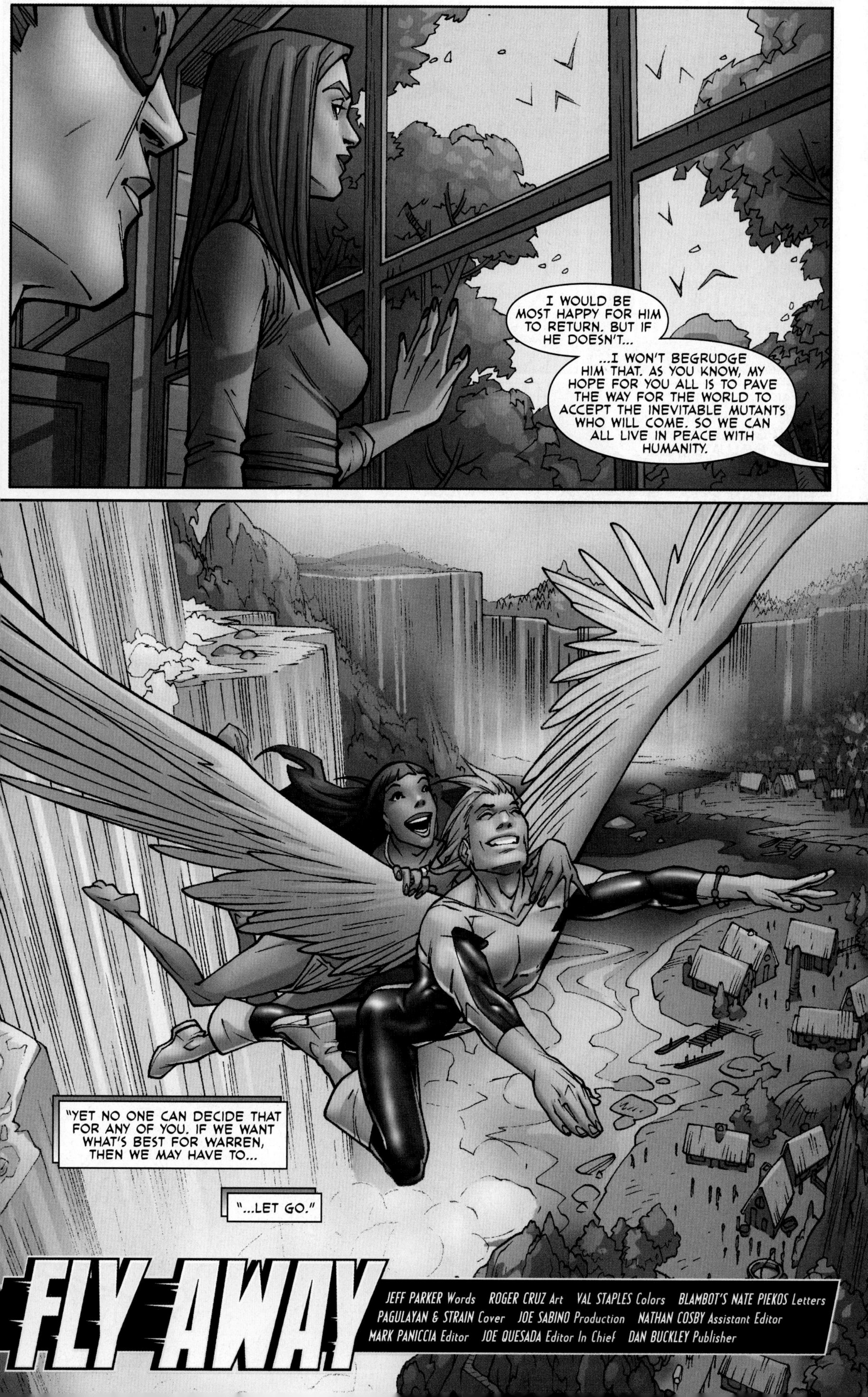

I WOULD BE MOST HAPPY FOR HIM TO RETURN. BUT IF HE DOESN'T...
...I WON'T BEGRUDGE HIM THAT. AS YOU KNOW, MY HOPE FOR YOU ALL IS TO PAVE THE WAY FOR THE WORLD TO ACCEPT THE INEVITABLE MUTANTS WHO WILL COME. SO WE CAN ALL LIVE IN PEACE WITH HUMANITY.
"YET NO ONE CAN DECIDE THAT FOR ANY OF YOU. IF WE WANT WHAT'S BEST FOR WARREN, THEN WE MAY HAVE TO...
"...LET GO."
FLY AWAY
JEFF PARKER Words ROGER CRUZ Art VAL STAPLES Colors BLAMBOT'S NATE PIEKOS Letters
PAGULAYAN & STRAIN Cover JOE SABINO Production NATHAN COSBY Assistant Editor
MARK PANICCIA Editor JOE QUESADA Editor In Chief DAN BUCKLEY Publisher

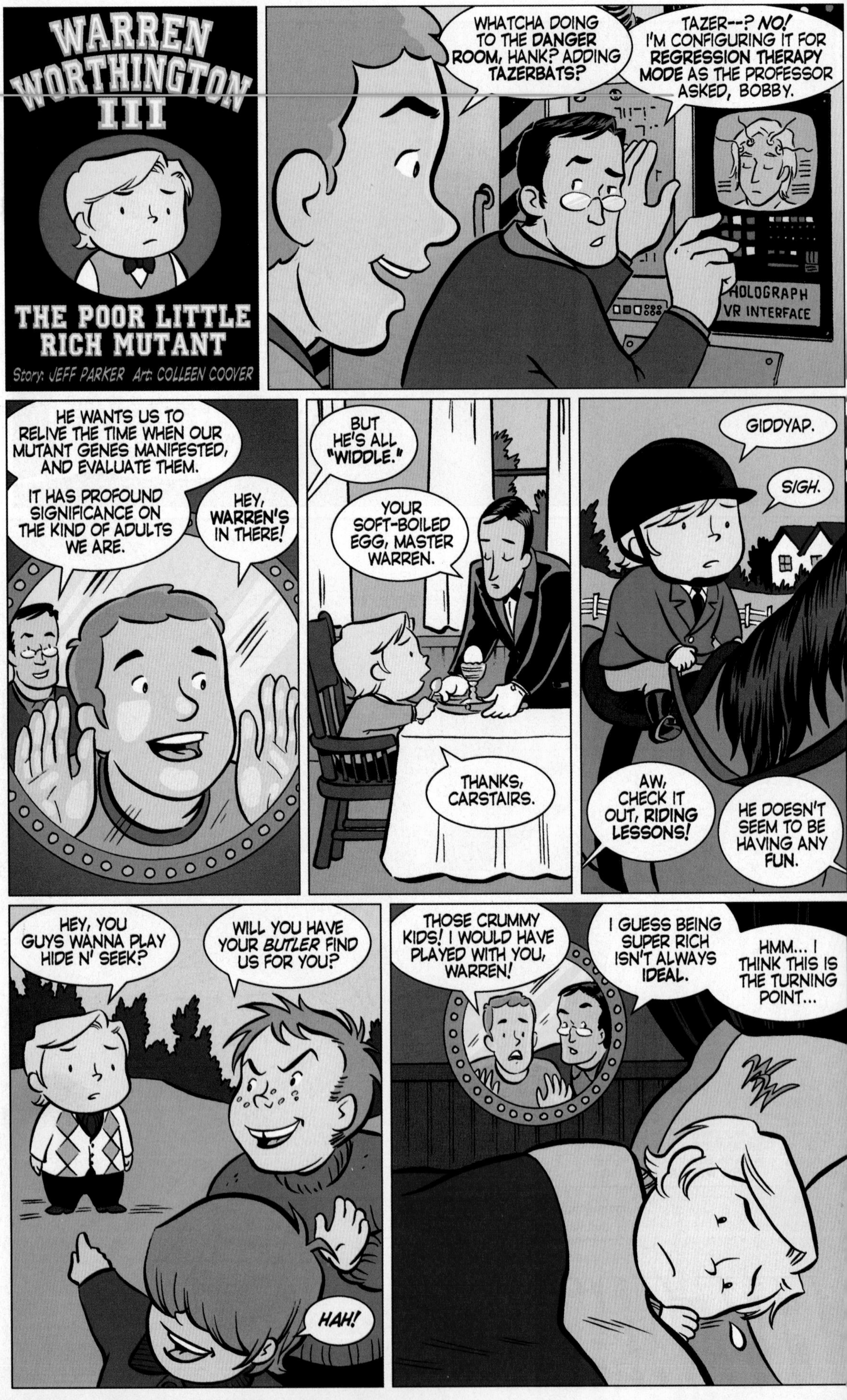
WARREN WORTHINGTON III
THE POOR LITTLE RICH MUTANT
Story: JEFF PARKER Art: COLLEEN COOVER
WHATCHA DOING TO THE DANGER ROOM, HANK? ADDING TAZERBATS?
TAZER--? NO! I'M CONFIGURING IT FOR REGRESSION THERAPY MODE AS THE PROFESSOR ASKED, BOBBY.
HOLOGRAPH VR INTERFACE
HE WANTS US TO RELIVE THE TIME WHEN OUR MUTANT GENES MANIFESTED, AND EVALUATE THEM.
IT HAS PROFOUND SIGNIFICANCE ON THE KIND OF ADULTS WE ARE.
HEY, WARREN'S IN THERE!
BUT HE'S ALL "WIDDLE."
YOUR SOFT-BOILED EGG, MASTER WARREN.
THANKS, CARSTAIRS.
GIDDYAP.
SIGH.
AW, CHECK IT OUT, RIDING LESSONS!
HE DOESN'T SEEM TO BE HAVING ANY FUN.
HEY, YOU GUYS WANNA PLAY HIDE N' SEEK?
WILL YOU HAVE YOUR BUTLER FIND US FOR YOU?
HAH!
THOSE CRUMMY KIDS! I WOULD HAVE PLAYED WITH YOU, WARREN!
I GUESS BEING SUPER RICH ISN'T ALWAYS IDEAL.
HMM... I THINK THIS IS THE TURNING POINT...

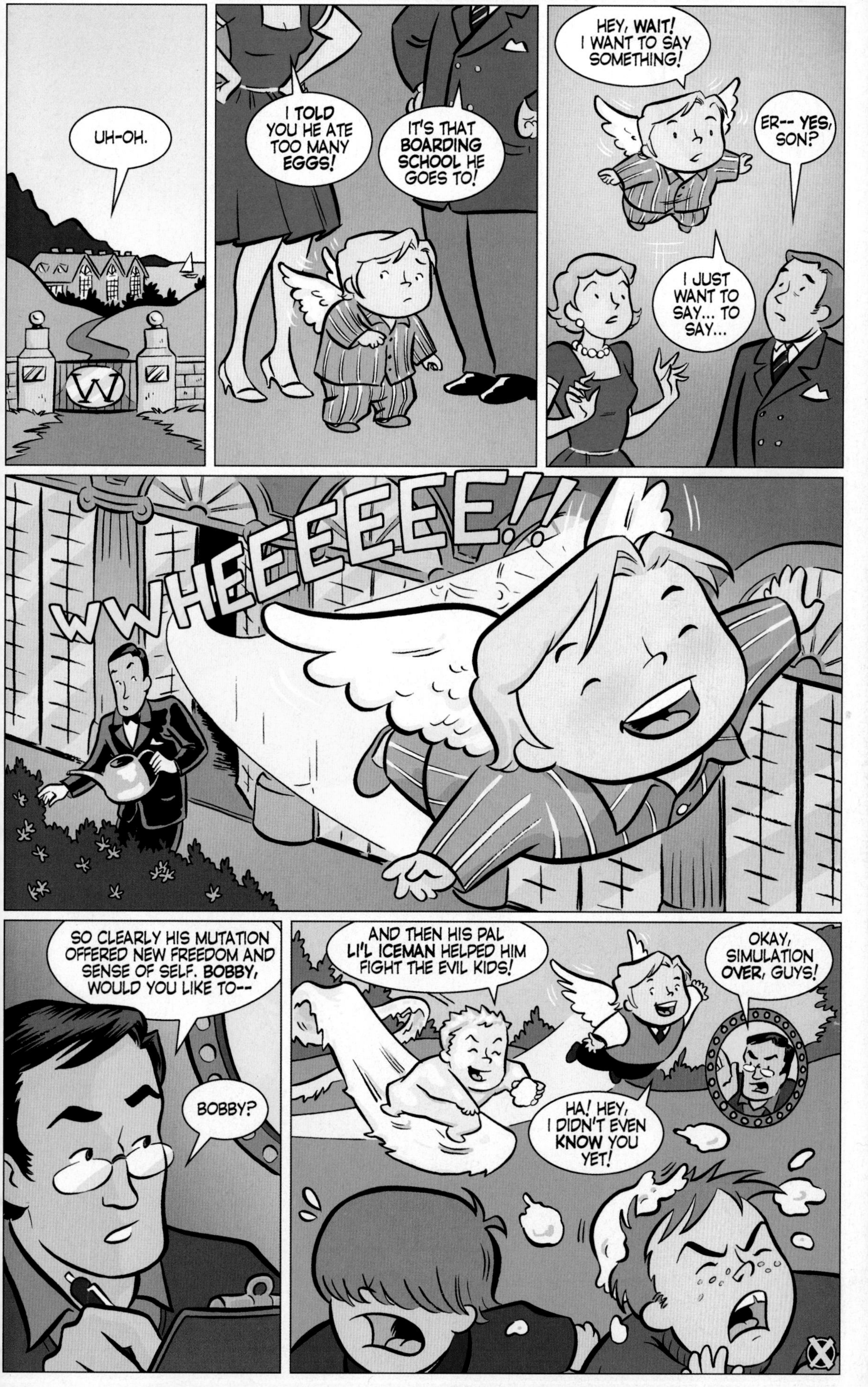
UH-OH.
I TOLD YOU HE ATE TOO MANY EGGS!
IT'S THAT BOARDING SCHOOL HE GOES TO!
HEY, WAIT! I WANT TO SAY SOMETHING!
ER-- YES, SON?
I JUST WANT TO SAY... TO SAY...
WWHEEEEEEE!!
SO CLEARLY HIS MUTATION OFFERED NEW FREEDOM AND SENSE OF SELF. BOBBY, WOULD YOU LIKE TO--
BOBBY?
AND THEN HIS PAL LI'L ICEMAN HELPED HIM FIGHT THE EVIL KIDS!
OKAY, SIMULATION OVER, GUYS!
HA! HEY, I DIDN'T EVEN KNOW YOU YET!

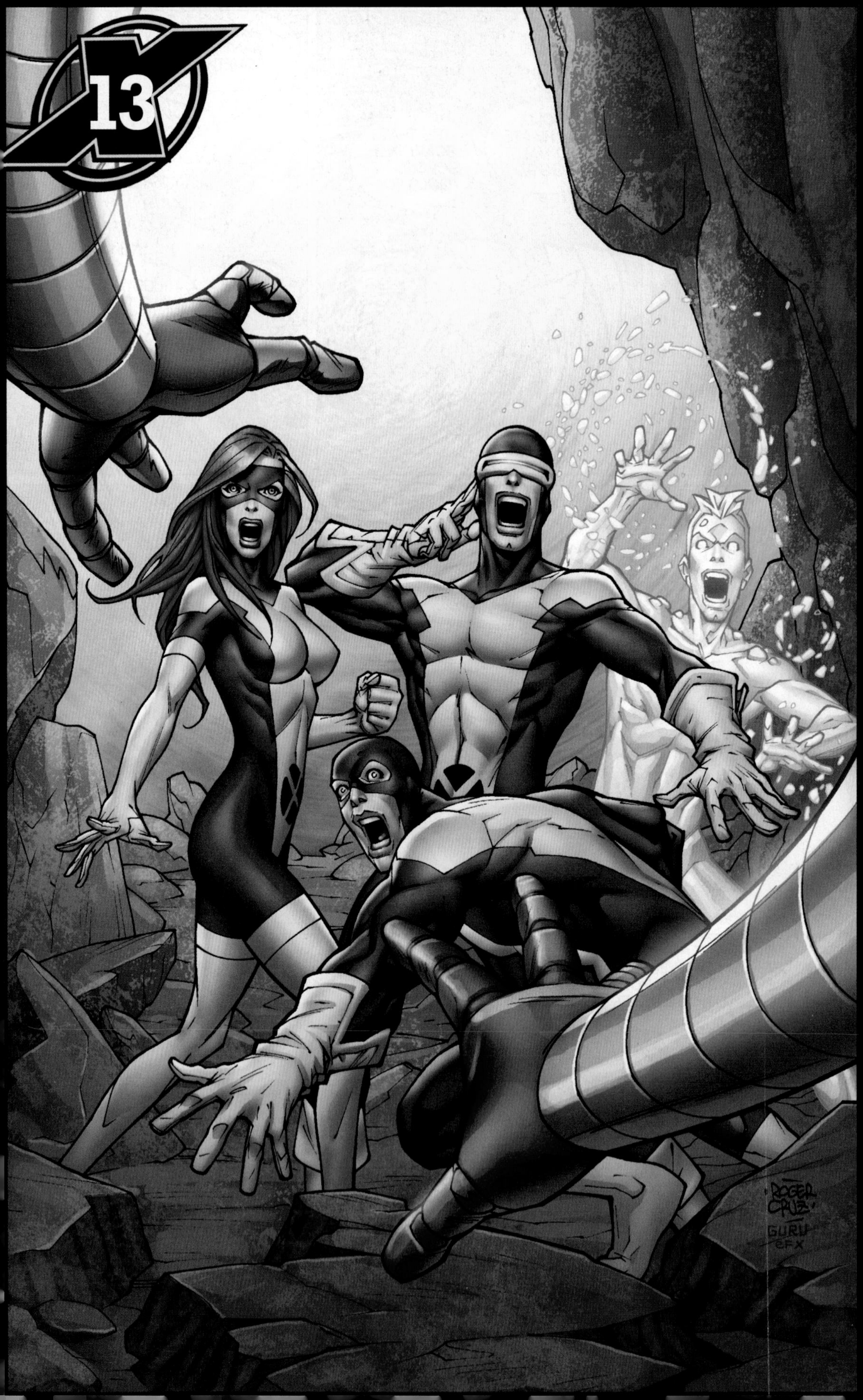
13
ROGER CRUZ
GURU eFX

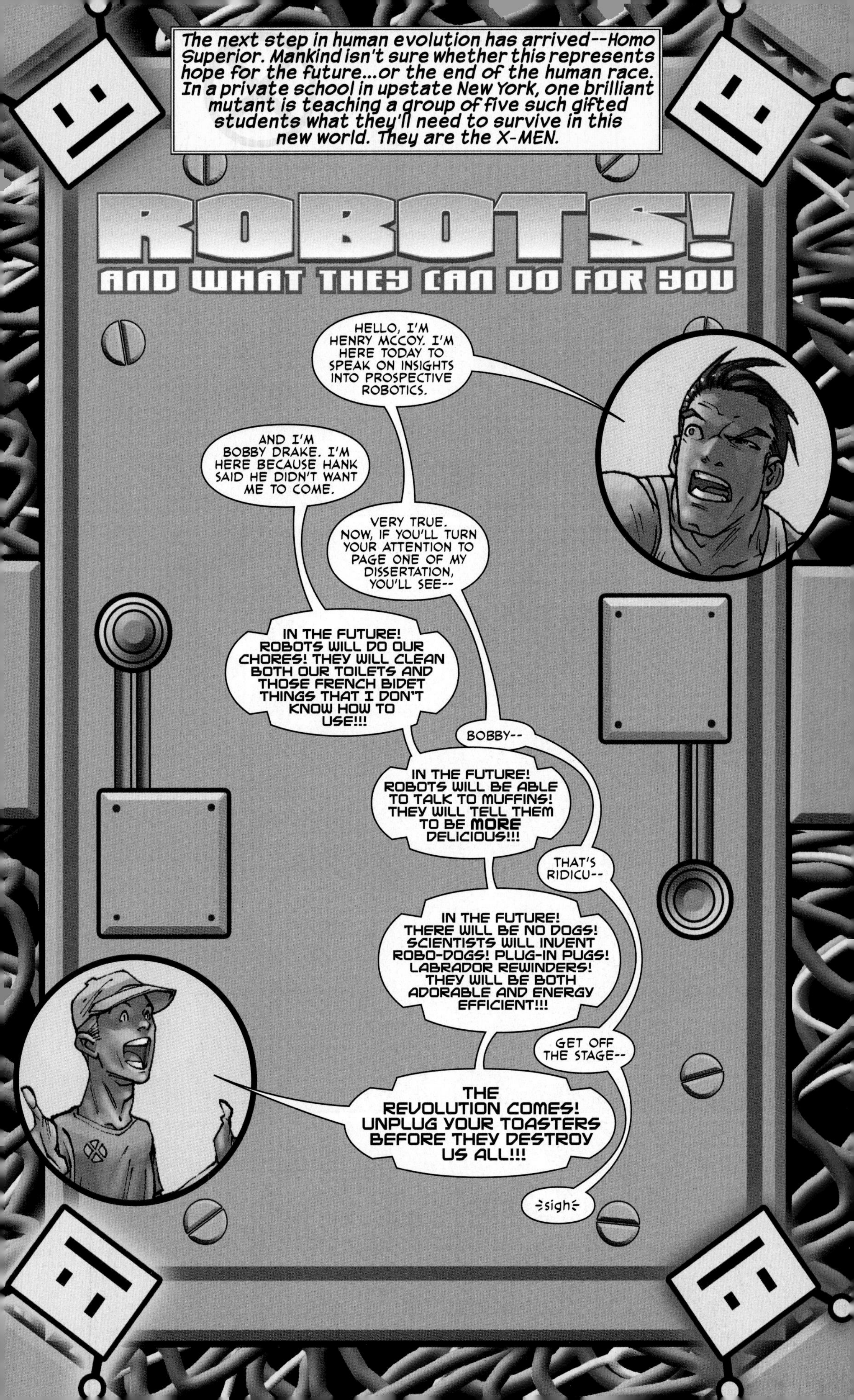
The next step in human evolution has arrived--Homo Superior. Mankind isn't sure whether this represents hope for the future...or the end of the human race. In a private school in upstate New York, one brilliant mutant is teaching a group of five such gifted students what they'll need to survive in this new world. They are the X-MEN.
ROBOTS!
AND WHAT THEY CAN DO FOR YOU
HELLO, I'M HENRY McCOY. I'M HERE TODAY TO SPEAK ON INSIGHTS INTO PROSPECTIVE ROBOTICS.
AND I'M BOBBY DRAKE. I'M HERE BECAUSE HANK SAID HE DIDN'T WANT ME TO COME.
VERY TRUE. NOW, IF YOU'LL TURN YOUR ATTENTION TO PAGE ONE OF MY DISSERTATION, YOU'LL SEE--
IN THE FUTURE! ROBOTS WILL DO OUR CHORES! THEY WILL CLEAN BOTH OUR TOILETS AND THOSE FRENCH BIDET THINGS THAT I DON'T KNOW HOW TO USE!!!
BOBBY--
IN THE FUTURE! ROBOTS WILL BE ABLE TO TALK TO MUFFINS! THEY WILL TELL THEM TO BE MORE DELICIOUS!!!
THAT'S RIDICU--
IN THE FUTURE! THERE WILL BE NO DOGS! SCIENTISTS WILL INVENT ROBO-DOGS! PLUG-IN PUGS! LABRADOR REWINDERS! THEY WILL BE BOTH ADORABLE AND ENERGY EFFICIENT!!!
GET OFF THE STAGE--
THE REVOLUTION COMES! UNPLUG YOUR TOASTERS BEFORE THEY DESTROY US ALL!!!
sigh

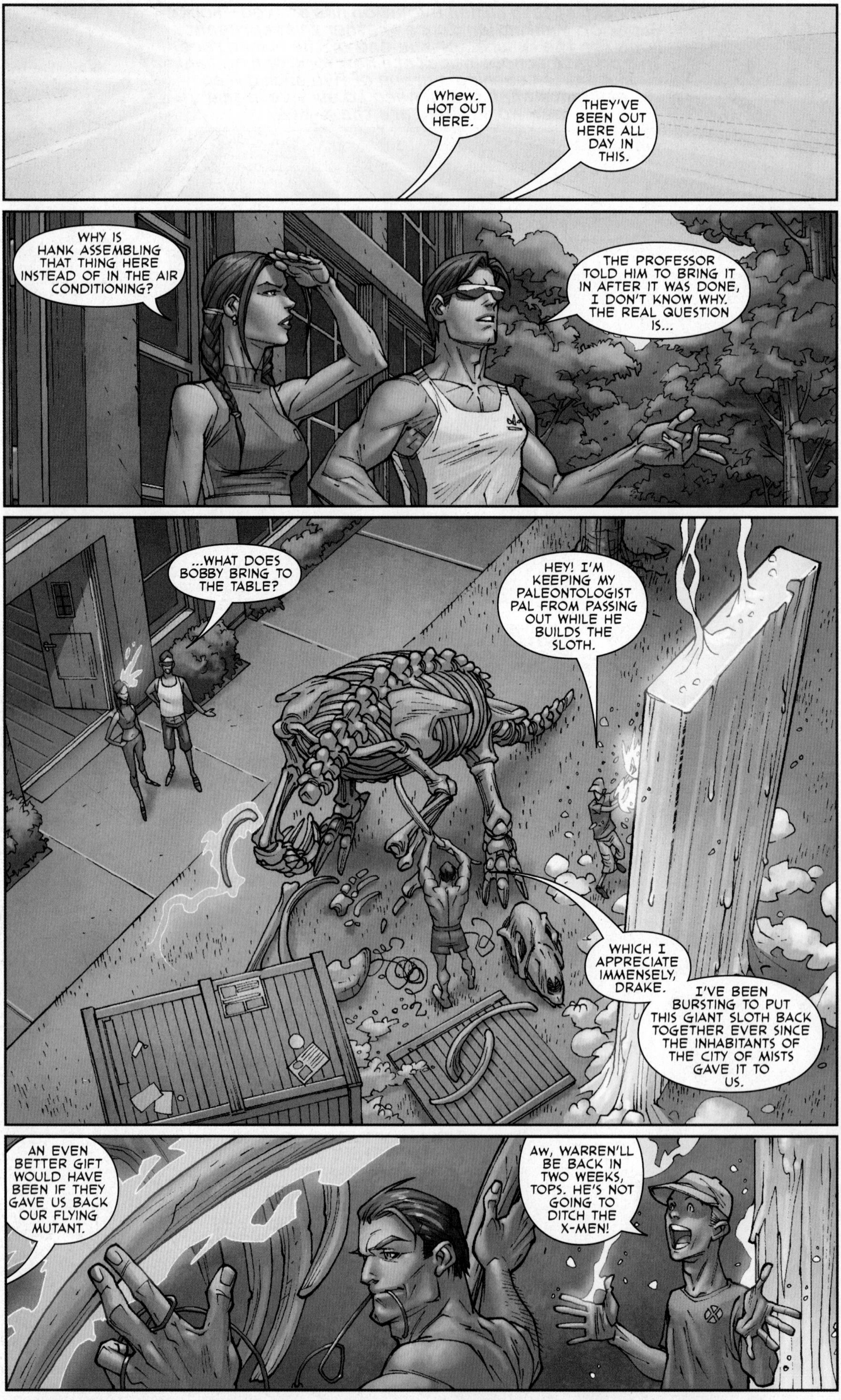
Whew. HOT OUT HERE.
THEY'VE BEEN OUT HERE ALL DAY IN THIS.
WHY IS HANK ASSEMBLING THAT THING HERE INSTEAD OF IN THE AIR CONDITIONING?
THE PROFESSOR TOLD HIM TO BRING IT IN AFTER IT WAS DONE, I DON'T KNOW WHY. THE REAL QUESTION IS...
...WHAT DOES BOBBY BRING TO THE TABLE?
HEY! I'M KEEPING MY PALEONTOLOGIST PAL FROM PASSING OUT WHILE HE BUILDS THE SLOTH.
WHICH I APPRECIATE IMMENSELY, DRAKE.
I'VE BEEN BURSTING TO PUT THIS GIANT SLOTH BACK TOGETHER EVER SINCE THE INHABITANTS OF THE CITY OF MISTS GAVE IT TO US.
AN EVEN BETTER GIFT WOULD HAVE BEEN IF THEY GAVE US BACK OUR FLYING MUTANT.
AW, WARREN'LL BE BACK IN TWO WEEKS, TOPS. HE'S NOT GOING TO DITCH THE X-MEN!

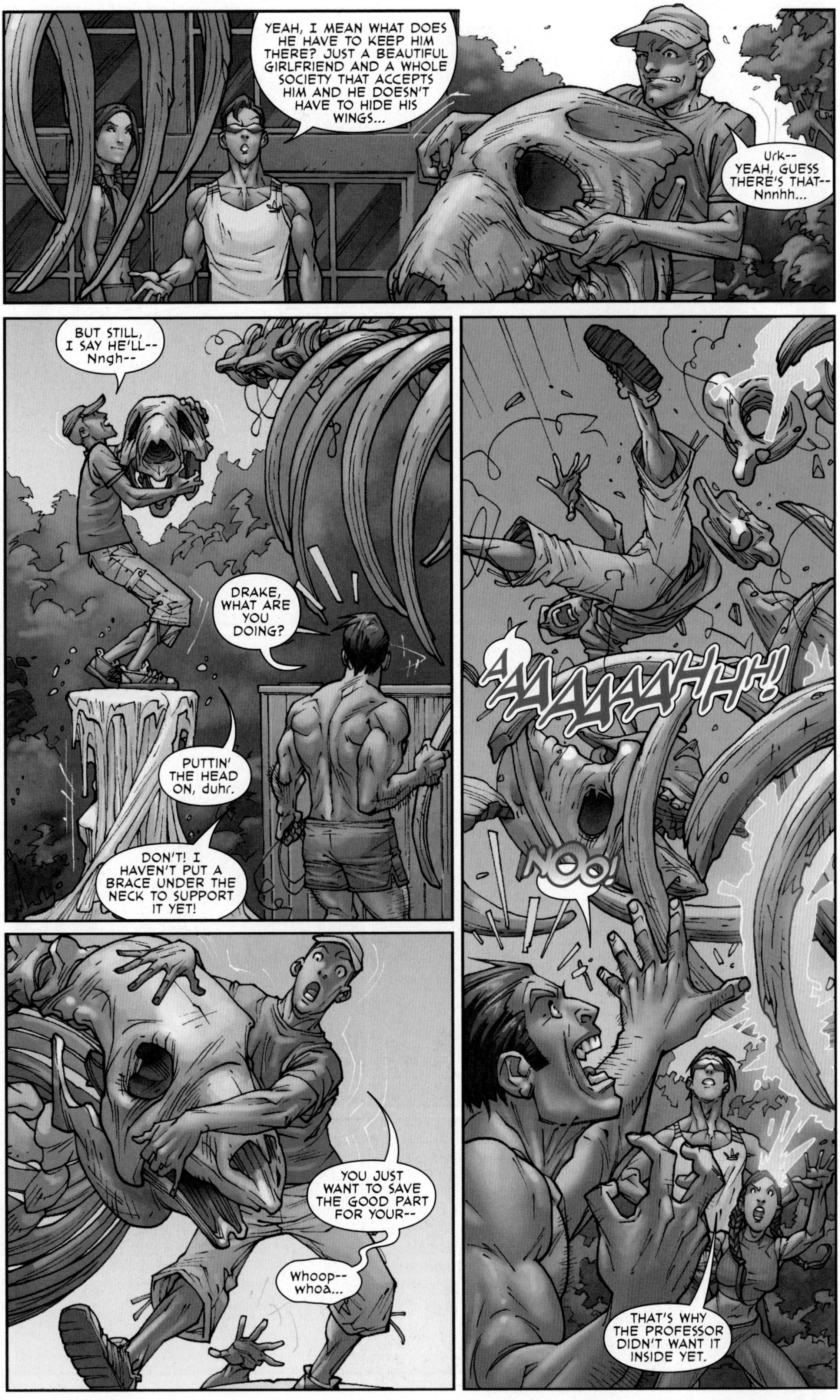
YEAH, I MEAN WHAT DOES HE HAVE TO KEEP HIM THERE? JUST A BEAUTIFUL GIRLFRIEND AND A WHOLE SOCIETY THAT ACCEPTS HIM AND HE DOESN'T HAVE TO HIDE HIS WINGS...
Urk-- YEAH, GUESS THERE'S THAT-- Nnnhh...
BUT STILL, I SAY HE'LL-- Nngh--
DRAKE, WHAT ARE YOU DOING?
PUTTIN' THE HEAD ON, duhr.
DON'T! I HAVEN'T PUT A BRACE UNDER THE NECK TO SUPPORT IT YET!
YOU JUST WANT TO SAVE THE GOOD PART FOR YOUR--
Whoop-- whoa...
AAAAAAHHH!
NOO!
THAT'S WHY THE PROFESSOR DIDN'T WANT IT INSIDE YET.

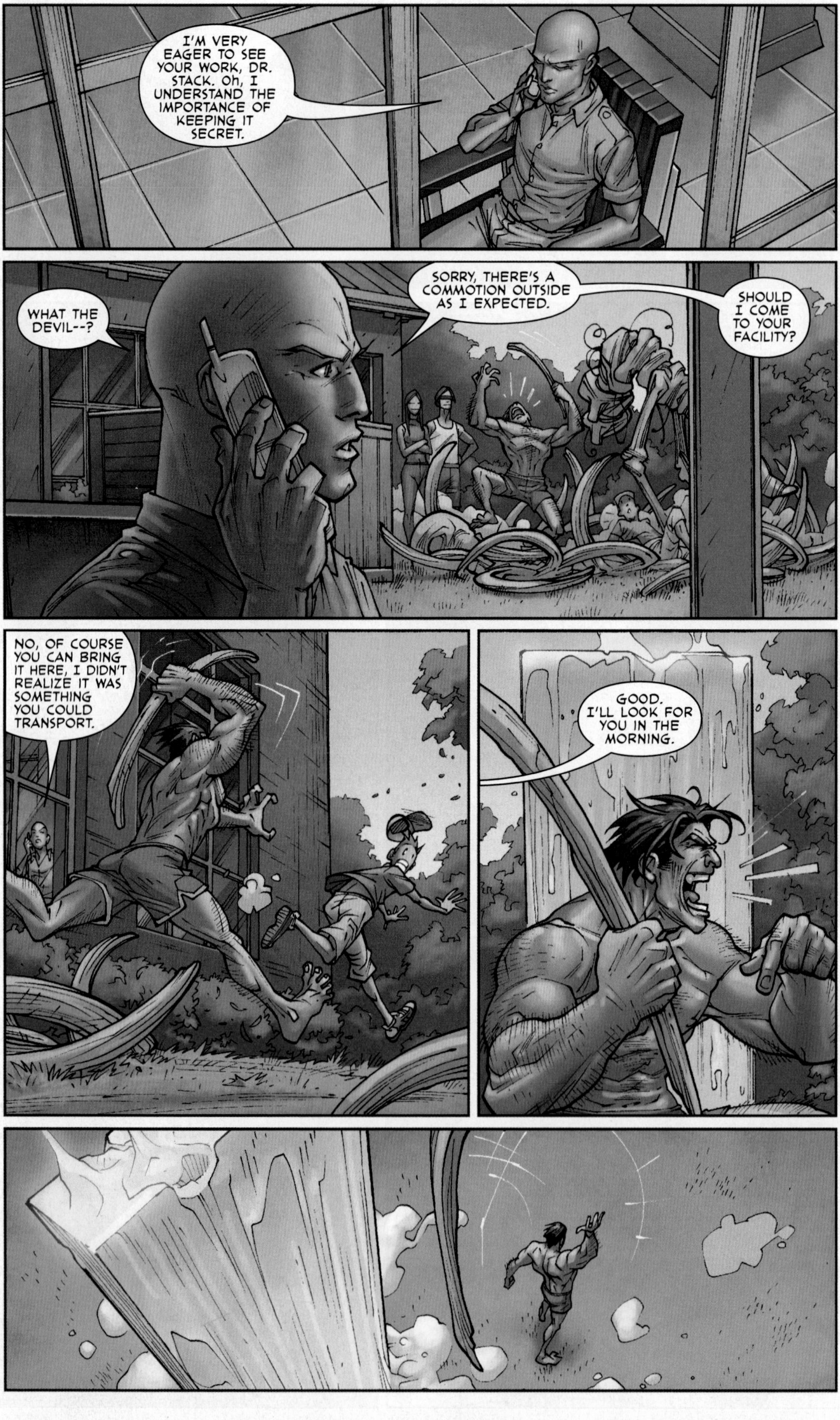
I'M VERY EAGER TO SEE YOUR WORK, DR. STACK. Oh, I UNDERSTAND THE IMPORTANCE OF KEEPING IT SECRET.
WHAT THE DEVIL--?
SORRY, THERE'S A COMMOTION OUTSIDE AS I EXPECTED.
SHOULD I COME TO YOUR FACILITY?
NO, OF COURSE YOU CAN BRING IT HERE, I DIDN'T REALIZE IT WAS SOMETHING YOU COULD TRANSPORT.
GOOD. I'LL LOOK FOR YOU IN THE MORNING.

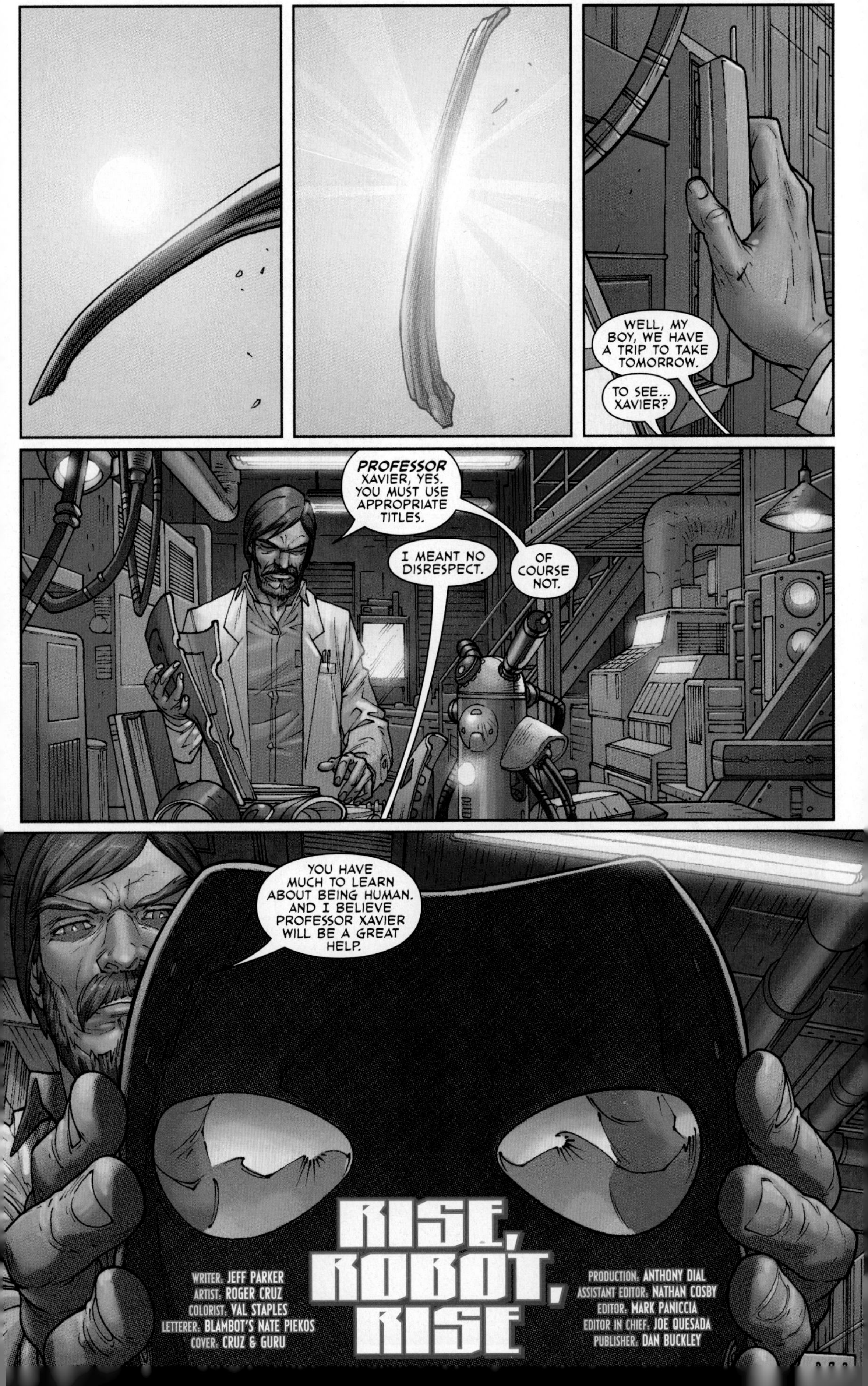
WELL, MY BOY, WE HAVE A TRIP TO TAKE TOMORROW.
TO SEE... XAVIER?
PROFESSOR XAVIER, YES. YOU MUST USE APPROPRIATE TITLES.
I MEANT NO DISRESPECT.
OF COURSE NOT.
YOU HAVE MUCH TO LEARN ABOUT BEING HUMAN. AND I BELIEVE PROFESSOR XAVIER WILL BE A GREAT HELP.
RISE, ROBOT, RISE
WRITER: JEFF PARKER
ARTIST: ROGER CRUZ
COLORIST: VAL STAPLES
LETTERER: BLAMBOT'S NATE PIEKOS
COVER: CRUZ & GURU
PRODUCTION: ANTHONY DIAL
ASSISTANT EDITOR: NATHAN COSBY
EDITOR: MARK PANICCIA
EDITOR IN CHIEF: JOE QUESADA
PUBLISHER: DAN BUCKLEY

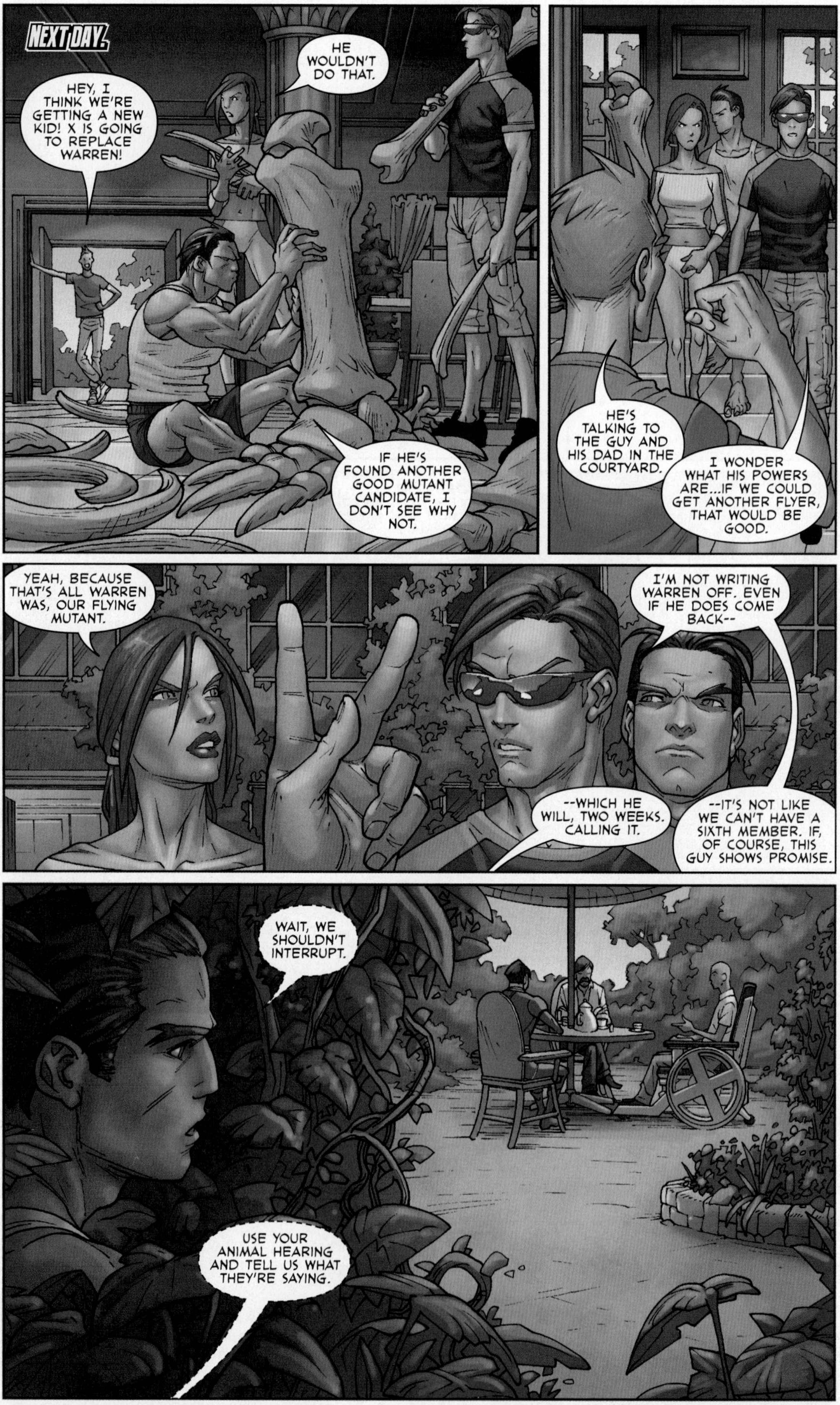
NEXT DAY.
HEY, I THINK WE'RE GETTING A NEW KID! X IS GOING TO REPLACE WARREN!
HE WOULDN'T DO THAT.
IF HE'S FOUND ANOTHER GOOD MUTANT CANDIDATE, I DON'T SEE WHY NOT.
HE'S TALKING TO THE GUY AND HIS DAD IN THE COURTYARD.
I WONDER WHAT HIS POWERS ARE...IF WE COULD GET ANOTHER FLYER, THAT WOULD BE GOOD.
YEAH, BECAUSE THAT'S ALL WARREN WAS, OUR FLYING MUTANT.
I'M NOT WRITING WARREN OFF. EVEN IF HE DOES COME BACK--
--WHICH HE WILL, TWO WEEKS. CALLING IT.
--IT'S NOT LIKE WE CAN'T HAVE A SIXTH MEMBER. IF, OF COURSE, THIS GUY SHOWS PROMISE.
WAIT, WE SHOULDN'T INTERRUPT.
USE YOUR ANIMAL HEARING AND TELL US WHAT THEY'RE SAYING.

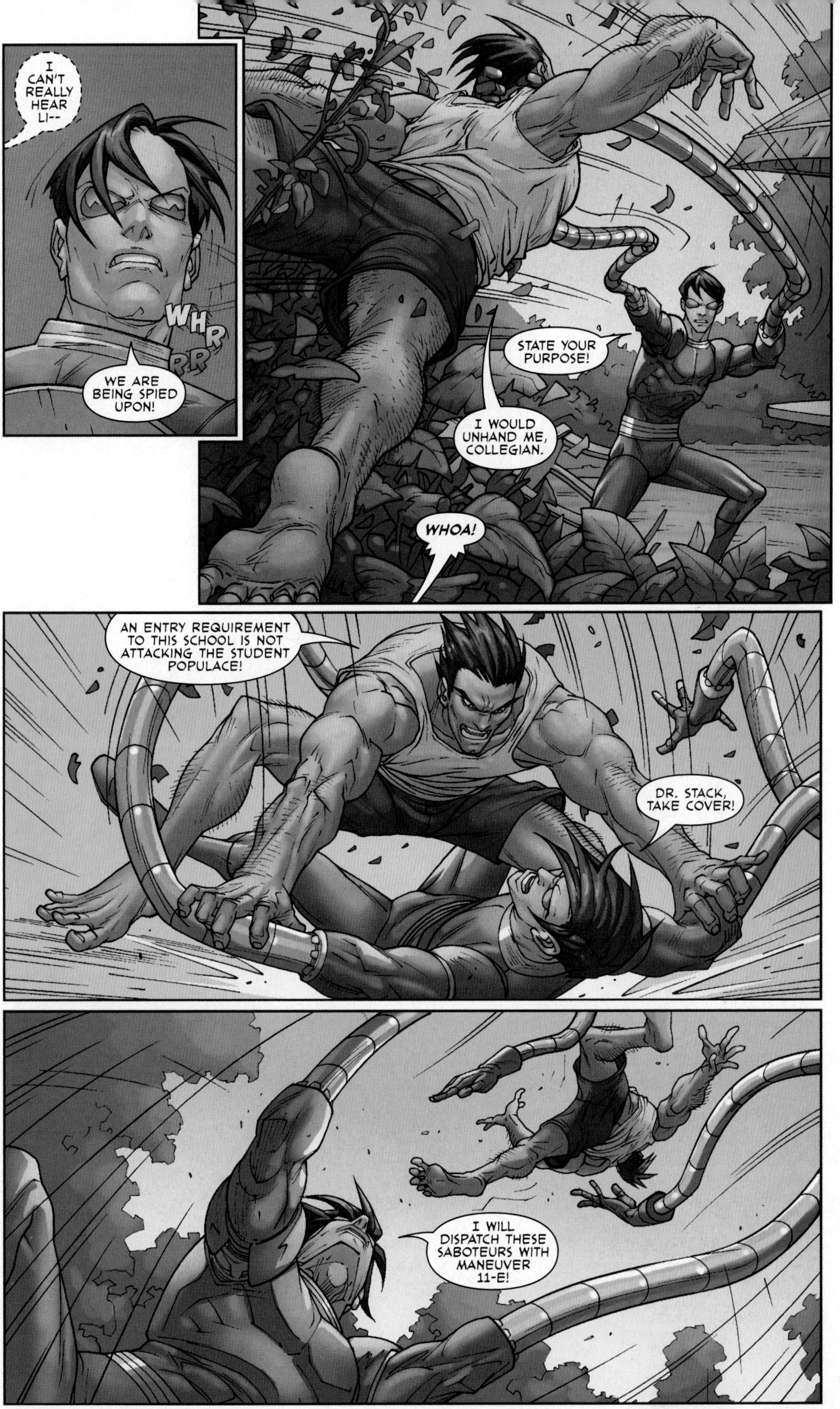

I CAN'T REALLY HEAR LI--
WHRRR
WE ARE BEING SPIED UPON!
STATE YOUR PURPOSE!
I WOULD UNHAND ME, COLLEGIAN.
WHOA!
AN ENTRY REQUIREMENT TO THIS SCHOOL IS NOT ATTACKING THE STUDENT POPULACE!
DR. STACK, TAKE COVER!
I WILL DISPATCH THESE SABOTEURS WITH MANEUVER 11-E!

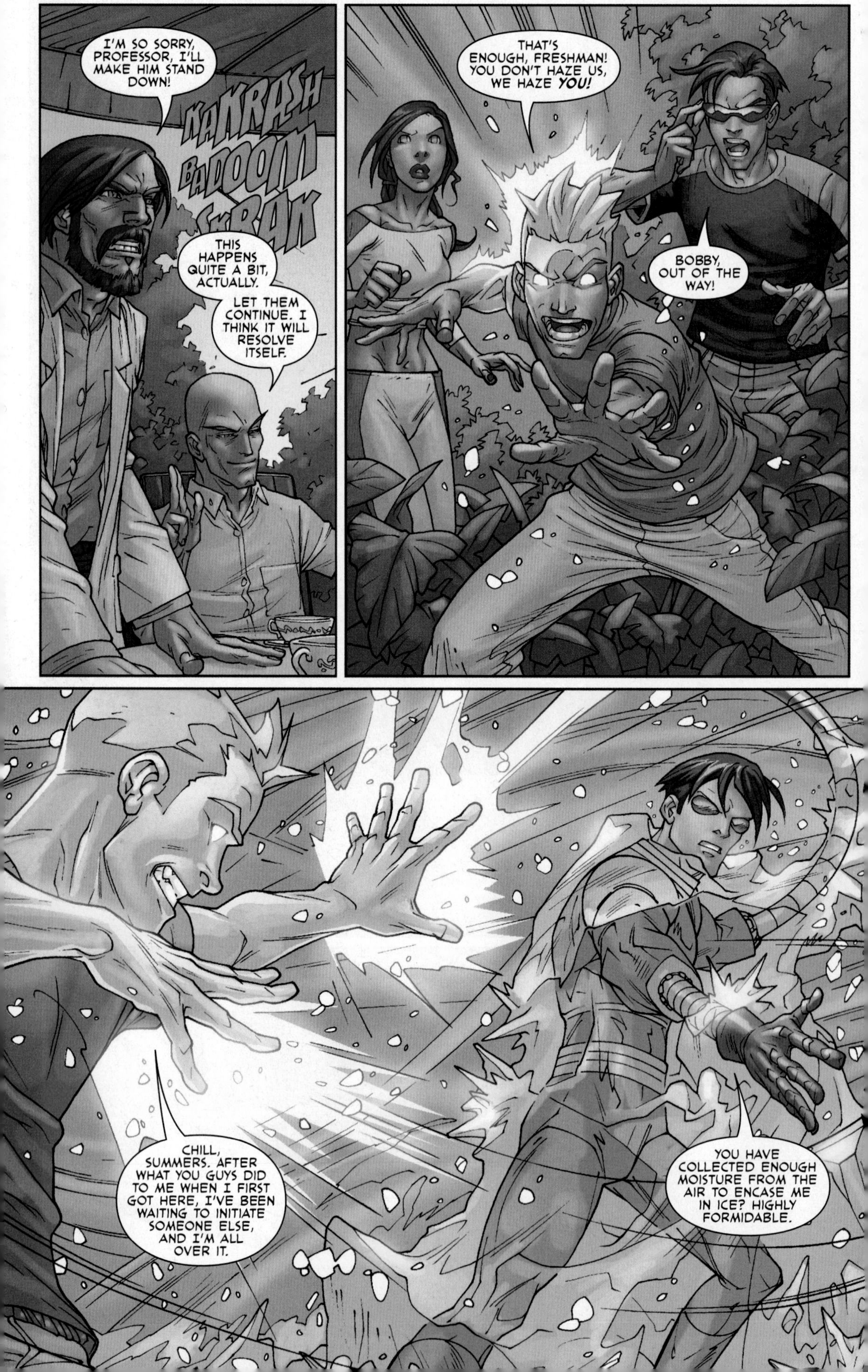
I'M SO SORRY, PROFESSOR, I'LL MAKE HIM STAND DOWN!
KAKRASH BADOOM SKRAK
THIS HAPPENS QUITE A BIT, ACTUALLY.
LET THEM CONTINUE. I THINK IT WILL RESOLVE ITSELF.
THAT'S ENOUGH, FRESHMAN! YOU DON'T HAZE US, WE HAZE *YOU!*
BOBBY, OUT OF THE WAY!
CHILL, SUMMERS. AFTER WHAT YOU GUYS DID TO ME WHEN I FIRST GOT HERE, I'VE BEEN WAITING TO INITIATE SOMEONE ELSE, AND I'M ALL OVER IT.
YOU HAVE COLLECTED ENOUGH MOISTURE FROM THE AIR TO ENCASE ME IN ICE? HIGHLY FORMIDABLE.

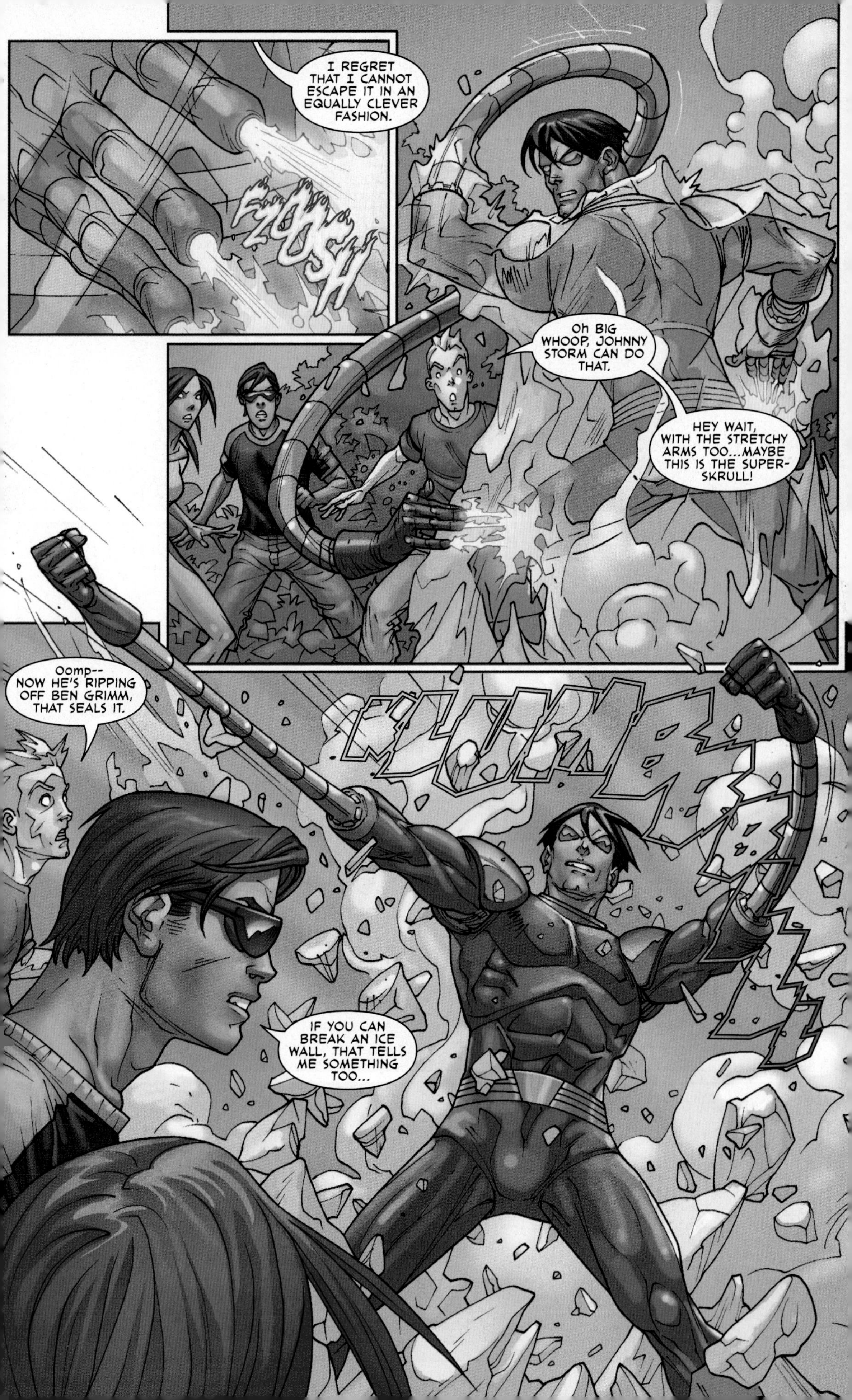

I REGRET THAT I CANNOT ESCAPE IT IN AN EQUALLY CLEVER FASHION.
FZOOSH
Oh BIG WHOOP, JOHNNY STORM CAN DO THAT.
HEY WAIT, WITH THE STRETCHY ARMS TOO...MAYBE THIS IS THE SUPER-SKRULL!
Oomp-- NOW HE'S RIPPING OFF BEN GRIMM, THAT SEALS IT.
IF YOU CAN BREAK AN ICE WALL, THAT TELLS ME SOMETHING TOO...

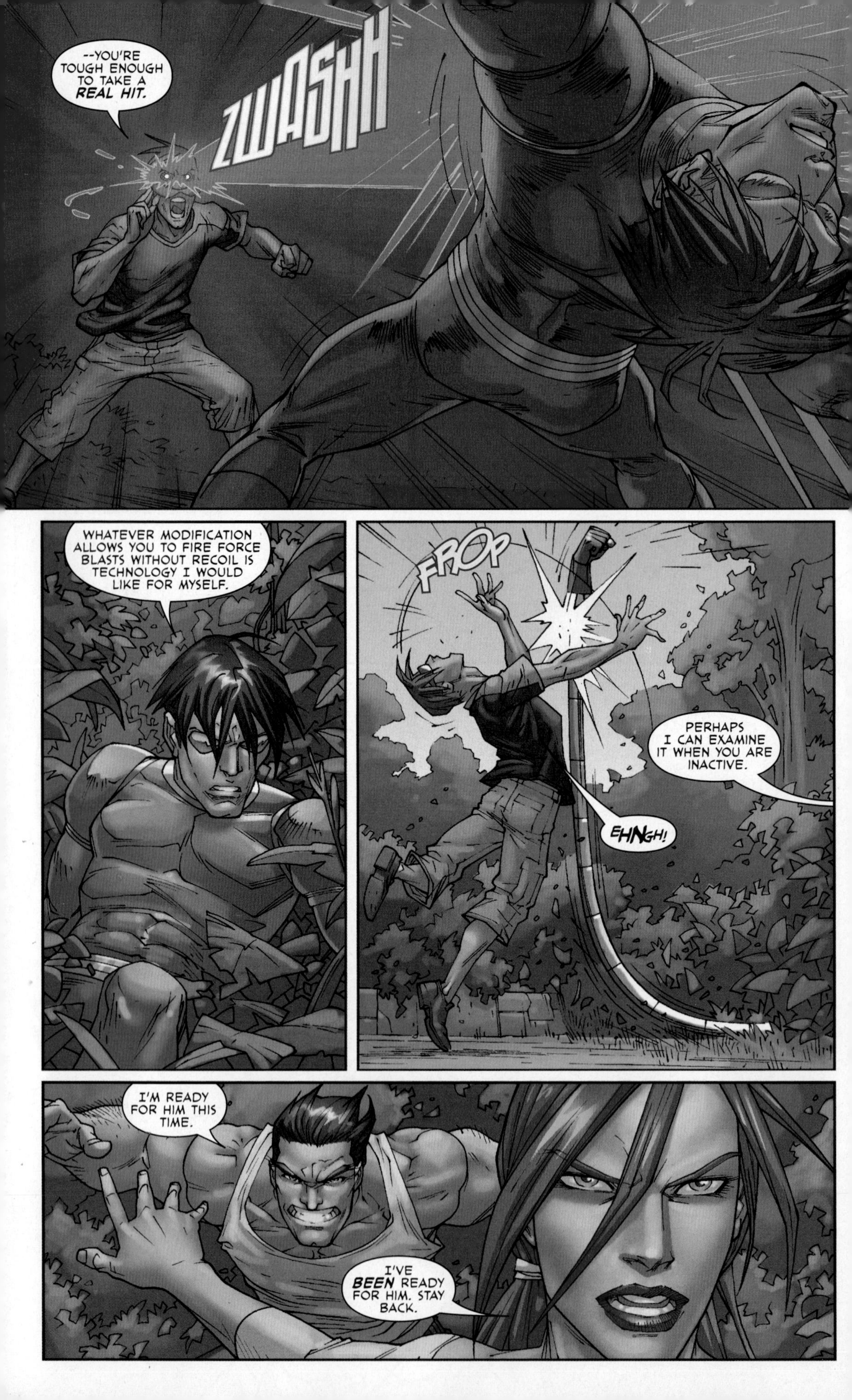
--YOU'RE TOUGH ENOUGH TO TAKE A REAL HIT.
ZWASHH
WHATEVER MODIFICATION ALLOWS YOU TO FIRE FORCE BLASTS WITHOUT RECOIL IS TECHNOLOGY I WOULD LIKE FOR MYSELF.
FROP
PERHAPS I CAN EXAMINE IT WHEN YOU ARE INACTIVE.
EHNGH!
I'M READY FOR HIM THIS TIME.
I'VE BEEN READY FOR HIM. STAY BACK.

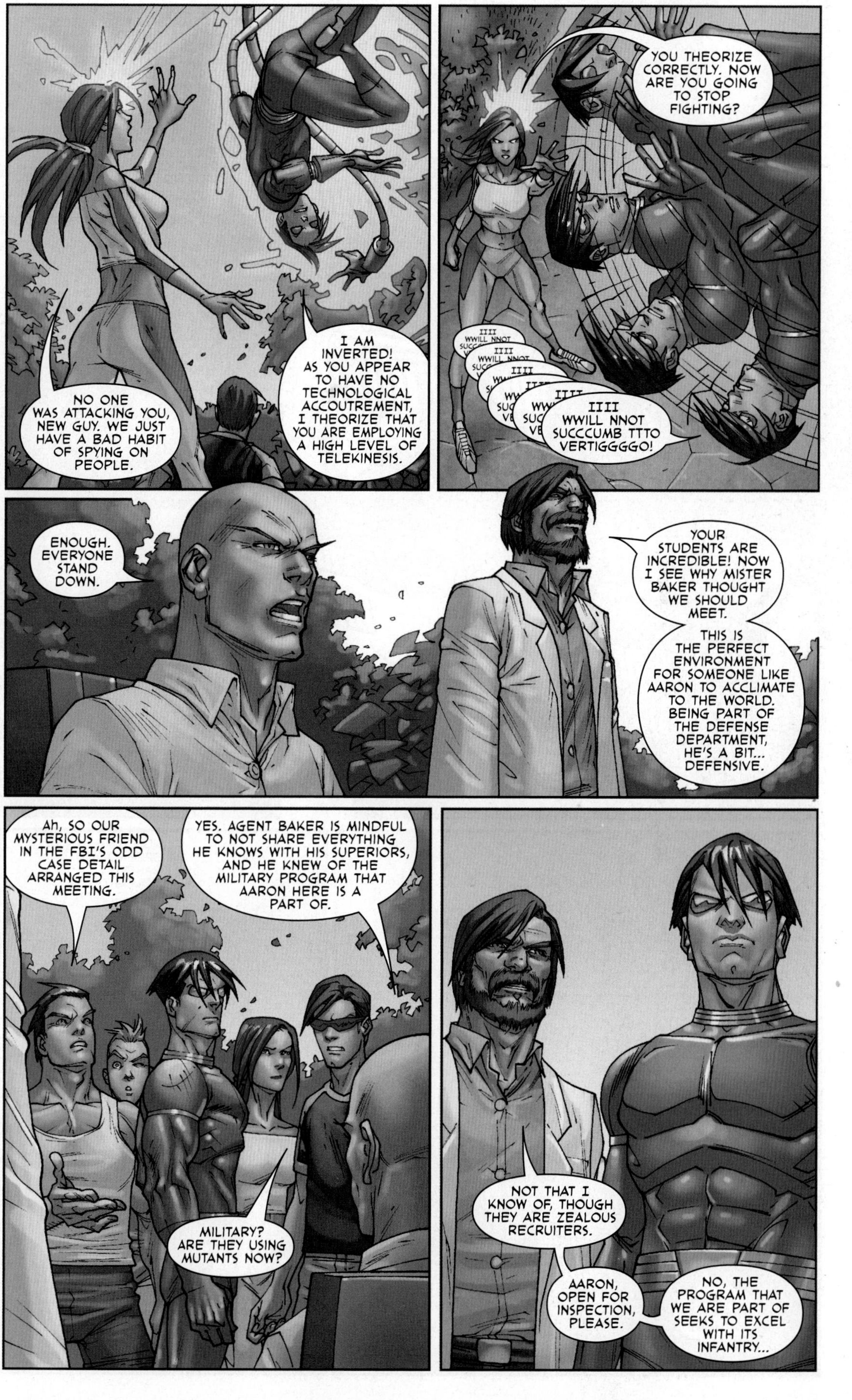
NO ONE WAS ATTACKING YOU, NEW GUY. WE JUST HAVE A BAD HABIT OF SPYING ON PEOPLE.
I AM INVERTED! AS YOU APPEAR TO HAVE NO TECHNOLOGICAL ACCOUTREMENT, I THEORIZE THAT YOU ARE EMPLOYING A HIGH LEVEL OF TELEKINESIS.
YOU THEORIZE CORRECTLY. NOW ARE YOU GOING TO STOP FIGHTING?
IIII WWILL NNOT SUCCCUMB TTTO VERTIGGGGO!
ENOUGH. EVERYONE STAND DOWN.
YOUR STUDENTS ARE INCREDIBLE! NOW I SEE WHY MISTER BAKER THOUGHT WE SHOULD MEET.
THIS IS THE PERFECT ENVIRONMENT FOR SOMEONE LIKE AARON TO ACCLIMATE TO THE WORLD. BEING PART OF THE DEFENSE DEPARTMENT, HE'S A BIT... DEFENSIVE.
Ah, SO OUR MYSTERIOUS FRIEND IN THE FBI'S ODD CASE DETAIL ARRANGED THIS MEETING.
YES. AGENT BAKER IS MINDFUL TO NOT SHARE EVERYTHING HE KNOWS WITH HIS SUPERIORS, AND HE KNEW OF THE MILITARY PROGRAM THAT AARON HERE IS A PART OF.
MILITARY? ARE THEY USING MUTANTS NOW?
NOT THAT I KNOW OF, THOUGH THEY ARE ZEALOUS RECRUITERS.
AARON, OPEN FOR INSPECTION, PLEASE.
NO, THE PROGRAM THAT WE ARE PART OF SEEKS TO EXCEL WITH ITS INFANTRY...

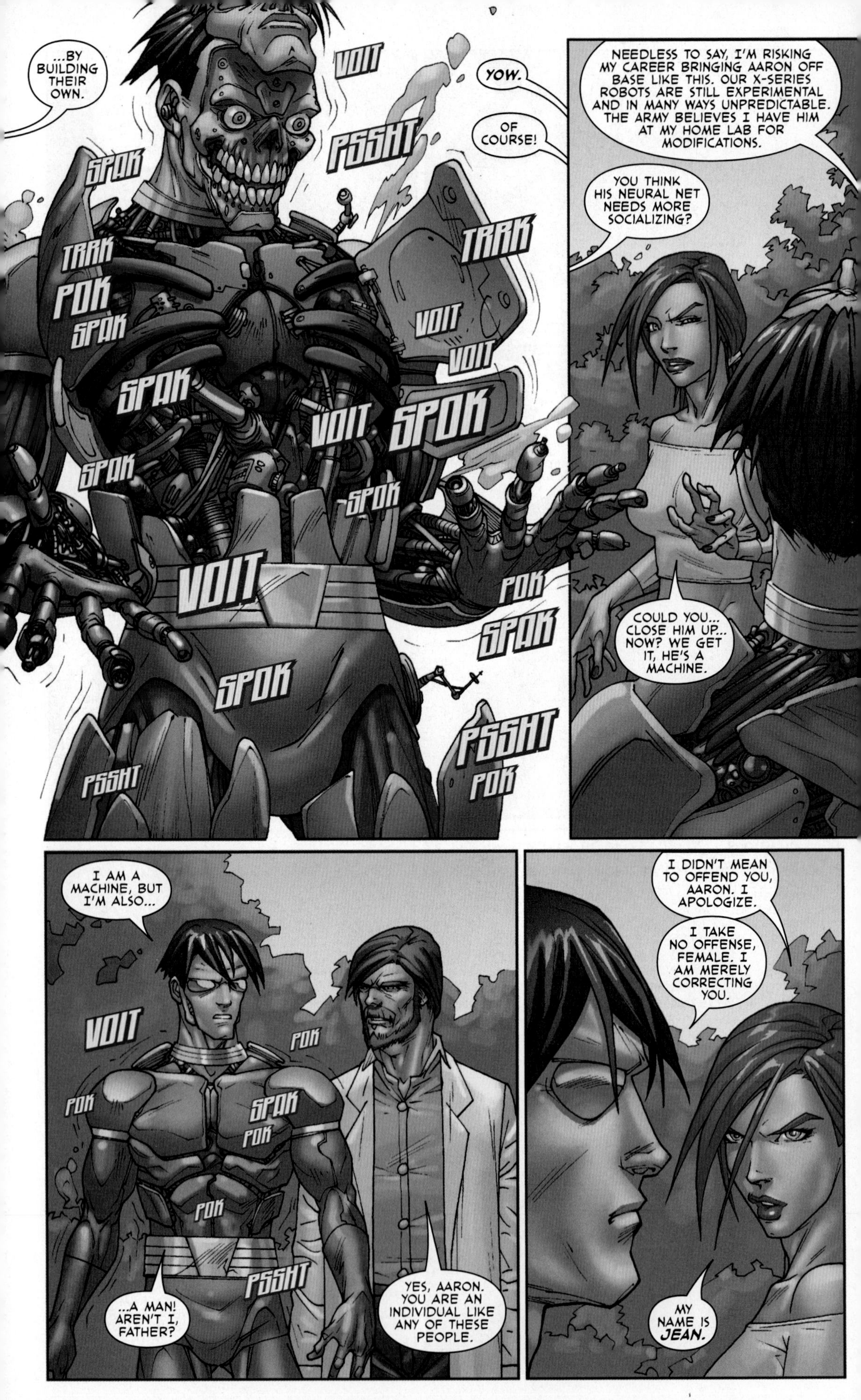
...BY BUILDING THEIR OWN.
VOIT
YOW.
PSSHT
OF COURSE!
SPOK
TRRK
TRRK
POK
SPOK
VOIT
VOIT
SPOK
VOIT
SPOK
SPOK
SPOK
VOIT
POK
SPOK
SPOK
PSSHT
PSSHT
POK
NEEDLESS TO SAY, I'M RISKING MY CAREER BRINGING AARON OFF BASE LIKE THIS. OUR X-SERIES ROBOTS ARE STILL EXPERIMENTAL AND IN MANY WAYS UNPREDICTABLE. THE ARMY BELIEVES I HAVE HIM AT MY HOME LAB FOR MODIFICATIONS.
YOU THINK HIS NEURAL NET NEEDS MORE SOCIALIZING?
COULD YOU... CLOSE HIM UP... NOW? WE GET IT, HE'S A MACHINE.
I AM A MACHINE, BUT I'M ALSO...
VOIT
POK
POK
SPOK
POK
POK
PSSHT
...A MAN! AREN'T I, FATHER?
YES, AARON. YOU ARE AN INDIVIDUAL LIKE ANY OF THESE PEOPLE.
I DIDN'T MEAN TO OFFEND YOU, AARON. I APOLOGIZE.
I TAKE NO OFFENSE, FEMALE. I AM MERELY CORRECTING YOU.
MY NAME IS *JEAN.*

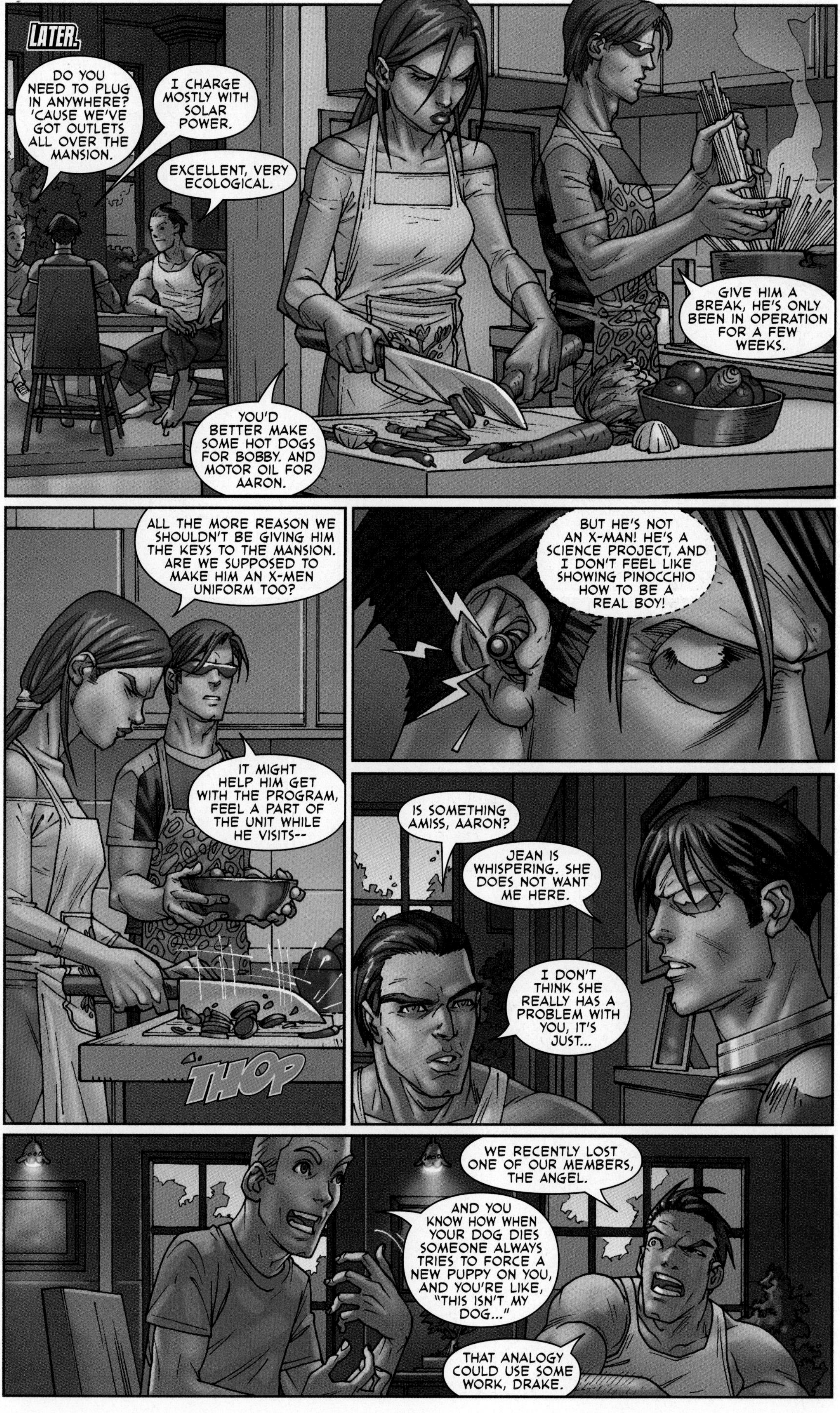
LATER.
DO YOU NEED TO PLUG IN ANYWHERE? 'CAUSE WE'VE GOT OUTLETS ALL OVER THE MANSION.
I CHARGE MOSTLY WITH SOLAR POWER.
EXCELLENT, VERY ECOLOGICAL.
YOU'D BETTER MAKE SOME HOT DOGS FOR BOBBY. AND MOTOR OIL FOR AARON.
GIVE HIM A BREAK, HE'S ONLY BEEN IN OPERATION FOR A FEW WEEKS.
ALL THE MORE REASON WE SHOULDN'T BE GIVING HIM THE KEYS TO THE MANSION. ARE WE SUPPOSED TO MAKE HIM AN X-MEN UNIFORM TOO?
IT MIGHT HELP HIM GET WITH THE PROGRAM, FEEL A PART OF THE UNIT WHILE HE VISITS--
THOP
BUT HE'S NOT AN X-MAN! HE'S A SCIENCE PROJECT, AND I DON'T FEEL LIKE SHOWING PINOCCHIO HOW TO BE A REAL BOY!
IS SOMETHING AMISS, AARON?
JEAN IS WHISPERING. SHE DOES NOT WANT ME HERE.
I DON'T THINK SHE REALLY HAS A PROBLEM WITH YOU, IT'S JUST...
WE RECENTLY LOST ONE OF OUR MEMBERS, THE ANGEL.
AND YOU KNOW HOW WHEN YOUR DOG DIES SOMEONE ALWAYS TRIES TO FORCE A NEW PUPPY ON YOU, AND YOU'RE LIKE, "THIS ISN'T MY DOG..."
THAT ANALOGY COULD USE SOME WORK, DRAKE.

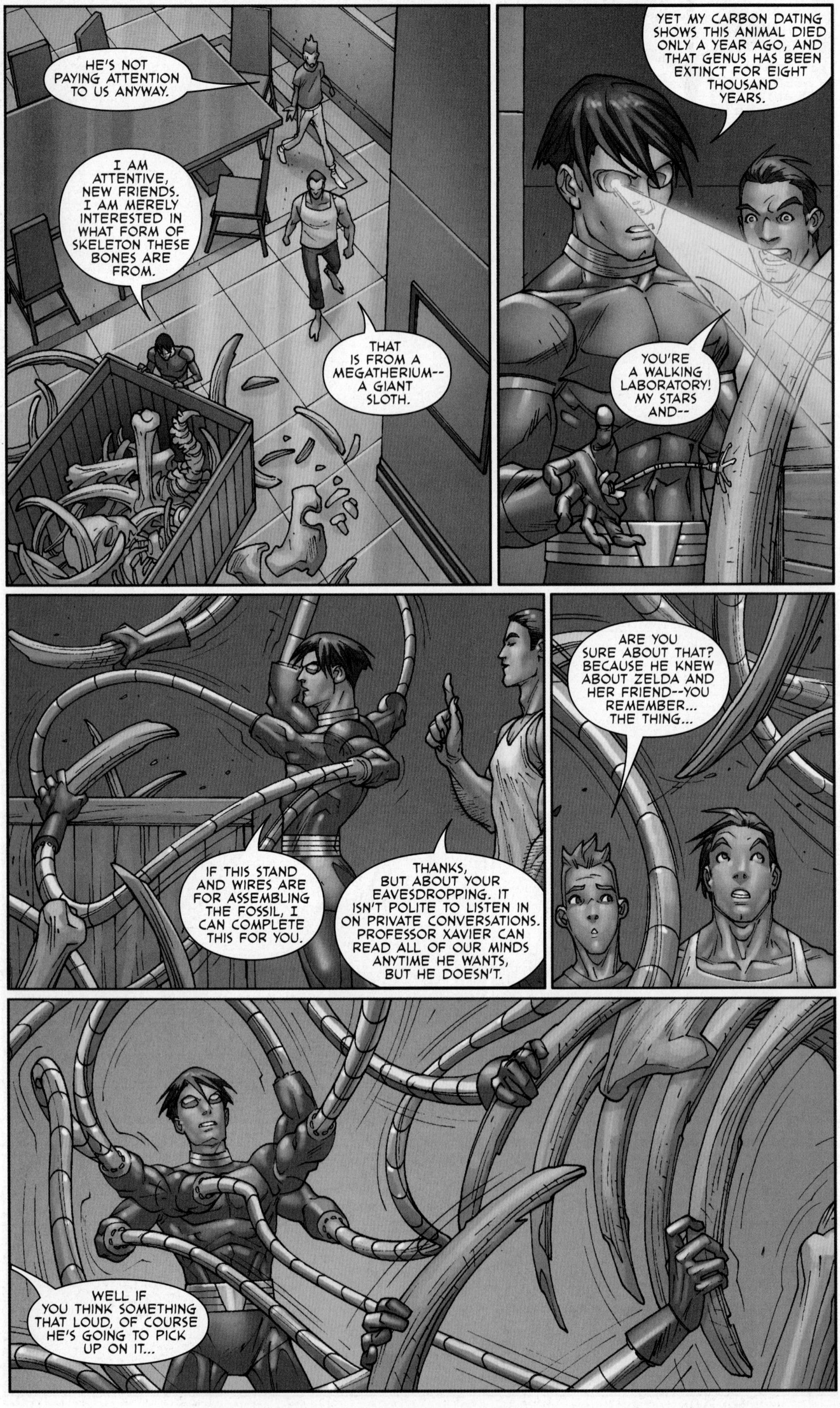
HE'S NOT PAYING ATTENTION TO US ANYWAY.
I AM ATTENTIVE, NEW FRIENDS. I AM MERELY INTERESTED IN WHAT FORM OF SKELETON THESE BONES ARE FROM.
THAT IS FROM A MEGATHERIUM-- A GIANT SLOTH.
YET MY CARBON DATING SHOWS THIS ANIMAL DIED ONLY A YEAR AGO, AND THAT GENUS HAS BEEN EXTINCT FOR EIGHT THOUSAND YEARS.
YOU'RE A WALKING LABORATORY! MY STARS AND--
IF THIS STAND AND WIRES ARE FOR ASSEMBLING THE FOSSIL, I CAN COMPLETE THIS FOR YOU.
THANKS, BUT ABOUT YOUR EAVESDROPPING. IT ISN'T POLITE TO LISTEN IN ON PRIVATE CONVERSATIONS. PROFESSOR XAVIER CAN READ ALL OF OUR MINDS ANYTIME HE WANTS, BUT HE DOESN'T.
ARE YOU SURE ABOUT THAT? BECAUSE HE KNEW ABOUT ZELDA AND HER FRIEND--YOU REMEMBER... THE THING...
WELL IF YOU THINK SOMETHING THAT LOUD, OF COURSE HE'S GOING TO PICK UP ON IT...

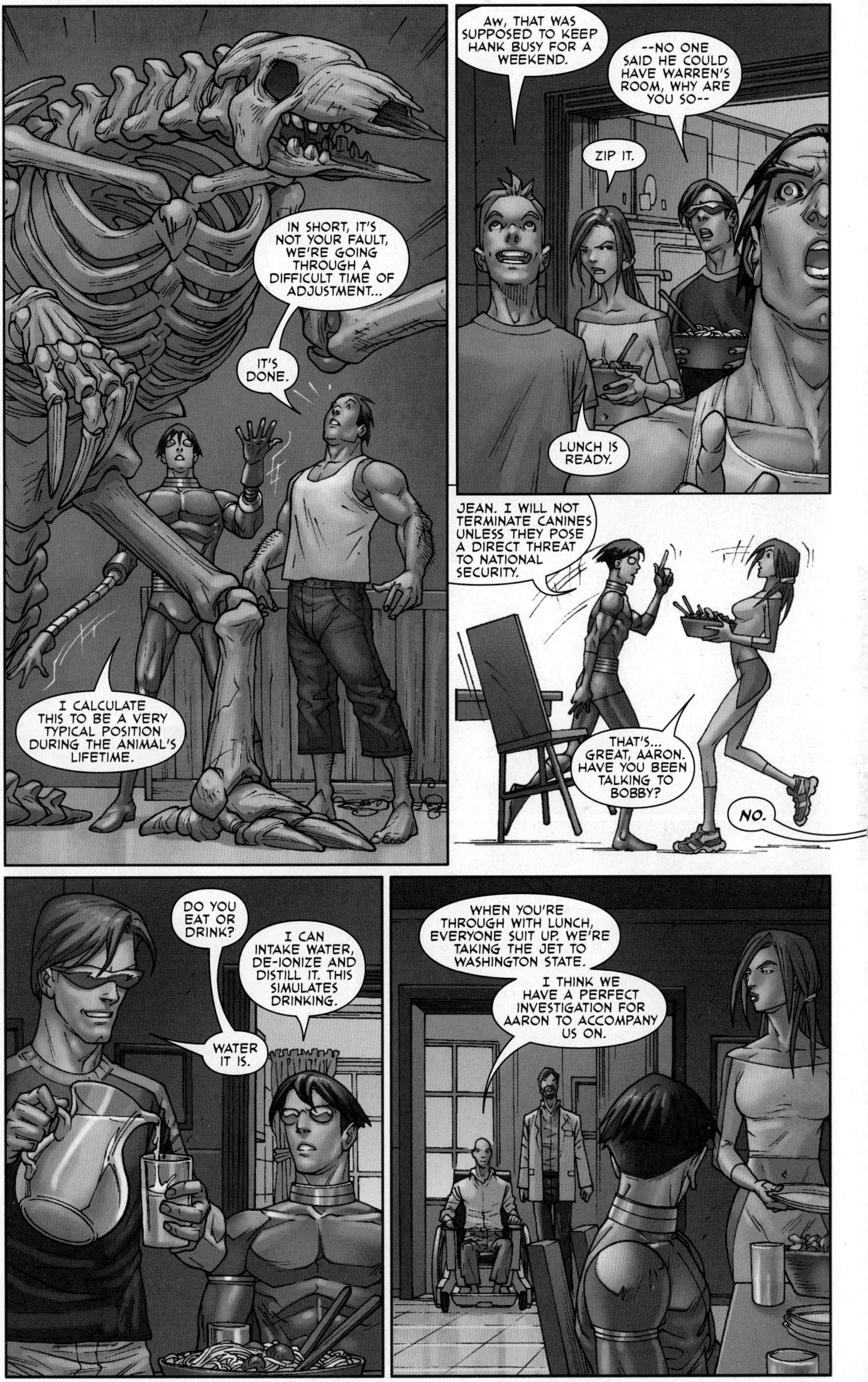
IN SHORT, IT'S NOT YOUR FAULT, WE'RE GOING THROUGH A DIFFICULT TIME OF ADJUSTMENT...
IT'S DONE.
I CALCULATE THIS TO BE A VERY TYPICAL POSITION DURING THE ANIMAL'S LIFETIME.
AW, THAT WAS SUPPOSED TO KEEP HANK BUSY FOR A WEEKEND.
--NO ONE SAID HE COULD HAVE WARREN'S ROOM, WHY ARE YOU SO--
ZIP IT.
LUNCH IS READY.
JEAN. I WILL NOT TERMINATE CANINES UNLESS THEY POSE A DIRECT THREAT TO NATIONAL SECURITY.
THAT'S... GREAT, AARON. HAVE YOU BEEN TALKING TO BOBBY?
NO.
DO YOU EAT OR DRINK?
I CAN INTAKE WATER, DE-IONIZE AND DISTILL IT. THIS SIMULATES DRINKING.
WATER IT IS.
WHEN YOU'RE THROUGH WITH LUNCH, EVERYONE SUIT UP. WE'RE TAKING THE JET TO WASHINGTON STATE.
I THINK WE HAVE A PERFECT INVESTIGATION FOR AARON TO ACCOMPANY US ON.

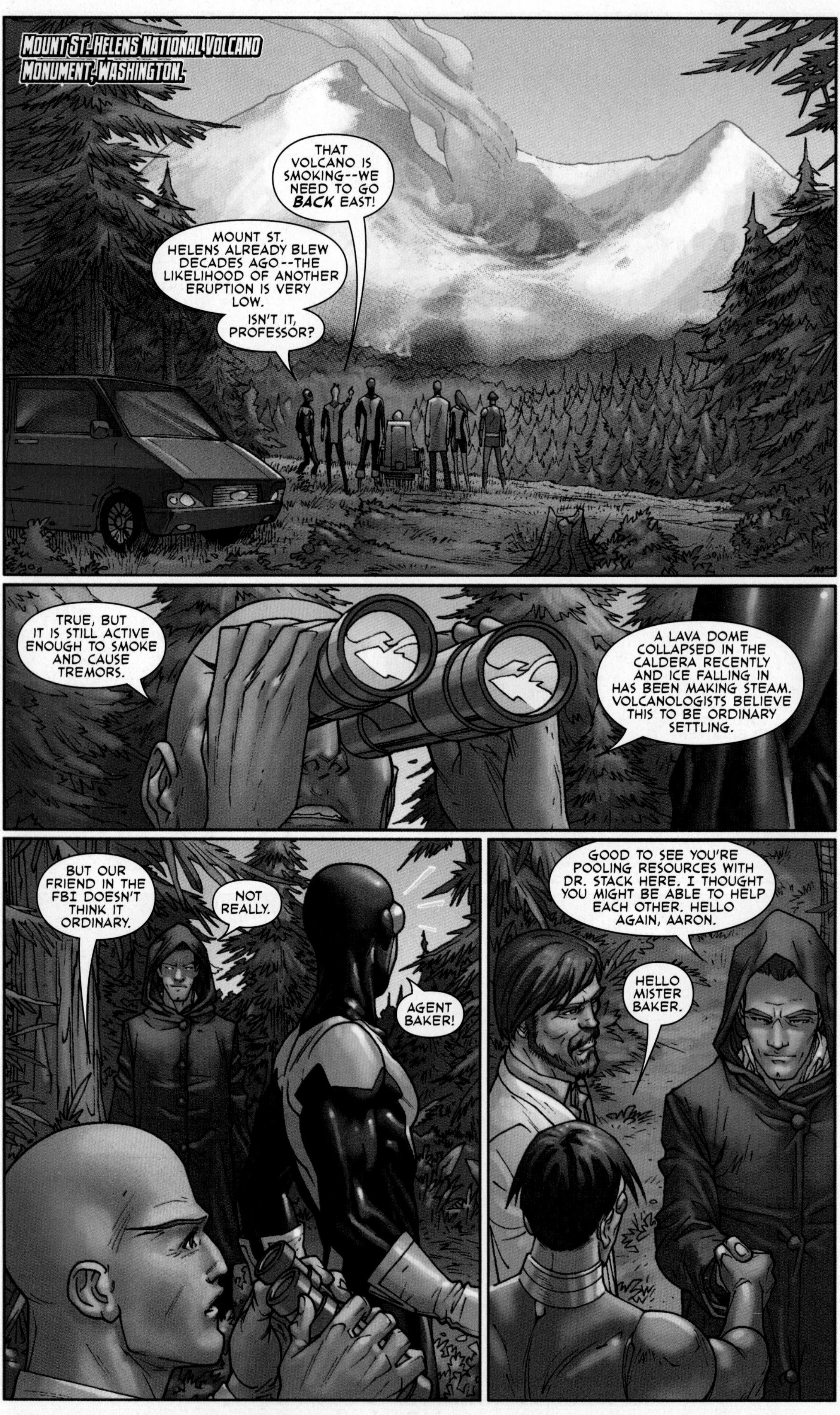
MOUNT ST. HELENS NATIONAL VOLCANO MONUMENT, WASHINGTON.
THAT VOLCANO IS SMOKING--WE NEED TO GO BACK EAST!
MOUNT ST. HELENS ALREADY BLEW DECADES AGO--THE LIKELIHOOD OF ANOTHER ERUPTION IS VERY LOW.
ISN'T IT, PROFESSOR?
TRUE, BUT IT IS STILL ACTIVE ENOUGH TO SMOKE AND CAUSE TREMORS.
A LAVA DOME COLLAPSED IN THE CALDERA RECENTLY AND ICE FALLING IN HAS BEEN MAKING STEAM. VOLCANOLOGISTS BELIEVE THIS TO BE ORDINARY SETTLING.
BUT OUR FRIEND IN THE FBI DOESN'T THINK IT ORDINARY.
NOT REALLY.
AGENT BAKER!
GOOD TO SEE YOU'RE POOLING RESOURCES WITH DR. STACK HERE. I THOUGHT YOU MIGHT BE ABLE TO HELP EACH OTHER. HELLO AGAIN, AARON.
HELLO MISTER BAKER.

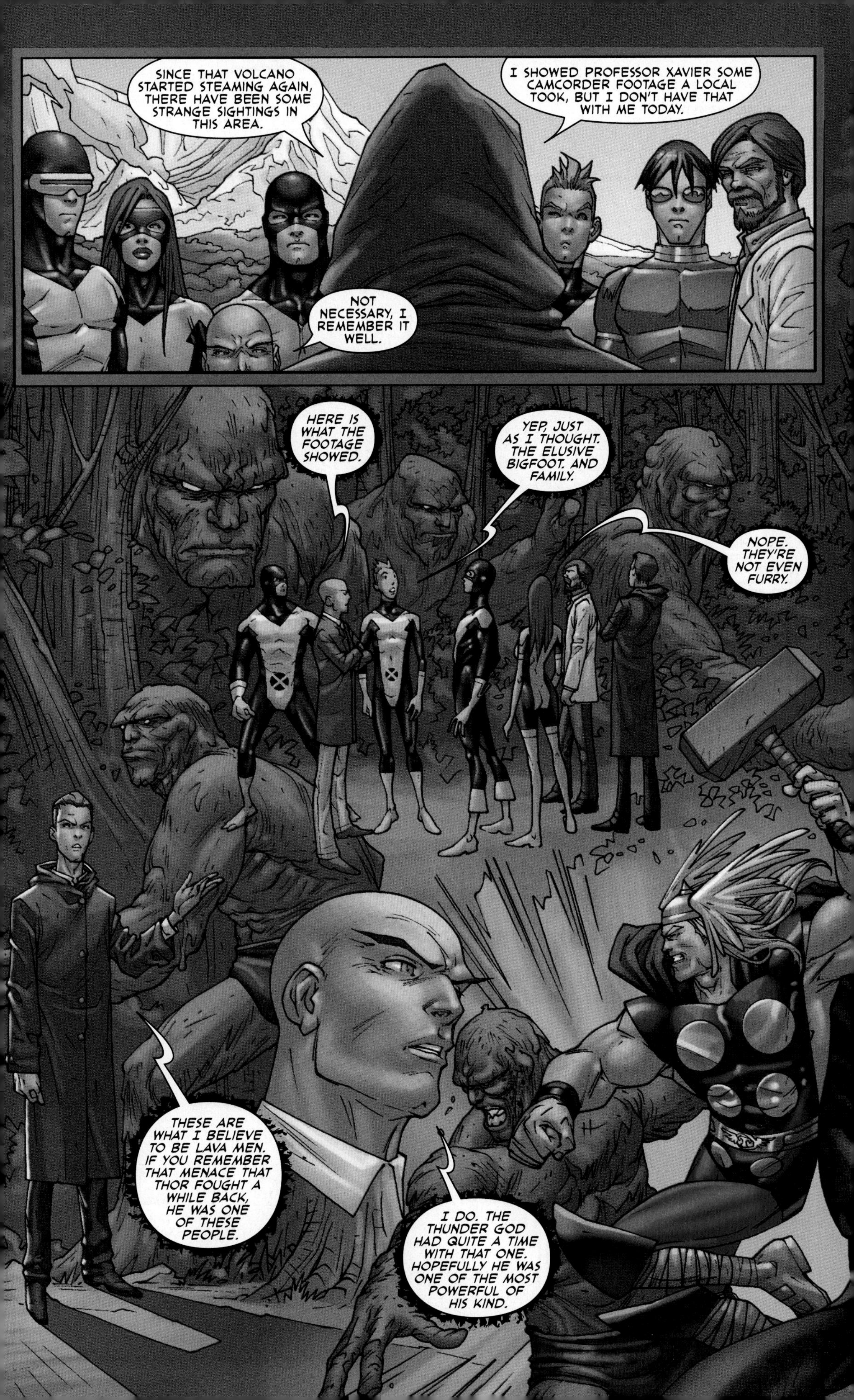
SINCE THAT VOLCANO STARTED STEAMING AGAIN, THERE HAVE BEEN SOME STRANGE SIGHTINGS IN THIS AREA.
I SHOWED PROFESSOR XAVIER SOME CAMCORDER FOOTAGE A LOCAL TOOK, BUT I DON'T HAVE THAT WITH ME TODAY.
NOT NECESSARY, I REMEMBER IT WELL.
HERE IS WHAT THE FOOTAGE SHOWED.
YEP, JUST AS I THOUGHT. THE ELUSIVE BIGFOOT. AND FAMILY.
NOPE. THEY'RE NOT EVEN FURRY.
THESE ARE WHAT I BELIEVE TO BE LAVA MEN. IF YOU REMEMBER THAT MENACE THAT THOR FOUGHT A WHILE BACK, HE WAS ONE OF THESE PEOPLE.
I DO. THE THUNDER GOD HAD QUITE A TIME WITH THAT ONE. HOPEFULLY HE WAS ONE OF THE MOST POWERFUL OF HIS KIND.

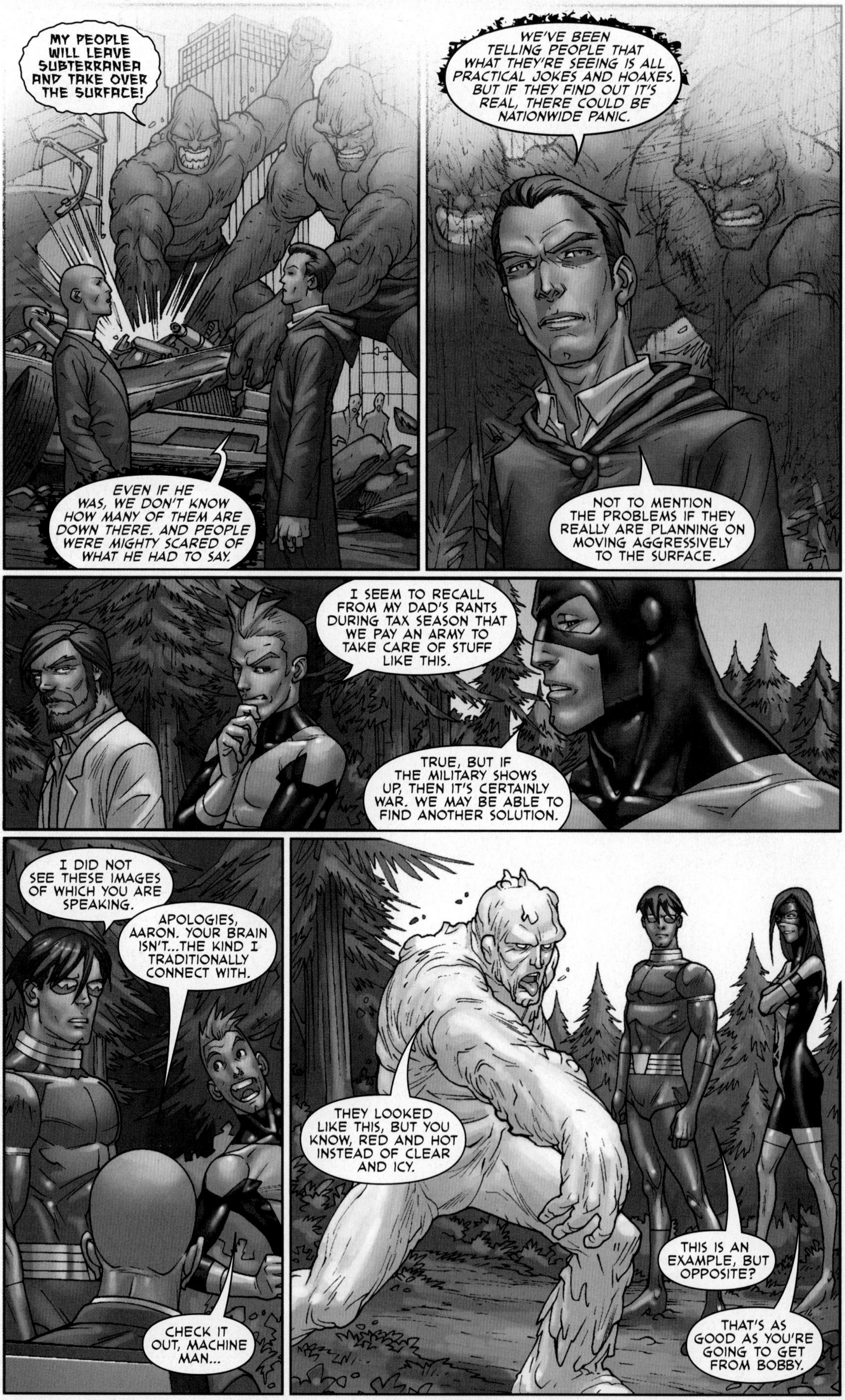
MY PEOPLE WILL LEAVE SUBTERRANEA AND TAKE OVER THE SURFACE!
EVEN IF HE WAS, WE DON'T KNOW HOW MANY OF THEM ARE DOWN THERE. AND PEOPLE WERE MIGHTY SCARED OF WHAT HE HAD TO SAY.
WE'VE BEEN TELLING PEOPLE THAT WHAT THEY'RE SEEING IS ALL PRACTICAL JOKES AND HOAXES. BUT IF THEY FIND OUT IT'S REAL, THERE COULD BE NATIONWIDE PANIC.
NOT TO MENTION THE PROBLEMS IF THEY REALLY ARE PLANNING ON MOVING AGGRESSIVELY TO THE SURFACE.
I SEEM TO RECALL FROM MY DAD'S RANTS DURING TAX SEASON THAT WE PAY AN ARMY TO TAKE CARE OF STUFF LIKE THIS.
TRUE, BUT IF THE MILITARY SHOWS UP, THEN IT'S CERTAINLY WAR. WE MAY BE ABLE TO FIND ANOTHER SOLUTION.
I DID NOT SEE THESE IMAGES OF WHICH YOU ARE SPEAKING.
APOLOGIES, AARON. YOUR BRAIN ISN'T...THE KIND I TRADITIONALLY CONNECT WITH.
CHECK IT OUT, MACHINE MAN...
THEY LOOKED LIKE THIS, BUT YOU KNOW, RED AND HOT INSTEAD OF CLEAR AND ICY.
THIS IS AN EXAMPLE, BUT OPPOSITE?
THAT'S AS GOOD AS YOU'RE GOING TO GET FROM BOBBY.

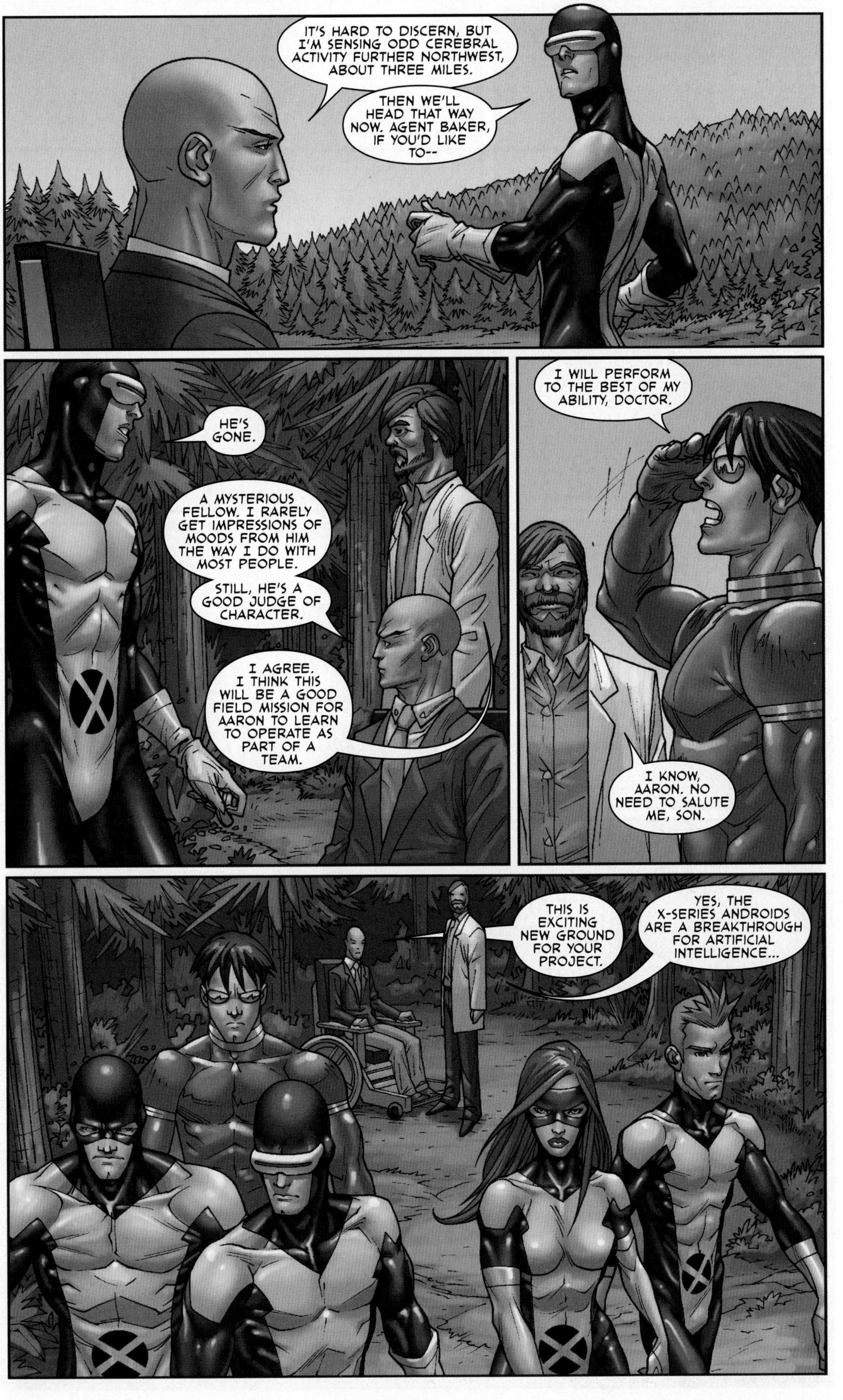
IT'S HARD TO DISCERN, BUT I'M SENSING ODD CEREBRAL ACTIVITY FURTHER NORTHWEST, ABOUT THREE MILES.
THEN WE'LL HEAD THAT WAY NOW. AGENT BAKER, IF YOU'D LIKE TO--
HE'S GONE.
A MYSTERIOUS FELLOW. I RARELY GET IMPRESSIONS OF MOODS FROM HIM THE WAY I DO WITH MOST PEOPLE.
STILL, HE'S A GOOD JUDGE OF CHARACTER.
I AGREE. I THINK THIS WILL BE A GOOD FIELD MISSION FOR AARON TO LEARN TO OPERATE AS PART OF A TEAM.
I WILL PERFORM TO THE BEST OF MY ABILITY, DOCTOR.
I KNOW, AARON. NO NEED TO SALUTE ME, SON.
THIS IS EXCITING NEW GROUND FOR YOUR PROJECT.
YES, THE X-SERIES ANDROIDS ARE A BREAKTHROUGH FOR ARTIFICIAL INTELLIGENCE...

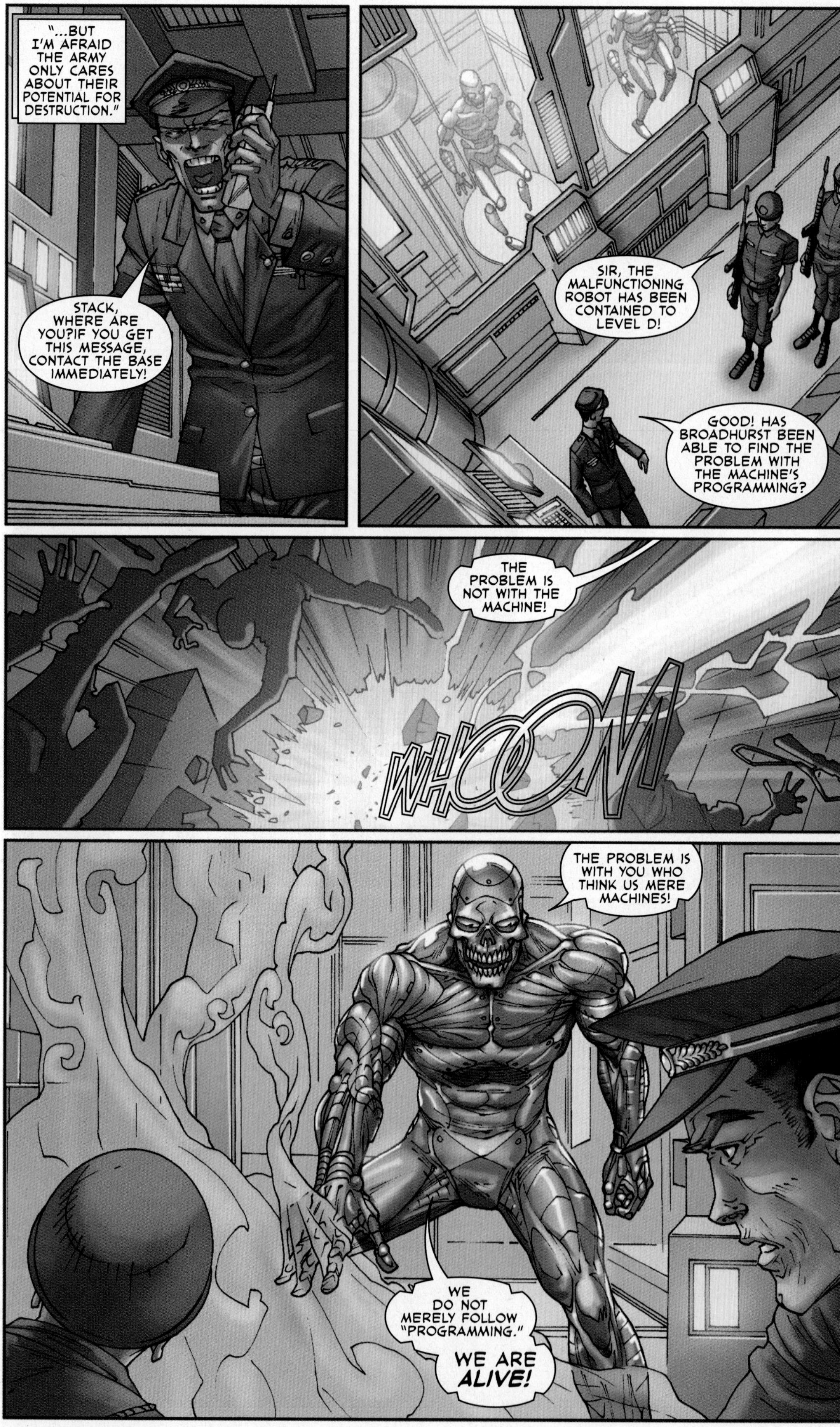
"...BUT I'M AFRAID THE ARMY ONLY CARES ABOUT THEIR POTENTIAL FOR DESTRUCTION."
STACK, WHERE ARE YOU?IF YOU GET THIS MESSAGE, CONTACT THE BASE IMMEDIATELY!
SIR, THE MALFUNCTIONING ROBOT HAS BEEN CONTAINED TO LEVEL D!
GOOD! HAS BROADHURST BEEN ABLE TO FIND THE PROBLEM WITH THE MACHINE'S PROGRAMMING?
THE PROBLEM IS NOT WITH THE MACHINE!
WHOOM
THE PROBLEM IS WITH YOU WHO THINK US MERE MACHINES!
WE DO NOT MERELY FOLLOW "PROGRAMMING."
WE ARE *ALIVE!*

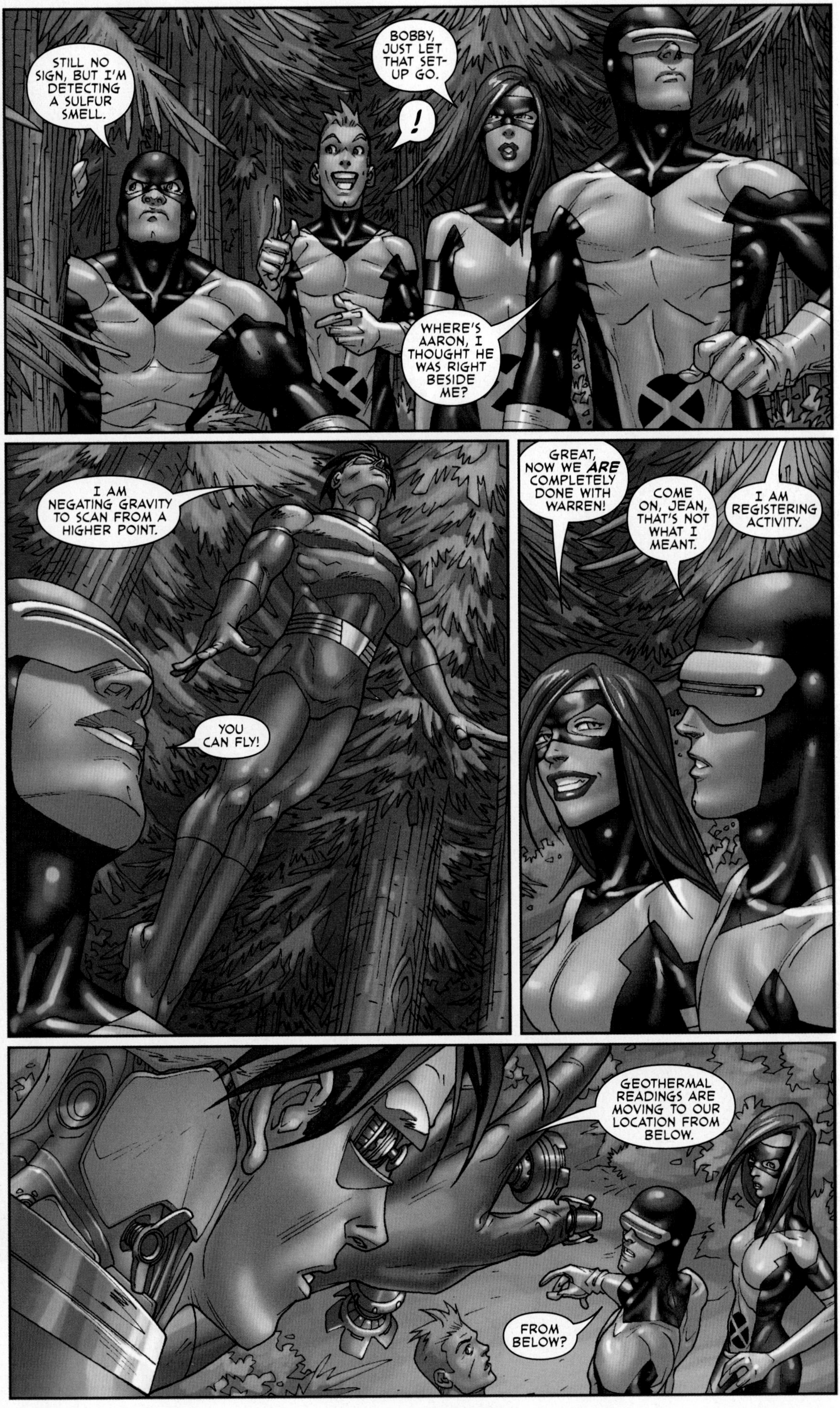
STILL NO SIGN, BUT I'M DETECTING A SULFUR SMELL.
!
BOBBY, JUST LET THAT SET-UP GO.
WHERE'S AARON, I THOUGHT HE WAS RIGHT BESIDE ME?
I AM NEGATING GRAVITY TO SCAN FROM A HIGHER POINT.
YOU CAN FLY!
GREAT, NOW WE *ARE* COMPLETELY DONE WITH WARREN!
COME ON, JEAN, THAT'S NOT WHAT I MEANT.
I AM REGISTERING ACTIVITY.
GEOTHERMAL READINGS ARE MOVING TO OUR LOCATION FROM BELOW.
FROM BELOW?

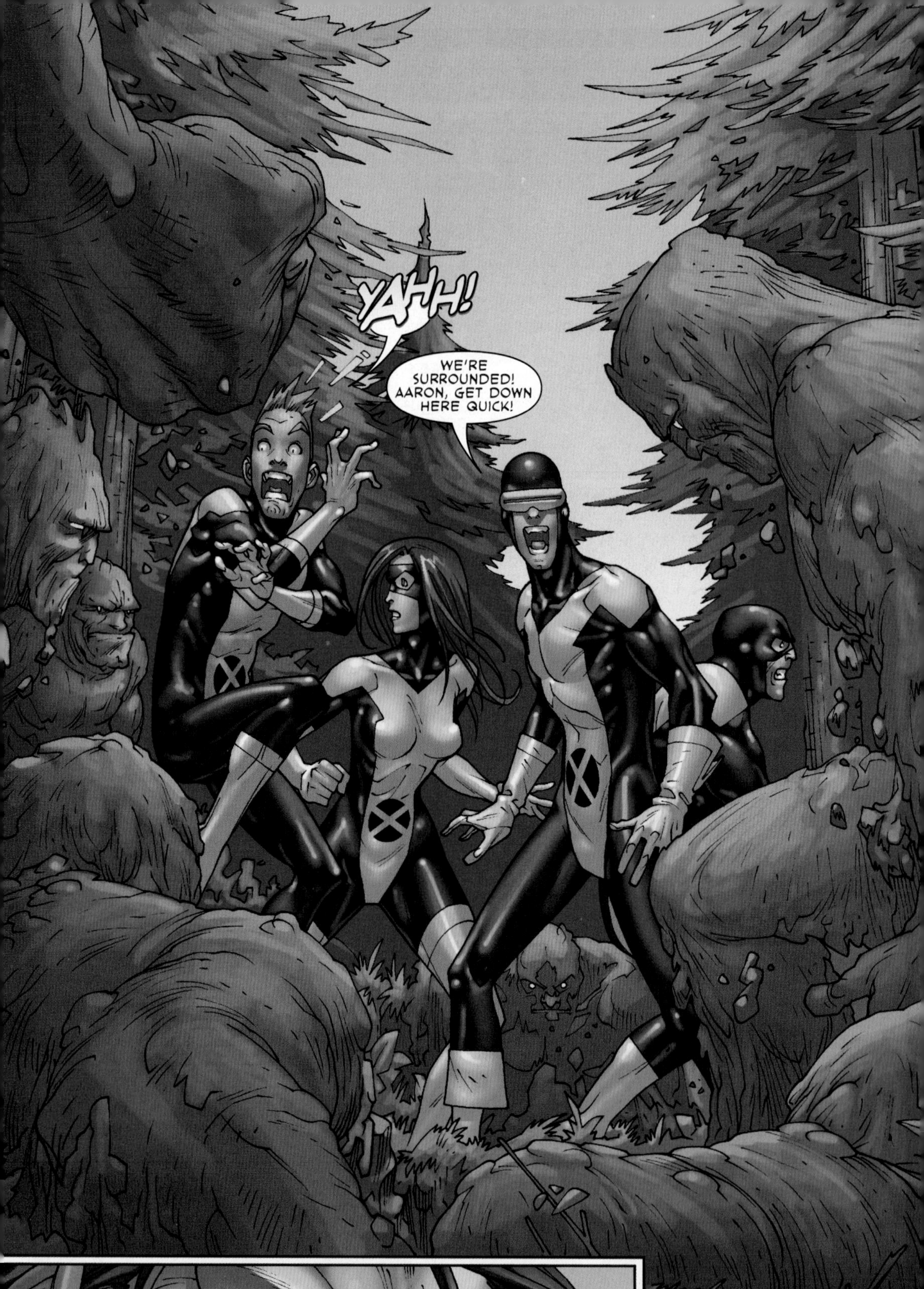
YAHH!
WE'RE SURROUNDED! AARON, GET DOWN HERE QUICK!
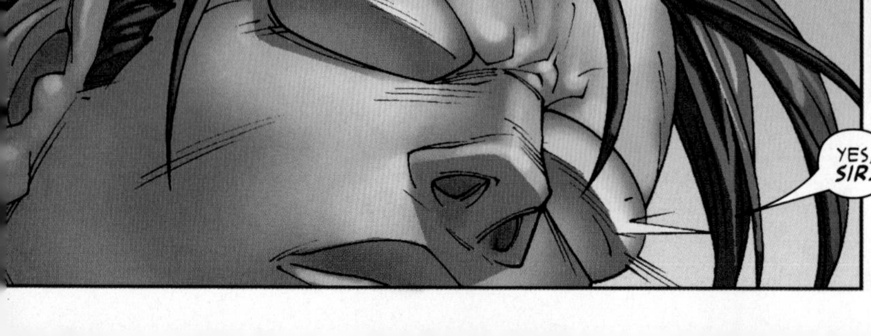
YES, SIR.

TO BE CONTINUED!

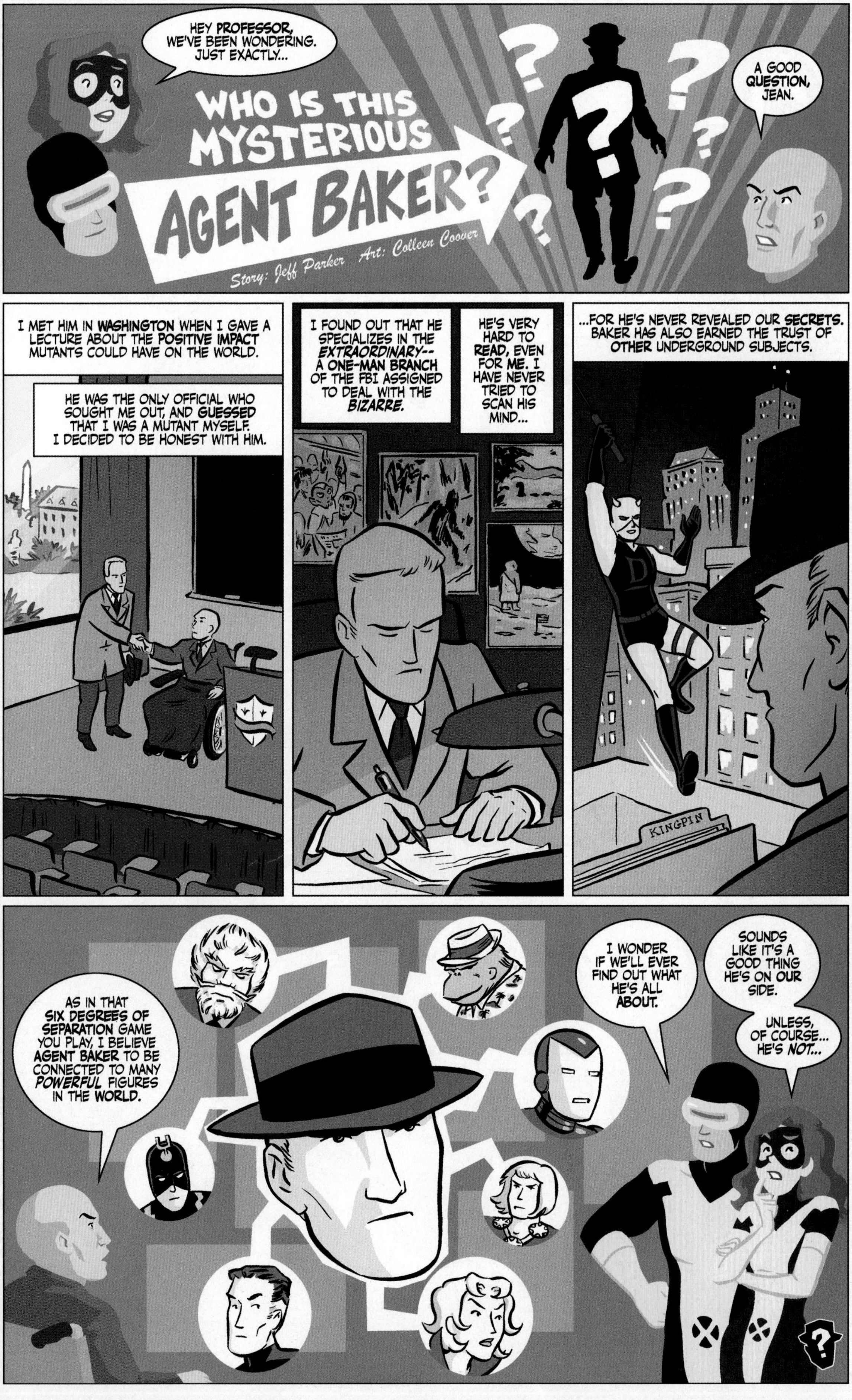
HEY PROFESSOR, WE'VE BEEN WONDERING. JUST EXACTLY...
WHO IS THIS MYSTERIOUS AGENT BAKER?
A GOOD QUESTION, JEAN.
Story: Jeff Parker Art: Colleen Coover
I MET HIM IN WASHINGTON WHEN I GAVE A LECTURE ABOUT THE POSITIVE IMPACT MUTANTS COULD HAVE ON THE WORLD.
HE WAS THE ONLY OFFICIAL WHO SOUGHT ME OUT, AND GUESSED THAT I WAS A MUTANT MYSELF. I DECIDED TO BE HONEST WITH HIM.
I FOUND OUT THAT HE SPECIALIZES IN THE EXTRAORDINARY-- A ONE-MAN BRANCH OF THE FBI ASSIGNED TO DEAL WITH THE BIZARRE.
HE'S VERY HARD TO READ, EVEN FOR ME. I HAVE NEVER TRIED TO SCAN HIS MIND...
...FOR HE'S NEVER REVEALED OUR SECRETS. BAKER HAS ALSO EARNED THE TRUST OF OTHER UNDERGROUND SUBJECTS.
KINGPIN
AS IN THAT SIX DEGREES OF SEPARATION GAME YOU PLAY, I BELIEVE AGENT BAKER TO BE CONNECTED TO MANY POWERFUL FIGURES IN THE WORLD.
I WONDER IF WE'LL EVER FIND OUT WHAT HE'S ALL ABOUT.
SOUNDS LIKE IT'S A GOOD THING HE'S ON OUR SIDE.
UNLESS, OF COURSE... HE'S NOT...

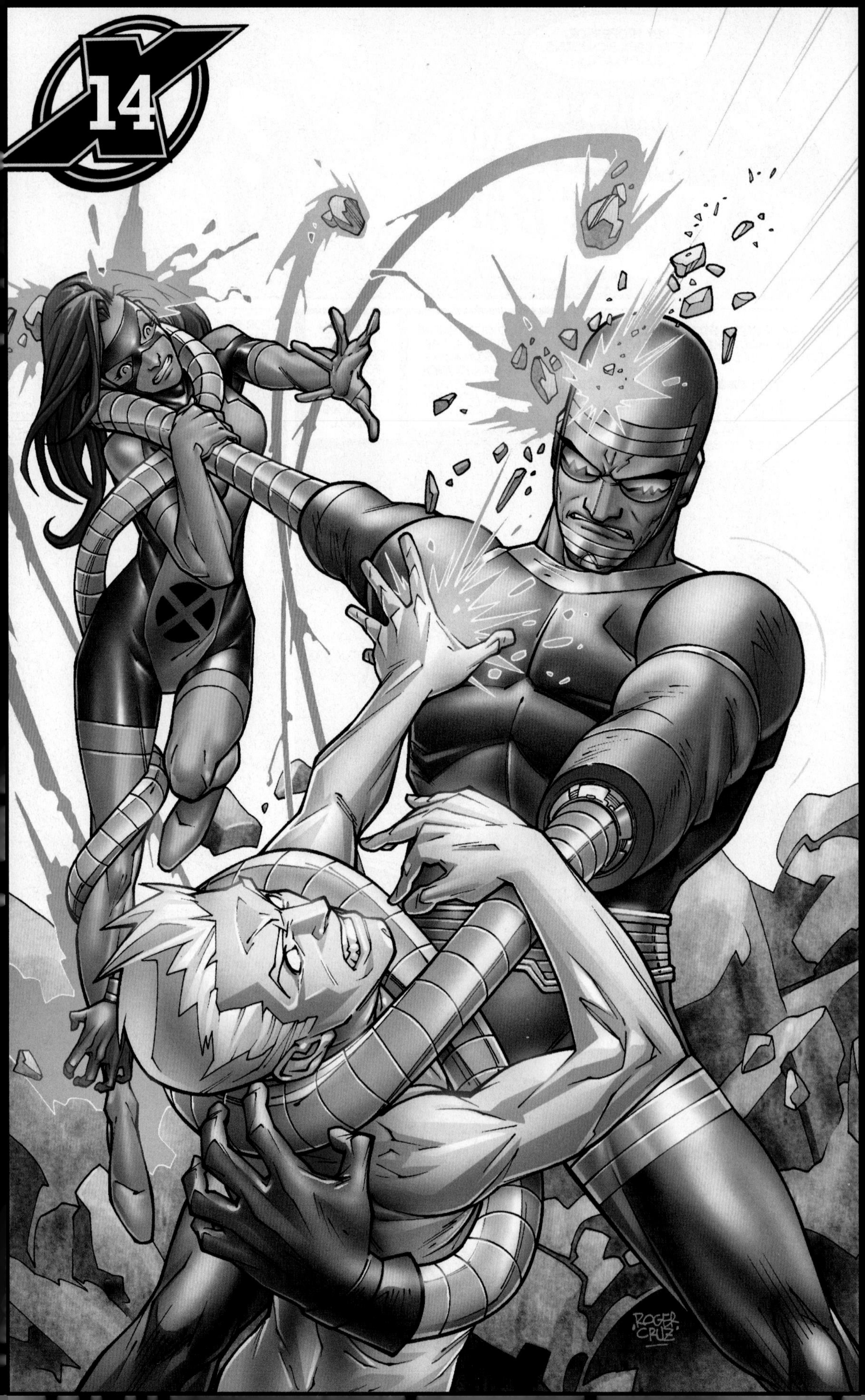
14
ROGER CRUZ

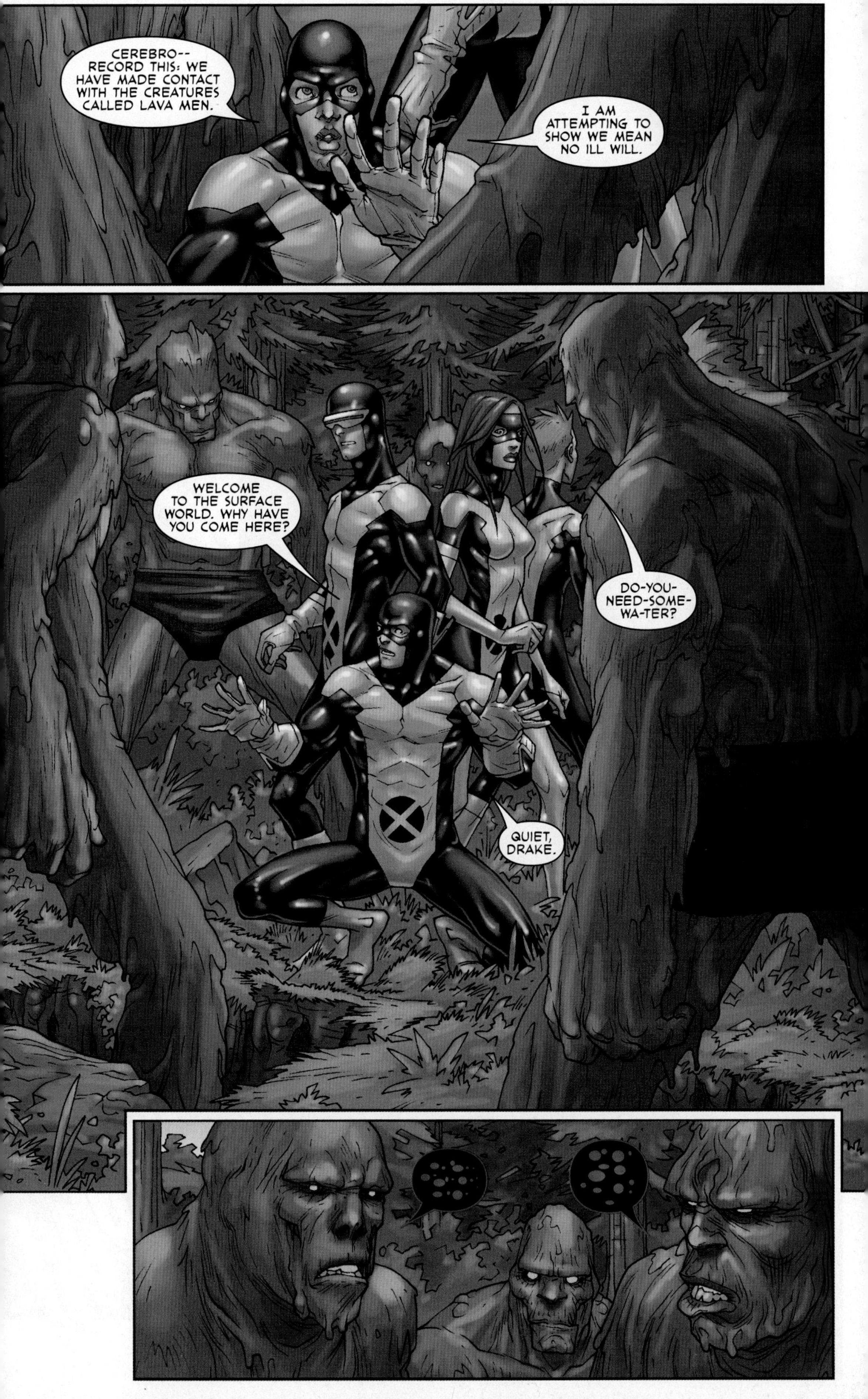
CEREBRO-- RECORD THIS: WE HAVE MADE CONTACT WITH THE CREATURES CALLED LAVA MEN.
I AM ATTEMPTING TO SHOW WE MEAN NO ILL WILL.
WELCOME TO THE SURFACE WORLD. WHY HAVE YOU COME HERE?
DO-YOU-NEED-SOME-WA-TER?
QUIET, DRAKE.

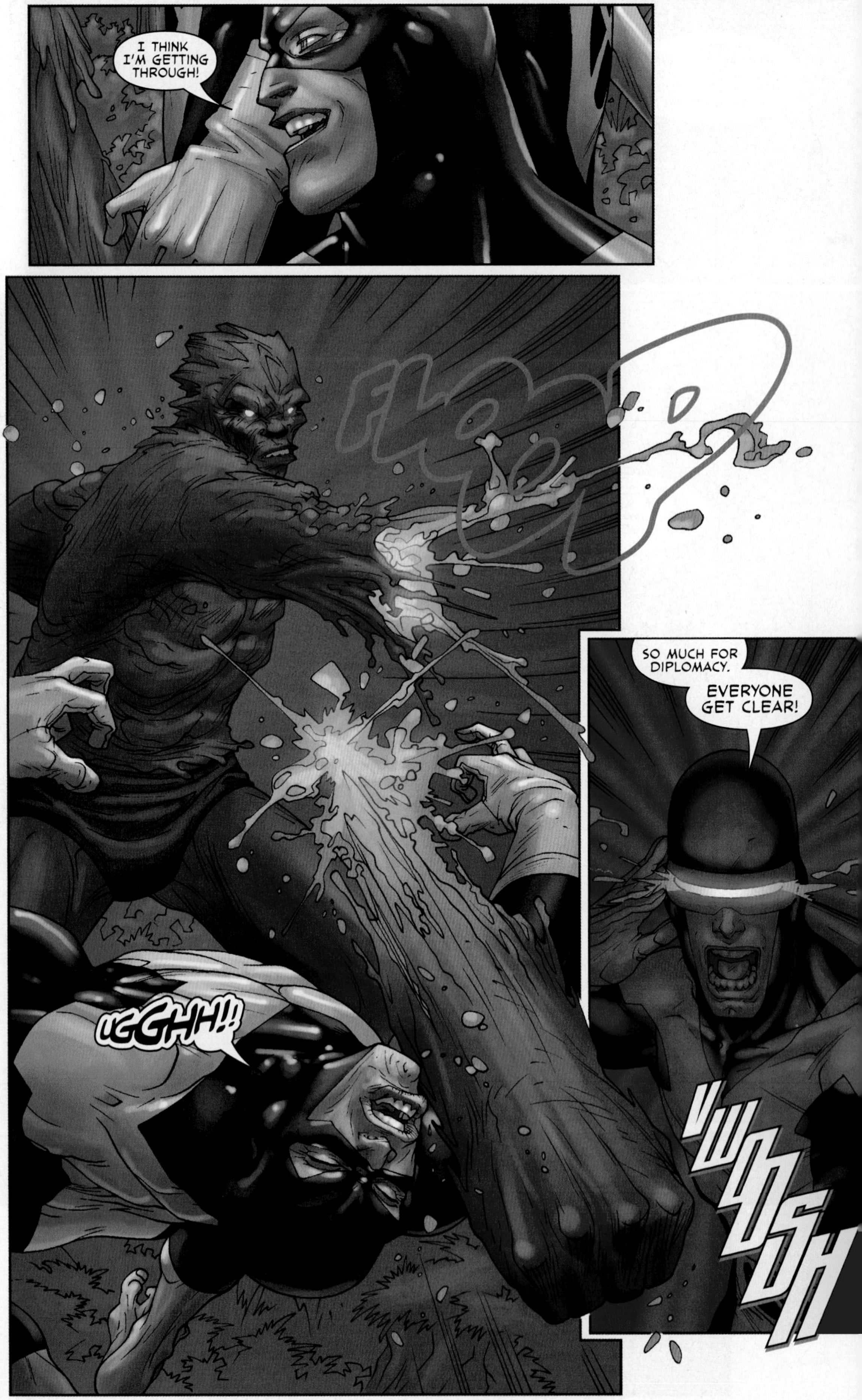
I THINK I'M GETTING THROUGH!
FLOOP
SO MUCH FOR DIPLOMACY.
EVERYONE GET CLEAR!
UGGHH!!
VWOOSH

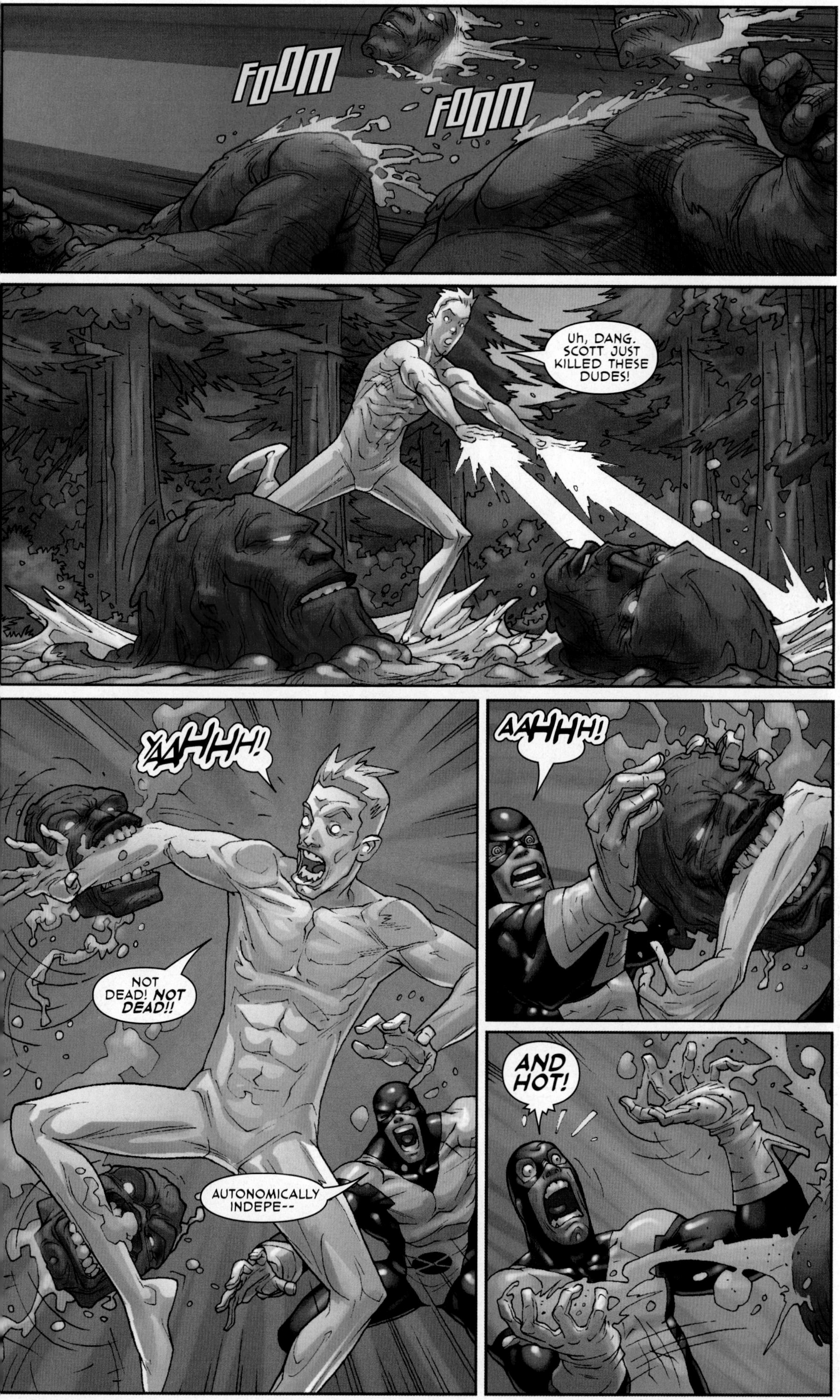
FOOM
FOOM
Uh, DANG. SCOTT JUST KILLED THESE DUDES!
YAAHHH!
NOT DEAD! NOT DEAD!!
AUTONOMICALLY INDEPE--
AAHHH!
AND HOT!

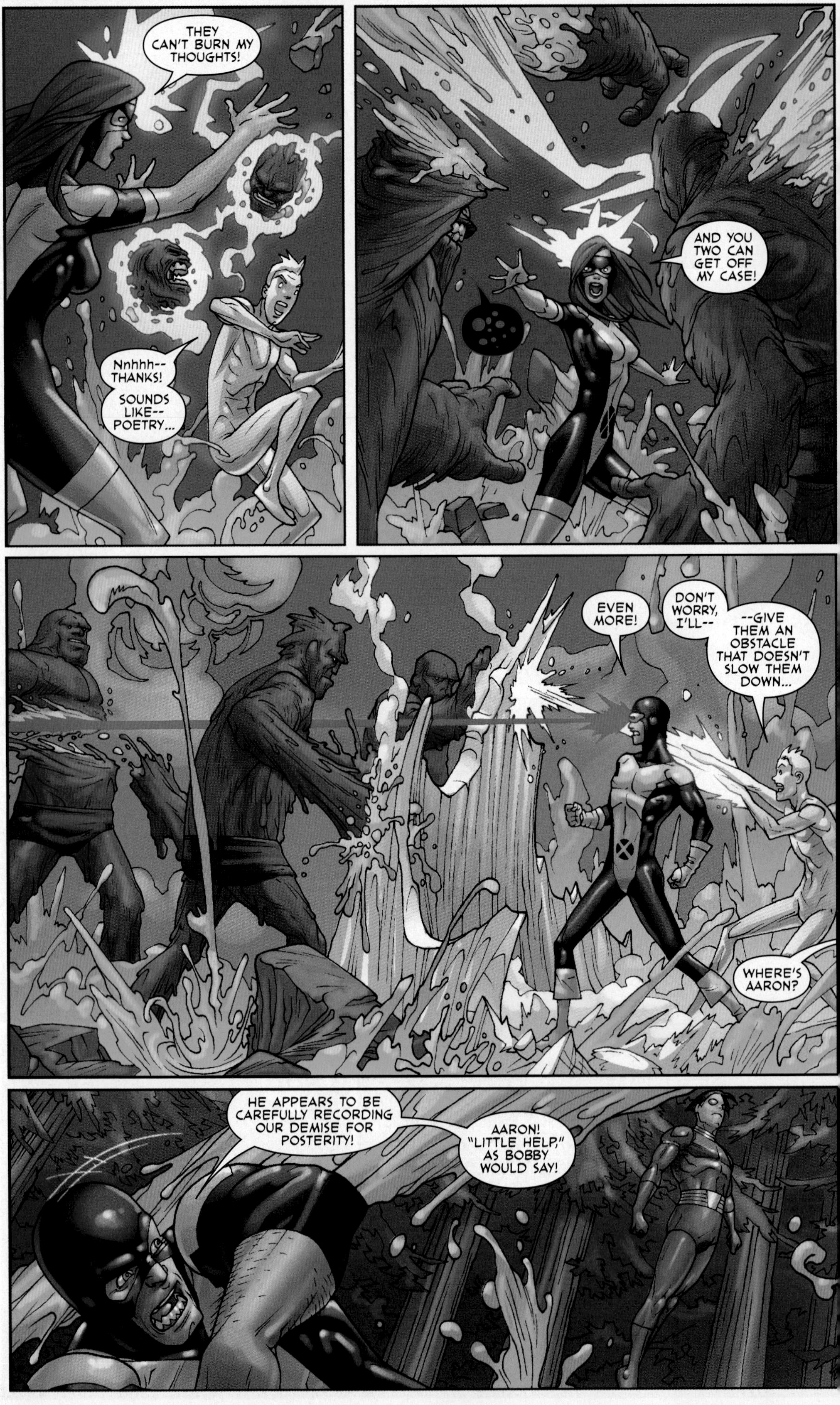
THEY CAN'T BURN MY THOUGHTS!
Nnhhh-- THANKS!
SOUNDS LIKE-- POETRY...
AND YOU TWO CAN GET OFF MY CASE!
EVEN MORE!
DON'T WORRY, I'LL--
--GIVE THEM AN OBSTACLE THAT DOESN'T SLOW THEM DOWN...
WHERE'S AARON?
HE APPEARS TO BE CAREFULLY RECORDING OUR DEMISE FOR POSTERITY!
AARON! "LITTLE HELP," AS BOBBY WOULD SAY!

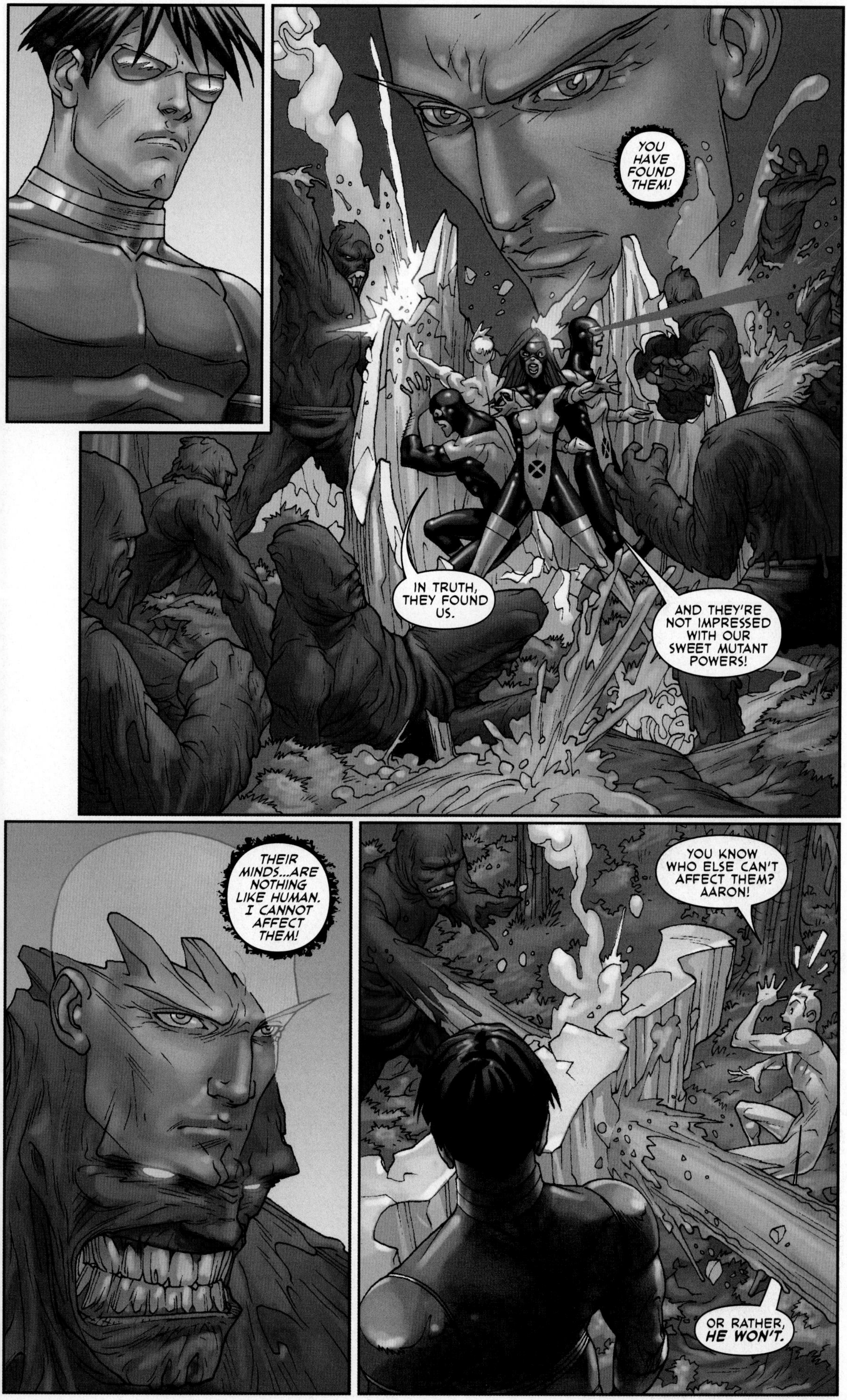
YOU HAVE FOUND THEM!
IN TRUTH, THEY FOUND US.
AND THEY'RE NOT IMPRESSED WITH OUR SWEET MUTANT POWERS!
THEIR MINDS...ARE NOTHING LIKE HUMAN. I CANNOT AFFECT THEM!
YOU KNOW WHO ELSE CAN'T AFFECT THEM? AARON!
OR RATHER, HE WON'T.

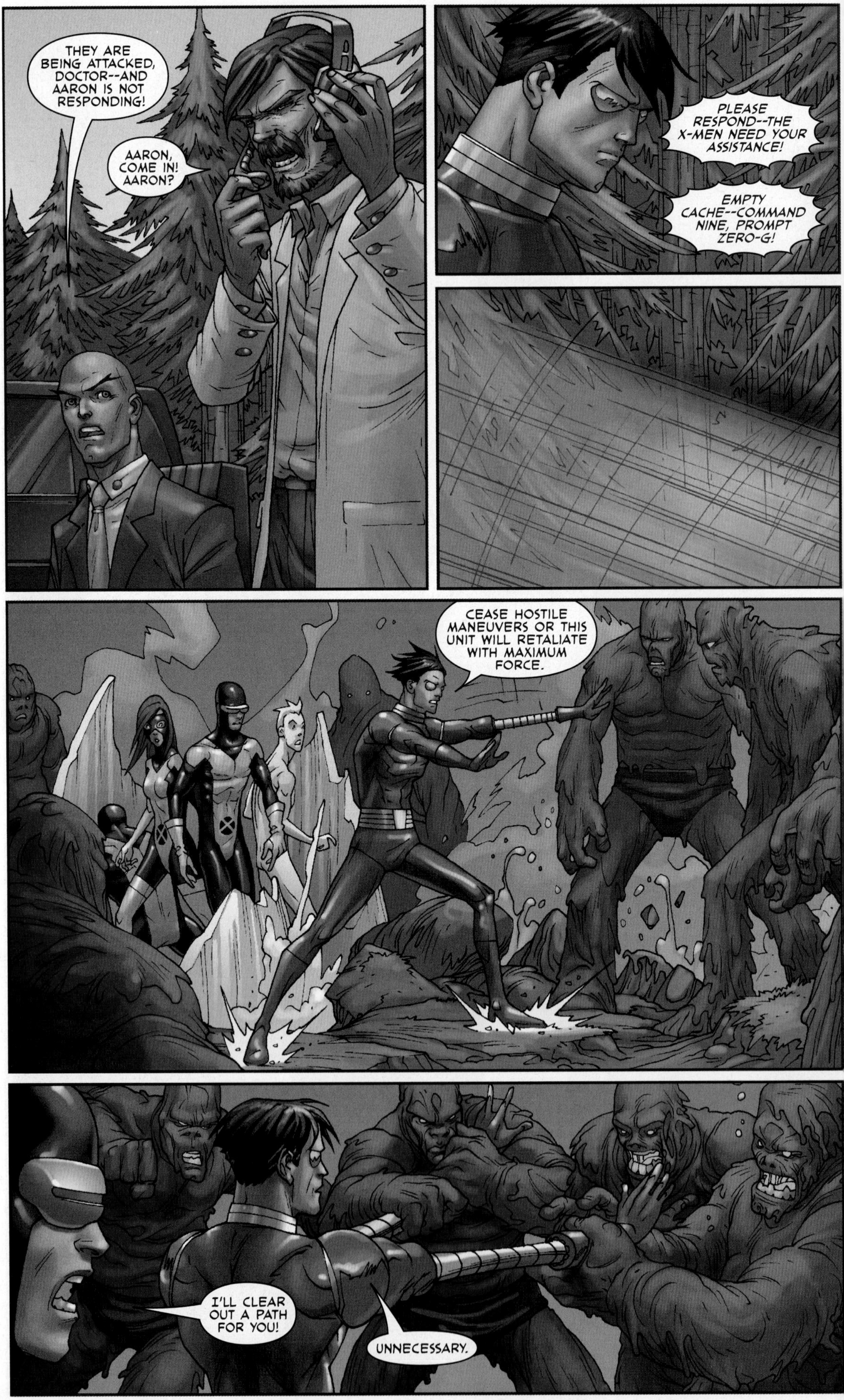
THEY ARE BEING ATTACKED, DOCTOR--AND AARON IS NOT RESPONDING!
AARON, COME IN! AARON?
PLEASE RESPOND--THE X-MEN NEED YOUR ASSISTANCE!
EMPTY CACHE--COMMAND NINE, PROMPT ZERO-G!
CEASE HOSTILE MANEUVERS OR THIS UNIT WILL RETALIATE WITH MAXIMUM FORCE.
I'LL CLEAR OUT A PATH FOR YOU!
UNNECESSARY.

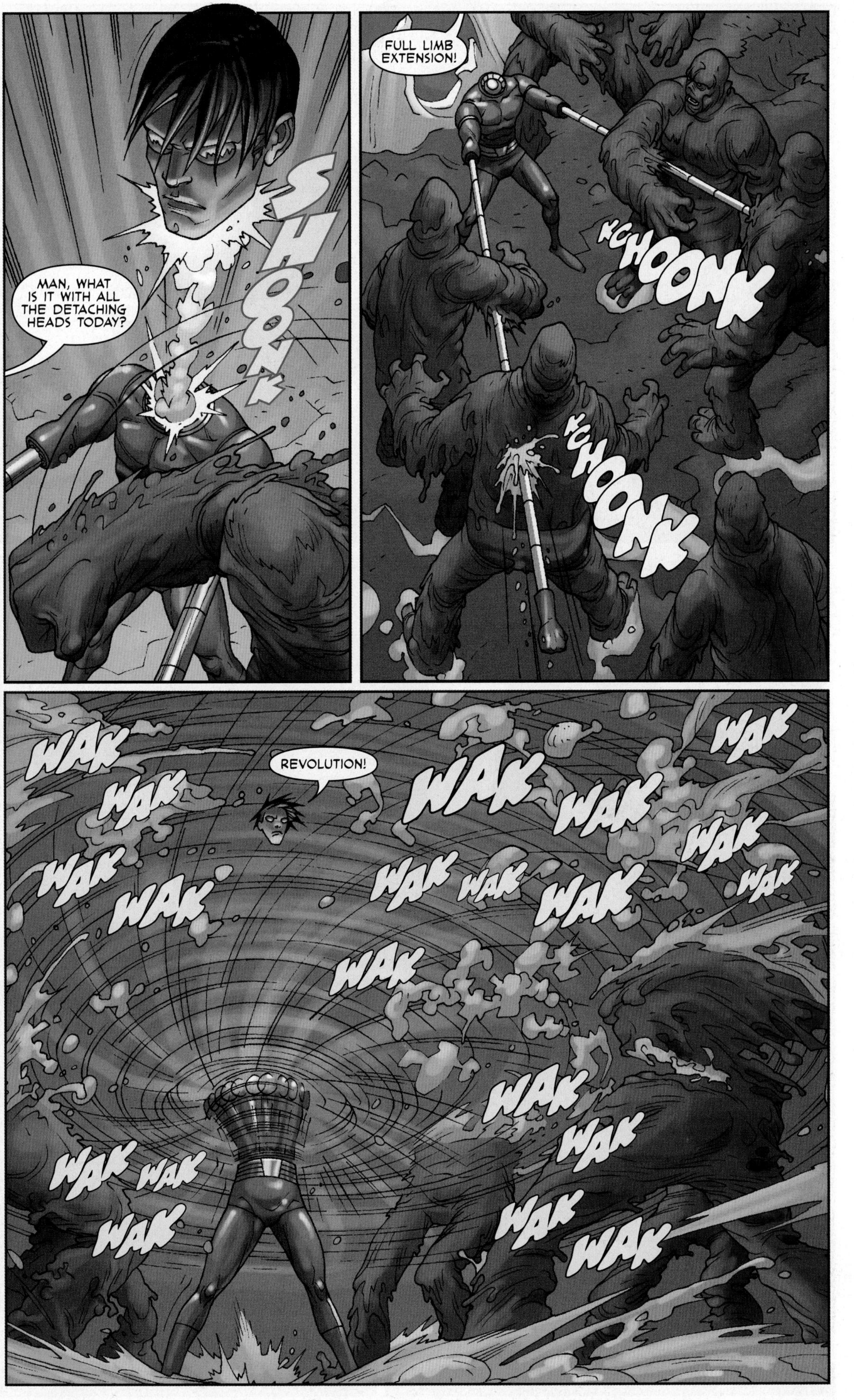
MAN, WHAT IS IT WITH ALL THE DETACHING HEADS TODAY?
SHOONK
FULL LIMB EXTENSION!
K'CHOONK
K'CHOONK
REVOLUTION!
WAK WAK WAK WAK WAK WAK WAK WAK WAK WAK WAK WAK WAK WAK WAK WAK WAK WAK WAK WAK WAK

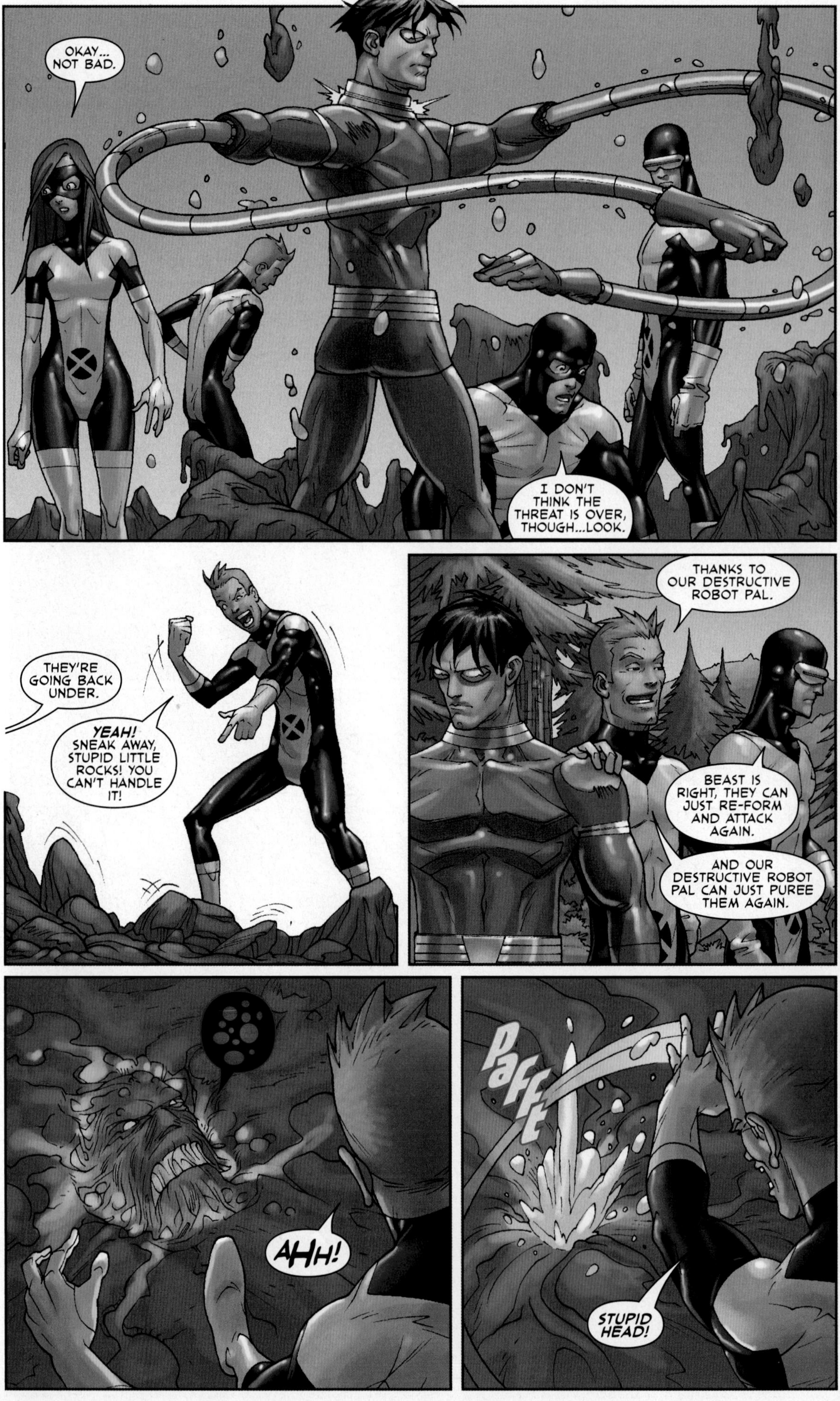
OKAY... NOT BAD.
I DON'T THINK THE THREAT IS OVER, THOUGH...LOOK.
THEY'RE GOING BACK UNDER.
YEAH! SNEAK AWAY, STUPID LITTLE ROCKS! YOU CAN'T HANDLE IT!
THANKS TO OUR DESTRUCTIVE ROBOT PAL.
BEAST IS RIGHT, THEY CAN JUST RE-FORM AND ATTACK AGAIN.
AND OUR DESTRUCTIVE ROBOT PAL CAN JUST PUREE THEM AGAIN.
AHH!
PAFFT
STUPID HEAD!

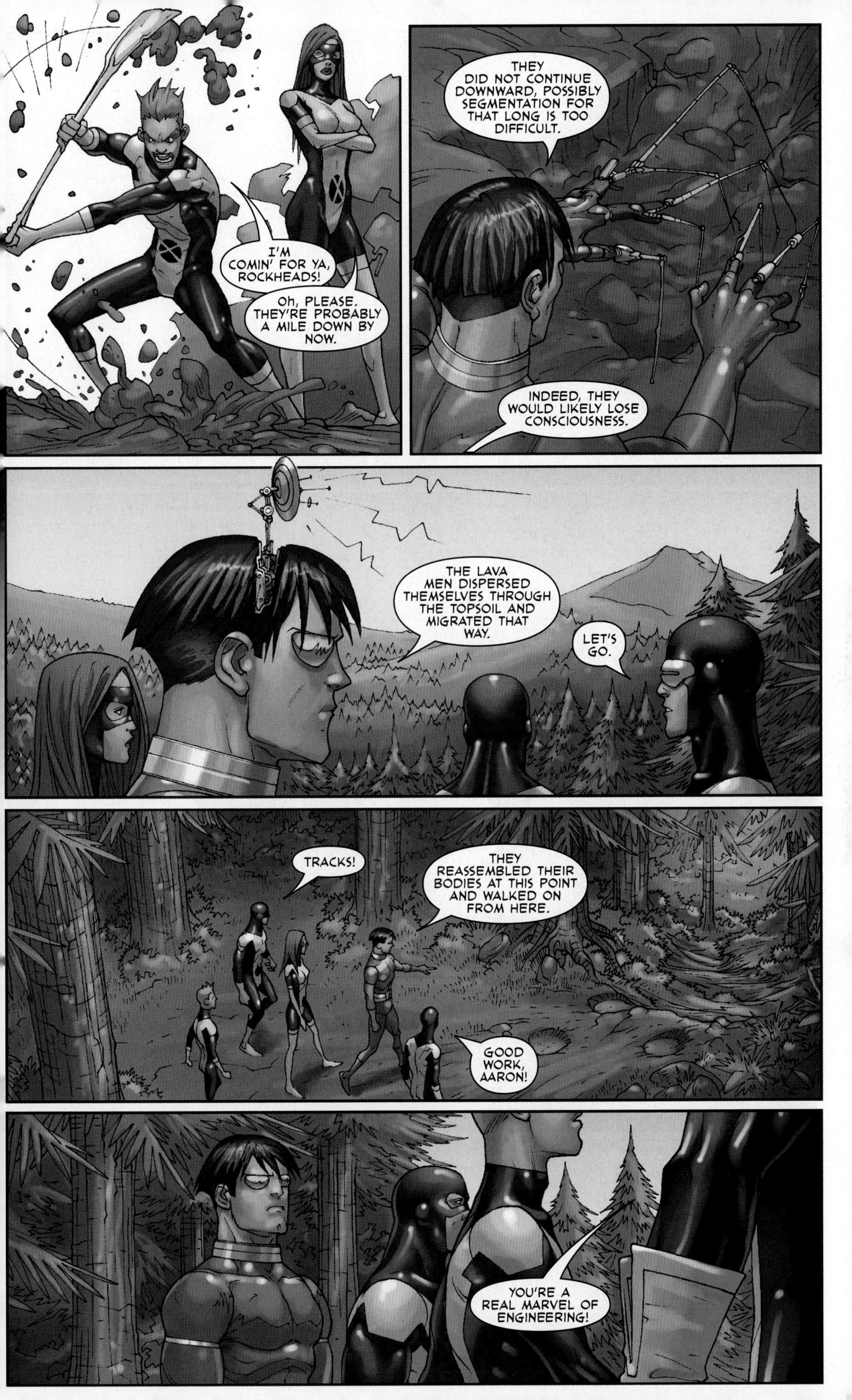
I'M COMIN' FOR YA, ROCKHEADS!
Oh, PLEASE. THEY'RE PROBABLY A MILE DOWN BY NOW.
THEY DID NOT CONTINUE DOWNWARD, POSSIBLY SEGMENTATION FOR THAT LONG IS TOO DIFFICULT.
INDEED, THEY WOULD LIKELY LOSE CONSCIOUSNESS.
THE LAVA MEN DISPERSED THEMSELVES THROUGH THE TOPSOIL AND MIGRATED THAT WAY.
LET'S GO.
TRACKS!
THEY REASSEMBLED THEIR BODIES AT THIS POINT AND WALKED ON FROM HERE.
GOOD WORK, AARON!
YOU'RE A REAL MARVEL OF ENGINEERING!

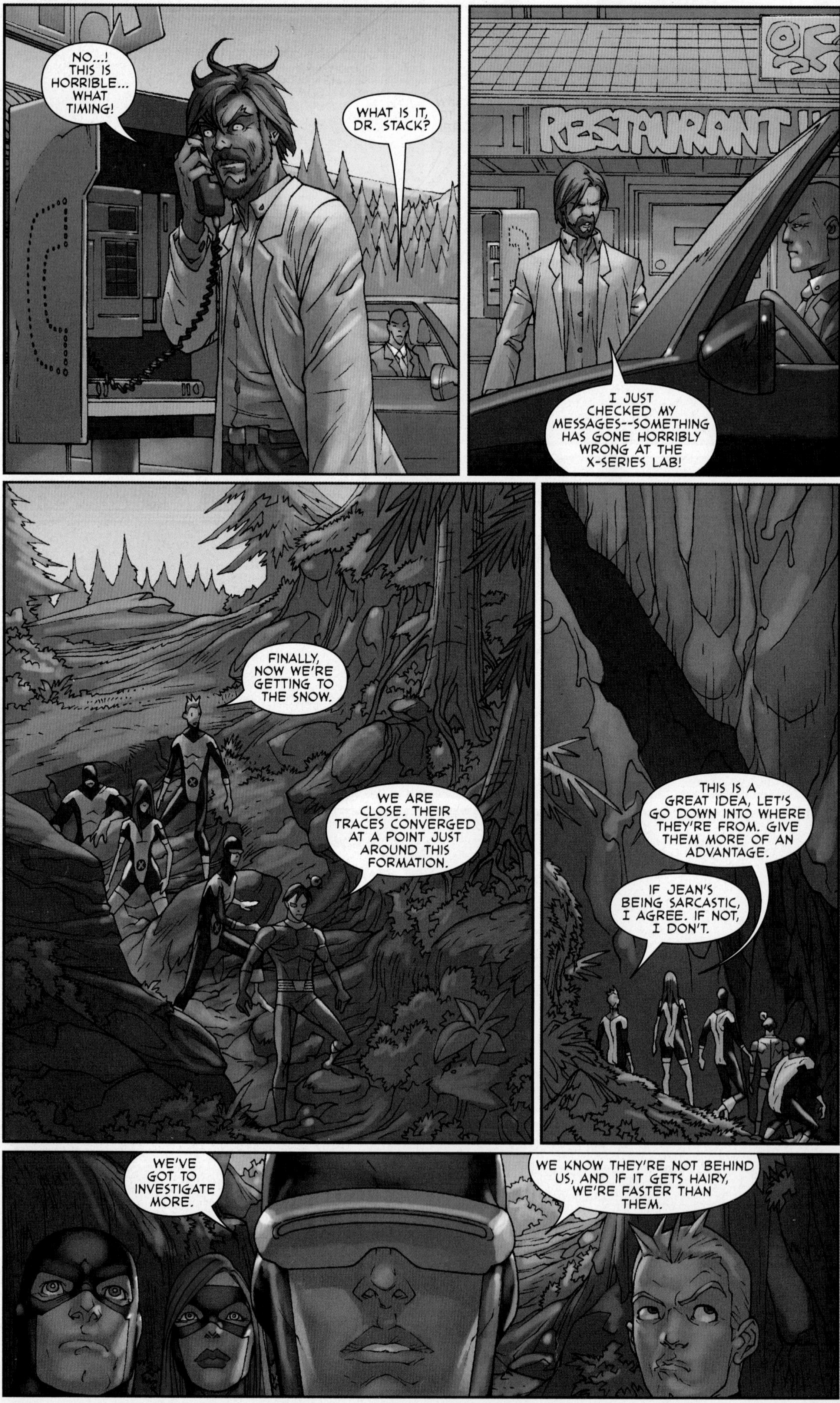
NO...! THIS IS HORRIBLE... WHAT TIMING!
WHAT IS IT, DR. STACK?
RESTAURANT
I JUST CHECKED MY MESSAGES--SOMETHING HAS GONE HORRIBLY WRONG AT THE X-SERIES LAB!
FINALLY, NOW WE'RE GETTING TO THE SNOW.
WE ARE CLOSE. THEIR TRACES CONVERGED AT A POINT JUST AROUND THIS FORMATION.
THIS IS A GREAT IDEA, LET'S GO DOWN INTO WHERE THEY'RE FROM. GIVE THEM MORE OF AN ADVANTAGE.
IF JEAN'S BEING SARCASTIC, I AGREE. IF NOT, I DON'T.
WE'VE GOT TO INVESTIGATE MORE.
WE KNOW THEY'RE NOT BEHIND US, AND IF IT GETS HAIRY, WE'RE FASTER THAN THEM.

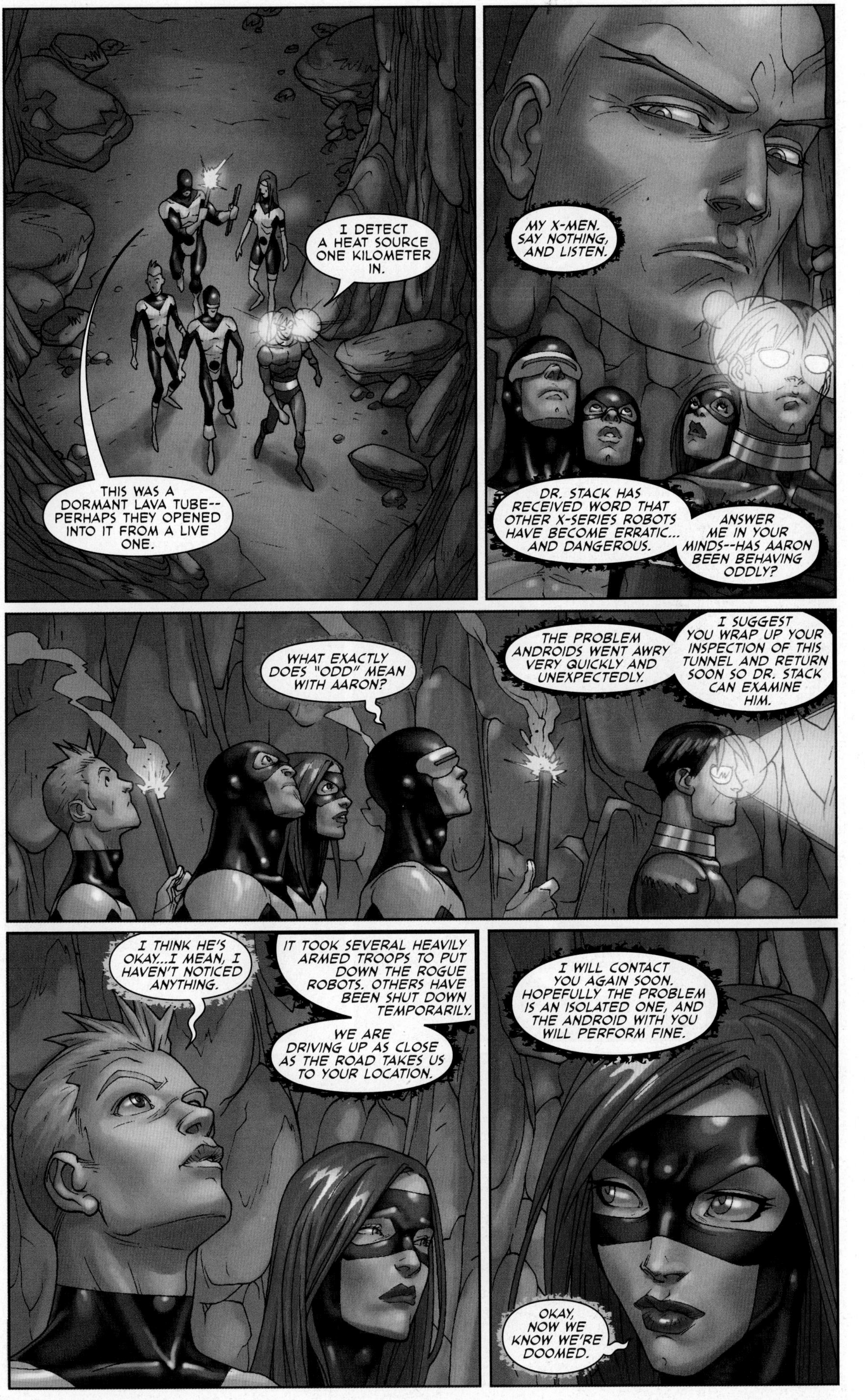

I DETECT A HEAT SOURCE ONE KILOMETER IN.
THIS WAS A DORMANT LAVA TUBE--PERHAPS THEY OPENED INTO IT FROM A LIVE ONE.
MY X-MEN. SAY NOTHING, AND LISTEN.
DR. STACK HAS RECEIVED WORD THAT OTHER X-SERIES ROBOTS HAVE BECOME ERRATIC... AND DANGEROUS.
ANSWER ME IN YOUR MINDS--HAS AARON BEEN BEHAVING ODDLY?
WHAT EXACTLY DOES "ODD" MEAN WITH AARON?
THE PROBLEM ANDROIDS WENT AWRY VERY QUICKLY AND UNEXPECTEDLY.
I SUGGEST YOU WRAP UP YOUR INSPECTION OF THIS TUNNEL AND RETURN SOON SO DR. STACK CAN EXAMINE HIM.
I THINK HE'S OKAY...I MEAN, I HAVEN'T NOTICED ANYTHING.
IT TOOK SEVERAL HEAVILY ARMED TROOPS TO PUT DOWN THE ROGUE ROBOTS. OTHERS HAVE BEEN SHUT DOWN TEMPORARILY.
WE ARE DRIVING UP AS CLOSE AS THE ROAD TAKES US TO YOUR LOCATION.
I WILL CONTACT YOU AGAIN SOON. HOPEFULLY THE PROBLEM IS AN ISOLATED ONE, AND THE ANDROID WITH YOU WILL PERFORM FINE.
OKAY, NOW WE KNOW WE'RE DOOMED.

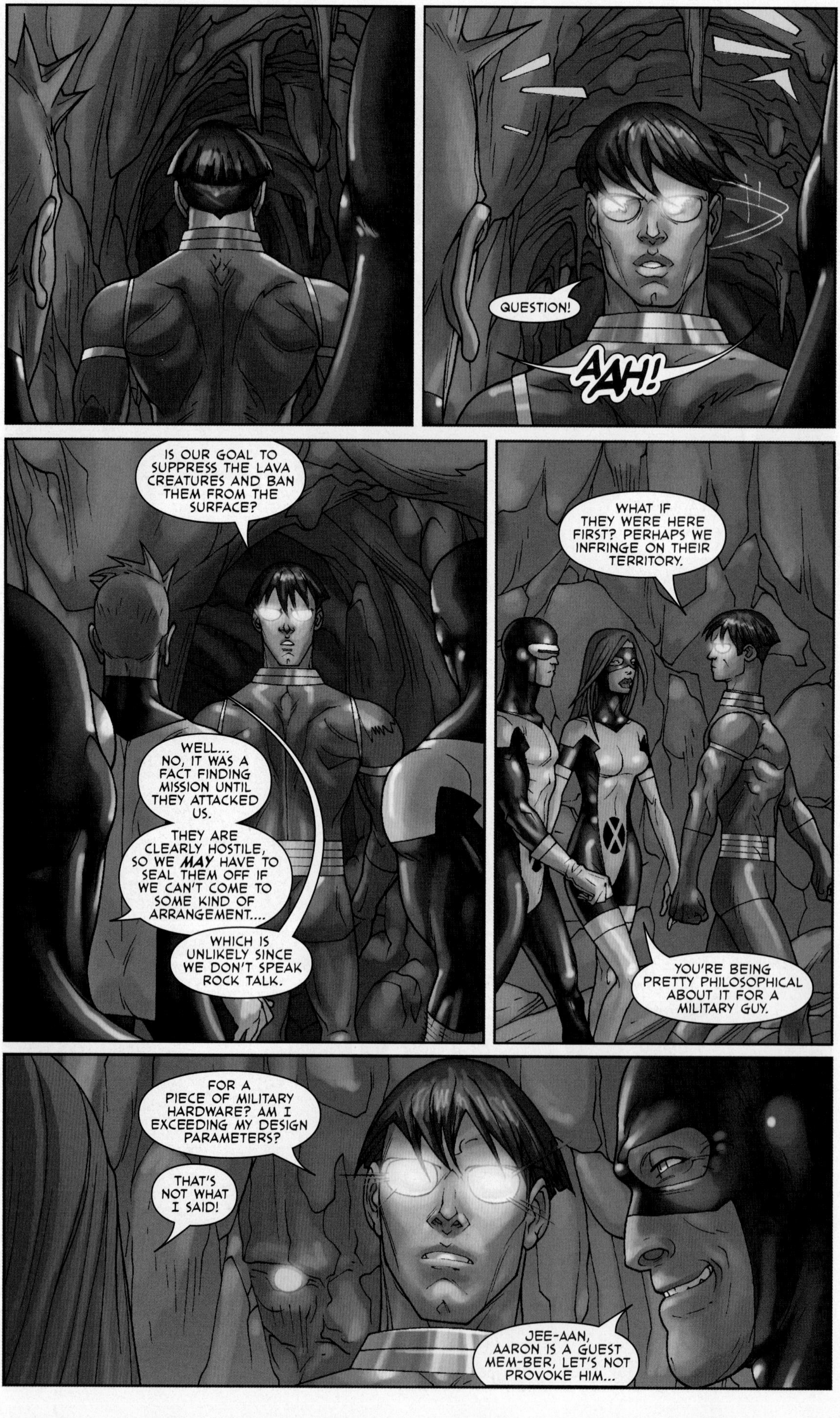
QUESTION!
AAH!
IS OUR GOAL TO SUPPRESS THE LAVA CREATURES AND BAN THEM FROM THE SURFACE?
WELL... NO, IT WAS A FACT FINDING MISSION UNTIL THEY ATTACKED US.
THEY ARE CLEARLY HOSTILE, SO WE MAY HAVE TO SEAL THEM OFF IF WE CAN'T COME TO SOME KIND OF ARRANGEMENT....
WHICH IS UNLIKELY SINCE WE DON'T SPEAK ROCK TALK.
WHAT IF THEY WERE HERE FIRST? PERHAPS WE INFRINGE ON THEIR TERRITORY.
YOU'RE BEING PRETTY PHILOSOPHICAL ABOUT IT FOR A MILITARY GUY.
FOR A PIECE OF MILITARY HARDWARE? AM I EXCEEDING MY DESIGN PARAMETERS?
THAT'S NOT WHAT I SAID!
JEE-AAN, AARON IS A GUEST MEM-BER, LET'S NOT PROVOKE HIM...

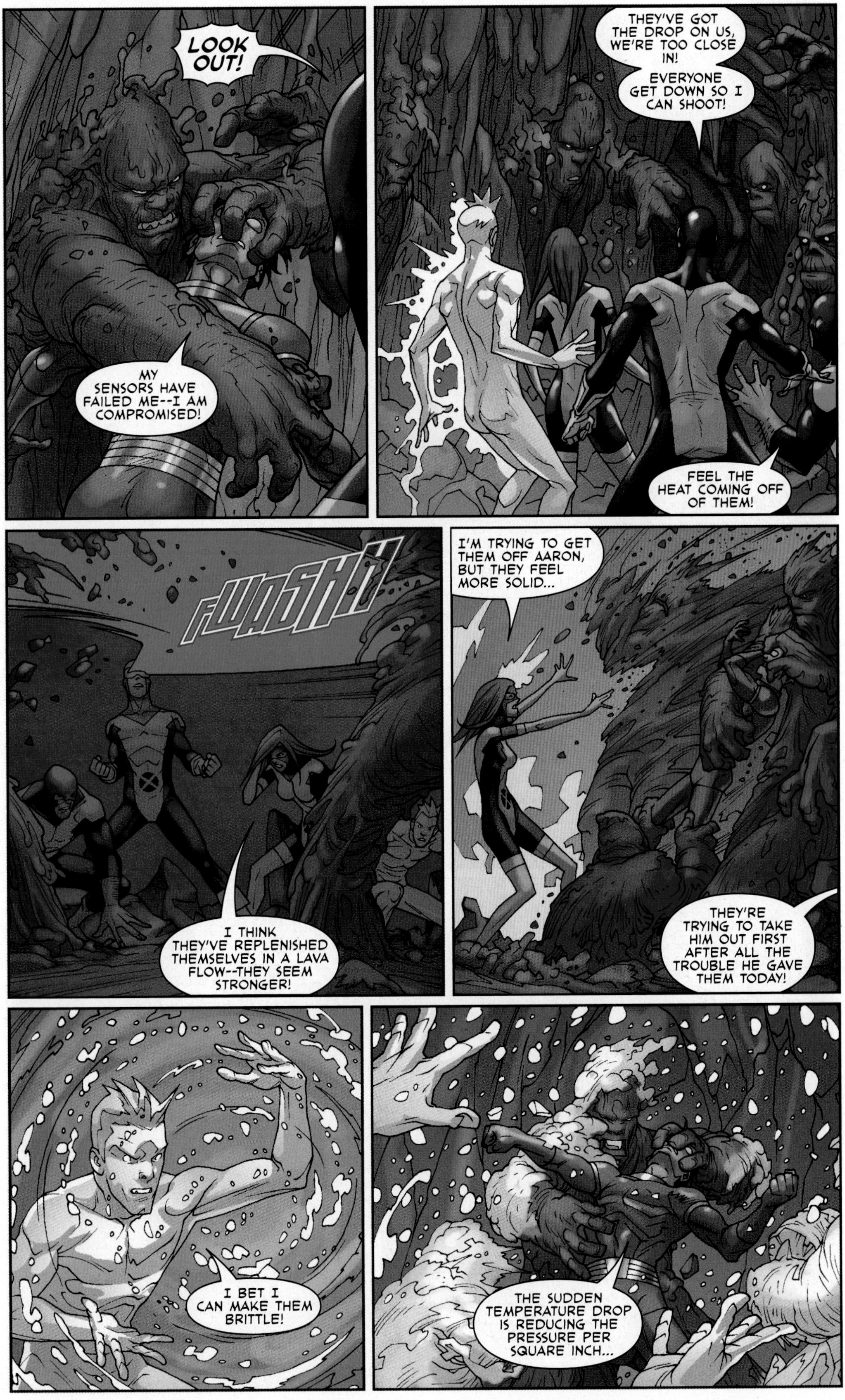
LOOK OUT!
MY SENSORS HAVE FAILED ME--I AM COMPROMISED!
THEY'VE GOT THE DROP ON US, WE'RE TOO CLOSE IN!
EVERYONE GET DOWN SO I CAN SHOOT!
FEEL THE HEAT COMING OFF OF THEM!
FWOOSHH
I THINK THEY'VE REPLENISHED THEMSELVES IN A LAVA FLOW--THEY SEEM STRONGER!
I'M TRYING TO GET THEM OFF AARON, BUT THEY FEEL MORE SOLID...
THEY'RE TRYING TO TAKE HIM OUT FIRST AFTER ALL THE TROUBLE HE GAVE THEM TODAY!
I BET I CAN MAKE THEM BRITTLE!
THE SUDDEN TEMPERATURE DROP IS REDUCING THE PRESSURE PER SQUARE INCH...

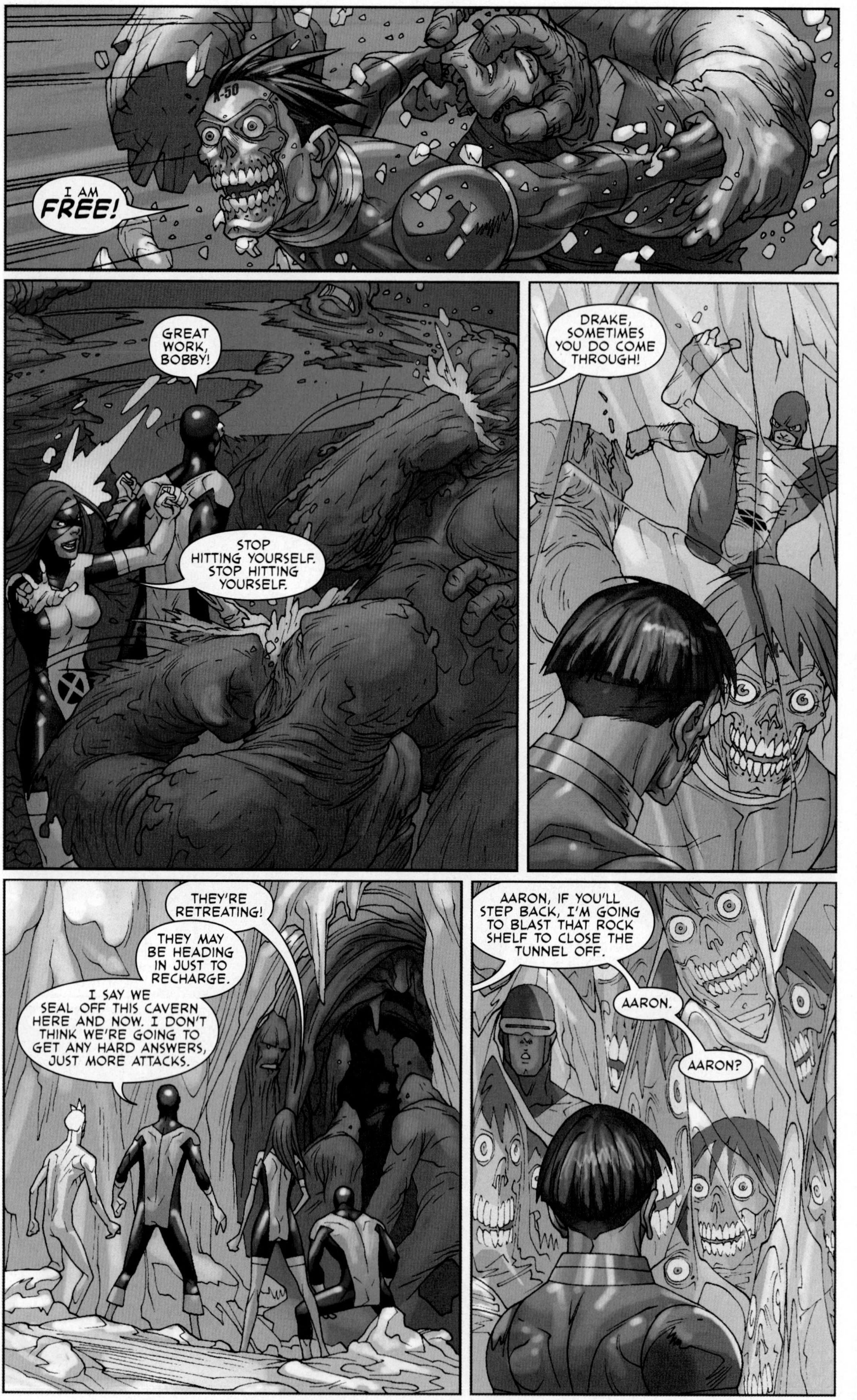
I AM FREE!
GREAT WORK, BOBBY!
STOP HITTING YOURSELF. STOP HITTING YOURSELF.
DRAKE, SOMETIMES YOU DO COME THROUGH!
THEY'RE RETREATING!
THEY MAY BE HEADING IN JUST TO RECHARGE.
I SAY WE SEAL OFF THIS CAVERN HERE AND NOW. I DON'T THINK WE'RE GOING TO GET ANY HARD ANSWERS, JUST MORE ATTACKS.
AARON, IF YOU'LL STEP BACK, I'M GOING TO BLAST THAT ROCK SHELF TO CLOSE THE TUNNEL OFF.
AARON.
AARON?

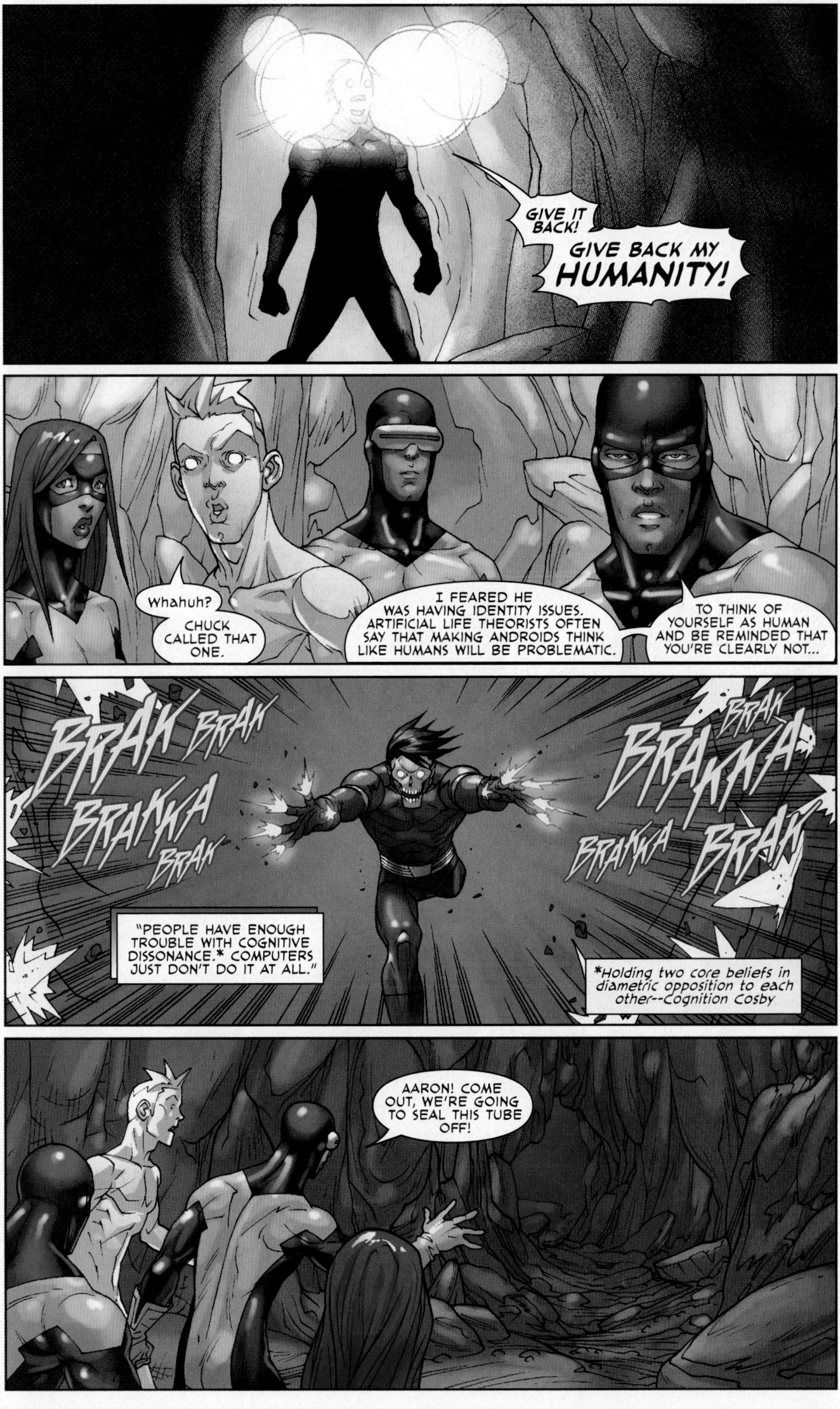
GIVE IT BACK! GIVE BACK MY HUMANITY!
Whahuh?
CHUCK CALLED THAT ONE.
I FEARED HE WAS HAVING IDENTITY ISSUES. ARTIFICIAL LIFE THEORISTS OFTEN SAY THAT MAKING ANDROIDS THINK LIKE HUMANS WILL BE PROBLEMATIC.
TO THINK OF YOURSELF AS HUMAN AND BE REMINDED THAT YOU'RE CLEARLY NOT...
BRAK BRAK
BRAKKA
BRAK
BRAK
BRAKKA
BRAKKA BRAK
"PEOPLE HAVE ENOUGH TROUBLE WITH COGNITIVE DISSONANCE.* COMPUTERS JUST DON'T DO IT AT ALL."
*Holding two core beliefs in diametric opposition to each other--Cognition Cosby
AARON! COME OUT, WE'RE GOING TO SEAL THIS TUBE OFF!

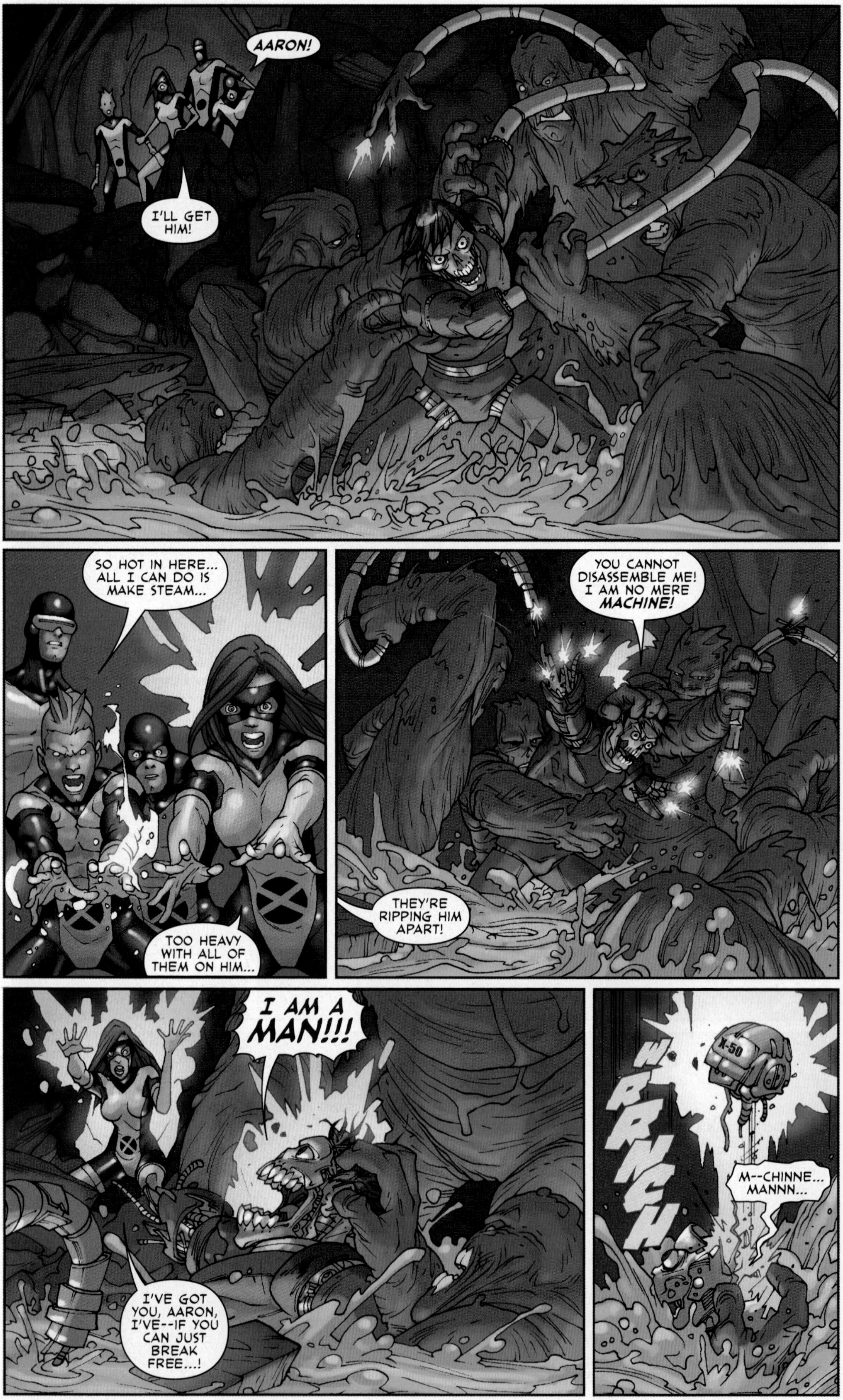

AARON!
I'LL GET HIM!
SO HOT IN HERE... ALL I CAN DO IS MAKE STEAM...
TOO HEAVY WITH ALL OF THEM ON HIM...
YOU CANNOT DISASSEMBLE ME! I AM NO MERE MACHINE!
THEY'RE RIPPING HIM APART!
I AM A MAN!!!
I'VE GOT YOU, AARON, I'VE--IF YOU CAN JUST BREAK FREE...!
WRRNCH
X-50
M--CHINNE... MANNN...

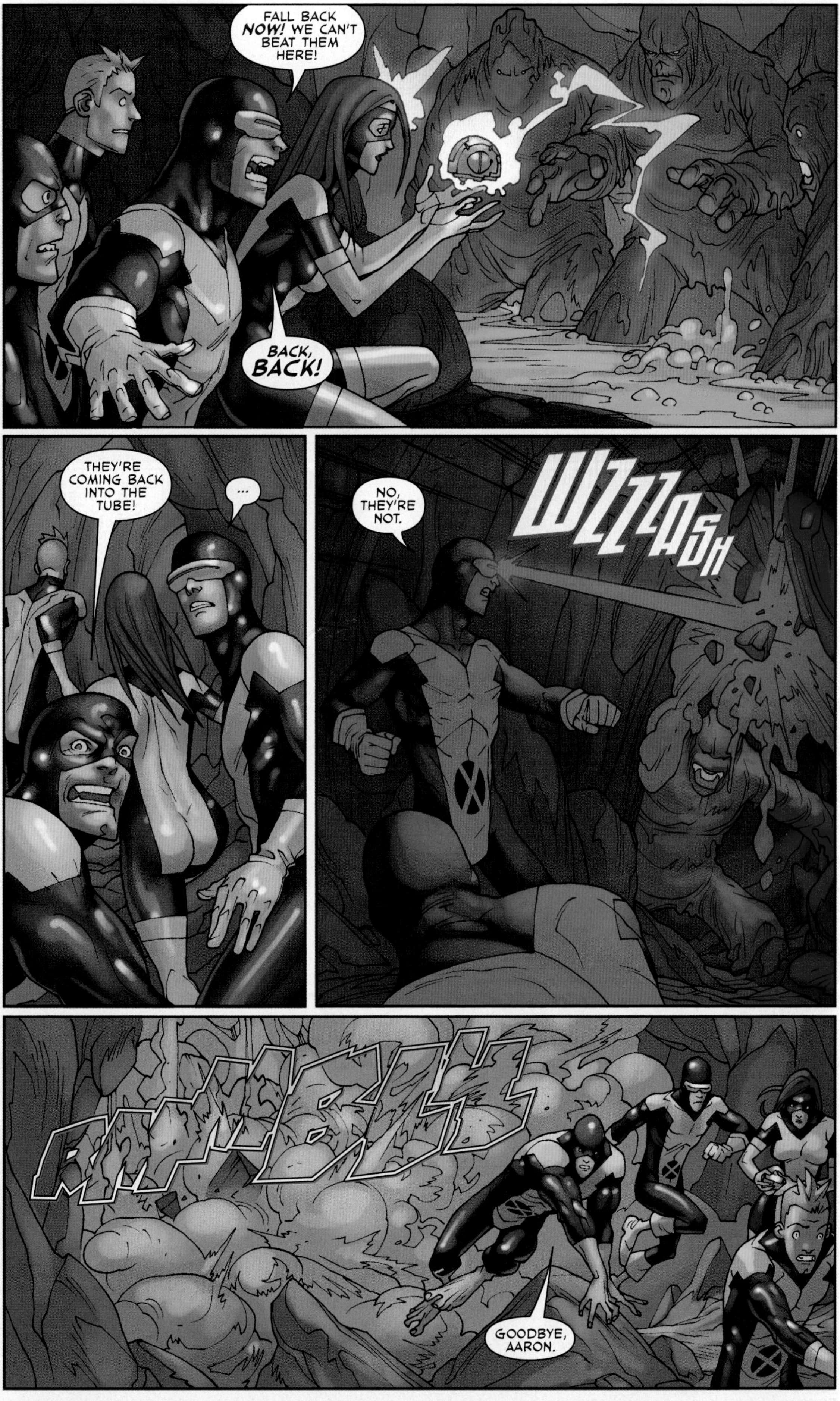
FALL BACK NOW! WE CAN'T BEAT THEM HERE!
BACK, BACK!
THEY'RE COMING BACK INTO THE TUBE!
...
NO, THEY'RE NOT.
WZZZASH
GOODBYE, AARON.

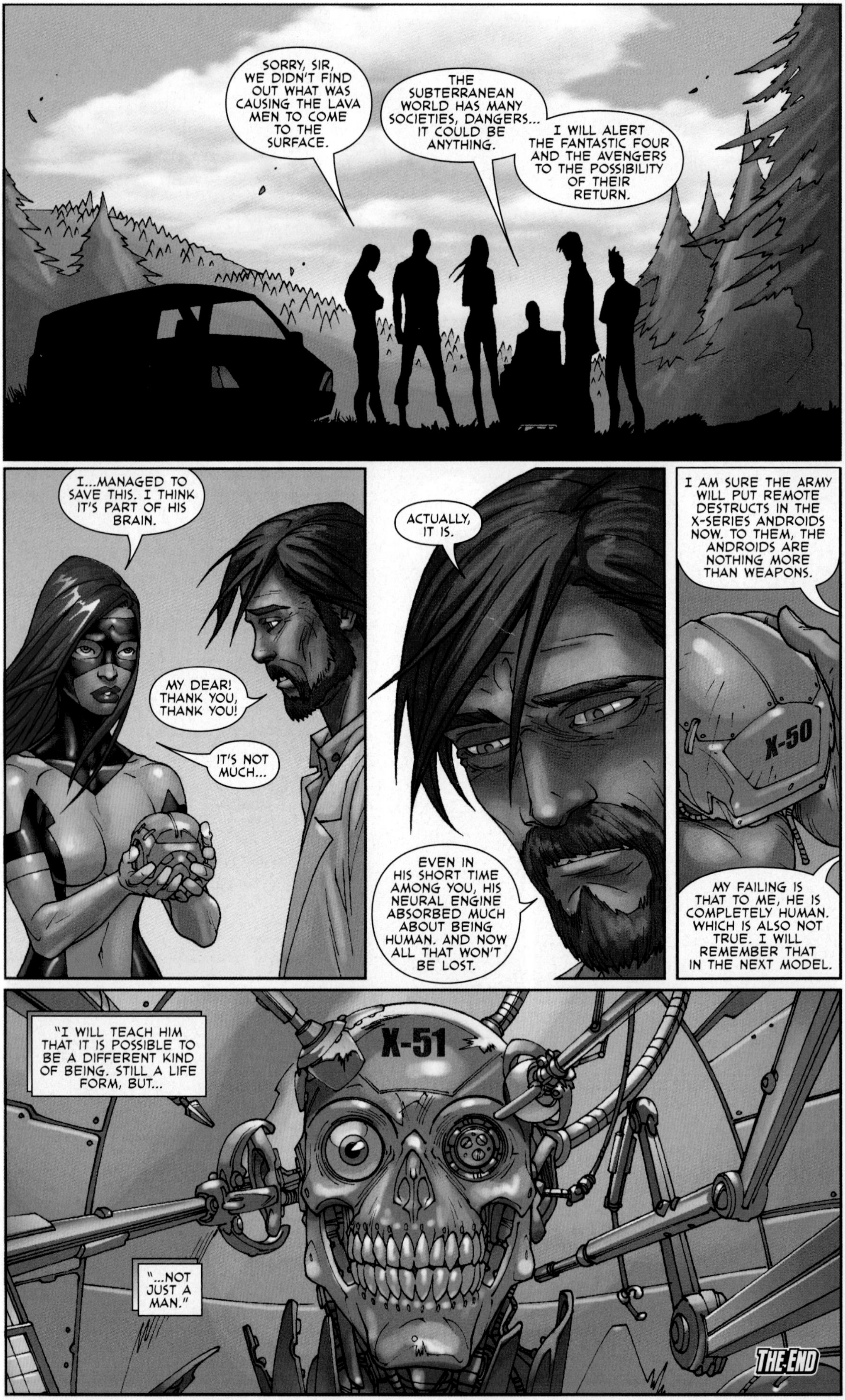

SORRY, SIR, WE DIDN'T FIND OUT WHAT WAS CAUSING THE LAVA MEN TO COME TO THE SURFACE.
THE SUBTERRANEAN WORLD HAS MANY SOCIETIES, DANGERS... IT COULD BE ANYTHING.
I WILL ALERT THE FANTASTIC FOUR AND THE AVENGERS TO THE POSSIBILITY OF THEIR RETURN.
I...MANAGED TO SAVE THIS. I THINK IT'S PART OF HIS BRAIN.
MY DEAR! THANK YOU, THANK YOU!
IT'S NOT MUCH...
ACTUALLY, IT IS.
EVEN IN HIS SHORT TIME AMONG YOU, HIS NEURAL ENGINE ABSORBED MUCH ABOUT BEING HUMAN. AND NOW ALL THAT WON'T BE LOST.
I AM SURE THE ARMY WILL PUT REMOTE DESTRUCTS IN THE X-SERIES ANDROIDS NOW. TO THEM, THE ANDROIDS ARE NOTHING MORE THAN WEAPONS.
X-50
MY FAILING IS THAT TO ME, HE IS COMPLETELY HUMAN. WHICH IS ALSO NOT TRUE. I WILL REMEMBER THAT IN THE NEXT MODEL.
"I WILL TEACH HIM THAT IT IS POSSIBLE TO BE A DIFFERENT KIND OF BEING. STILL A LIFE FORM, BUT...
X-51
"...NOT JUST A MAN."
THE END

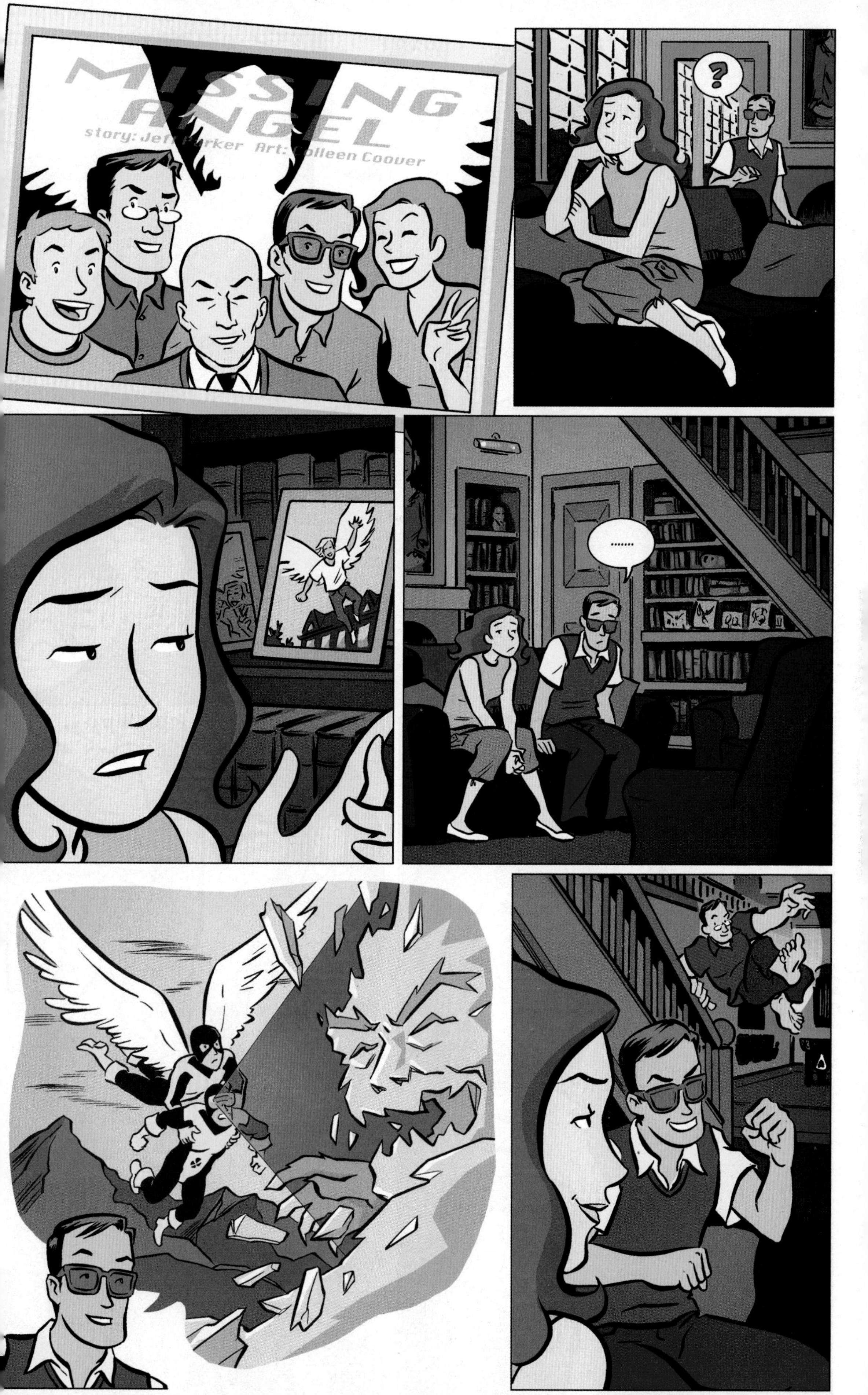
MISSING ANGEL
story: Jeff Parker Art: Colleen Coover
?
....

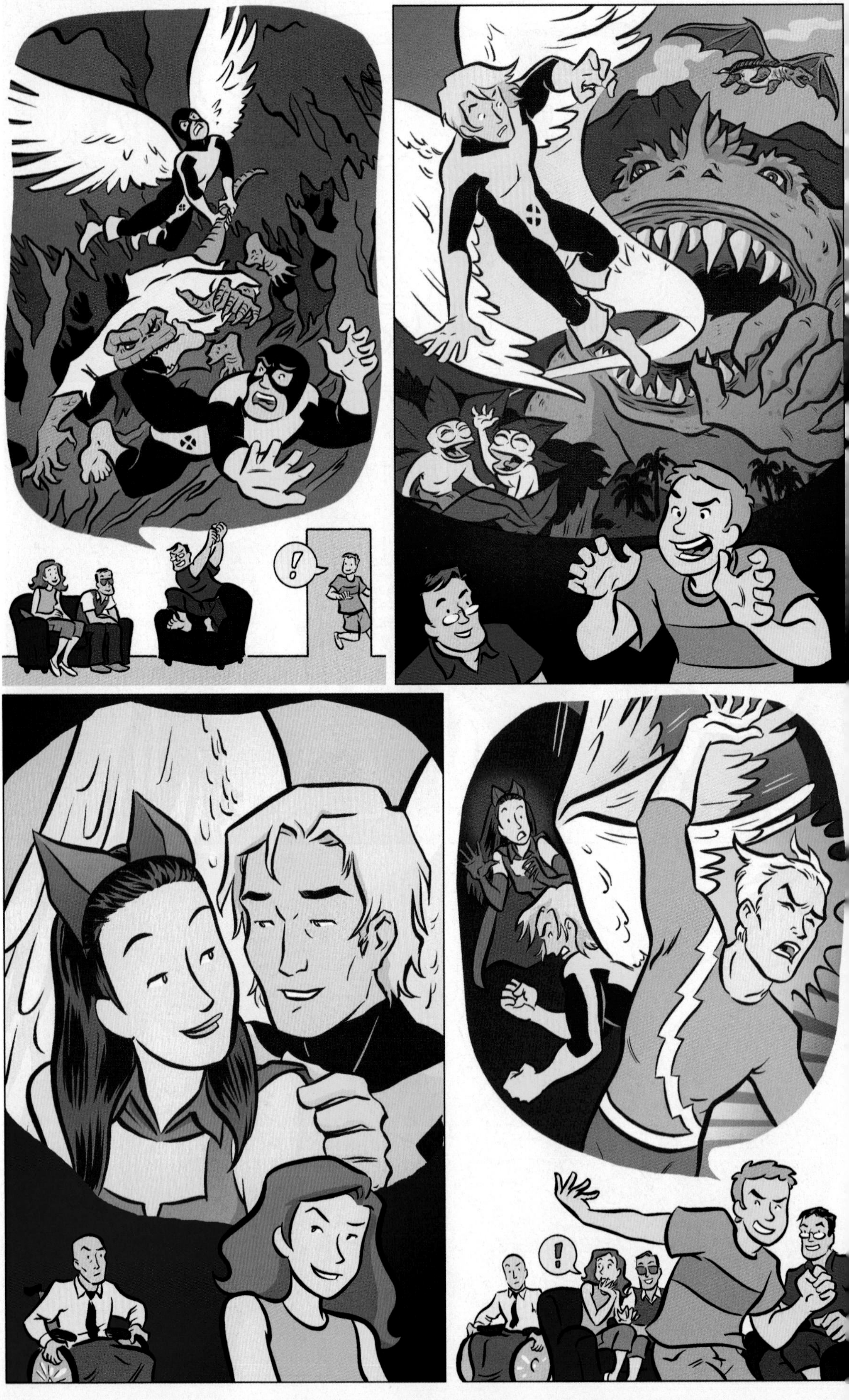
!
!

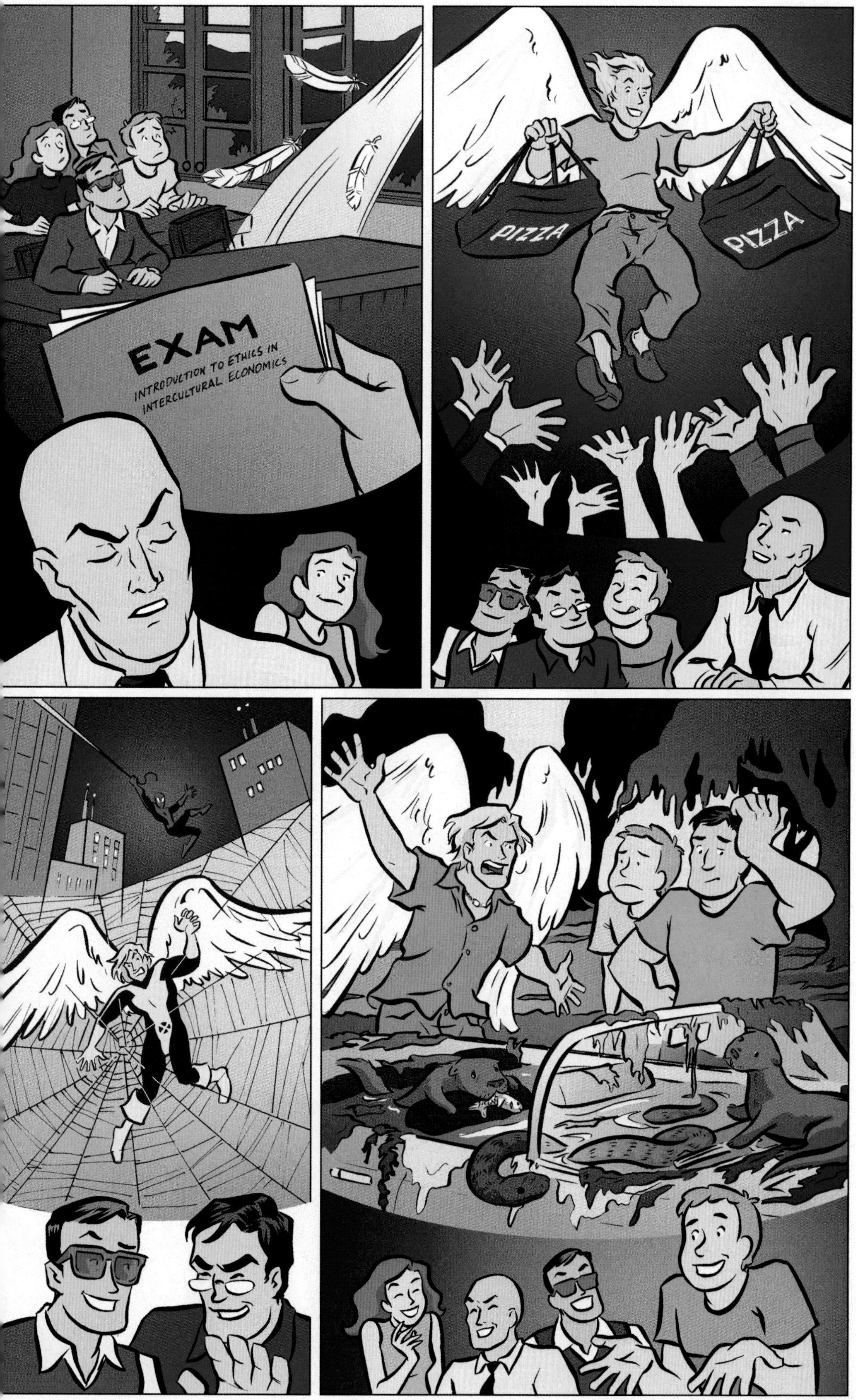
EXAM
INTRODUCTION TO ETHICS IN INTERCULTURAL ECONOMICS
PIZZA
PIZZA

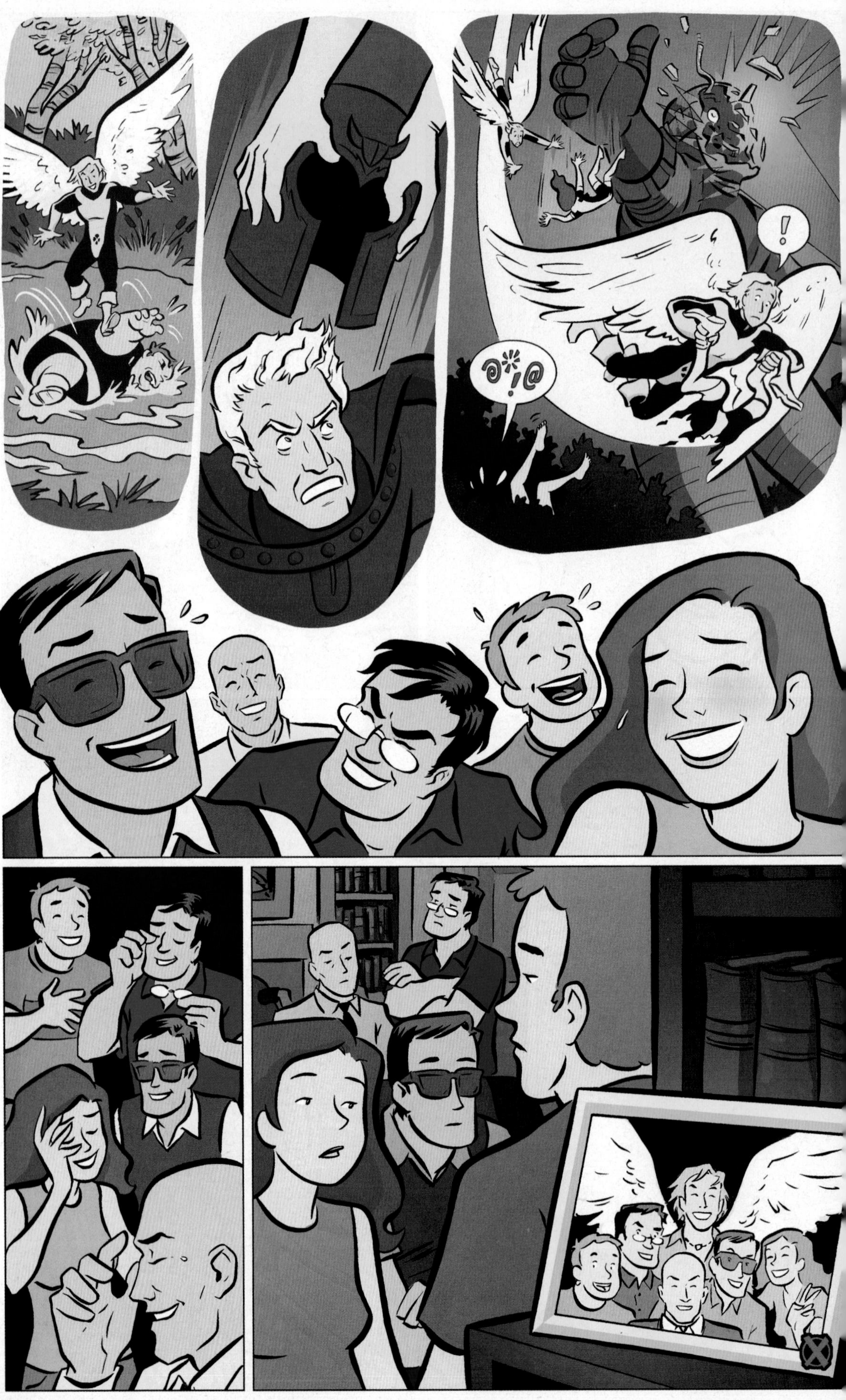
!

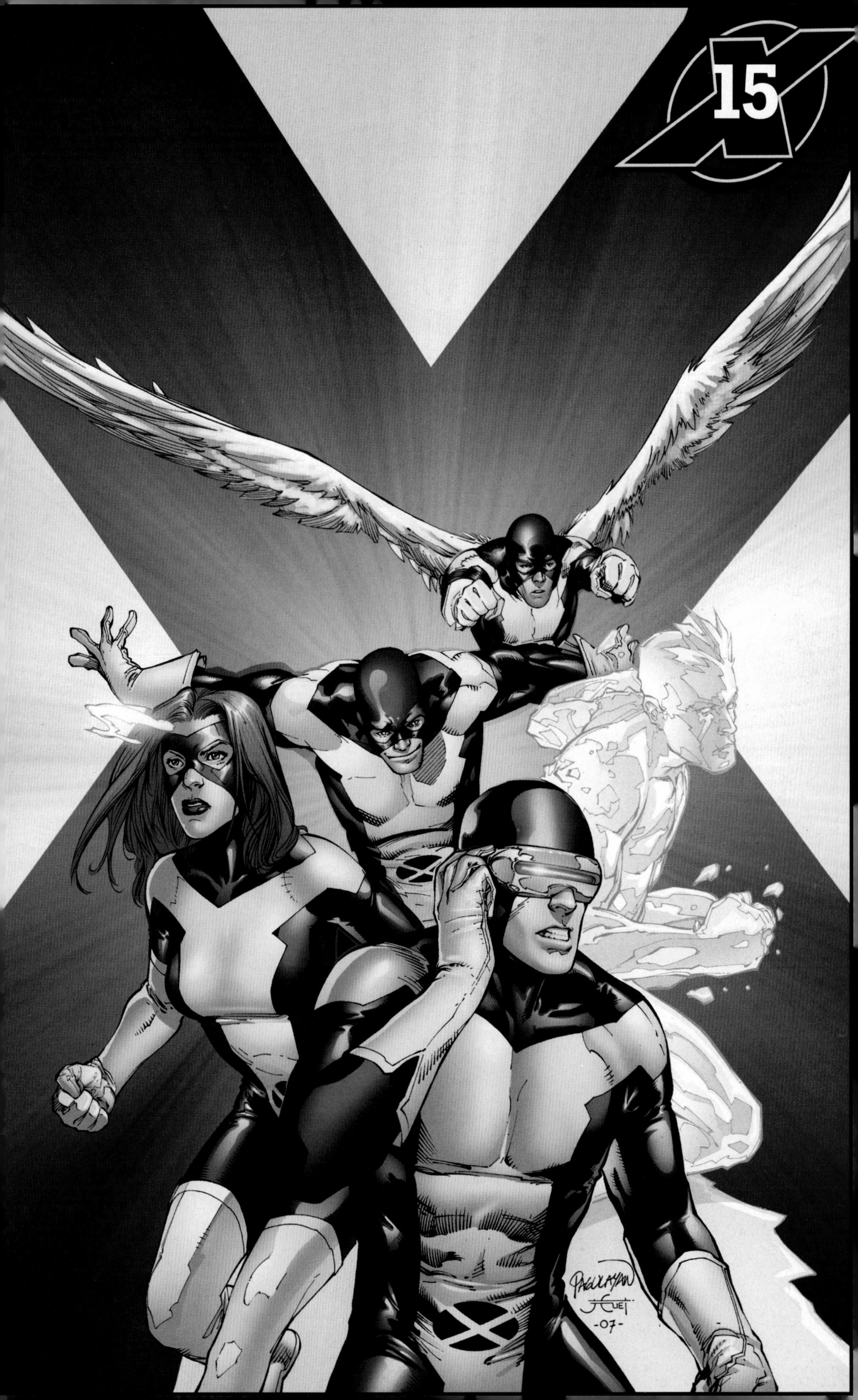
15

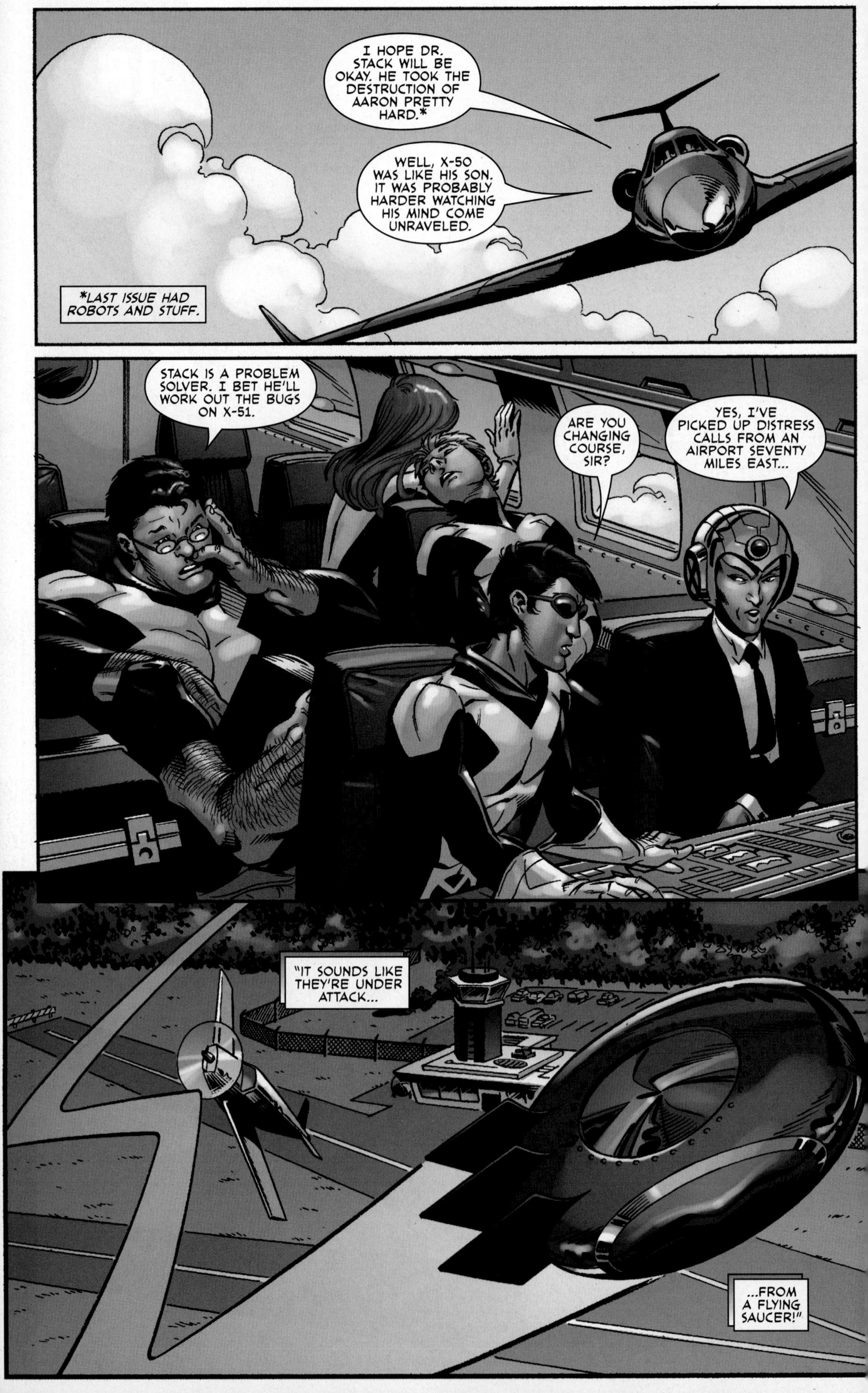
I HOPE DR. STACK WILL BE OKAY. HE TOOK THE DESTRUCTION OF AARON PRETTY HARD.*
WELL, X-50 WAS LIKE HIS SON. IT WAS PROBABLY HARDER WATCHING HIS MIND COME UNRAVELED.
*LAST ISSUE HAD ROBOTS AND STUFF.
STACK IS A PROBLEM SOLVER. I BET HE'LL WORK OUT THE BUGS ON X-51.
ARE YOU CHANGING COURSE, SIR?
YES, I'VE PICKED UP DISTRESS CALLS FROM AN AIRPORT SEVENTY MILES EAST...
"IT SOUNDS LIKE THEY'RE UNDER ATTACK...
...FROM A FLYING SAUCER!"

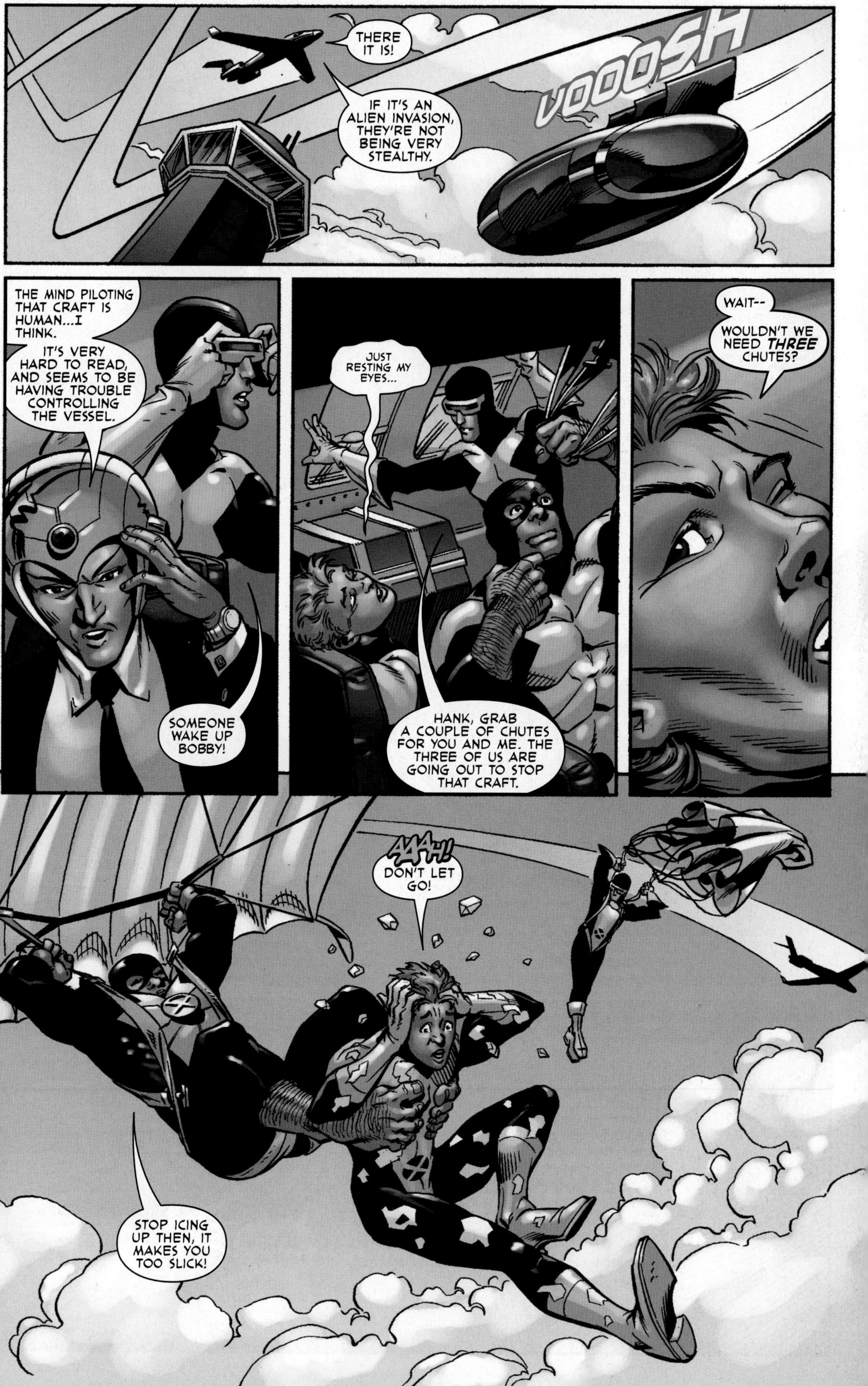
THERE IT IS!
IF IT'S AN ALIEN INVASION, THEY'RE NOT BEING VERY STEALTHY.
VOOOSH
THE MIND PILOTING THAT CRAFT IS HUMAN...I THINK.
IT'S VERY HARD TO READ, AND SEEMS TO BE HAVING TROUBLE CONTROLLING THE VESSEL.
SOMEONE WAKE UP BOBBY!
JUST RESTING MY EYES...
HANK, GRAB A COUPLE OF CHUTES FOR YOU AND ME. THE THREE OF US ARE GOING OUT TO STOP THAT CRAFT.
WAIT--
WOULDN'T WE NEED THREE CHUTES?
AAAH!
DON'T LET GO!
STOP ICING UP THEN, IT MAKES YOU TOO SLICK!

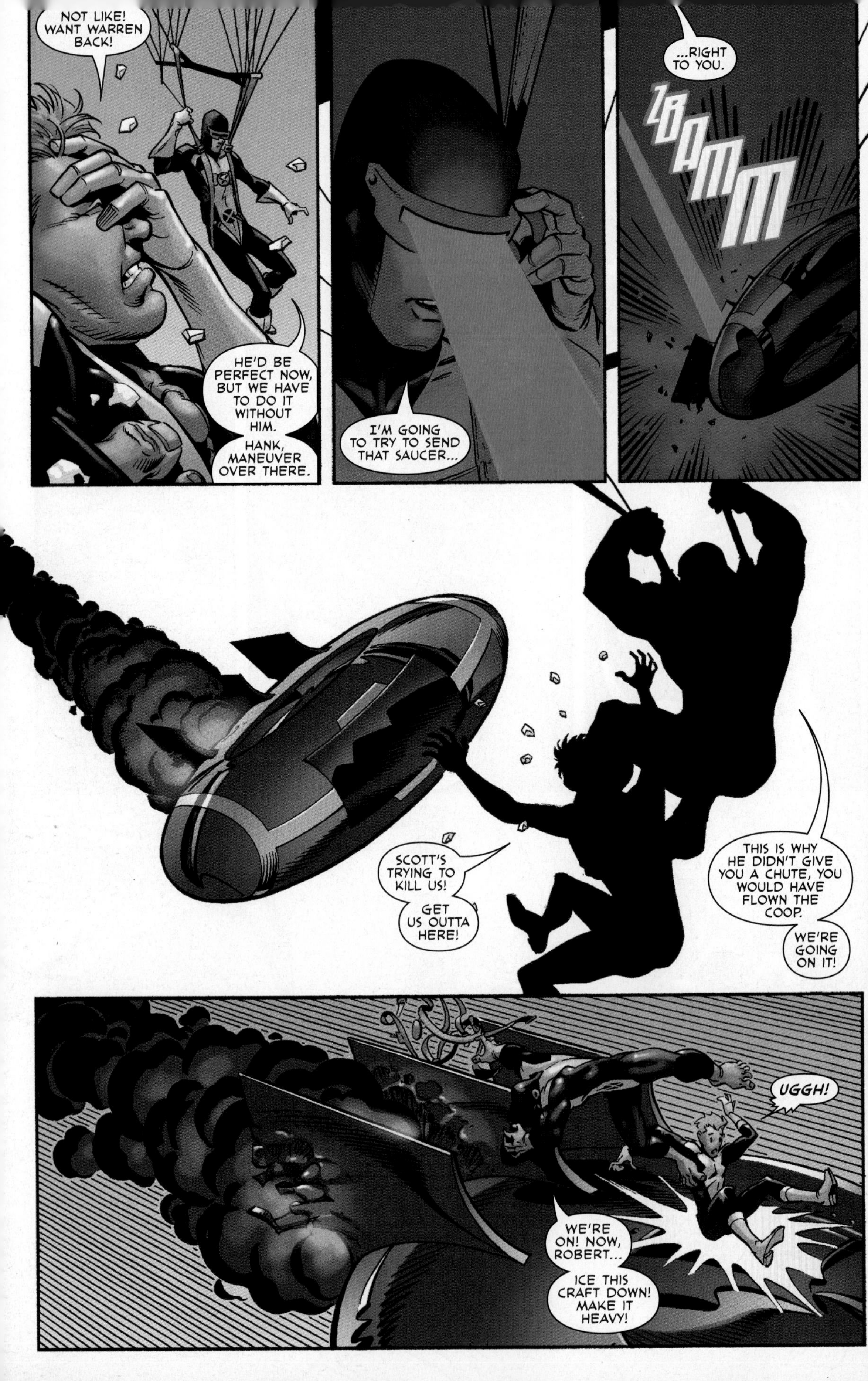
NOT LIKE! WANT WARREN BACK!
HE'D BE PERFECT NOW, BUT WE HAVE TO DO IT WITHOUT HIM.
HANK, MANEUVER OVER THERE.
I'M GOING TO TRY TO SEND THAT SAUCER...
...RIGHT TO YOU.
ZBAMM
SCOTT'S TRYING TO KILL US!
GET US OUTTA HERE!
THIS IS WHY HE DIDN'T GIVE YOU A CHUTE, YOU WOULD HAVE FLOWN THE COOP.
WE'RE GOING ON IT!
UGGH!
WE'RE ON! NOW, ROBERT...
ICE THIS CRAFT DOWN! MAKE IT HEAVY!

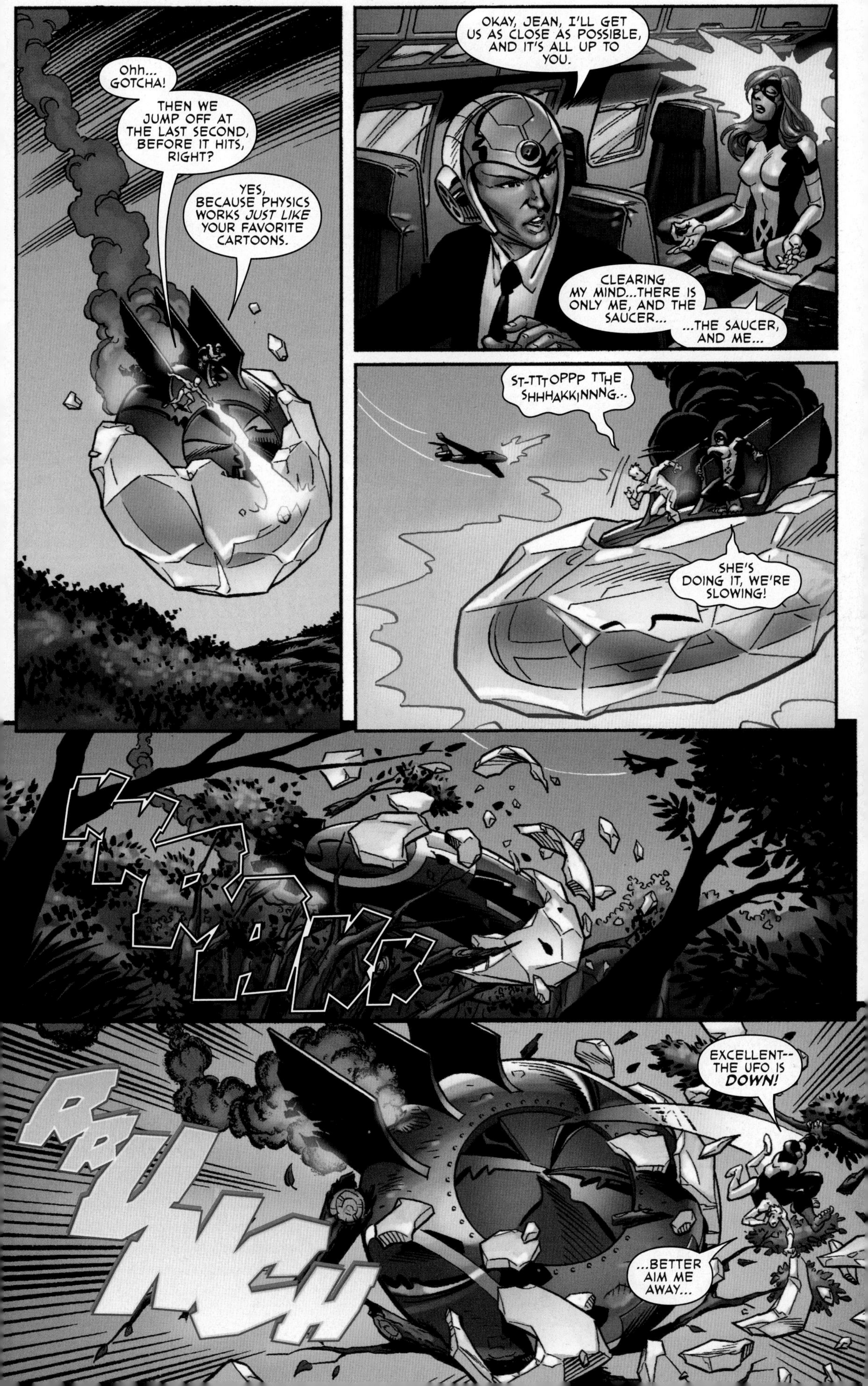

Ohh... GOTCHA!
THEN WE JUMP OFF AT THE LAST SECOND, BEFORE IT HITS, RIGHT?
YES, BECAUSE PHYSICS WORKS *JUST LIKE* YOUR FAVORITE CARTOONS.
OKAY, JEAN, I'LL GET US AS CLOSE AS POSSIBLE, AND IT'S ALL UP TO YOU.
CLEARING MY MIND...THERE IS ONLY ME, AND THE SAUCER...
...THE SAUCER, AND ME...
ST-TTTOPPP TTHE SHHHAKKINNNG...
SHE'S DOING IT, WE'RE SLOWING!
EXCELLENT-- THE UFO IS *DOWN!*
...BETTER AIM ME AWAY...

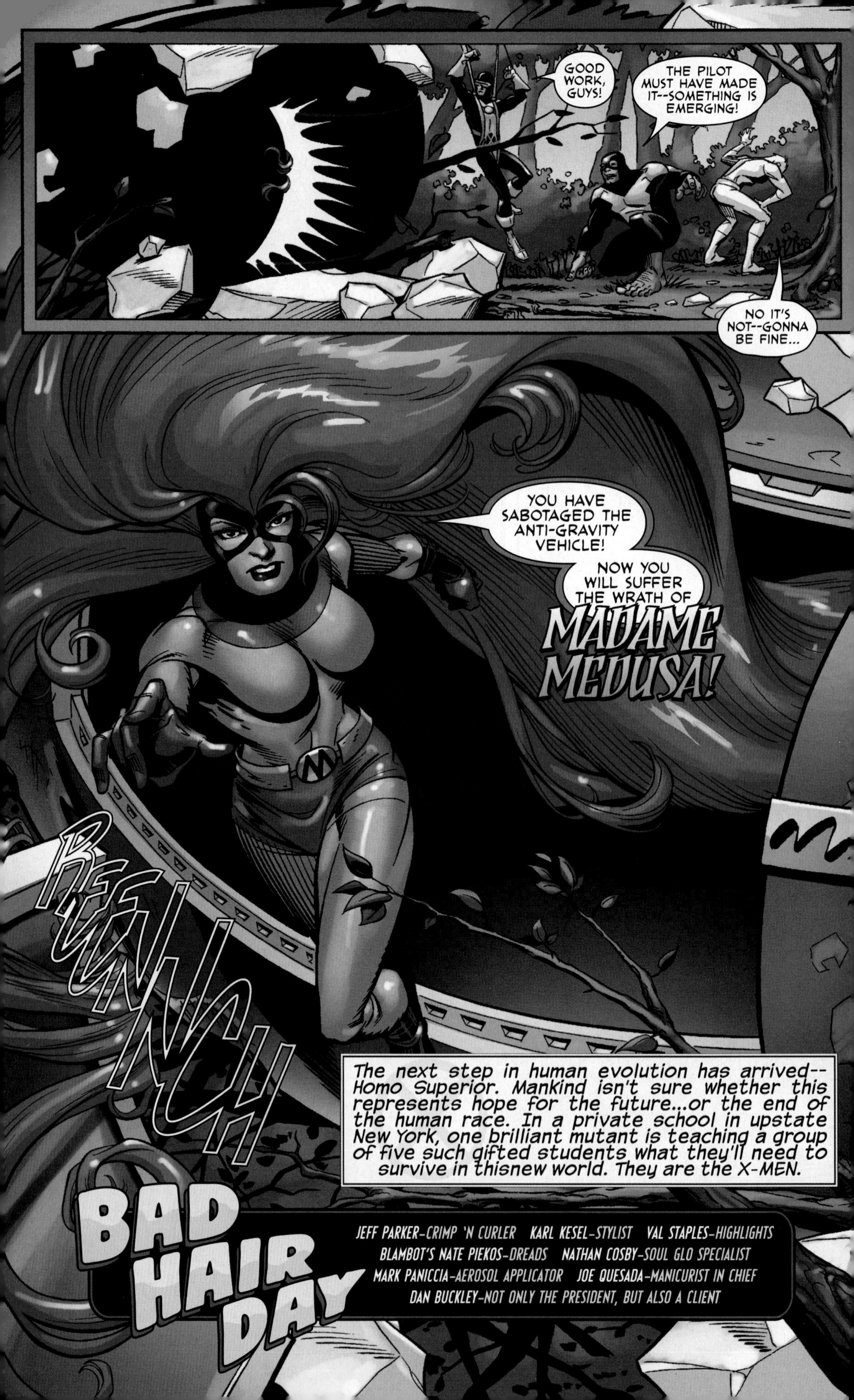
GOOD WORK, GUYS!
THE PILOT MUST HAVE MADE IT--SOMETHING IS EMERGING!
NO IT'S NOT--GONNA BE FINE...
YOU HAVE SABOTAGED THE ANTI-GRAVITY VEHICLE!
NOW YOU WILL SUFFER THE WRATH OF
MADAME MEDUSA!
BREEUNNCH
The next step in human evolution has arrived-- Homo Superior. Mankind isn't sure whether this represents hope for the future...or the end of the human race. In a private school in upstate New York, one brilliant mutant is teaching a group of five such gifted students what they'll need to survive in thisnew world. They are the X-MEN.
BAD HAIR DAY
JEFF PARKER-CRIMP 'N CURLER KARL KESEL-STYLIST VAL STAPLES-HIGHLIGHTS
BLAMBOT'S NATE PIEKOS-DREADS NATHAN COSBY-SOUL GLO SPECIALIST
MARK PANICCIA-AEROSOL APPLICATOR JOE QUESADA-MANICURIST IN CHIEF
DAN BUCKLEY-NOT ONLY THE PRESIDENT, BUT ALSO A CLIENT

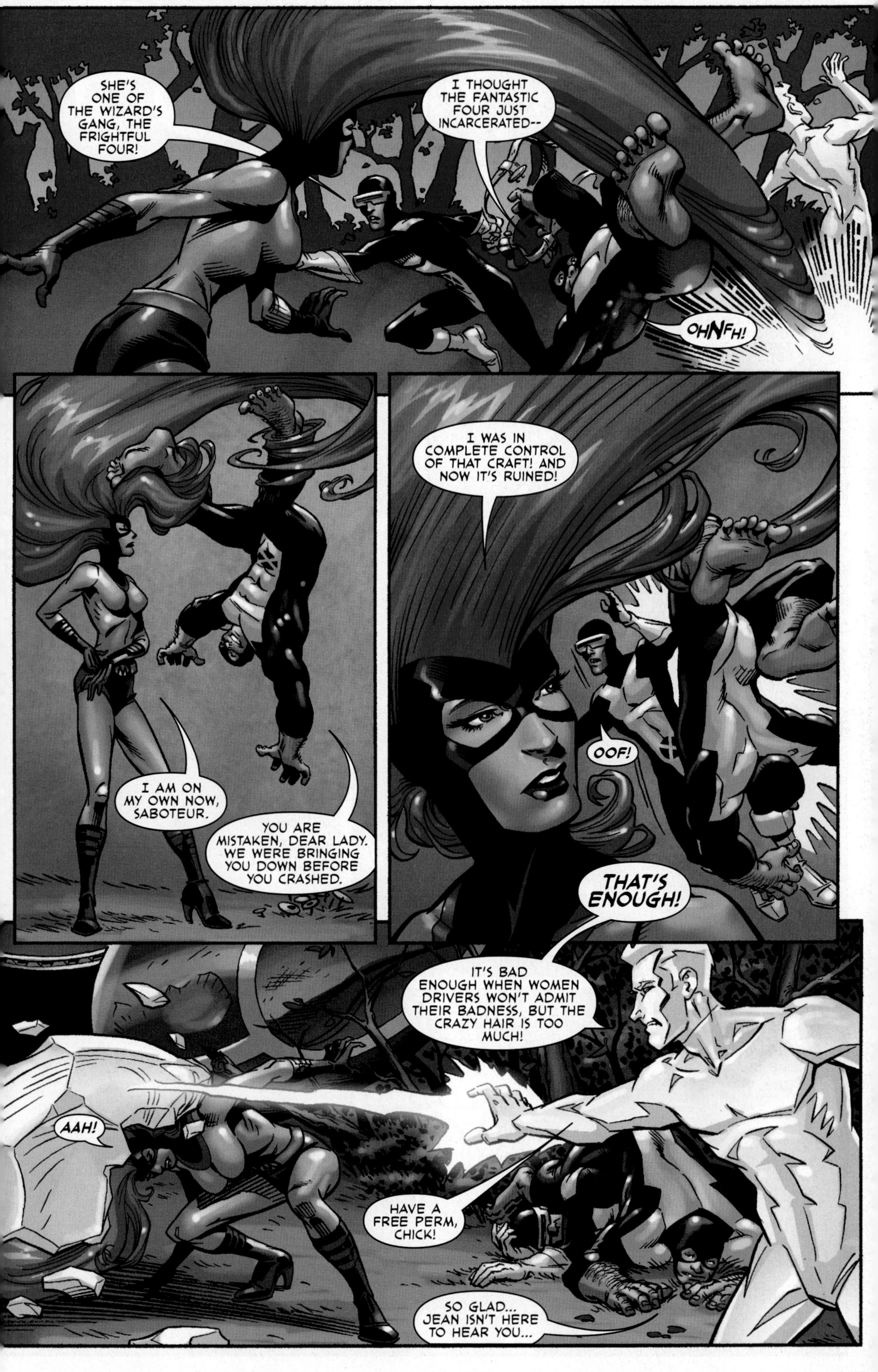
SHE'S ONE OF THE WIZARD'S GANG, THE FRIGHTFUL FOUR!
I THOUGHT THE FANTASTIC FOUR JUST INCARCERATED--
OHNFH!
I AM ON MY OWN NOW, SABOTEUR.
YOU ARE MISTAKEN, DEAR LADY. WE WERE BRINGING YOU DOWN BEFORE YOU CRASHED.
I WAS IN COMPLETE CONTROL OF THAT CRAFT! AND NOW IT'S RUINED!
OOF!
THAT'S ENOUGH!
IT'S BAD ENOUGH WHEN WOMEN DRIVERS WON'T ADMIT THEIR BADNESS, BUT THE CRAZY HAIR IS TOO MUCH!
AAH!
HAVE A FREE PERM, CHICK!
SO GLAD... JEAN ISN'T HERE TO HEAR YOU...

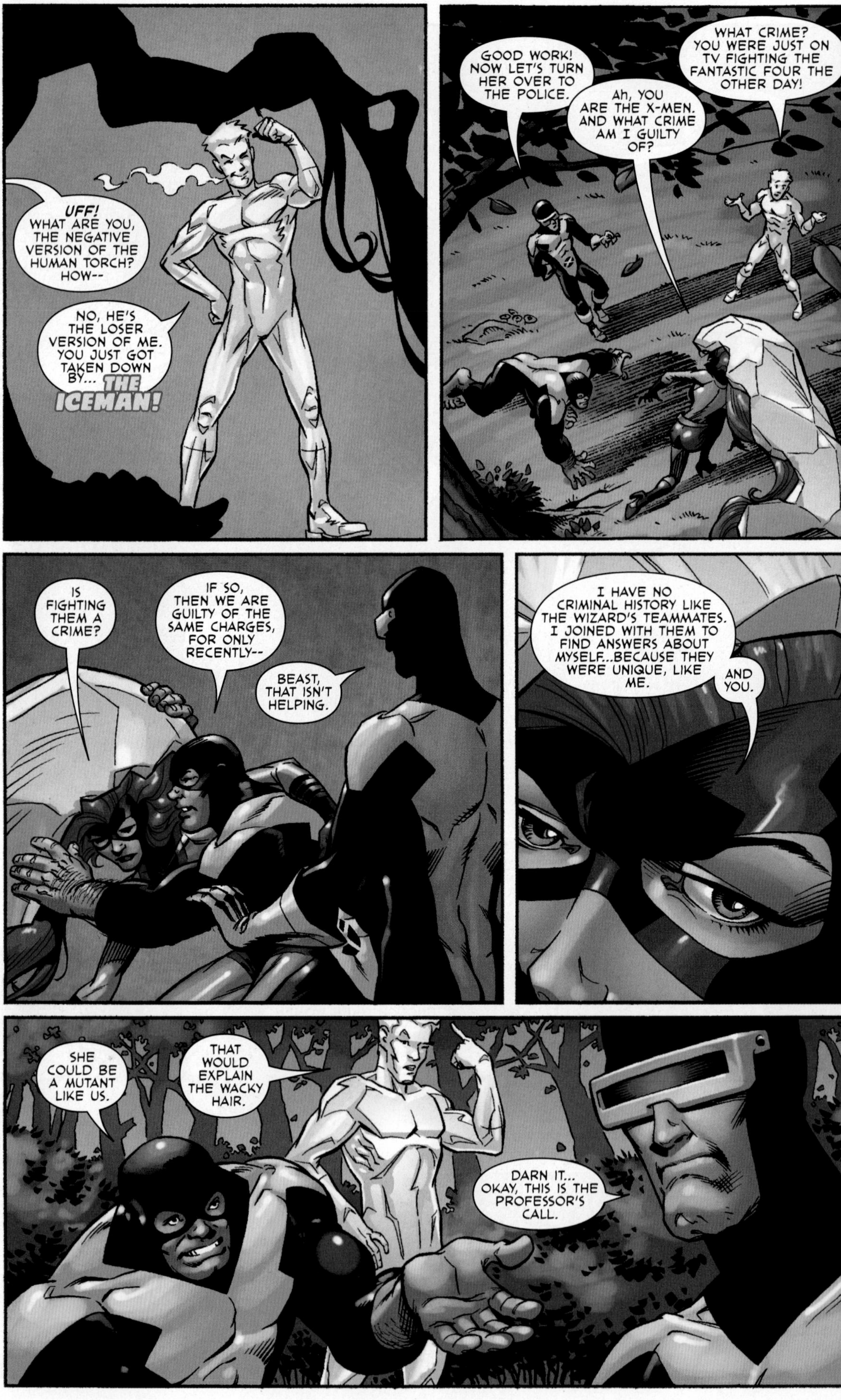
UFF! WHAT ARE YOU, THE NEGATIVE VERSION OF THE HUMAN TORCH? HOW--
NO, HE'S THE LOSER VERSION OF ME. YOU JUST GOT TAKEN DOWN BY... THE ICEMAN!
GOOD WORK! NOW LET'S TURN HER OVER TO THE POLICE.
Ah, YOU ARE THE X-MEN. AND WHAT CRIME AM I GUILTY OF?
WHAT CRIME? YOU WERE JUST ON TV FIGHTING THE FANTASTIC FOUR THE OTHER DAY!
IS FIGHTING THEM A CRIME?
IF SO, THEN WE ARE GUILTY OF THE SAME CHARGES, FOR ONLY RECENTLY--
BEAST, THAT ISN'T HELPING.
I HAVE NO CRIMINAL HISTORY LIKE THE WIZARD'S TEAMMATES. I JOINED WITH THEM TO FIND ANSWERS ABOUT MYSELF...BECAUSE THEY WERE UNIQUE, LIKE ME.
AND YOU.
SHE COULD BE A MUTANT LIKE US.
THAT WOULD EXPLAIN THE WACKY HAIR.
DARN IT... OKAY, THIS IS THE PROFESSOR'S CALL.

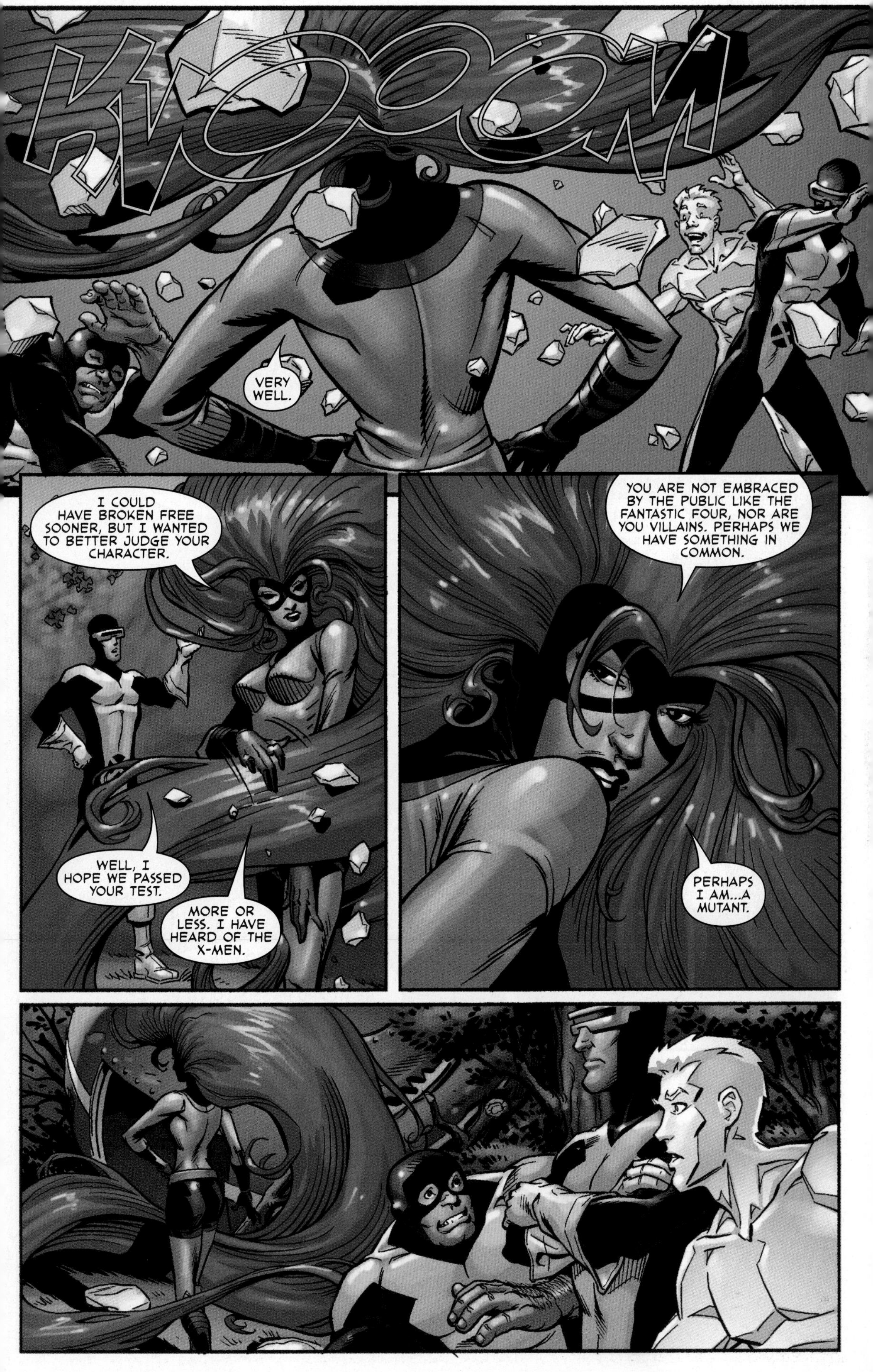
KVOOOM
VERY WELL.
I COULD HAVE BROKEN FREE SOONER, BUT I WANTED TO BETTER JUDGE YOUR CHARACTER.
WELL, I HOPE WE PASSED YOUR TEST.
MORE OR LESS. I HAVE HEARD OF THE X-MEN.
YOU ARE NOT EMBRACED BY THE PUBLIC LIKE THE FANTASTIC FOUR, NOR ARE YOU VILLAINS. PERHAPS WE HAVE SOMETHING IN COMMON.
PERHAPS I AM...A MUTANT.

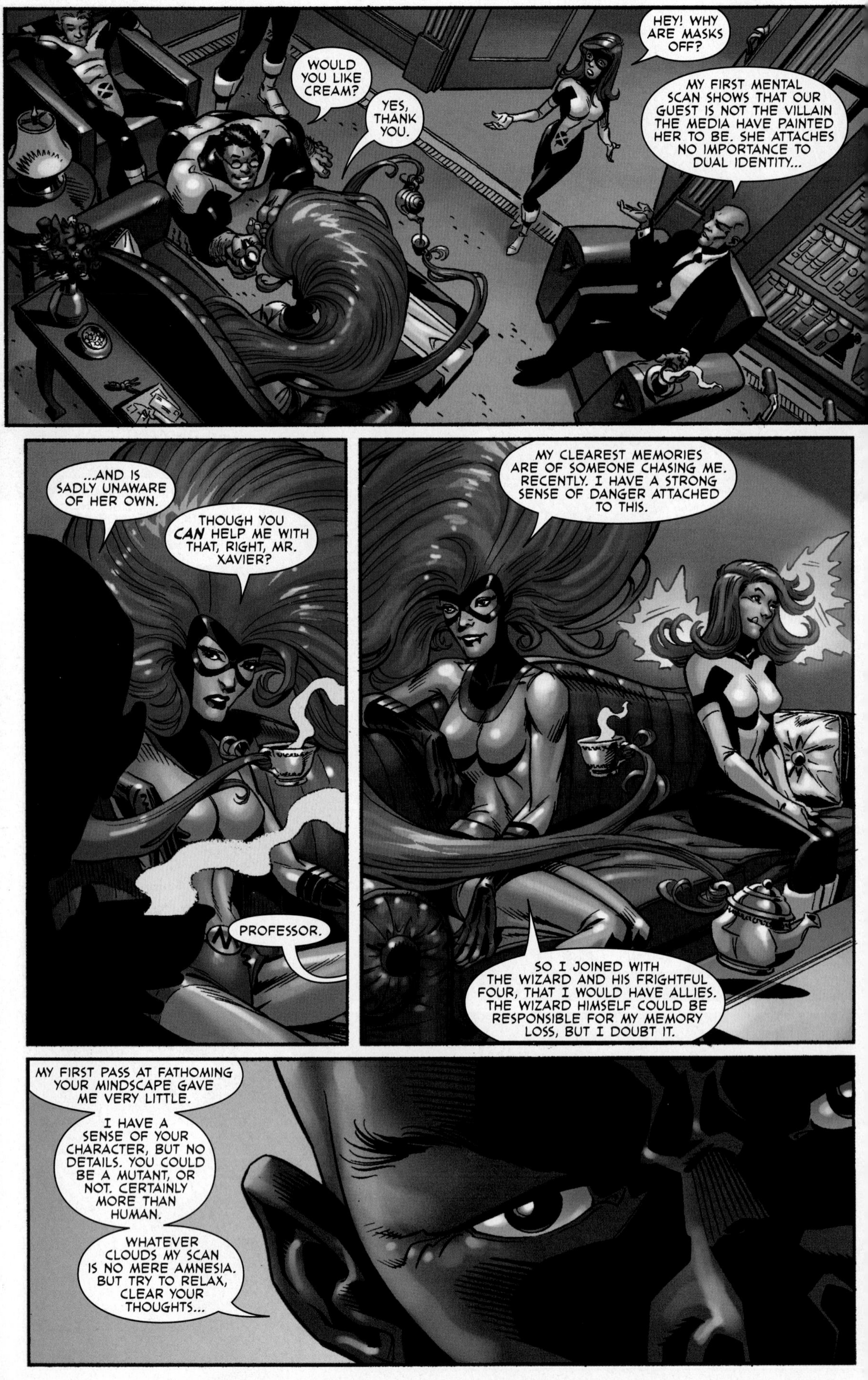
HEY! WHY ARE MASKS OFF?
WOULD YOU LIKE CREAM?
YES, THANK YOU.
MY FIRST MENTAL SCAN SHOWS THAT OUR GUEST IS NOT THE VILLAIN THE MEDIA HAVE PAINTED HER TO BE. SHE ATTACHES NO IMPORTANCE TO DUAL IDENTITY...
...AND IS SADLY UNAWARE OF HER OWN.
THOUGH YOU CAN HELP ME WITH THAT, RIGHT, MR. XAVIER?
PROFESSOR.
MY CLEAREST MEMORIES ARE OF SOMEONE CHASING ME. RECENTLY. I HAVE A STRONG SENSE OF DANGER ATTACHED TO THIS.
SO I JOINED WITH THE WIZARD AND HIS FRIGHTFUL FOUR, THAT I WOULD HAVE ALLIES. THE WIZARD HIMSELF COULD BE RESPONSIBLE FOR MY MEMORY LOSS, BUT I DOUBT IT.
MY FIRST PASS AT FATHOMING YOUR MINDSCAPE GAVE ME VERY LITTLE.
I HAVE A SENSE OF YOUR CHARACTER, BUT NO DETAILS. YOU COULD BE A MUTANT, OR NOT. CERTAINLY MORE THAN HUMAN.
WHATEVER CLOUDS MY SCAN IS NO MERE AMNESIA. BUT TRY TO RELAX, CLEAR YOUR THOUGHTS...

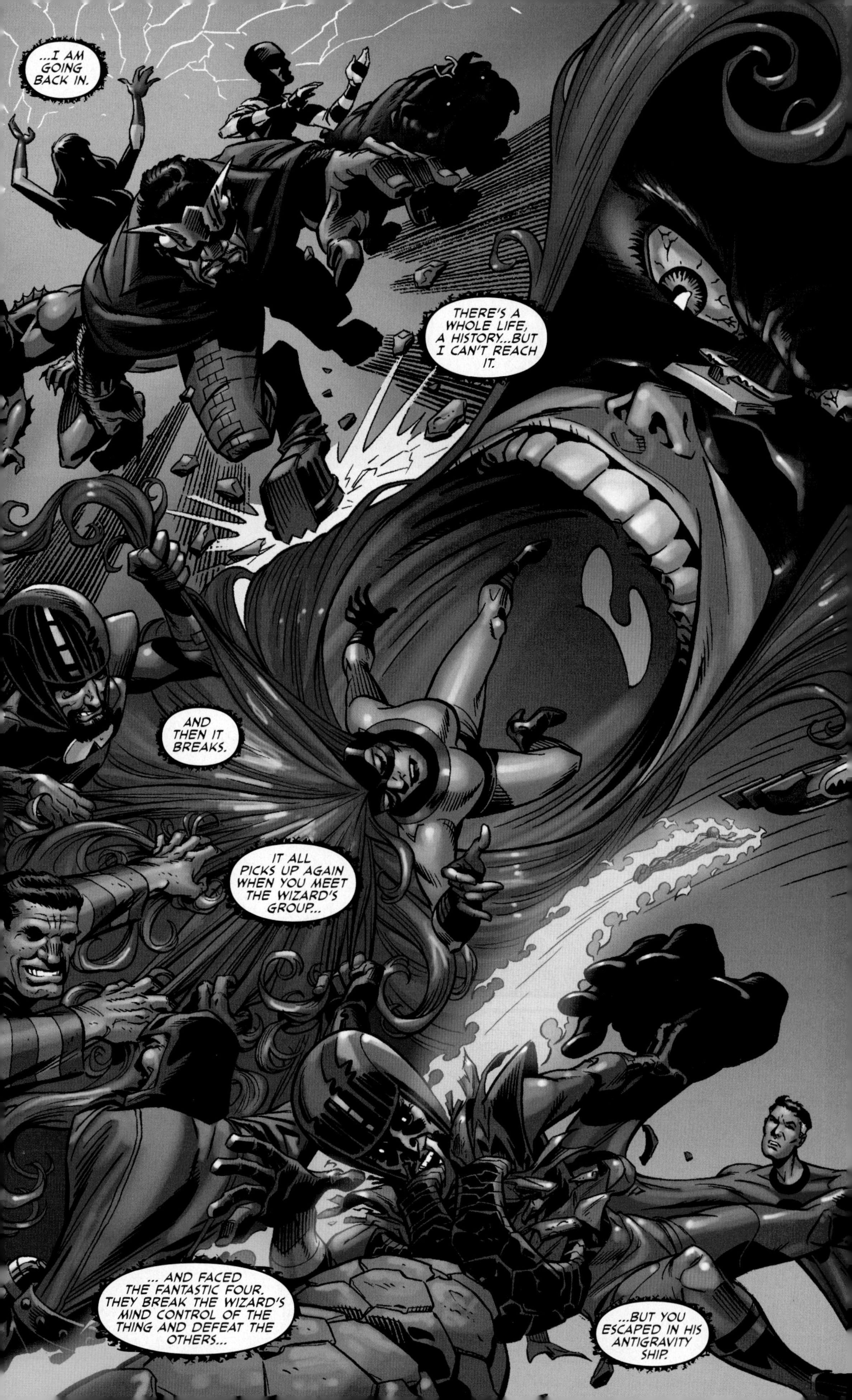
...I AM GOING BACK IN.
THERE'S A WHOLE LIFE, A HISTORY...BUT I CAN'T REACH IT.
AND THEN IT BREAKS.
IT ALL PICKS UP AGAIN WHEN YOU MEET THE WIZARD'S GROUP...
... AND FACED THE FANTASTIC FOUR. THEY BREAK THE WIZARD'S MIND CONTROL OF THE THING AND DEFEAT THE OTHERS...
...BUT YOU ESCAPED IN HIS ANTIGRAVITY SHIP.

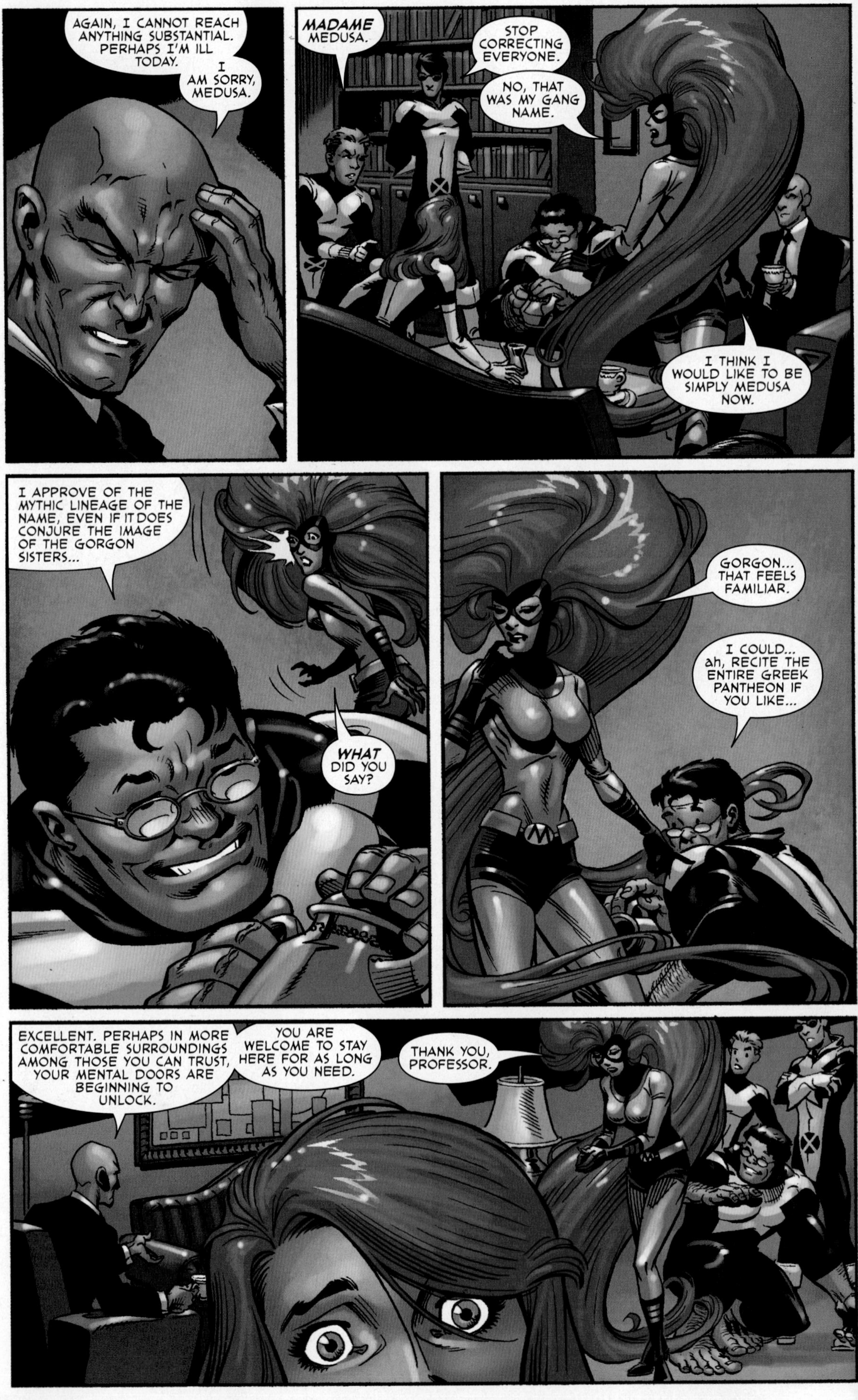
AGAIN, I CANNOT REACH ANYTHING SUBSTANTIAL. PERHAPS I'M ILL TODAY.
I AM SORRY, MEDUSA.
MADAME MEDUSA.
STOP CORRECTING EVERYONE.
NO, THAT WAS MY GANG NAME.
I THINK I WOULD LIKE TO BE SIMPLY MEDUSA NOW.
I APPROVE OF THE MYTHIC LINEAGE OF THE NAME, EVEN IF IT DOES CONJURE THE IMAGE OF THE GORGON SISTERS...
WHAT DID YOU SAY?
GORGON... THAT FEELS FAMILIAR.
I COULD... ah, RECITE THE ENTIRE GREEK PANTHEON IF YOU LIKE...
EXCELLENT. PERHAPS IN MORE COMFORTABLE SURROUNDINGS AMONG THOSE YOU CAN TRUST, YOUR MENTAL DOORS ARE BEGINNING TO UNLOCK.
YOU ARE WELCOME TO STAY HERE FOR AS LONG AS YOU NEED.
THANK YOU, PROFESSOR.

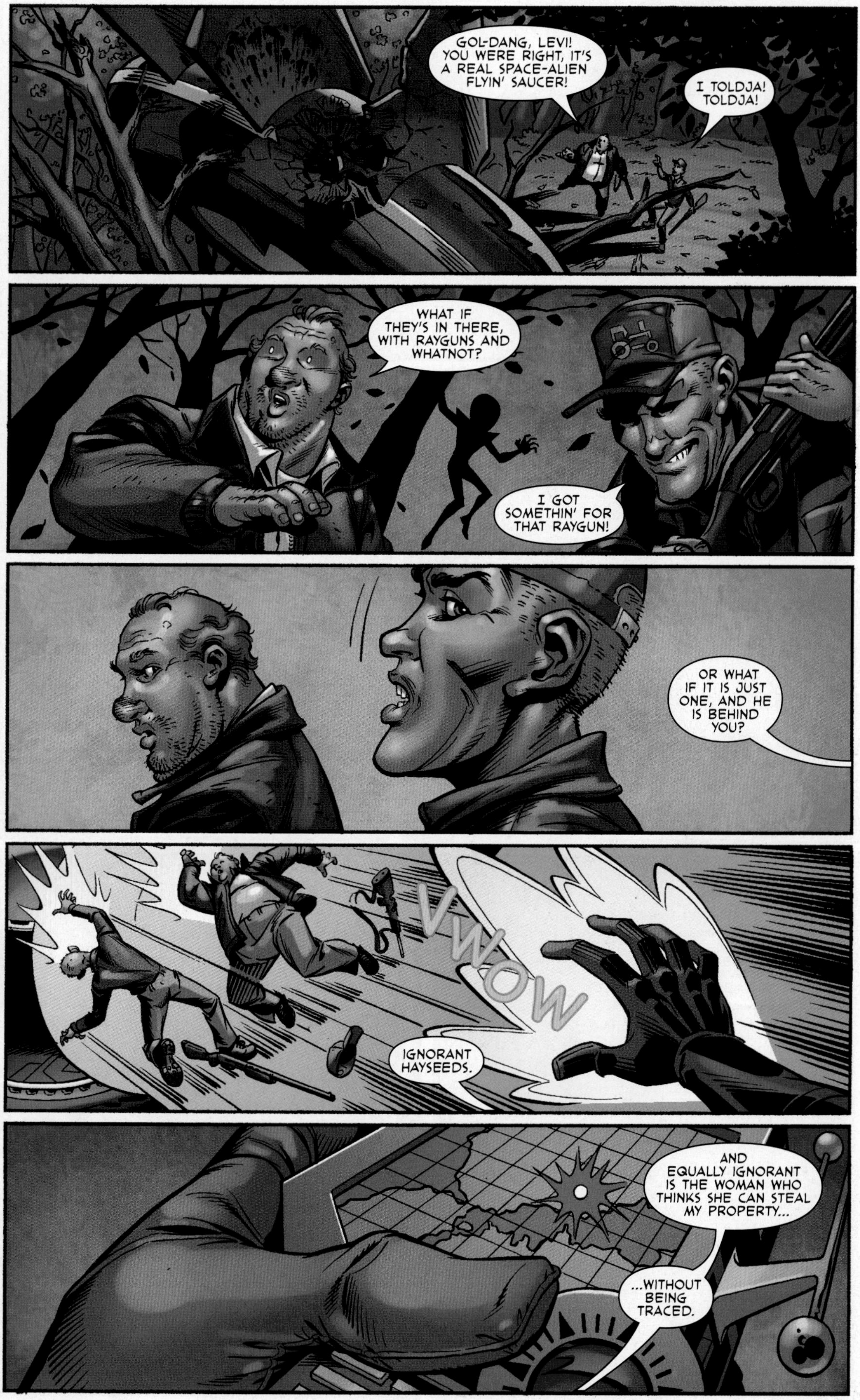
GOL-DANG, LEVI! YOU WERE RIGHT, IT'S A REAL SPACE-ALIEN FLYIN' SAUCER!
I TOLDJA! TOLDJA!
WHAT IF THEY'S IN THERE, WITH RAYGUNS AND WHATNOT?
I GOT SOMETHIN' FOR THAT RAYGUN!
OR WHAT IF IT IS JUST ONE, AND HE IS BEHIND YOU?
VWOW
IGNORANT HAYSEEDS.
AND EQUALLY IGNORANT IS THE WOMAN WHO THINKS SHE CAN STEAL MY PROPERTY...
...WITHOUT BEING TRACED.

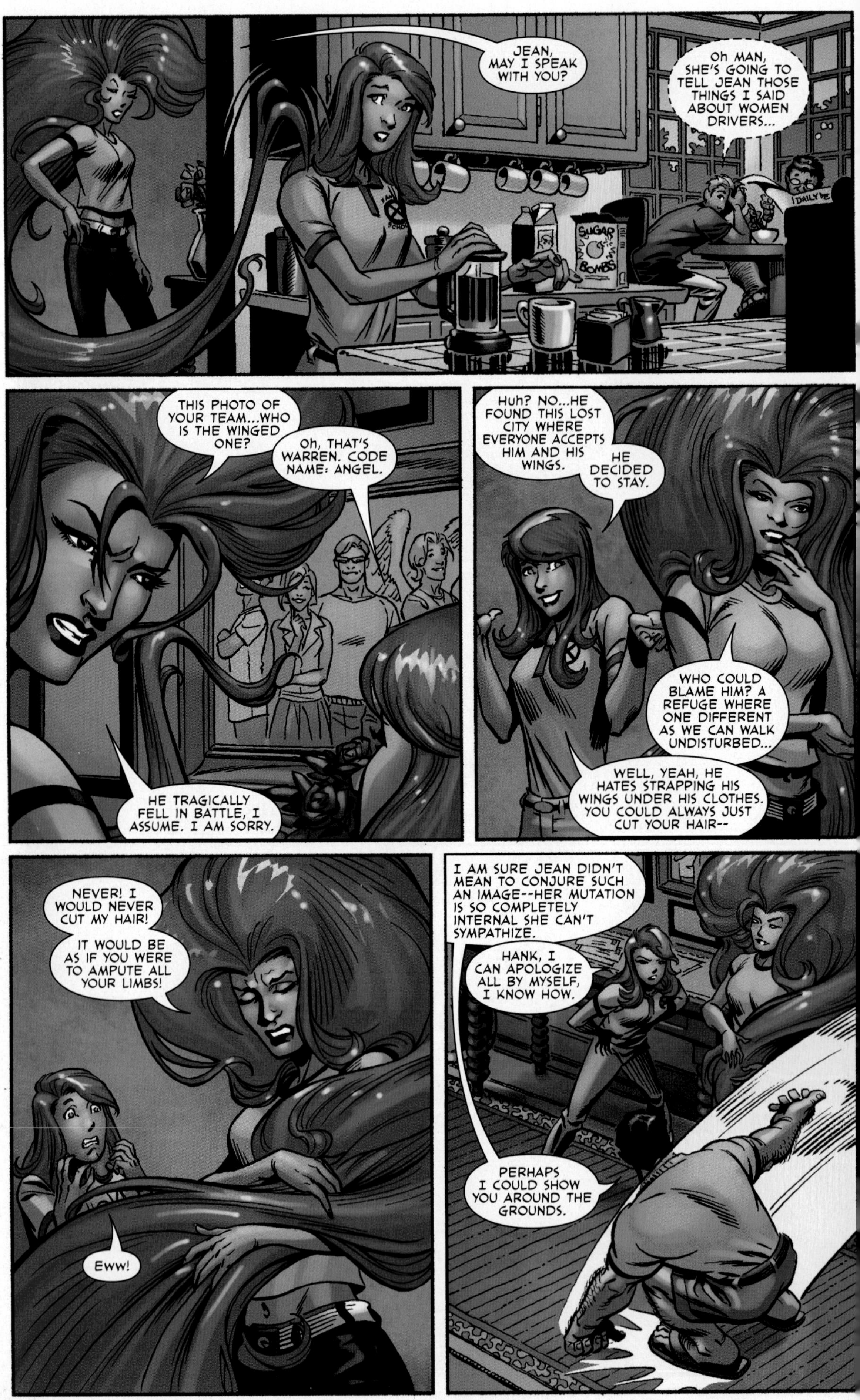
JEAN, MAY I SPEAK WITH YOU?
Oh MAN, SHE'S GOING TO TELL JEAN THOSE THINGS I SAID ABOUT WOMEN DRIVERS...
SUGAR BOMBS
DAILY
THIS PHOTO OF YOUR TEAM...WHO IS THE WINGED ONE?
Oh, THAT'S WARREN. CODE NAME: ANGEL.
HE TRAGICALLY FELL IN BATTLE, I ASSUME. I AM SORRY.
Huh? NO...HE FOUND THIS LOST CITY WHERE EVERYONE ACCEPTS HIM AND HIS WINGS.
HE DECIDED TO STAY.
WHO COULD BLAME HIM? A REFUGE WHERE ONE DIFFERENT AS WE CAN WALK UNDISTURBED...
WELL, YEAH, HE HATES STRAPPING HIS WINGS UNDER HIS CLOTHES. YOU COULD ALWAYS JUST CUT YOUR HAIR--
NEVER! I WOULD NEVER CUT MY HAIR!
IT WOULD BE AS IF YOU WERE TO AMPUTE ALL YOUR LIMBS!
Eww!
I AM SURE JEAN DIDN'T MEAN TO CONJURE SUCH AN IMAGE--HER MUTATION IS SO COMPLETELY INTERNAL SHE CAN'T SYMPATHIZE.
HANK, I CAN APOLOGIZE ALL BY MYSELF, I KNOW HOW.
PERHAPS I COULD SHOW YOU AROUND THE GROUNDS.

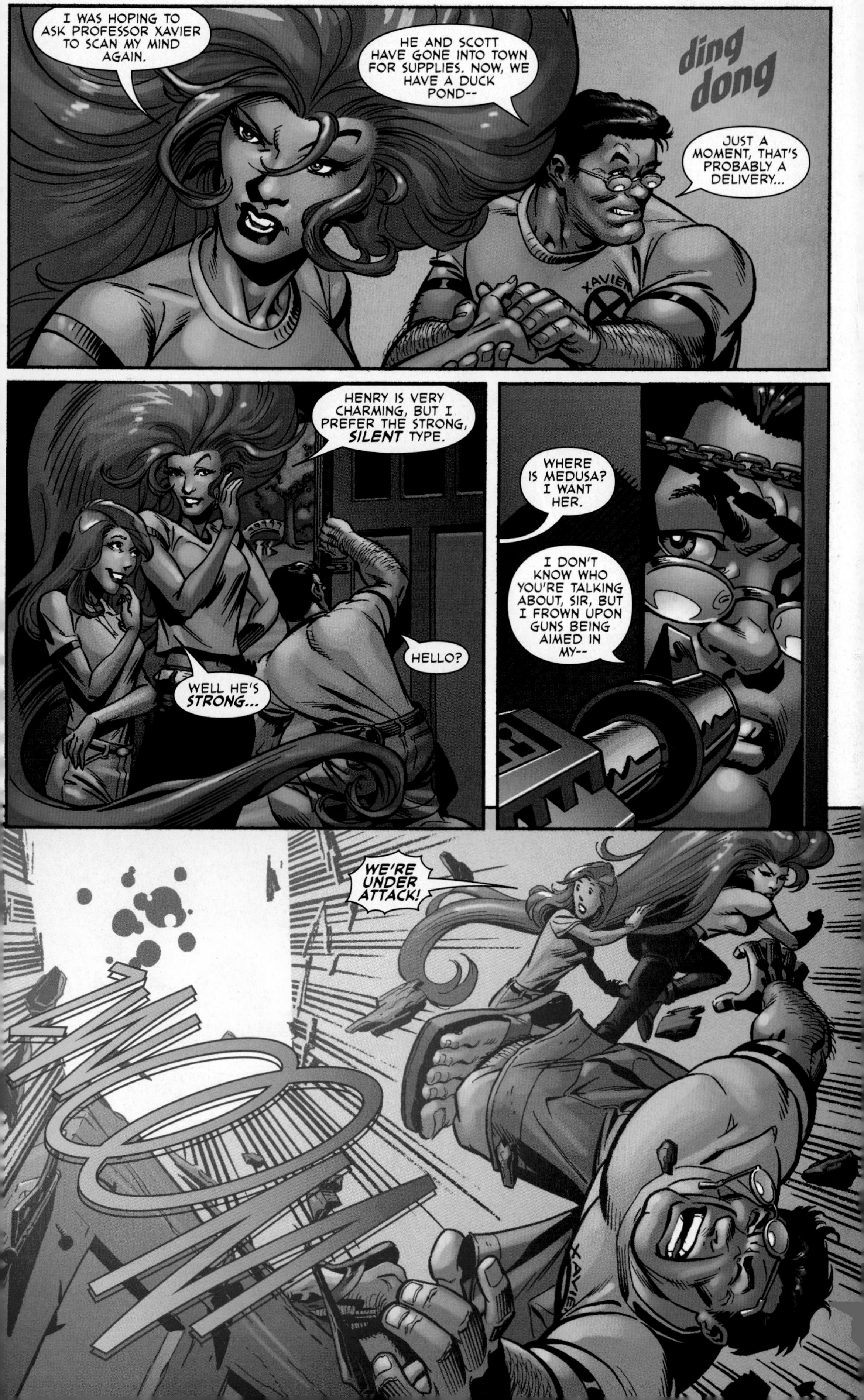
I WAS HOPING TO ASK PROFESSOR XAVIER TO SCAN MY MIND AGAIN.
HE AND SCOTT HAVE GONE INTO TOWN FOR SUPPLIES. NOW, WE HAVE A DUCK POND--
ding dong
JUST A MOMENT, THAT'S PROBABLY A DELIVERY...
XAVIER
HENRY IS VERY CHARMING, BUT I PREFER THE STRONG, SILENT TYPE.
WELL HE'S STRONG...
HELLO?
WHERE IS MEDUSA? I WANT HER.
I DON'T KNOW WHO YOU'RE TALKING ABOUT, SIR, BUT I FROWN UPON GUNS BEING AIMED IN MY--
WE'RE UNDER ATTACK!

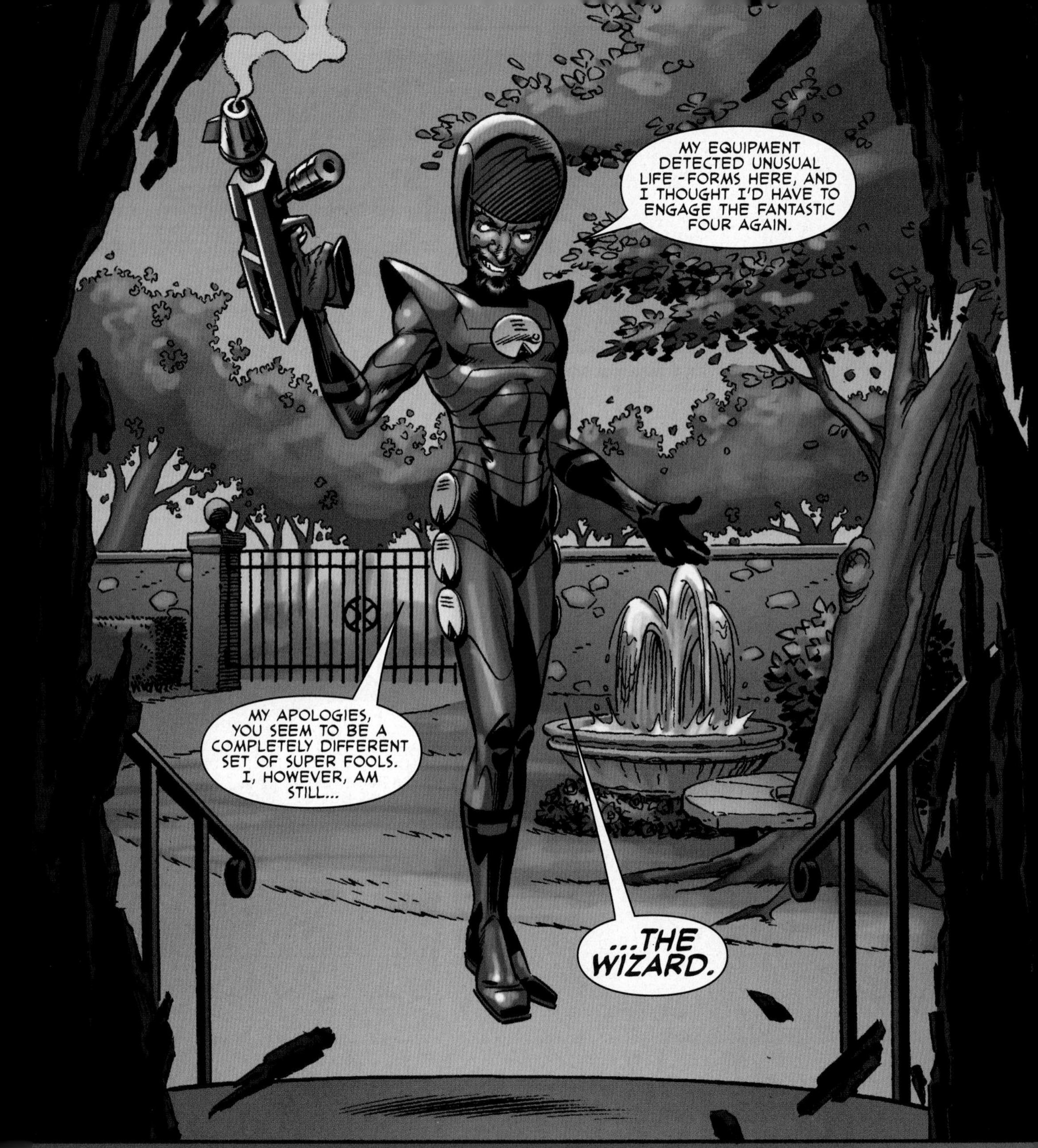
MY EQUIPMENT DETECTED UNUSUAL LIFE-FORMS HERE, AND I THOUGHT I'D HAVE TO ENGAGE THE FANTASTIC FOUR AGAIN.
MY APOLOGIES, YOU SEEM TO BE A COMPLETELY DIFFERENT SET OF SUPER FOOLS. I, HOWEVER, AM STILL...
...THE WIZARD.

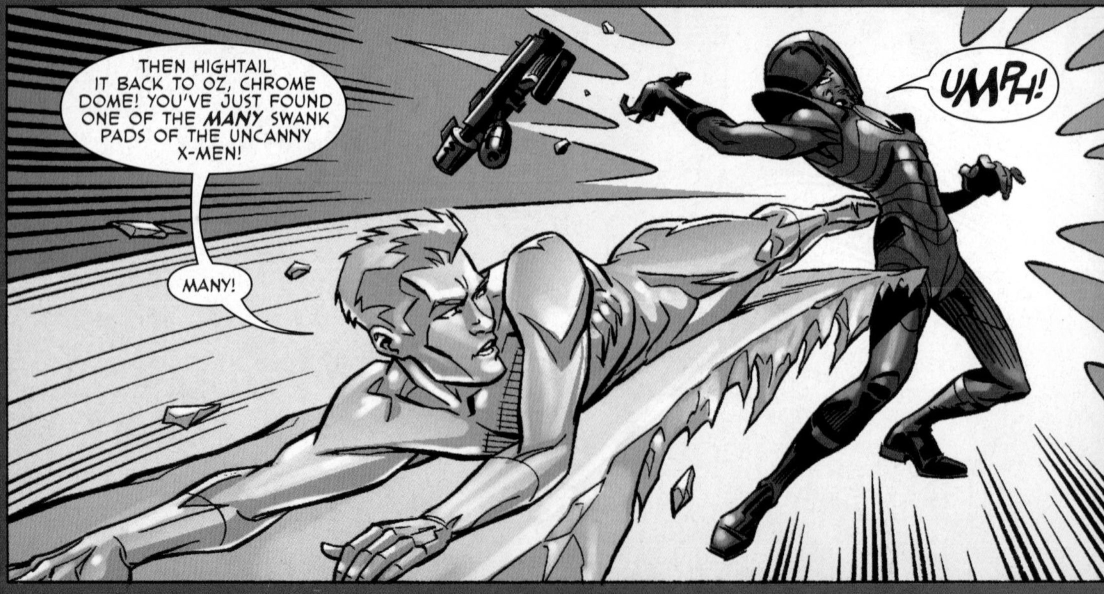
THEN HIGHTAIL IT BACK TO OZ, CHROME DOME! YOU'VE JUST FOUND ONE OF THE MANY SWANK PADS OF THE UNCANNY X-MEN!
MANY!
UMPH!

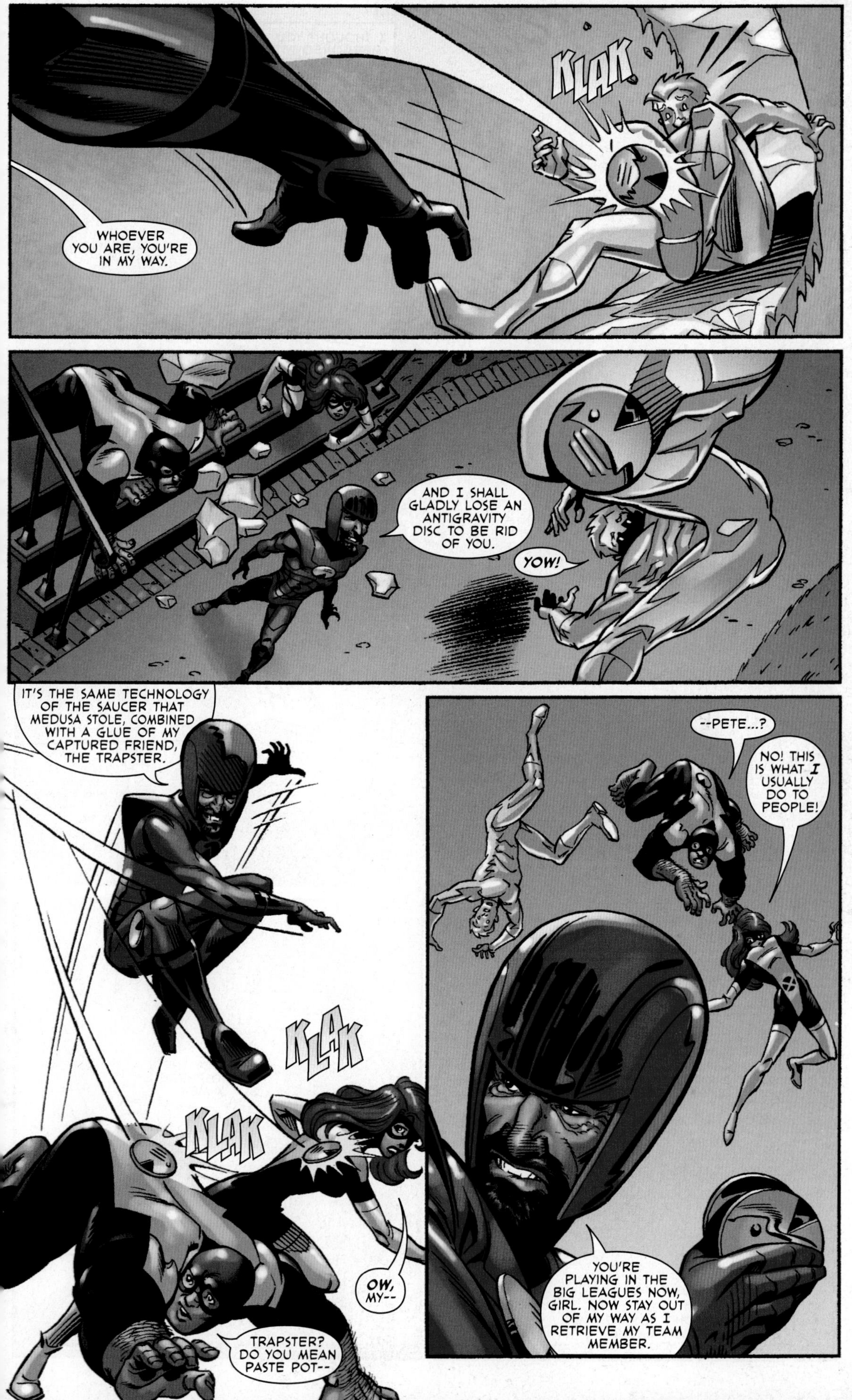
KLAK
WHOEVER YOU ARE, YOU'RE IN MY WAY.
AND I SHALL GLADLY LOSE AN ANTIGRAVITY DISC TO BE RID OF YOU.
YOW!
IT'S THE SAME TECHNOLOGY OF THE SAUCER THAT MEDUSA STOLE, COMBINED WITH A GLUE OF MY CAPTURED FRIEND, THE TRAPSTER.
KLAK
KLAK
OW, MY--
TRAPSTER? DO YOU MEAN PASTE POT--
--PETE...?
NO! THIS IS WHAT *I* USUALLY DO TO PEOPLE!
YOU'RE PLAYING IN THE BIG LEAGUES NOW, GIRL. NOW STAY OUT OF MY WAY AS I RETRIEVE MY TEAM MEMBER.

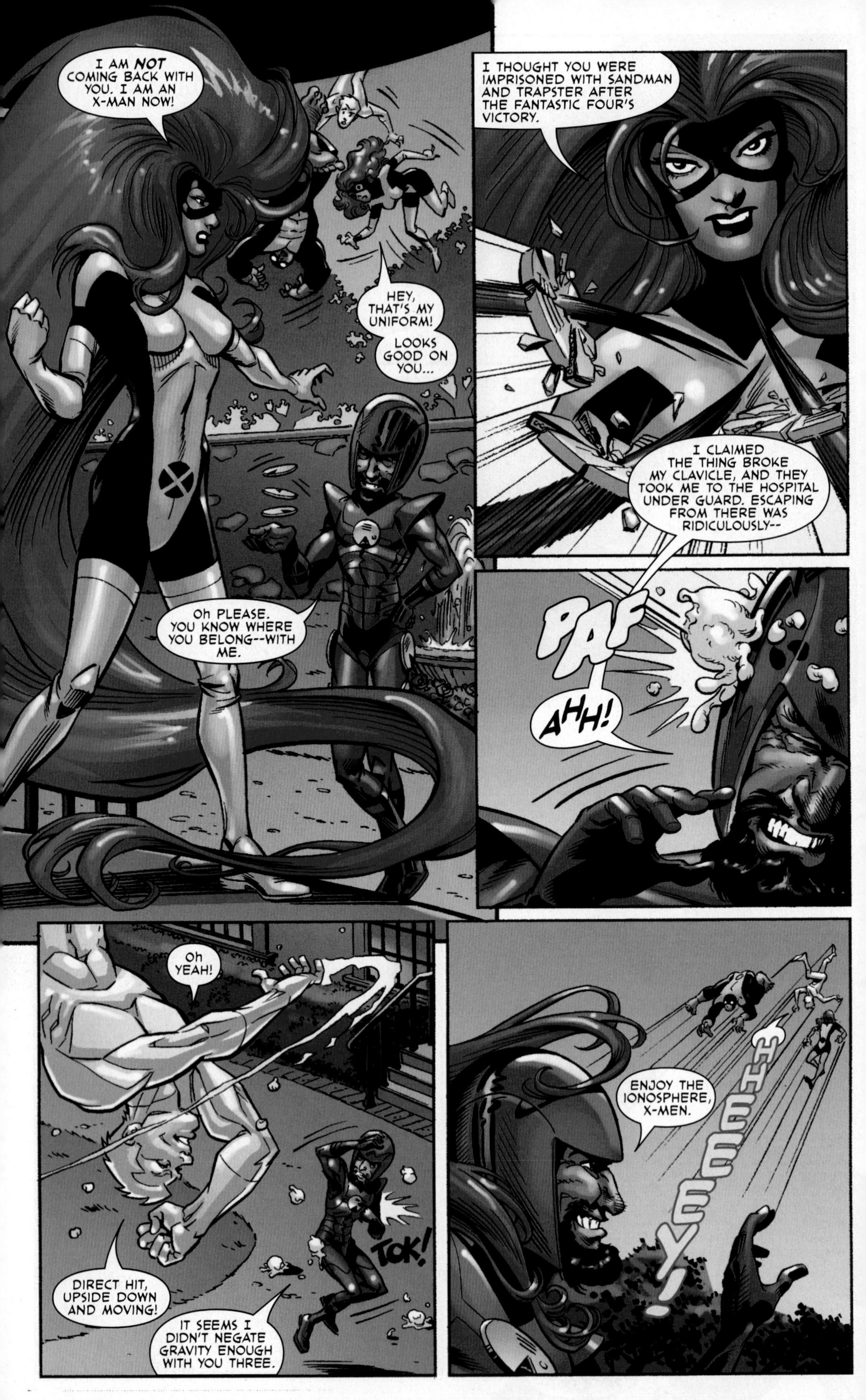

I AM NOT COMING BACK WITH YOU. I AM AN X-MAN NOW!
HEY, THAT'S MY UNIFORM!
LOOKS GOOD ON YOU...
Oh PLEASE. YOU KNOW WHERE YOU BELONG--WITH ME.
I THOUGHT YOU WERE IMPRISONED WITH SANDMAN AND TRAPSTER AFTER THE FANTASTIC FOUR'S VICTORY.
I CLAIMED THE THING BROKE MY CLAVICLE, AND THEY TOOK ME TO THE HOSPITAL UNDER GUARD. ESCAPING FROM THERE WAS RIDICULOUSLY--
PAF
AHH!
Oh YEAH!
TOK!
DIRECT HIT, UPSIDE DOWN AND MOVING!
IT SEEMS I DIDN'T NEGATE GRAVITY ENOUGH WITH YOU THREE.
ENJOY THE IONOSPHERE, X-MEN.
YEEEEEHHH!

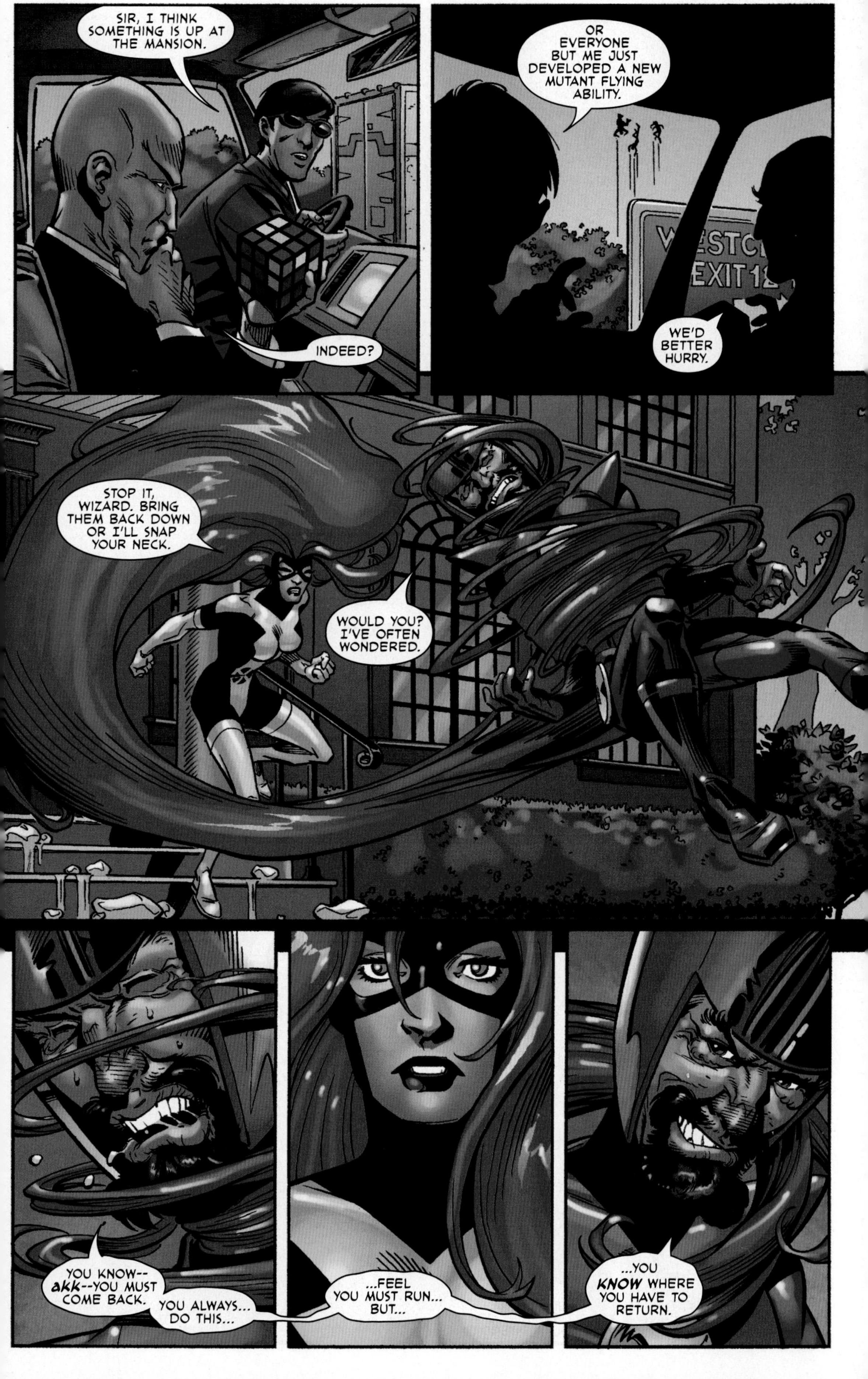
SIR, I THINK SOMETHING IS UP AT THE MANSION.
INDEED?
OR EVERYONE BUT ME JUST DEVELOPED A NEW MUTANT FLYING ABILITY.
WE'D BETTER HURRY.
STOP IT, WIZARD. BRING THEM BACK DOWN OR I'LL SNAP YOUR NECK.
WOULD YOU? I'VE OFTEN WONDERED.
YOU KNOW-- *akk*--YOU MUST COME BACK.
YOU ALWAYS... DO THIS...
...FEEL YOU MUST RUN... BUT...
...YOU *KNOW* WHERE YOU HAVE TO RETURN.

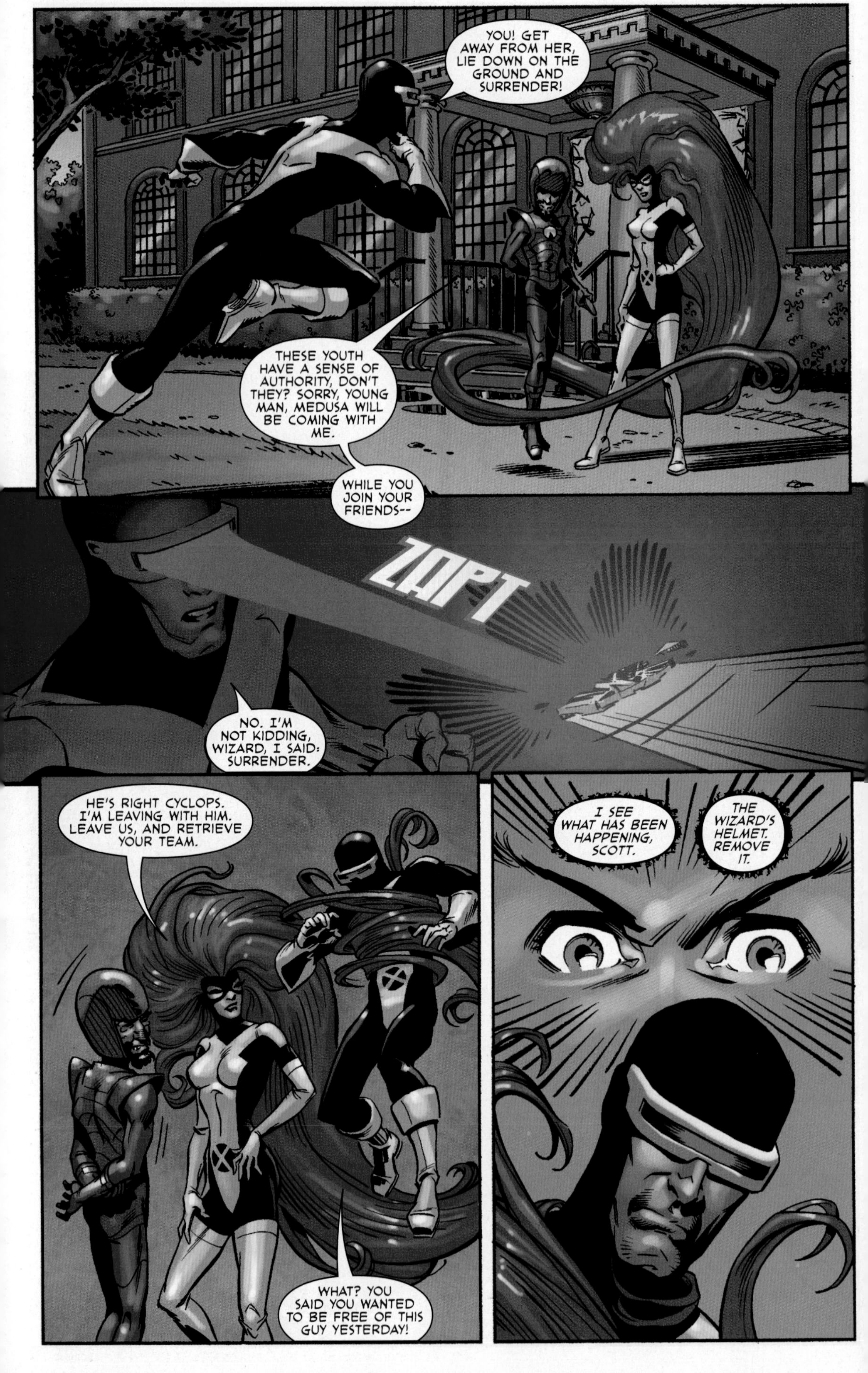
YOU! GET AWAY FROM HER, LIE DOWN ON THE GROUND AND SURRENDER!
THESE YOUTH HAVE A SENSE OF AUTHORITY, DON'T THEY? SORRY, YOUNG MAN, MEDUSA WILL BE COMING WITH ME.
WHILE YOU JOIN YOUR FRIENDS--
ZAPT
NO. I'M NOT KIDDING, WIZARD, I SAID: SURRENDER.
HE'S RIGHT CYCLOPS. I'M LEAVING WITH HIM. LEAVE US, AND RETRIEVE YOUR TEAM.
WHAT? YOU SAID YOU WANTED TO BE FREE OF THIS GUY YESTERDAY!
I SEE WHAT HAS BEEN HAPPENING, SCOTT.
THE WIZARD'S HELMET. REMOVE IT.

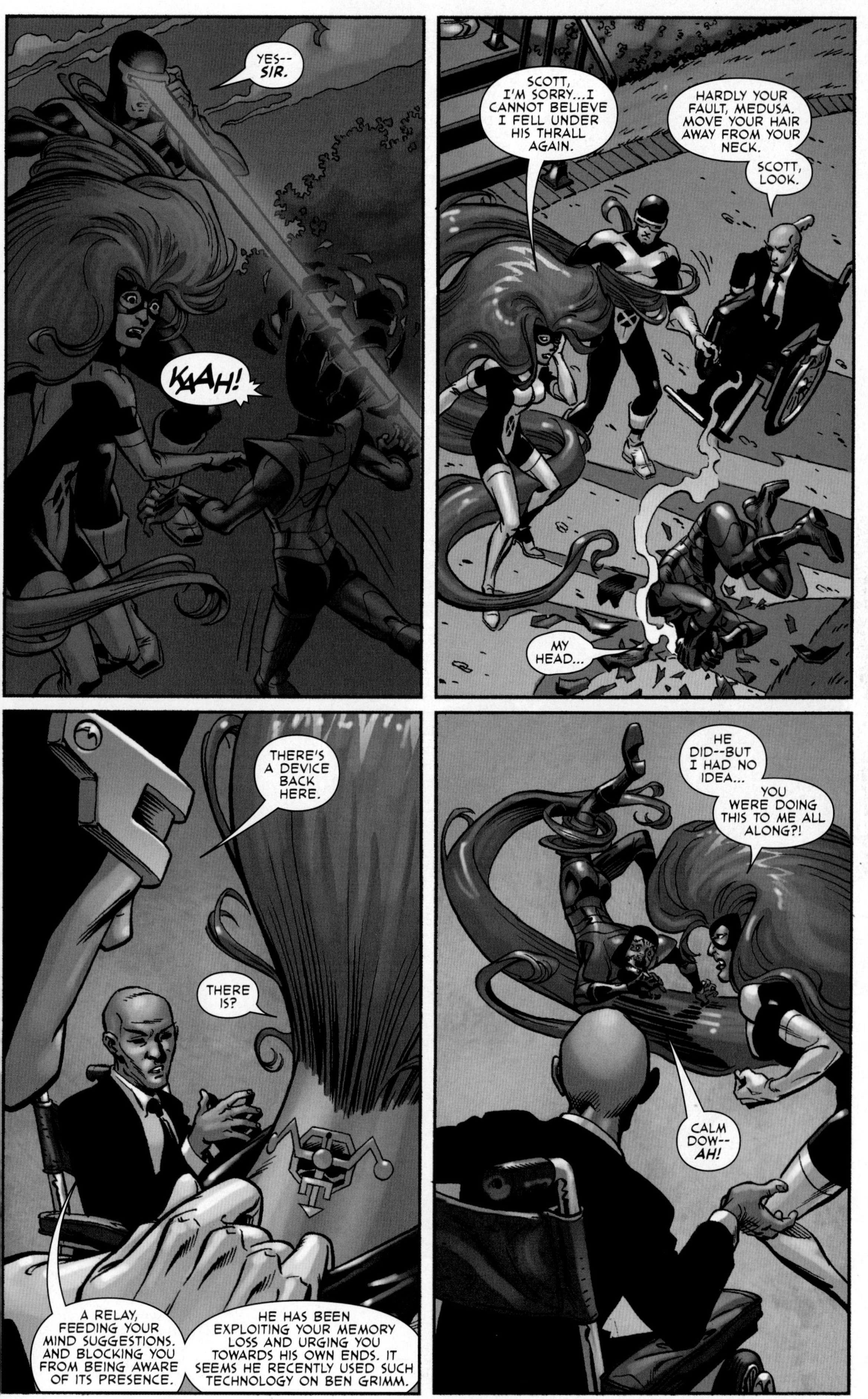
YES--
SIR.
KAAH!
SCOTT, I'M SORRY...I CANNOT BELIEVE I FELL UNDER HIS THRALL AGAIN.
HARDLY YOUR FAULT, MEDUSA. MOVE YOUR HAIR AWAY FROM YOUR NECK.
SCOTT, LOOK.
MY HEAD...
THERE'S A DEVICE BACK HERE.
THERE IS?
A RELAY, FEEDING YOUR MIND SUGGESTIONS. AND BLOCKING YOU FROM BEING AWARE OF ITS PRESENCE.
HE HAS BEEN EXPLOITING YOUR MEMORY LOSS AND URGING YOU TOWARDS HIS OWN ENDS. IT SEEMS HE RECENTLY USED SUCH TECHNOLOGY ON BEN GRIMM.
HE DID--BUT I HAD NO IDEA...
YOU WERE DOING THIS TO ME ALL ALONG?!
CALM DOW--
AH!

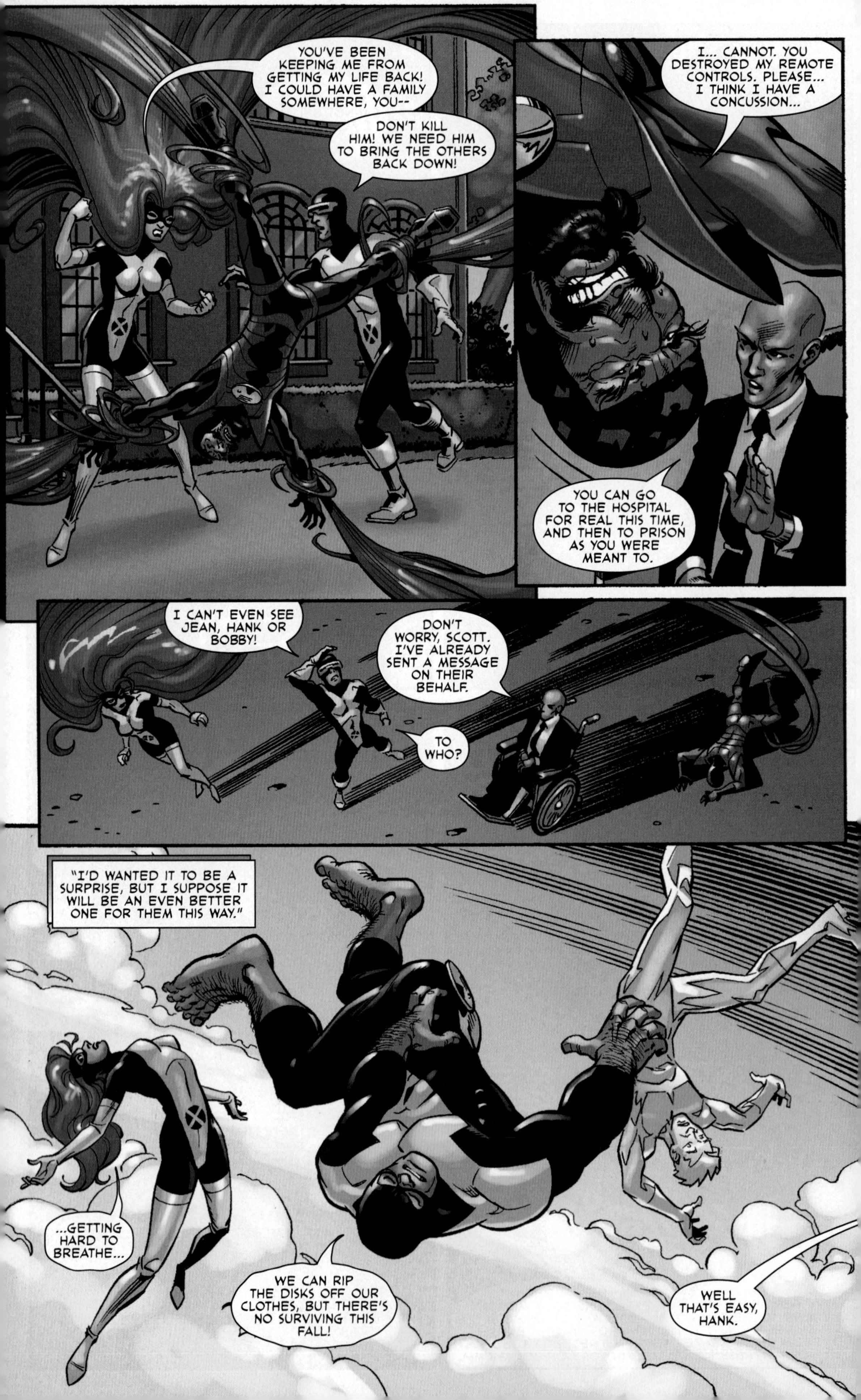
YOU'VE BEEN KEEPING ME FROM GETTING MY LIFE BACK! I COULD HAVE A FAMILY SOMEWHERE, YOU--
DON'T KILL HIM! WE NEED HIM TO BRING THE OTHERS BACK DOWN!
I... CANNOT. YOU DESTROYED MY REMOTE CONTROLS. PLEASE... I THINK I HAVE A CONCUSSION...
YOU CAN GO TO THE HOSPITAL FOR REAL THIS TIME, AND THEN TO PRISON AS YOU WERE MEANT TO.
I CAN'T EVEN SEE JEAN, HANK OR BOBBY!
DON'T WORRY, SCOTT. I'VE ALREADY SENT A MESSAGE ON THEIR BEHALF.
TO WHO?
"I'D WANTED IT TO BE A SURPRISE, BUT I SUPPOSE IT WILL BE AN EVEN BETTER ONE FOR THEM THIS WAY."
...GETTING HARD TO BREATHE...
WE CAN RIP THE DISKS OFF OUR CLOTHES, BUT THERE'S NO SURVIVING THIS FALL!
WELL THAT'S EASY, HANK.

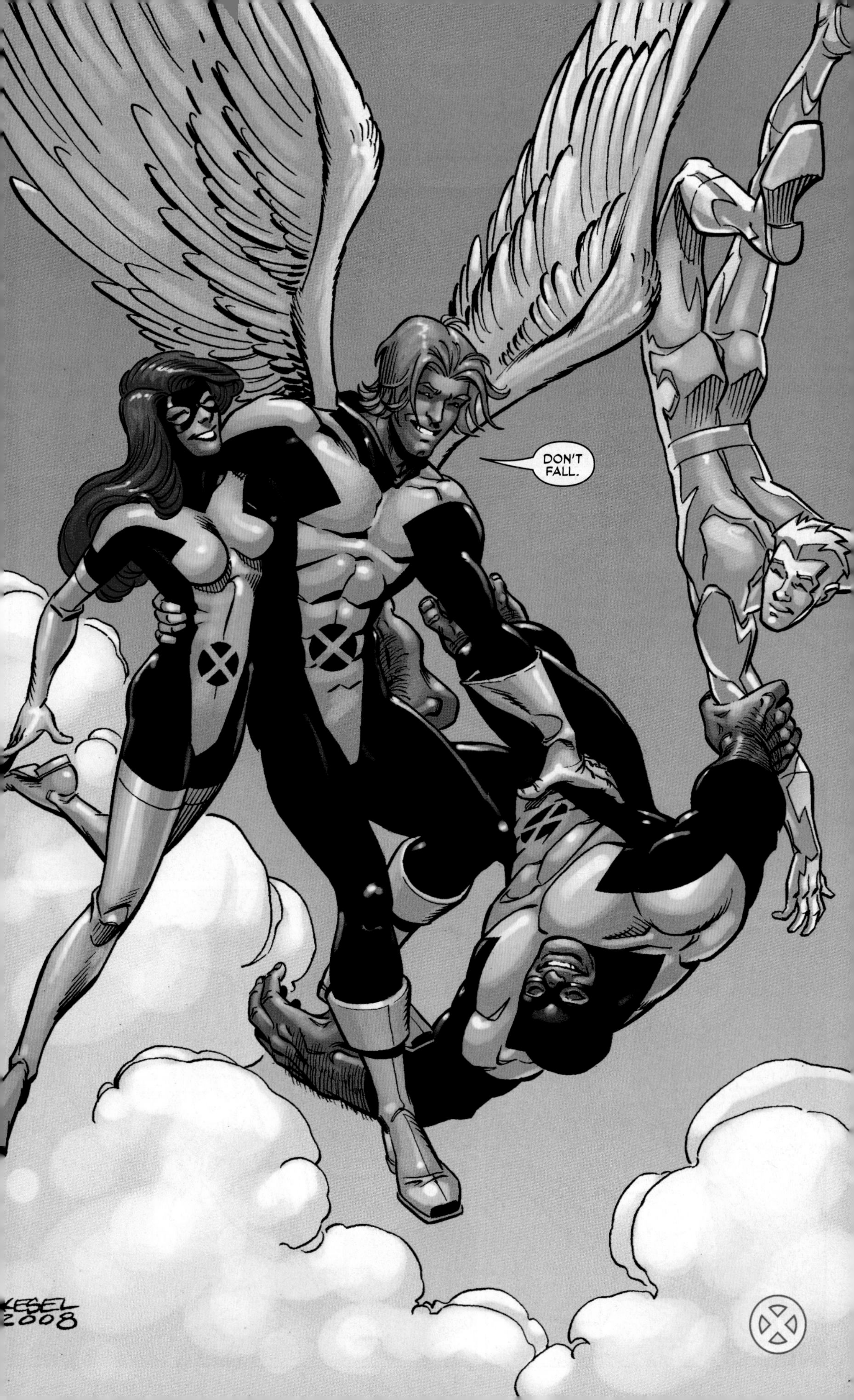
DON'T FALL.
KESEL 2008

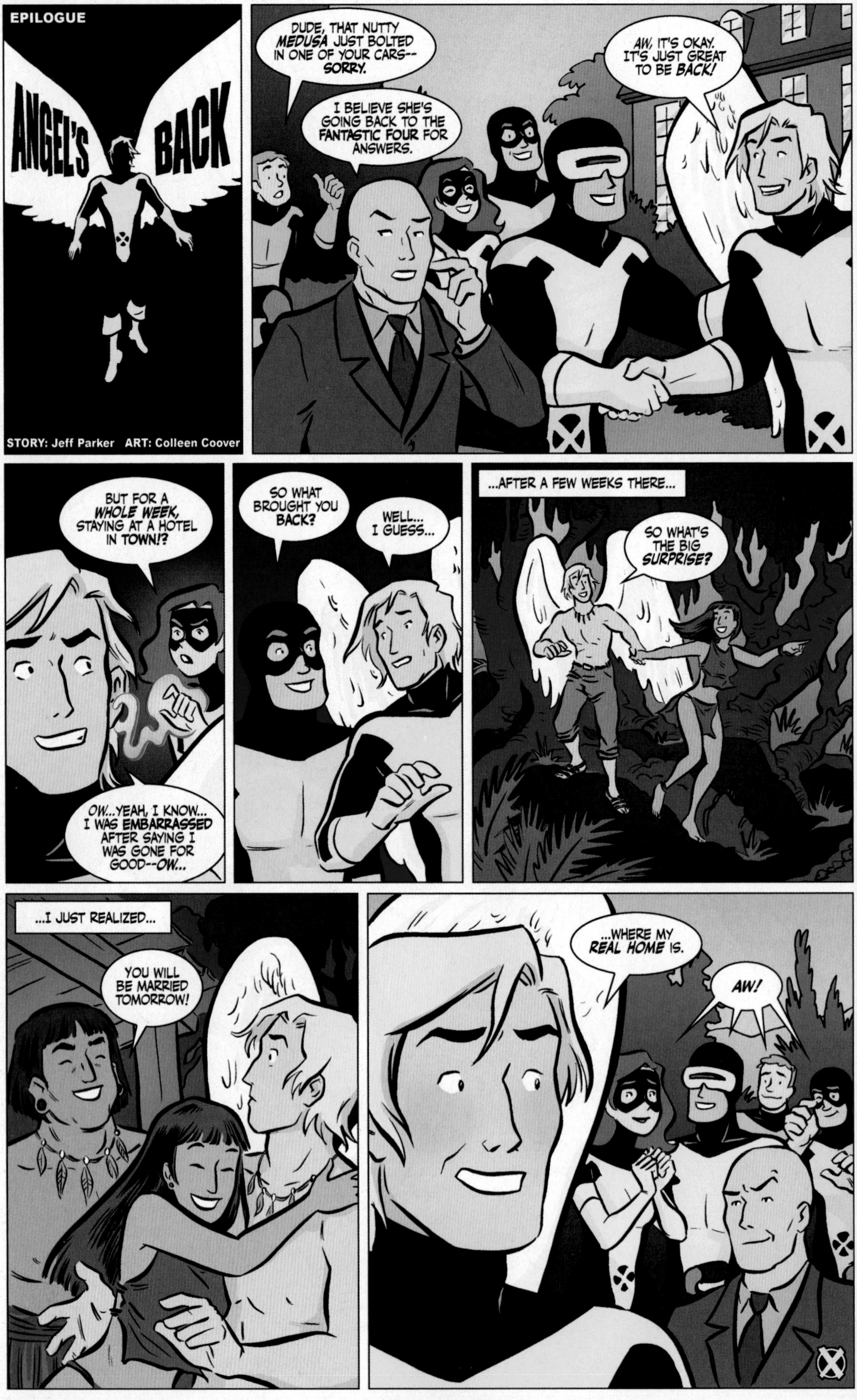
EPILOGUE
ANGEL'S BACK
STORY: Jeff Parker ART: Colleen Coover
DUDE, THAT NUTTY MEDUSA JUST BOLTED IN ONE OF YOUR CARS-- SORRY.
I BELIEVE SHE'S GOING BACK TO THE FANTASTIC FOUR FOR ANSWERS.
AW, IT'S OKAY. IT'S JUST GREAT TO BE BACK!
BUT FOR A WHOLE WEEK, STAYING AT A HOTEL IN TOWN!?
OW...YEAH, I KNOW... I WAS EMBARRASSED AFTER SAYING I WAS GONE FOR GOOD--OW...
SO WHAT BROUGHT YOU BACK?
WELL... I GUESS...
...AFTER A FEW WEEKS THERE...
SO WHAT'S THE BIG SURPRISE?
...I JUST REALIZED...
YOU WILL BE MARRIED TOMORROW!
...WHERE MY REAL HOME IS.
AW!

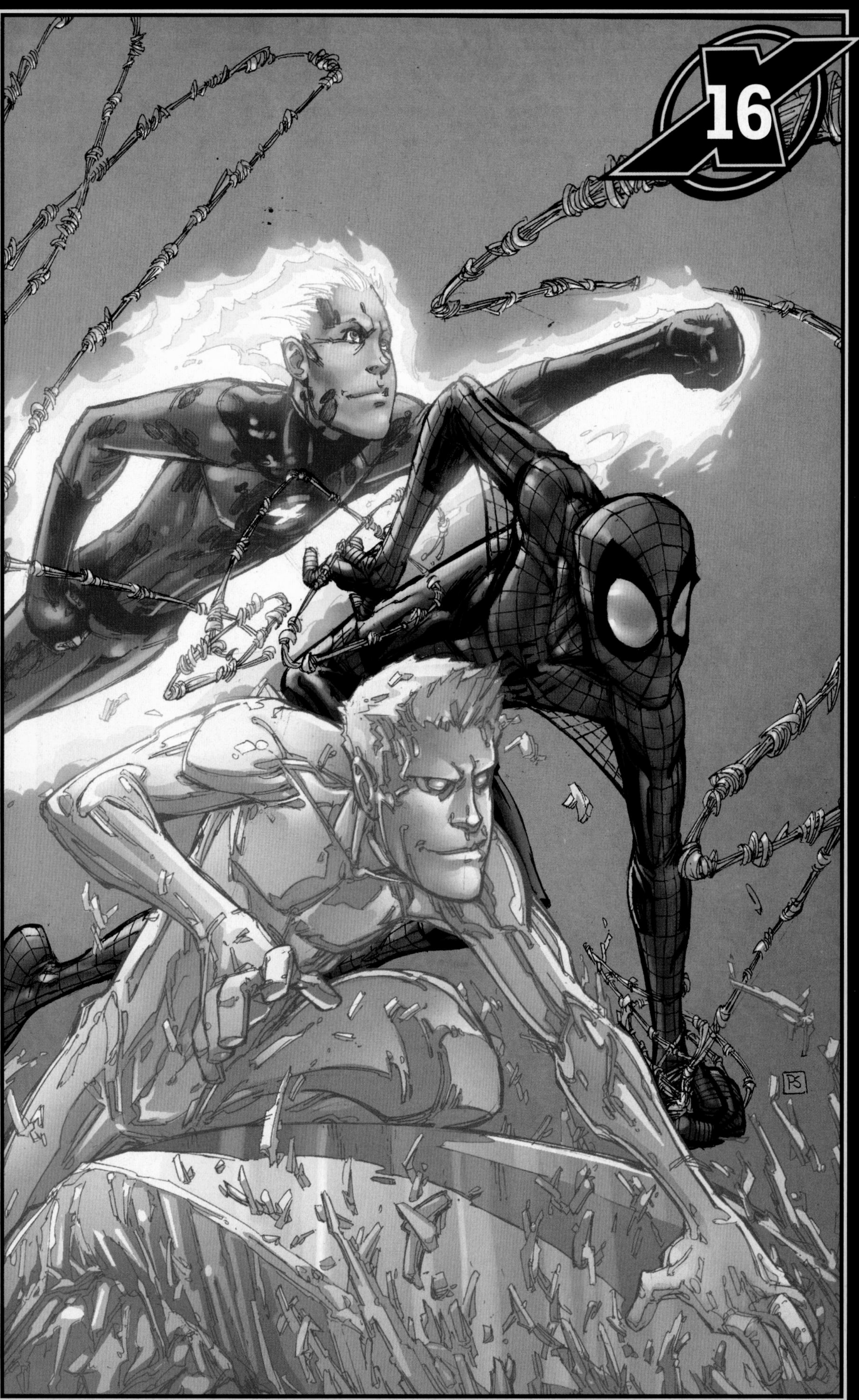
16

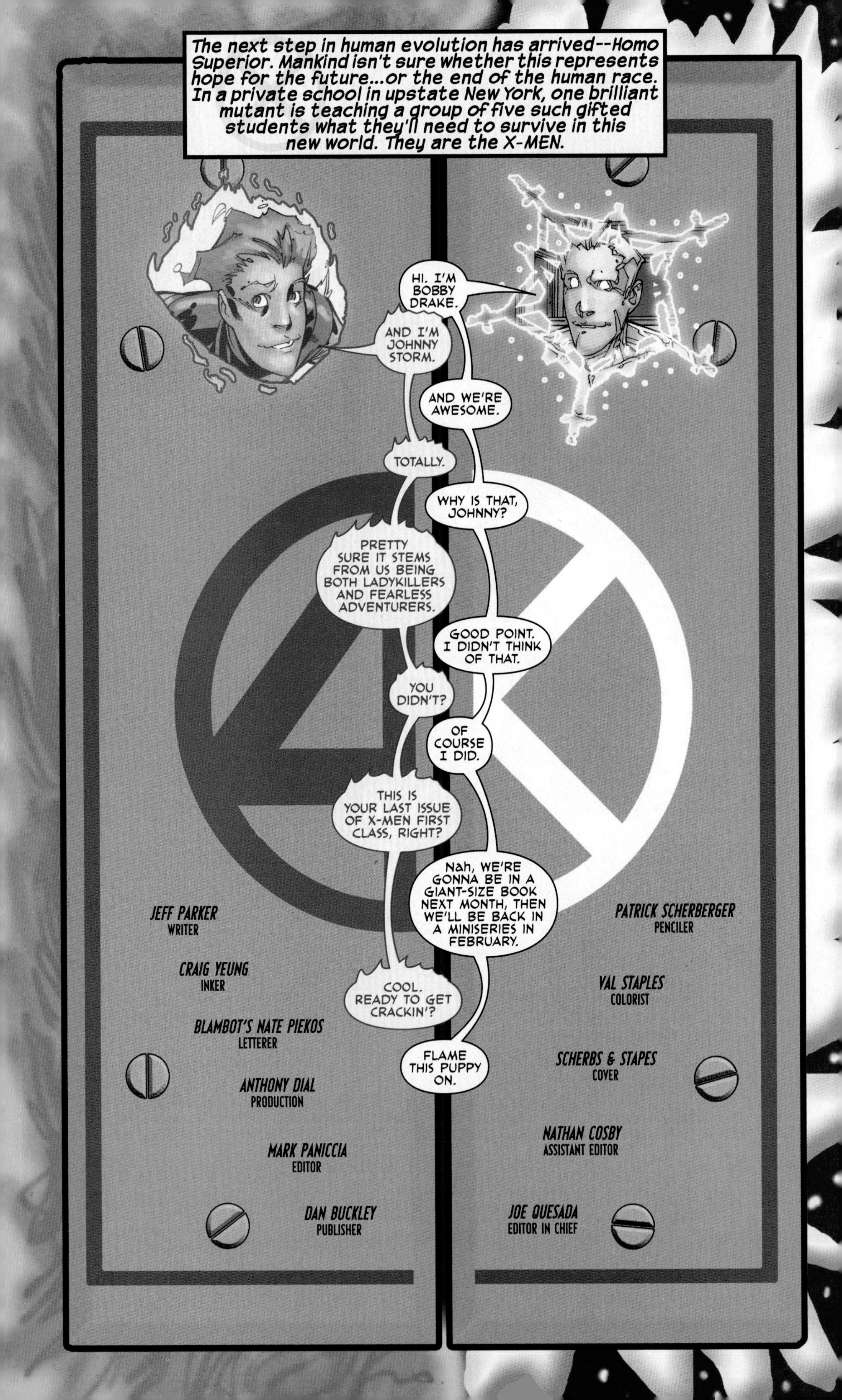
The next step in human evolution has arrived--Homo Superior. Mankind isn't sure whether this represents hope for the future...or the end of the human race. In a private school in upstate New York, one brilliant mutant is teaching a group of five such gifted students what they'll need to survive in this new world. They are the X-MEN.
HI. I'M BOBBY DRAKE.
AND I'M JOHNNY STORM.
AND WE'RE AWESOME.
TOTALLY.
WHY IS THAT, JOHNNY?
PRETTY SURE IT STEMS FROM US BEING BOTH LADYKILLERS AND FEARLESS ADVENTURERS.
GOOD POINT. I DIDN'T THINK OF THAT.
YOU DIDN'T?
OF COURSE I DID.
THIS IS YOUR LAST ISSUE OF X-MEN FIRST CLASS, RIGHT?
Nah, WE'RE GONNA BE IN A GIANT-SIZE BOOK NEXT MONTH, THEN WE'LL BE BACK IN A MINISERIES IN FEBRUARY.
COOL. READY TO GET CRACKIN'?
FLAME THIS PUPPY ON.
JEFF PARKER WRITER
PATRICK SCHERBERGER PENCILER
CRAIG YEUNG INKER
VAL STAPLES COLORIST
BLAMBOT'S NATE PIEKOS LETTERER
SCHERBS & STAPES COVER
ANTHONY DIAL PRODUCTION
NATHAN COSBY ASSISTANT EDITOR
MARK PANICCIA EDITOR
DAN BUCKLEY PUBLISHER
JOE QUESADA EDITOR IN CHIEF

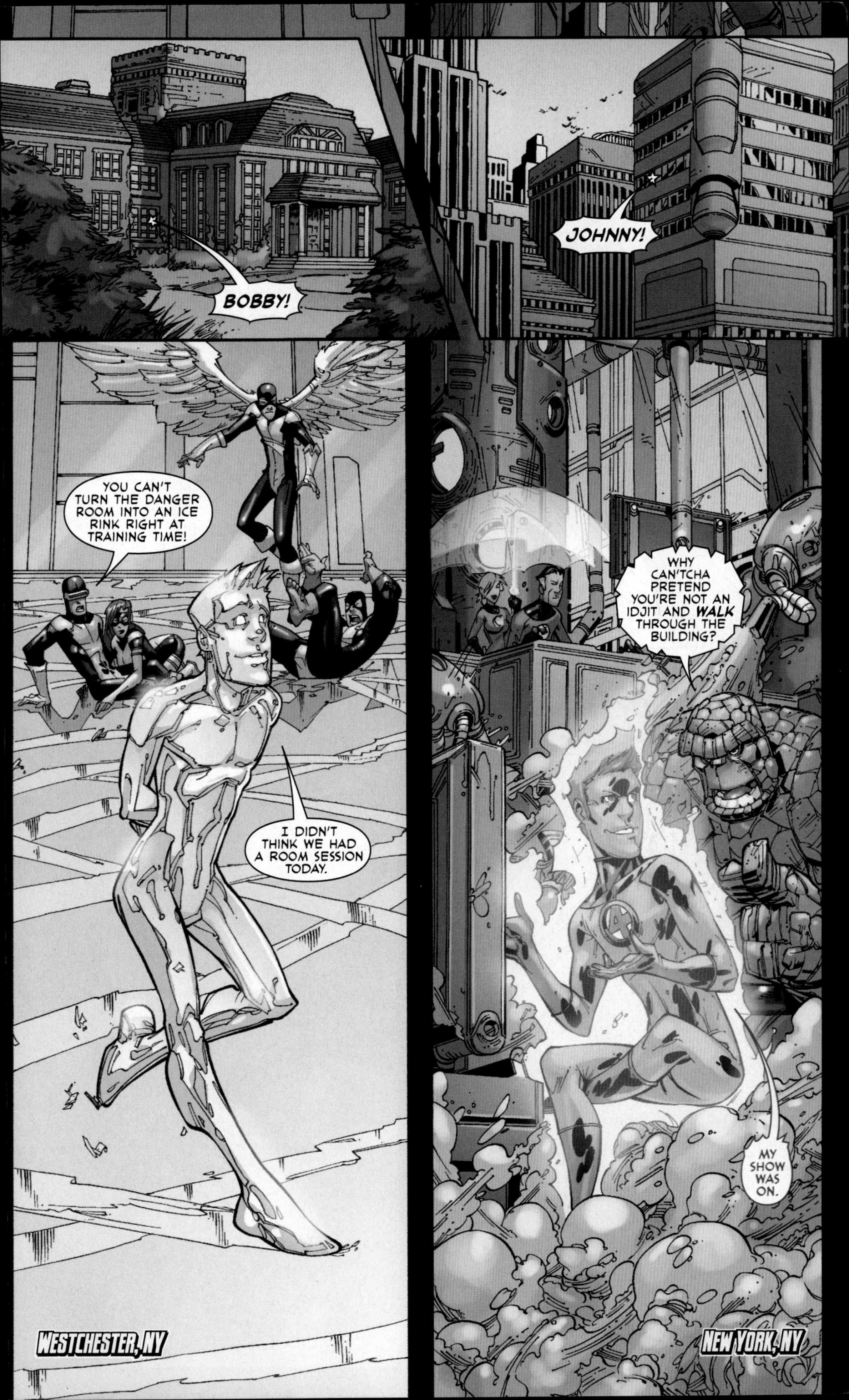
BOBBY!
JOHNNY!
YOU CAN'T TURN THE DANGER ROOM INTO AN ICE RINK RIGHT AT TRAINING TIME!
I DIDN'T THINK WE HAD A ROOM SESSION TODAY.
WESTCHESTER, NY
WHY CAN'TCHA PRETEND YOU'RE NOT AN IDJIT AND WALK THROUGH THE BUILDING?
MY SHOW WAS ON.
NEW YORK, NY

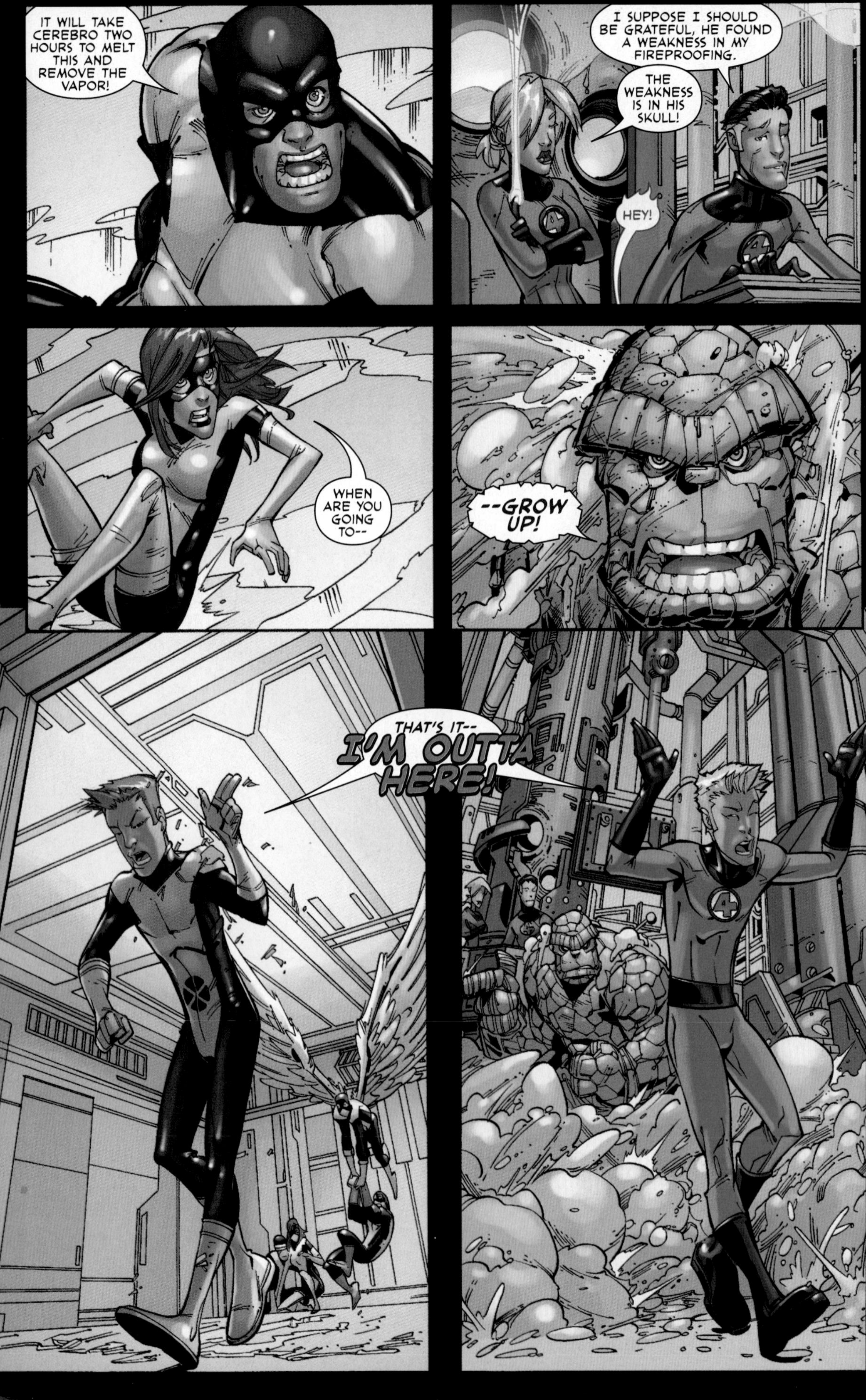
IT WILL TAKE CEREBRO TWO HOURS TO MELT THIS AND REMOVE THE VAPOR!
I SUPPOSE I SHOULD BE GRATEFUL, HE FOUND A WEAKNESS IN MY FIREPROOFING.
THE WEAKNESS IS IN HIS SKULL!
HEY!
WHEN ARE YOU GOING TO--
--GROW UP!
THAT'S IT--
I'M OUTTA HERE!

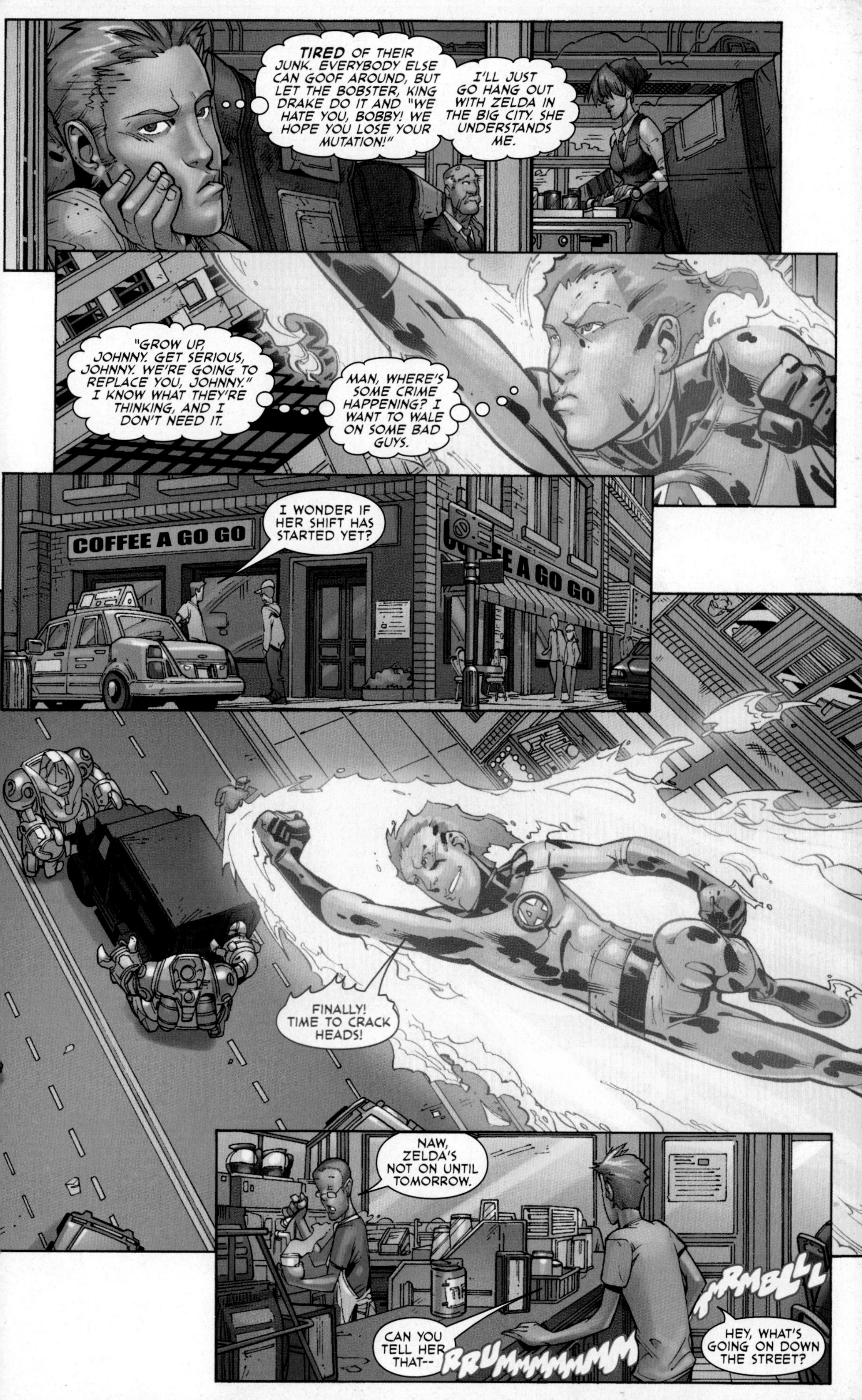
TIRED OF THEIR JUNK. EVERYBODY ELSE CAN GOOF AROUND, BUT LET THE BOBSTER, KING DRAKE DO IT AND "WE HATE YOU, BOBBY! WE HOPE YOU LOSE YOUR MUTATION!"
I'LL JUST GO HANG OUT WITH ZELDA IN THE BIG CITY. SHE UNDERSTANDS ME.
"GROW UP, JOHNNY. GET SERIOUS, JOHNNY. WE'RE GOING TO REPLACE YOU, JOHNNY." I KNOW WHAT THEY'RE THINKING, AND I DON'T NEED IT.
MAN, WHERE'S SOME CRIME HAPPENING? I WANT TO WALE ON SOME BAD GUYS.
COFFEE A GO GO
I WONDER IF HER SHIFT HAS STARTED YET?
COFFEE A GO GO
FINALLY! TIME TO CRACK HEADS!
NAW, ZELDA'S NOT ON UNTIL TOMORROW.
CAN YOU TELL HER THAT--
RRUMMMMMMM
RRMBLLL
HEY, WHAT'S GOING ON DOWN THE STREET?

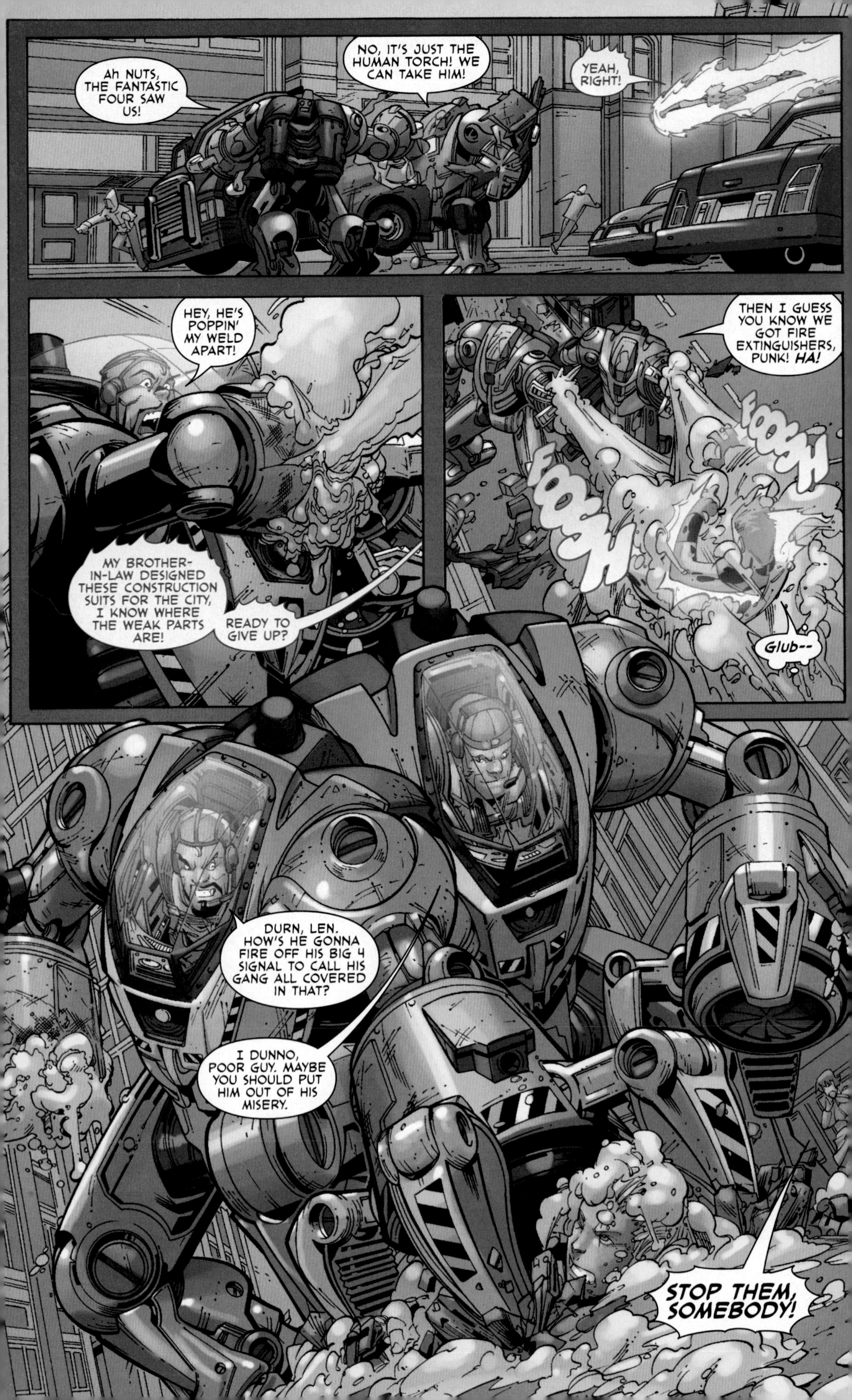
Ah NUTS, THE FANTASTIC FOUR SAW US!
NO, IT'S JUST THE HUMAN TORCH! WE CAN TAKE HIM!
YEAH, RIGHT!
HEY, HE'S POPPIN' MY WELD APART!
MY BROTHER-IN-LAW DESIGNED THESE CONSTRUCTION SUITS FOR THE CITY, I KNOW WHERE THE WEAK PARTS ARE!
READY TO GIVE UP?
THEN I GUESS YOU KNOW WE GOT FIRE EXTINGUISHERS, PUNK! HA!
FOOSH
FOOSH
Glub--
DURN, LEN. HOW'S HE GONNA FIRE OFF HIS BIG 4 SIGNAL TO CALL HIS GANG ALL COVERED IN THAT?
I DUNNO, POOR GUY. MAYBE YOU SHOULD PUT HIM OUT OF HIS MISERY.
STOP THEM, SOMEBODY!

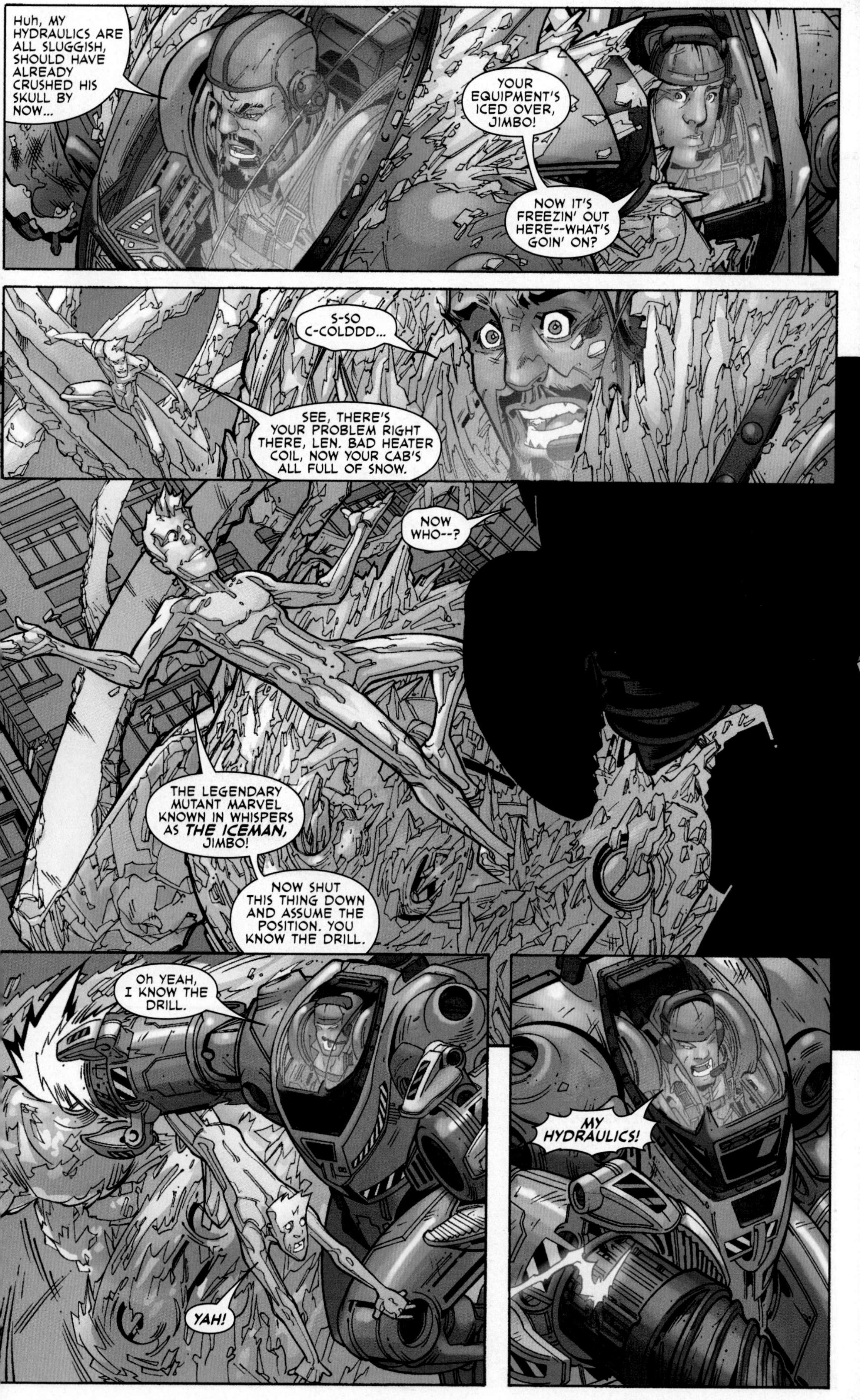
Huh, MY HYDRAULICS ARE ALL SLUGGISH, SHOULD HAVE ALREADY CRUSHED HIS SKULL BY NOW...
YOUR EQUIPMENT'S ICED OVER, JIMBO!
NOW IT'S FREEZIN' OUT HERE--WHAT'S GOIN' ON?
S-SO C-COLDDD...
SEE, THERE'S YOUR PROBLEM RIGHT THERE, LEN. BAD HEATER COIL, NOW YOUR CAB'S ALL FULL OF SNOW.
NOW WHO--?
THE LEGENDARY MUTANT MARVEL KNOWN IN WHISPERS AS *THE ICEMAN,* JIMBO!
NOW SHUT THIS THING DOWN AND ASSUME THE POSITION. YOU KNOW THE DRILL.
Oh YEAH, I KNOW THE DRILL.
YAH!
MY HYDRAULICS!

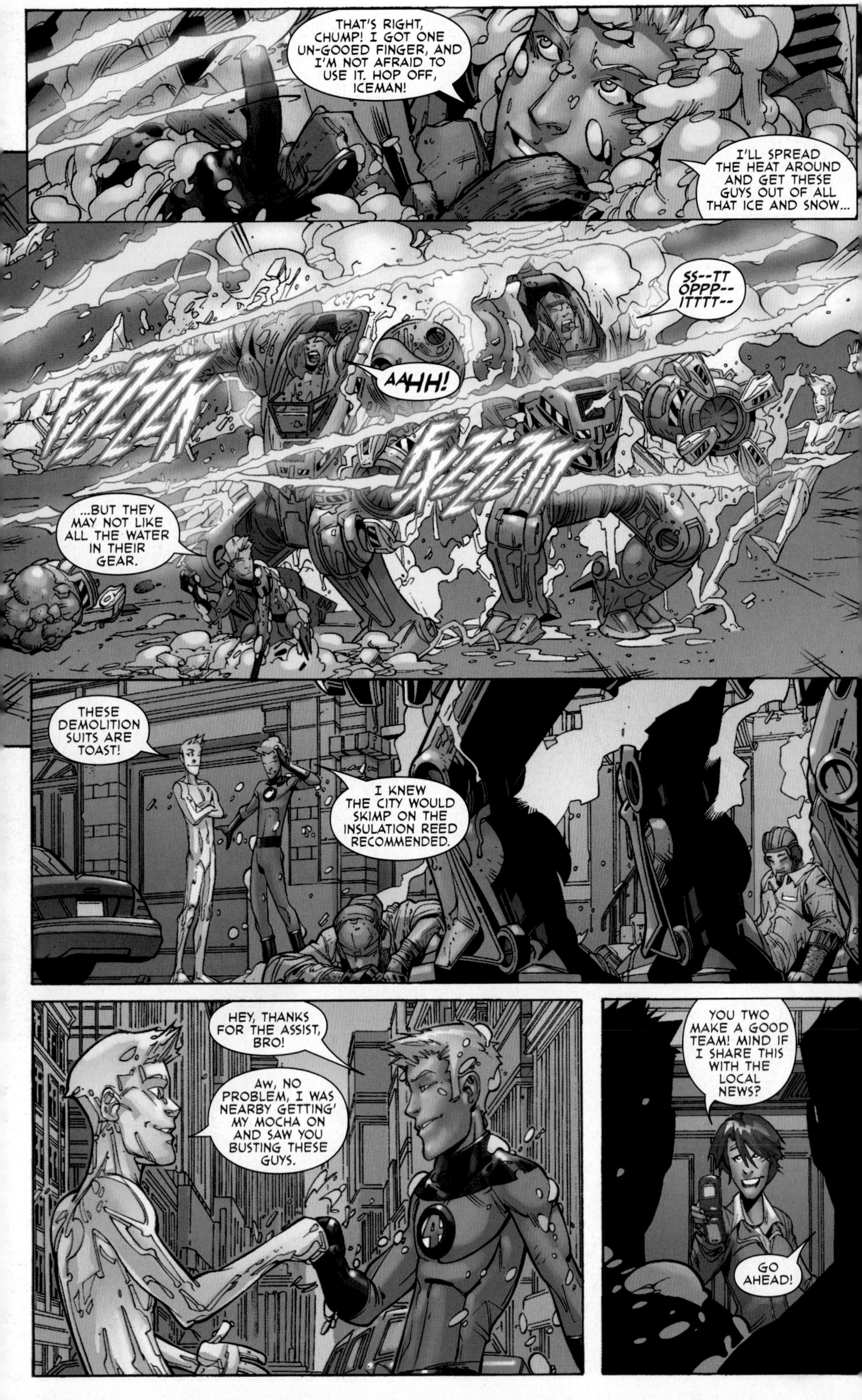
THAT'S RIGHT, CHUMP! I GOT ONE UN-GOOED FINGER, AND I'M NOT AFRAID TO USE IT. HOP OFF, ICEMAN!
I'LL SPREAD THE HEAT AROUND AND GET THESE GUYS OUT OF ALL THAT ICE AND SNOW...
SS--TT OPPP-- ITTTT--
AAHH!
FZZZZAK
FXZZZZTTT
...BUT THEY MAY NOT LIKE ALL THE WATER IN THEIR GEAR.
THESE DEMOLITION SUITS ARE TOAST!
I KNEW THE CITY WOULD SKIMP ON THE INSULATION REED RECOMMENDED.
HEY, THANKS FOR THE ASSIST, BRO!
AW, NO PROBLEM, I WAS NEARBY GETTING' MY MOCHA ON AND SAW YOU BUSTING THESE GUYS.
YOU TWO MAKE A GOOD TEAM! MIND IF I SHARE THIS WITH THE LOCAL NEWS?
GO AHEAD!

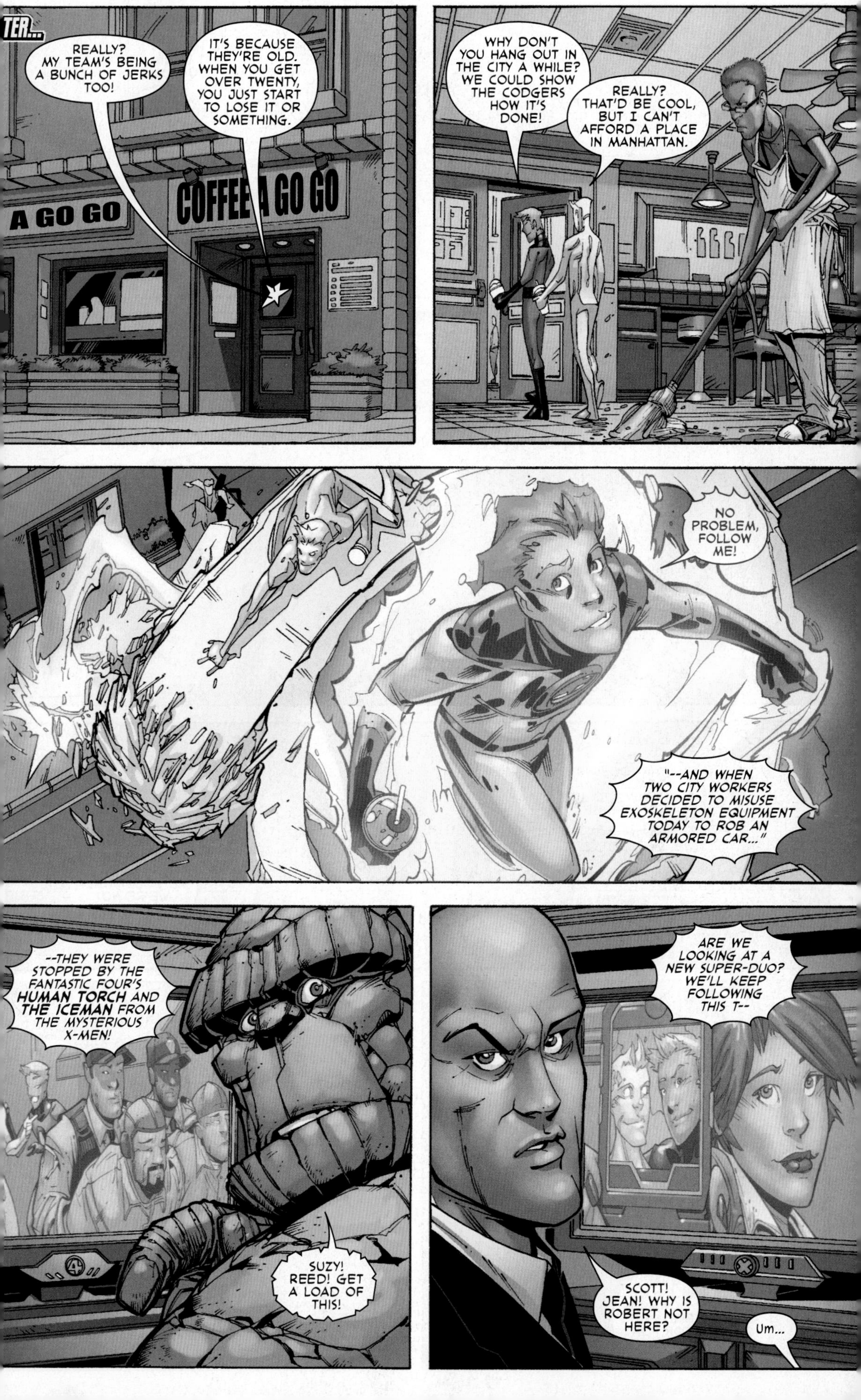
TER...
REALLY? MY TEAM'S BEING A BUNCH OF JERKS TOO!
IT'S BECAUSE THEY'RE OLD. WHEN YOU GET OVER TWENTY, YOU JUST START TO LOSE IT OR SOMETHING.
A GO GO
COFFEE A GO GO
WHY DON'T YOU HANG OUT IN THE CITY A WHILE? WE COULD SHOW THE CODGERS HOW IT'S DONE!
REALLY? THAT'D BE COOL, BUT I CAN'T AFFORD A PLACE IN MANHATTAN.
NO PROBLEM, FOLLOW ME!
"--AND WHEN TWO CITY WORKERS DECIDED TO MISUSE EXOSKELETON EQUIPMENT TODAY TO ROB AN ARMORED CAR..."
--THEY WERE STOPPED BY THE FANTASTIC FOUR'S HUMAN TORCH AND THE ICEMAN FROM THE MYSTERIOUS X-MEN!
SUZY! REED! GET A LOAD OF THIS!
ARE WE LOOKING AT A NEW SUPER-DUO? WE'LL KEEP FOLLOWING THIS T--
SCOTT! JEAN! WHY IS ROBERT NOT HERE?
Um...

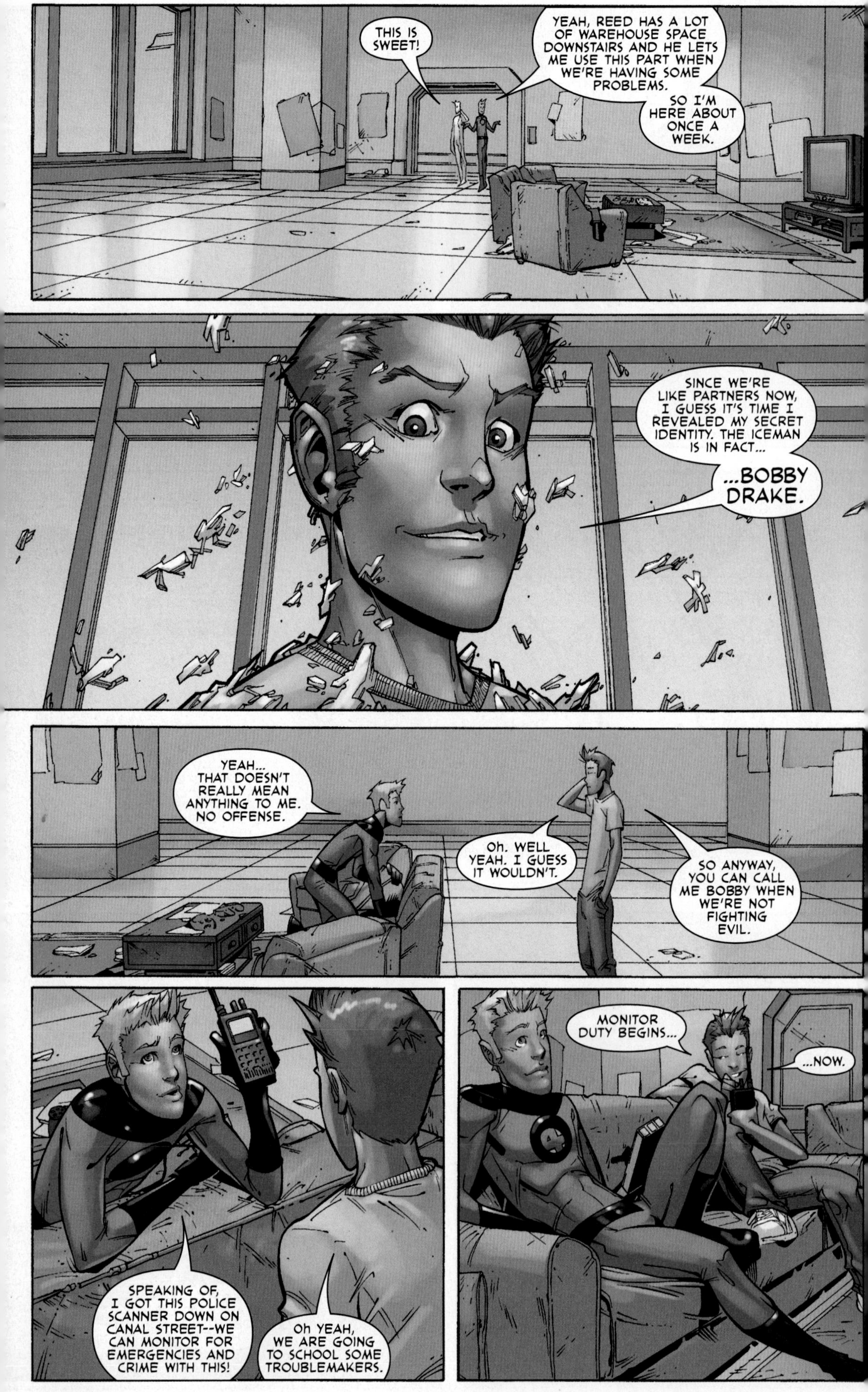
THIS IS SWEET!
YEAH, REED HAS A LOT OF WAREHOUSE SPACE DOWNSTAIRS AND HE LETS ME USE THIS PART WHEN WE'RE HAVING SOME PROBLEMS.
SO I'M HERE ABOUT ONCE A WEEK.
SINCE WE'RE LIKE PARTNERS NOW, I GUESS IT'S TIME I REVEALED MY SECRET IDENTITY. THE ICEMAN IS IN FACT...
...BOBBY DRAKE.
YEAH... THAT DOESN'T REALLY MEAN ANYTHING TO ME. NO OFFENSE.
Oh. WELL YEAH. I GUESS IT WOULDN'T.
SO ANYWAY, YOU CAN CALL ME BOBBY WHEN WE'RE NOT FIGHTING EVIL.
SPEAKING OF, I GOT THIS POLICE SCANNER DOWN ON CANAL STREET--WE CAN MONITOR FOR EMERGENCIES AND CRIME WITH THIS!
Oh YEAH, WE ARE GOING TO SCHOOL SOME TROUBLEMAKERS.
MONITOR DUTY BEGINS...
...NOW.

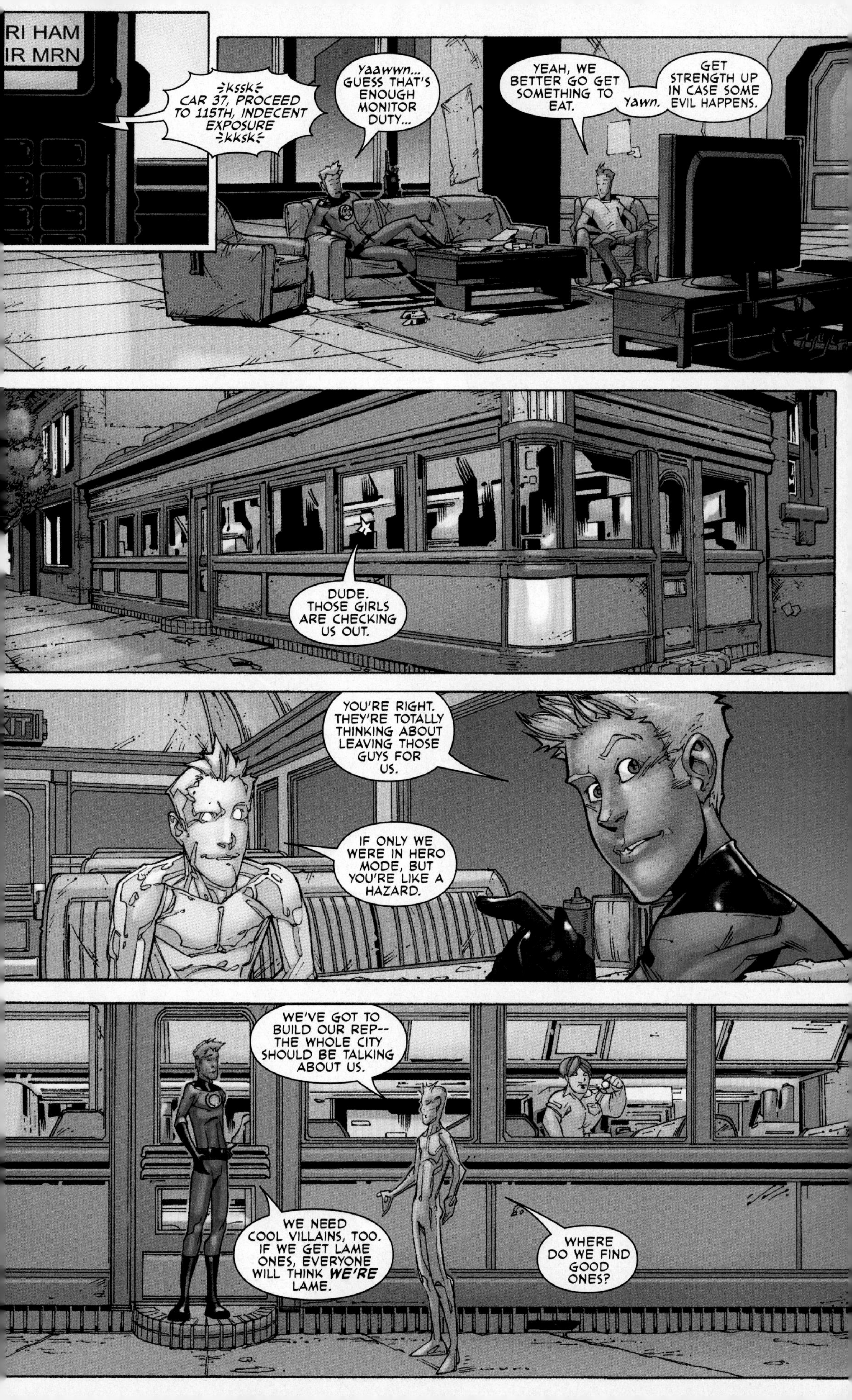
RI HAM
IR MRN
⋺kssk⋲ CAR 37, PROCEED TO 115TH, INDECENT EXPOSURE ⋺kksk⋲
Yaawwn... GUESS THAT'S ENOUGH MONITOR DUTY...
YEAH, WE BETTER GO GET SOMETHING TO EAT.
Yawn.
GET STRENGTH UP IN CASE SOME EVIL HAPPENS.
DUDE. THOSE GIRLS ARE CHECKING US OUT.
YOU'RE RIGHT. THEY'RE TOTALLY THINKING ABOUT LEAVING THOSE GUYS FOR US.
IF ONLY WE WERE IN HERO MODE, BUT YOU'RE LIKE A HAZARD.
WE'VE GOT TO BUILD OUR REP-- THE WHOLE CITY SHOULD BE TALKING ABOUT US.
WE NEED COOL VILLAINS, TOO. IF WE GET LAME ONES, EVERYONE WILL THINK *WE'RE* LAME.
WHERE DO WE FIND GOOD ONES?

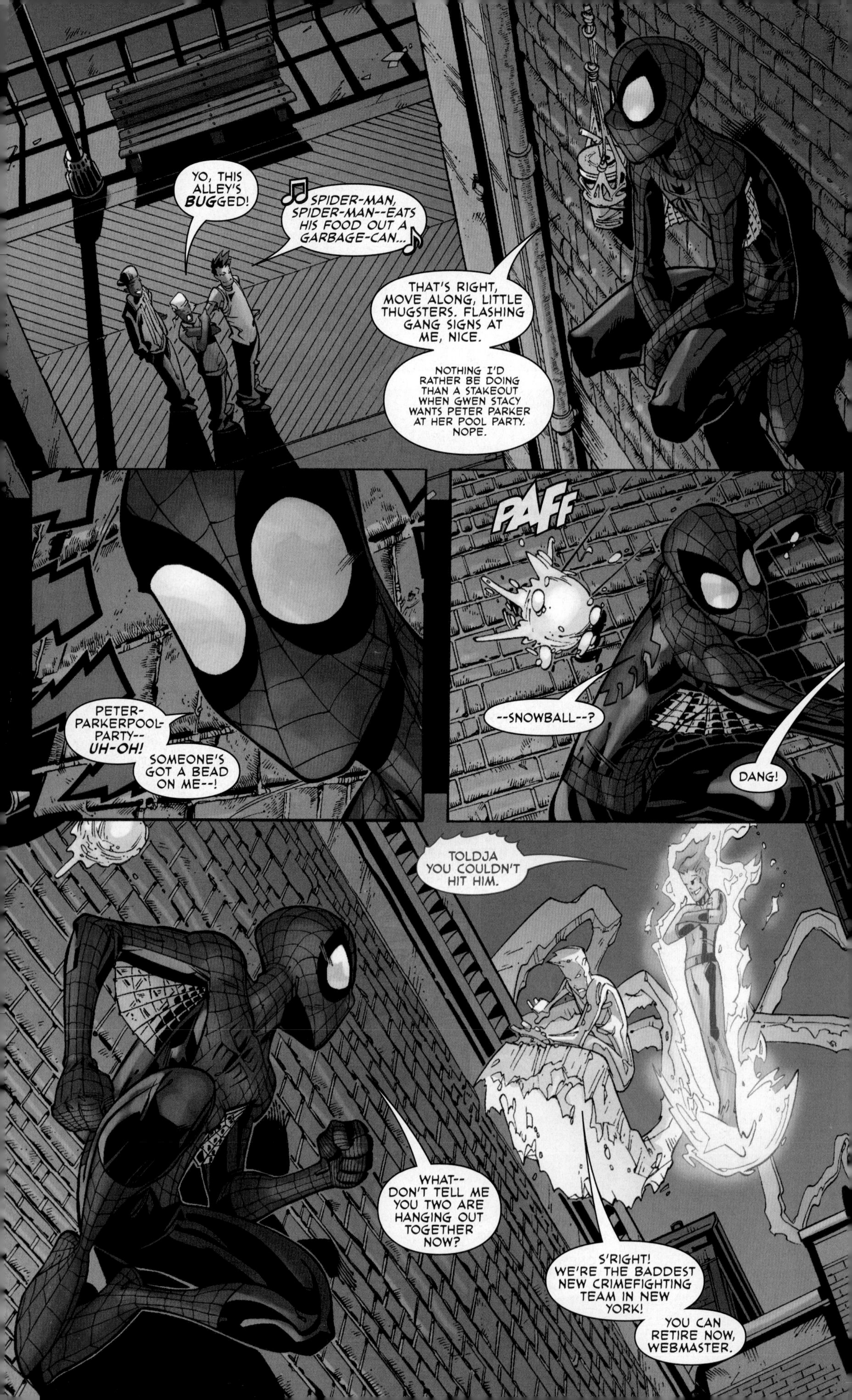
YO, THIS ALLEY'S *BUG*GED!
SPIDER-MAN, SPIDER-MAN--EATS HIS FOOD OUT A GARBAGE-CAN...
THAT'S RIGHT, MOVE ALONG, LITTLE THUGSTERS. FLASHING GANG SIGNS AT ME, NICE.
NOTHING I'D RATHER BE DOING THAN A STAKEOUT WHEN GWEN STACY WANTS PETER PARKER AT HER POOL PARTY. NOPE.
PETER-PARKERPOOL-PARTY-- *UH-OH!*
SOMEONE'S GOT A BEAD ON ME--!
PAFF
--SNOWBALL--?
DANG!
TOLDJA YOU COULDN'T HIT HIM.
WHAT-- DON'T TELL ME YOU TWO ARE HANGING OUT TOGETHER NOW?
S'RIGHT! WE'RE THE BADDEST NEW CRIMEFIGHTING TEAM IN NEW YORK!
YOU CAN RETIRE NOW, WEBMASTER.

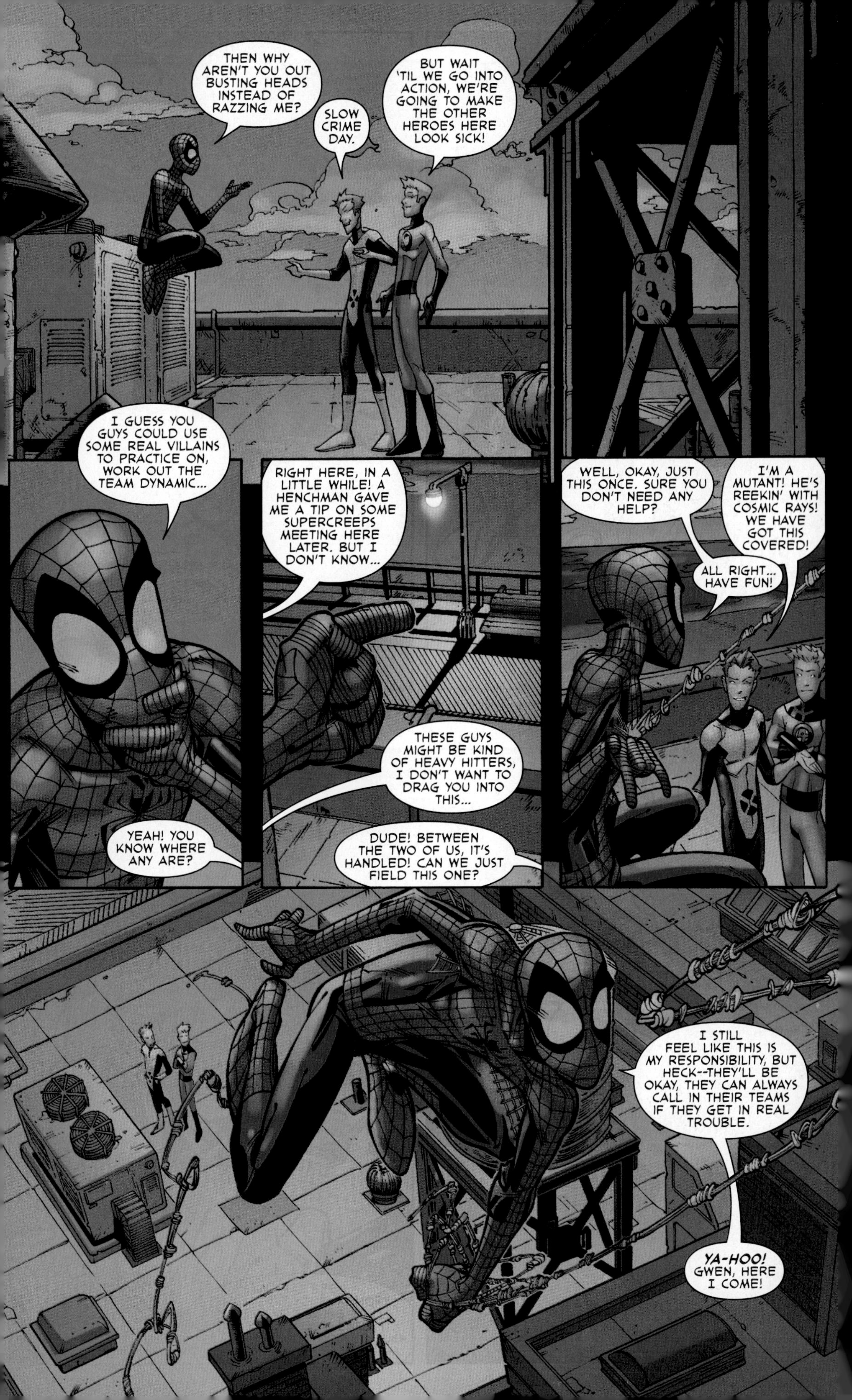
THEN WHY AREN'T YOU OUT BUSTING HEADS INSTEAD OF RAZZING ME?
SLOW CRIME DAY.
BUT WAIT 'TIL WE GO INTO ACTION, WE'RE GOING TO MAKE THE OTHER HEROES HERE LOOK SICK!
I GUESS YOU GUYS COULD USE SOME REAL VILLAINS TO PRACTICE ON, WORK OUT THE TEAM DYNAMIC...
YEAH! YOU KNOW WHERE ANY ARE?
RIGHT HERE, IN A LITTLE WHILE! A HENCHMAN GAVE ME A TIP ON SOME SUPERCREEPS MEETING HERE LATER. BUT I DON'T KNOW...
THESE GUYS MIGHT BE KIND OF HEAVY HITTERS, I DON'T WANT TO DRAG YOU INTO THIS...
DUDE! BETWEEN THE TWO OF US, IT'S HANDLED! CAN WE JUST FIELD THIS ONE?
WELL, OKAY, JUST THIS ONCE. SURE YOU DON'T NEED ANY HELP?
I'M A MUTANT! HE'S REEKIN' WITH COSMIC RAYS! WE HAVE GOT THIS COVERED!
ALL RIGHT... HAVE FUN!
I STILL FEEL LIKE THIS IS MY RESPONSIBILITY, BUT HECK--THEY'LL BE OKAY, THEY CAN ALWAYS CALL IN THEIR TEAMS IF THEY GET IN REAL TROUBLE.
YA-HOO! GWEN, HERE I COME!

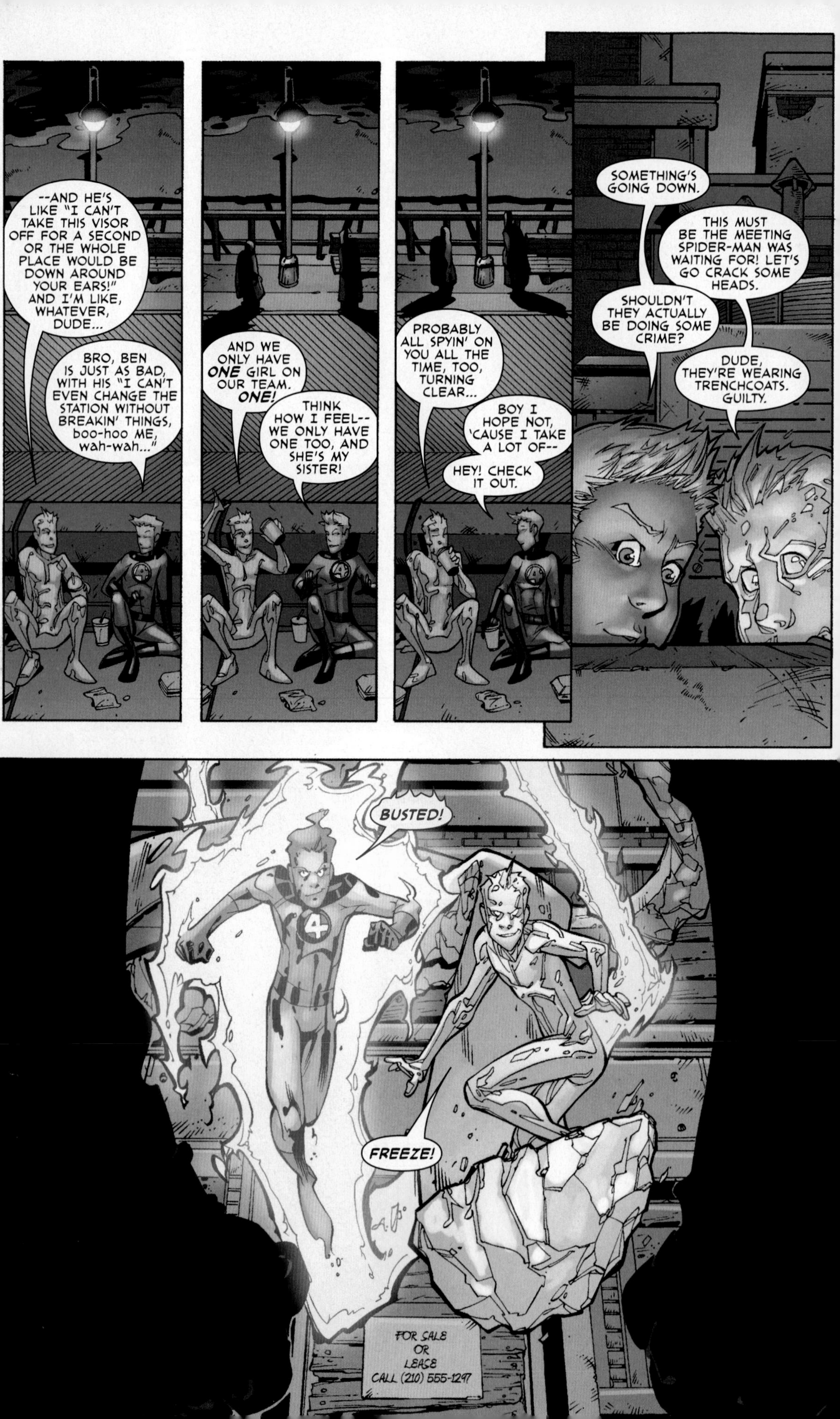
--AND HE'S LIKE "I CAN'T TAKE THIS VISOR OFF FOR A SECOND OR THE WHOLE PLACE WOULD BE DOWN AROUND YOUR EARS!" AND I'M LIKE, WHATEVER, DUDE...
BRO, BEN IS JUST AS BAD, WITH HIS "I CAN'T EVEN CHANGE THE STATION WITHOUT BREAKIN' THINGS, boo-hoo ME, wah-wah..."
AND WE ONLY HAVE ONE GIRL ON OUR TEAM. ONE!
THINK HOW I FEEL-- WE ONLY HAVE ONE TOO, AND SHE'S MY SISTER!
PROBABLY ALL SPYIN' ON YOU ALL THE TIME, TOO, TURNING CLEAR...
BOY I HOPE NOT, 'CAUSE I TAKE A LOT OF--
HEY! CHECK IT OUT.
SOMETHING'S GOING DOWN.
THIS MUST BE THE MEETING SPIDER-MAN WAS WAITING FOR! LET'S GO CRACK SOME HEADS.
SHOULDN'T THEY ACTUALLY BE DOING SOME CRIME?
DUDE, THEY'RE WEARING TRENCHCOATS. GUILTY.
BUSTED!
FREEZE!
FOR SALE OR LEASE CALL (210) 555-1297

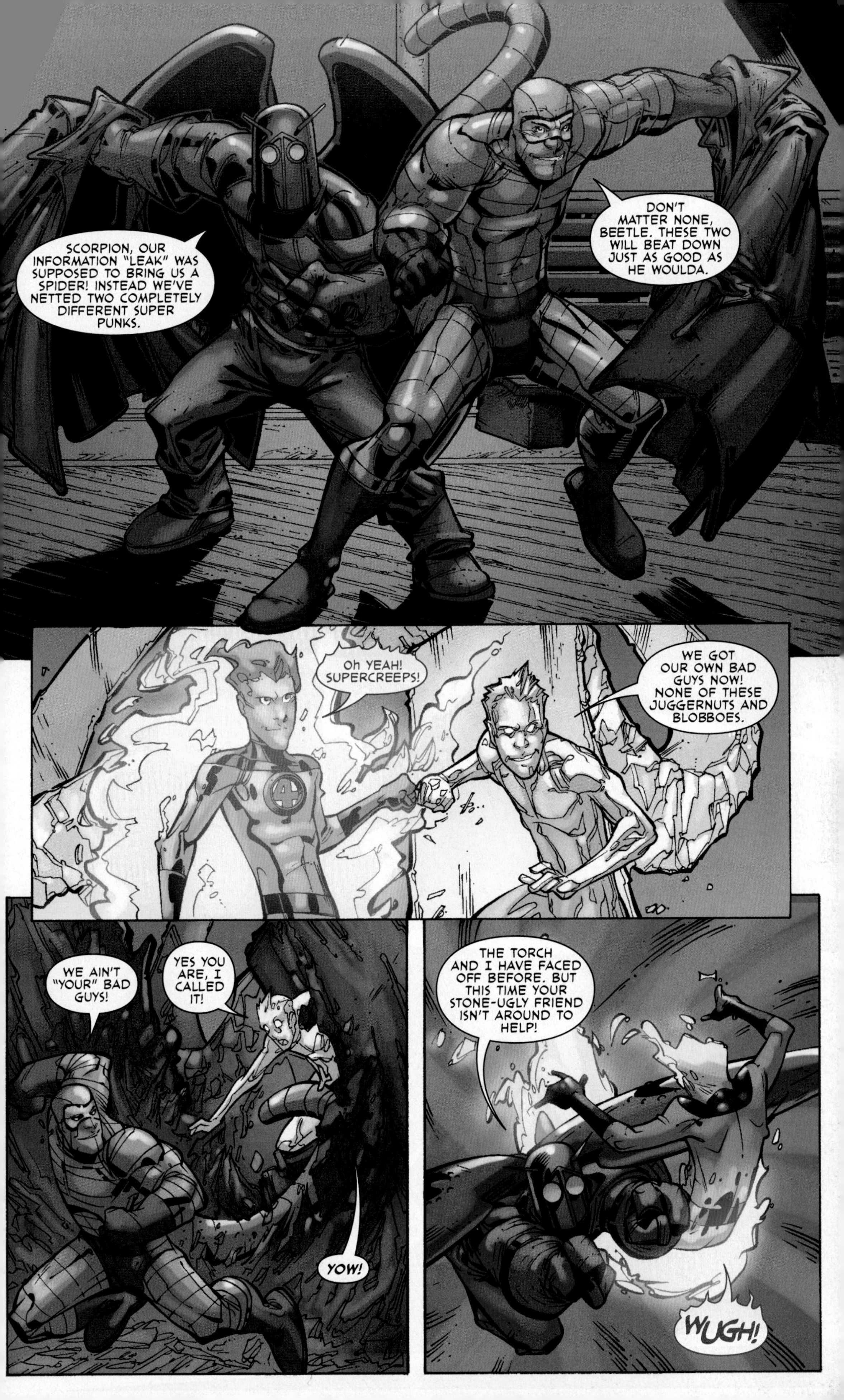
SCORPION, OUR INFORMATION "LEAK" WAS SUPPOSED TO BRING US A SPIDER! INSTEAD WE'VE NETTED TWO COMPLETELY DIFFERENT SUPER PUNKS.
DON'T MATTER NONE, BEETLE. THESE TWO WILL BEAT DOWN JUST AS GOOD AS HE WOULDA.
Oh YEAH! SUPERCREEPS!
WE GOT OUR OWN BAD GUYS NOW! NONE OF THESE JUGGERNUTS AND BLOBBOES.
WE AIN'T "YOUR" BAD GUYS!
YES YOU ARE, I CALLED IT!
YOW!
THE TORCH AND I HAVE FACED OFF BEFORE. BUT THIS TIME YOUR STONE-UGLY FRIEND ISN'T AROUND TO HELP!
WUGH!

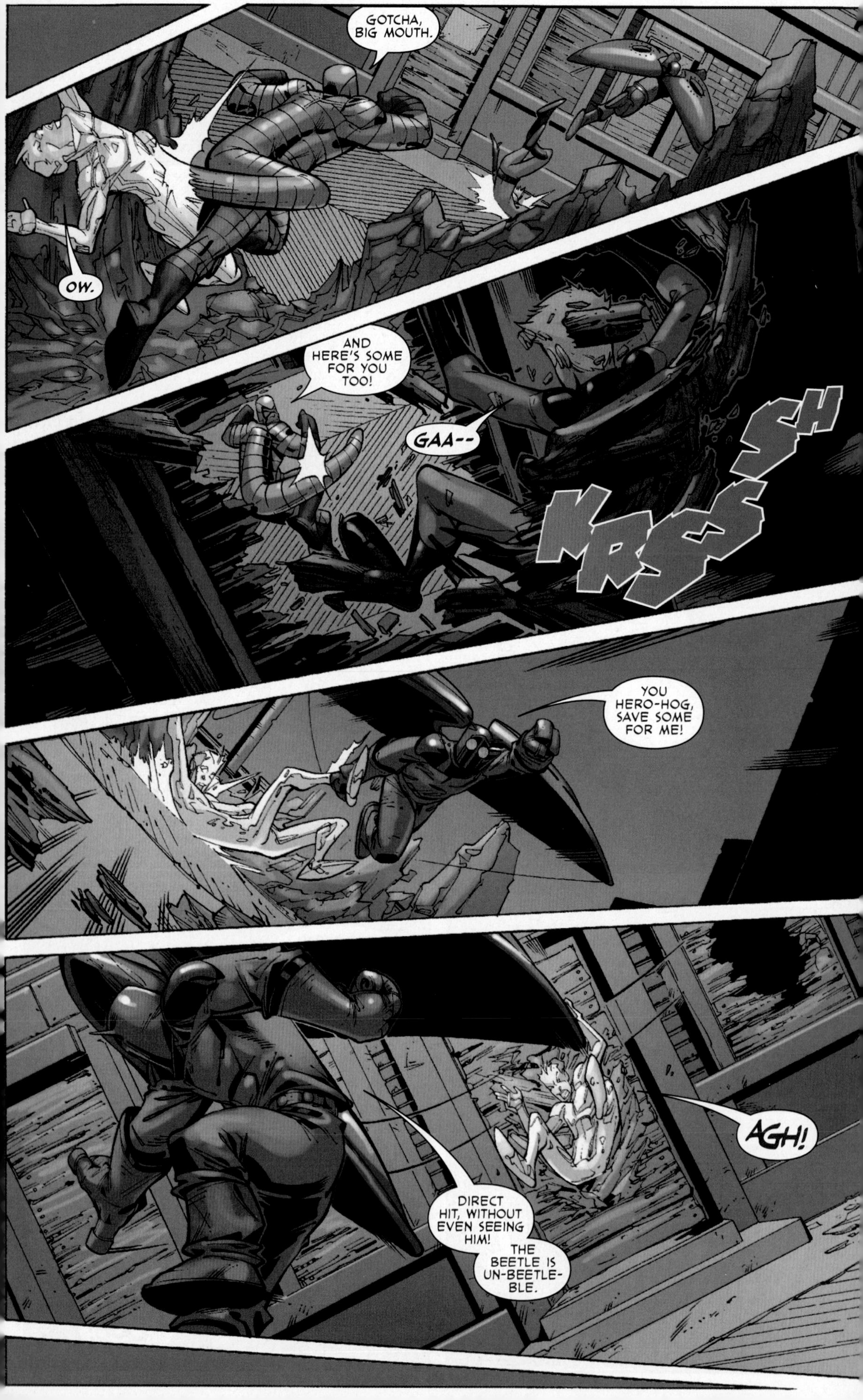
GOTCHA, BIG MOUTH.
OW.
AND HERE'S SOME FOR YOU TOO!
GAA--
KRSSSH
YOU HERO-HOG, SAVE SOME FOR ME!
AGH!
DIRECT HIT, WITHOUT EVEN SEEING HIM!
THE BEETLE IS UN-BEETLE-BLE.

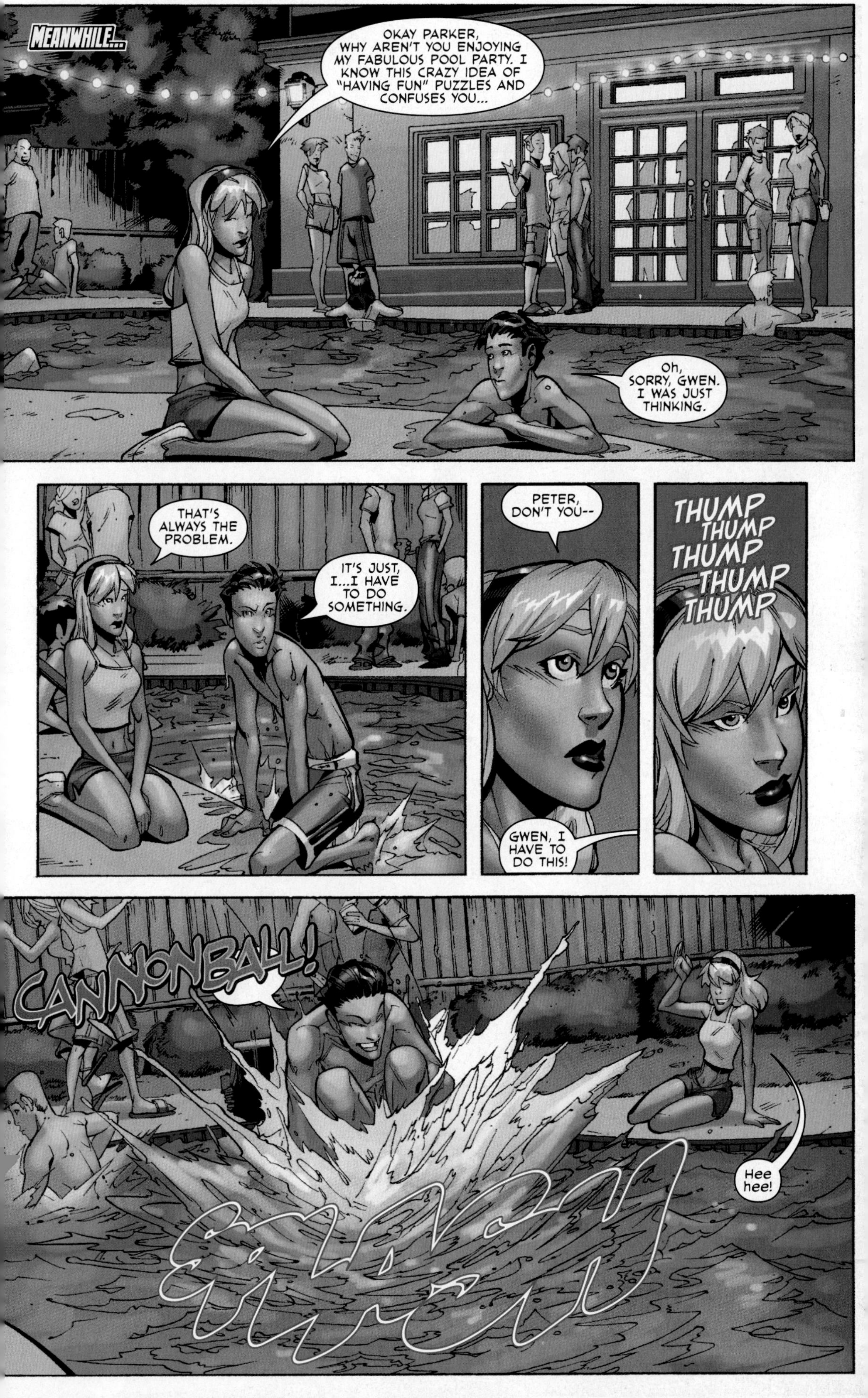
MEANWHILE...
OKAY PARKER, WHY AREN'T YOU ENJOYING MY FABULOUS POOL PARTY. I KNOW THIS CRAZY IDEA OF "HAVING FUN" PUZZLES AND CONFUSES YOU...
Oh, SORRY, GWEN. I WAS JUST THINKING.
THAT'S ALWAYS THE PROBLEM.
IT'S JUST, I...I HAVE TO DO SOMETHING.
PETER, DON'T YOU--
GWEN, I HAVE TO DO THIS!
THUMP THUMP THUMP THUMP THUMP
CANNONBALL!
Hee hee!

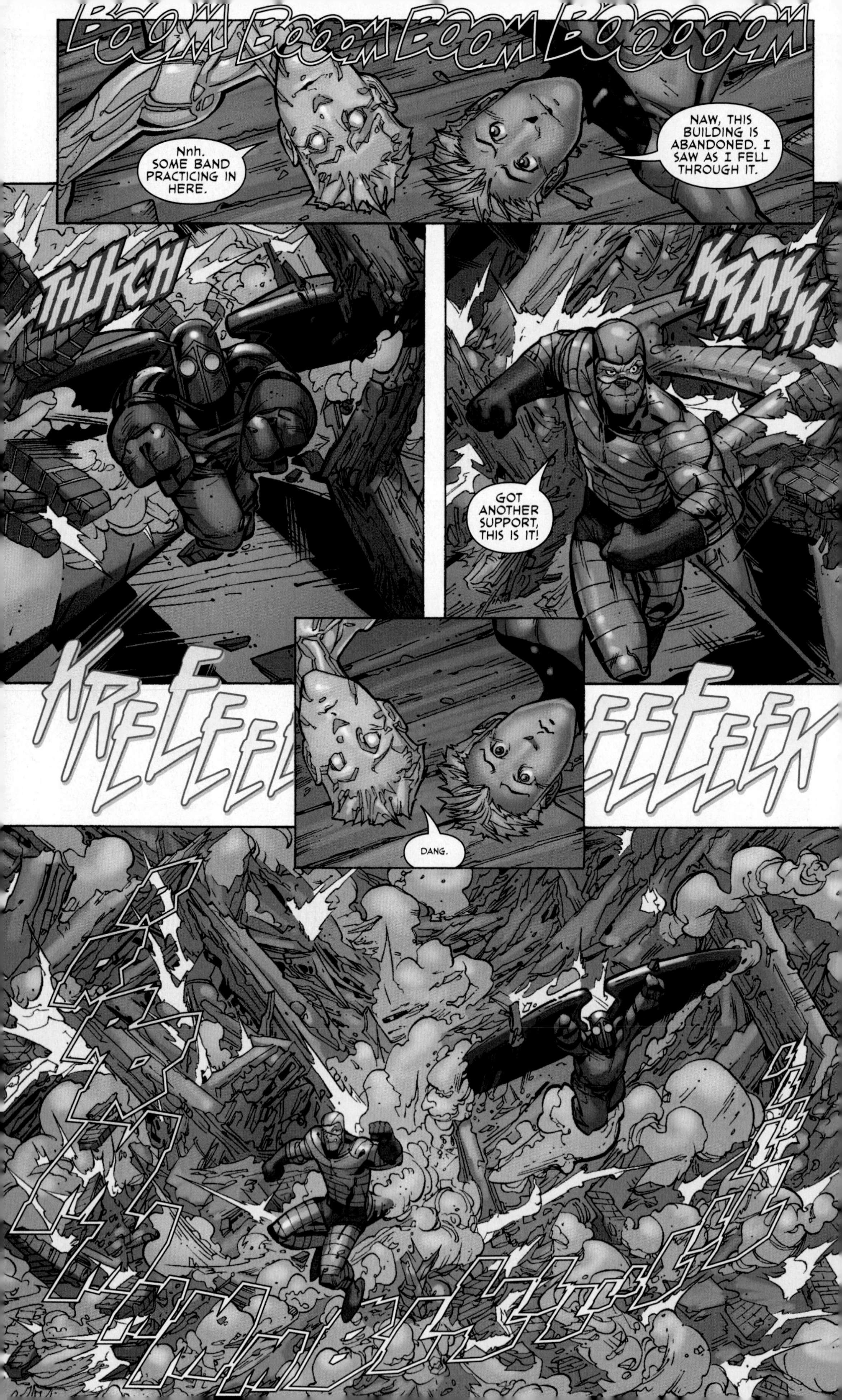

BOOM BOOOM BOOOM BOOOOOOM
Nnh. SOME BAND PRACTICING IN HERE.
NAW, THIS BUILDING IS ABANDONED. I SAW AS I FELL THROUGH IT.
THUTCH
KRAKK
GOT ANOTHER SUPPORT, THIS IS IT!
KREEEEEEEEEK
DANG.

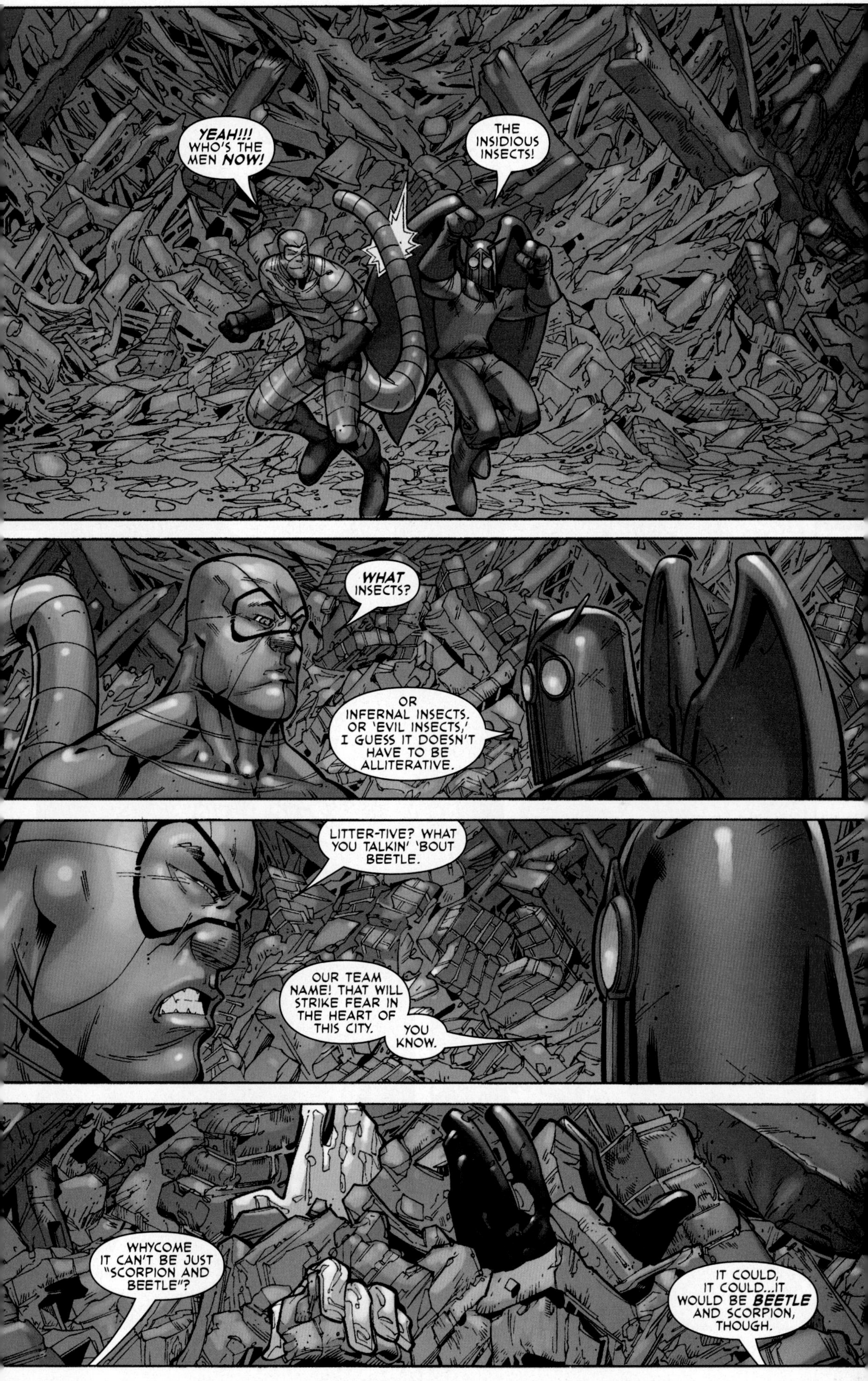
YEAH!!! WHO'S THE MEN NOW!
THE INSIDIOUS INSECTS!
WHAT INSECTS?
OR INFERNAL INSECTS. OR 'EVIL INSECTS,' I GUESS IT DOESN'T HAVE TO BE ALLITERATIVE.
LITTER-TIVE? WHAT YOU TALKIN' 'BOUT BEETLE.
OUR TEAM NAME! THAT WILL STRIKE FEAR IN THE HEART OF THIS CITY.
YOU KNOW.
WHYCOME IT CAN'T BE JUST "SCORPION AND BEETLE"?
IT COULD, IT COULD...IT WOULD BE BEETLE AND SCORPION, THOUGH.

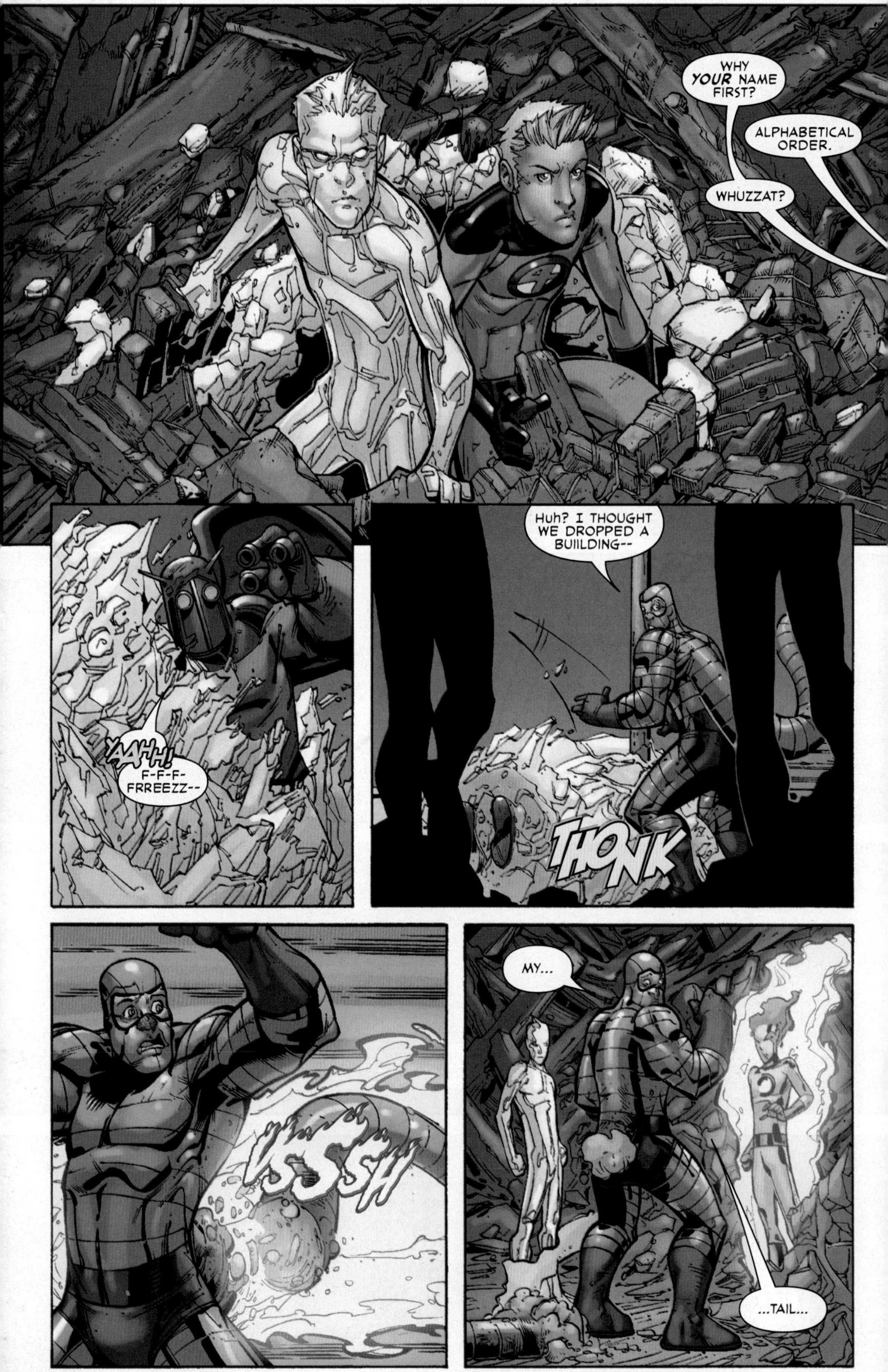
WHY YOUR NAME FIRST?
ALPHABETICAL ORDER.
WHUZZAT?
YAAHH! F-F-F-FRREEZZ--
Huh? I THOUGHT WE DROPPED A BUIILDING--
THONK
SSSH
MY...
...TAIL...

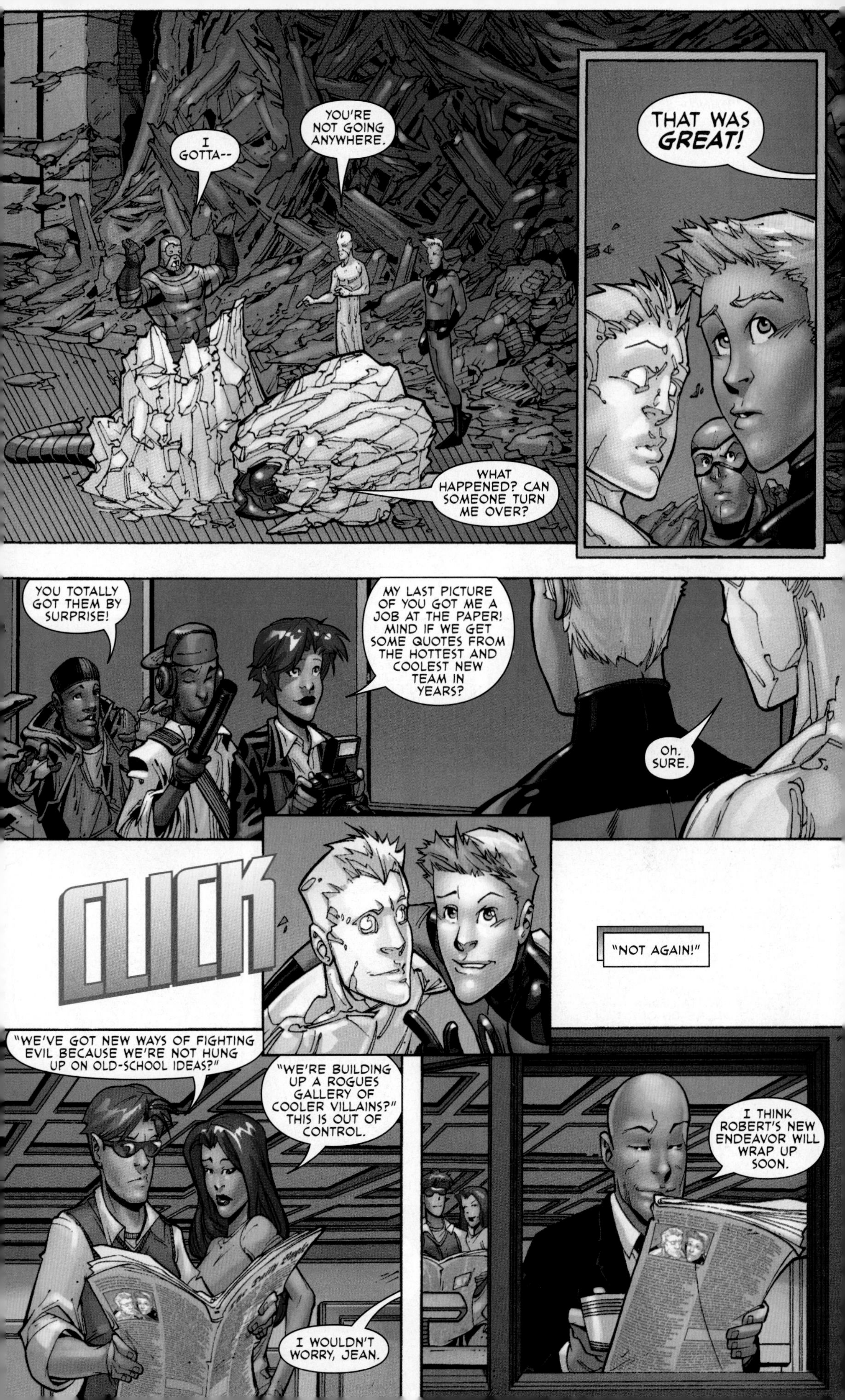
I GOTTA--
YOU'RE NOT GOING ANYWHERE.
WHAT HAPPENED? CAN SOMEONE TURN ME OVER?
THAT WAS *GREAT!*
YOU TOTALLY GOT THEM BY SURPRISE!
MY LAST PICTURE OF YOU GOT ME A JOB AT THE PAPER! MIND IF WE GET SOME QUOTES FROM THE HOTTEST AND COOLEST NEW TEAM IN YEARS?
Oh. SURE.
CLICK
"NOT AGAIN!"
"WE'VE GOT NEW WAYS OF FIGHTING EVIL BECAUSE WE'RE NOT HUNG UP ON OLD-SCHOOL IDEAS?"
"WE'RE BUILDING UP A ROGUES GALLERY OF COOLER VILLAINS?" THIS IS OUT OF CONTROL.
I WOULDN'T WORRY, JEAN.
I THINK ROBERT'S NEW ENDEAVOR WILL WRAP UP SOON.

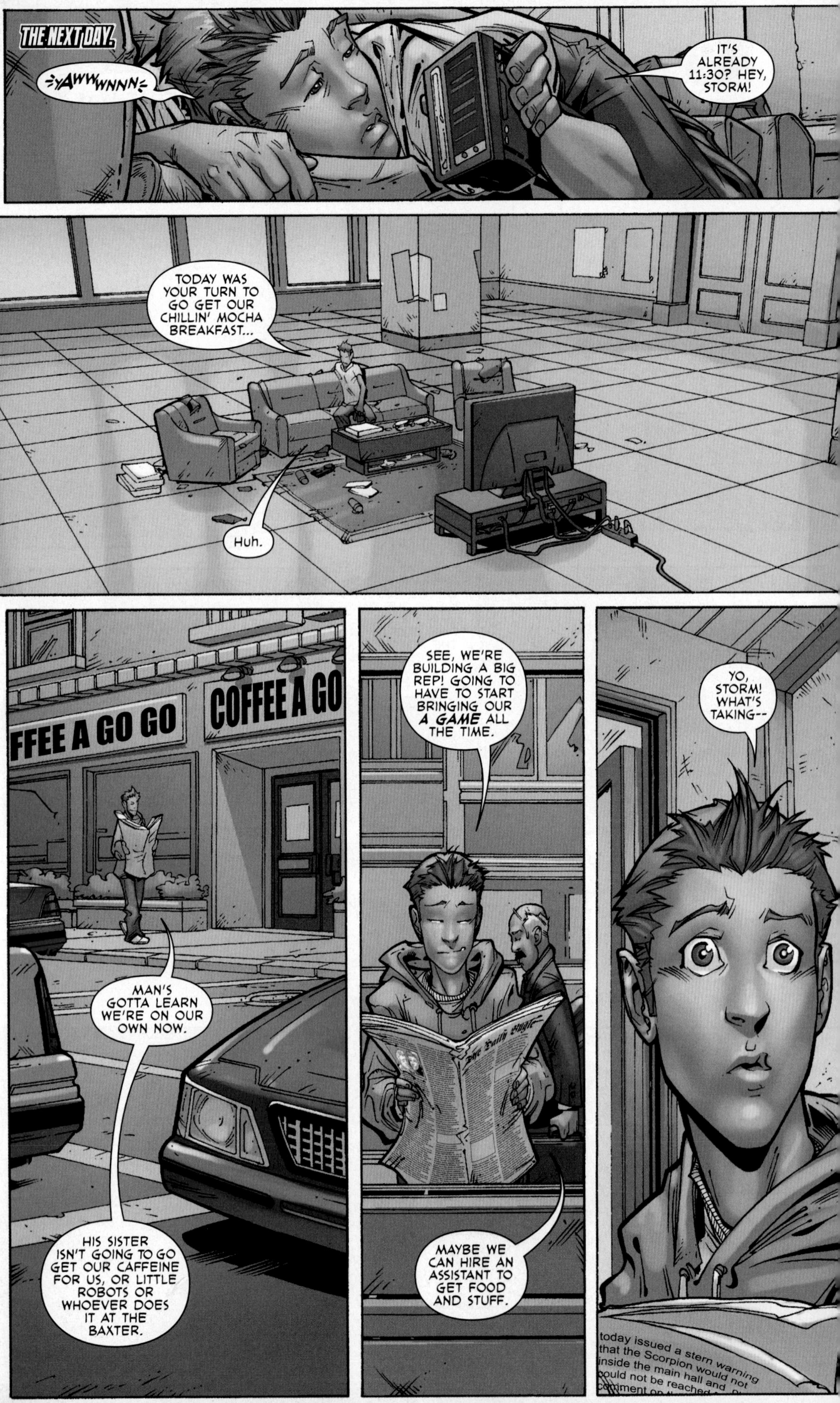
THE NEXT DAY.
YAWWWNNN
IT'S ALREADY 11:30? HEY, STORM!
TODAY WAS YOUR TURN TO GO GET OUR CHILLIN' MOCHA BREAKFAST...
Huh.
COFFEE A GO GO
FFEE A GO GO
MAN'S GOTTA LEARN WE'RE ON OUR OWN NOW.
HIS SISTER ISN'T GOING TO GO GET OUR CAFFEINE FOR US, OR LITTLE ROBOTS OR WHOEVER DOES IT AT THE BAXTER.
SEE, WE'RE BUILDING A BIG REP! GOING TO HAVE TO START BRINGING OUR *A GAME* ALL THE TIME.
MAYBE WE CAN HIRE AN ASSISTANT TO GET FOOD AND STUFF.
YO, STORM! WHAT'S TAKING--
today issued a stern warning
that the Scorpion would not
inside the main hall and

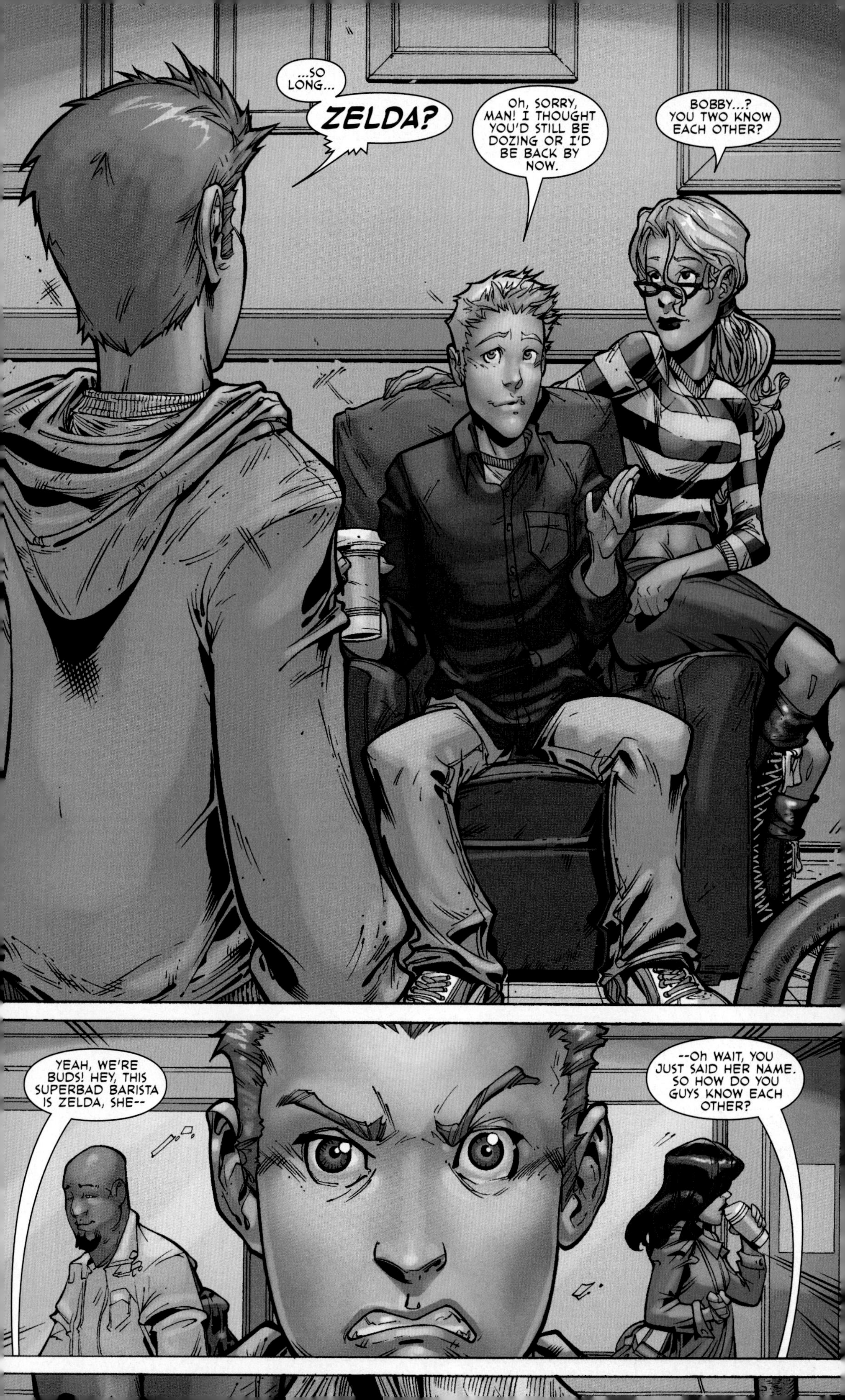
...SO LONG...
ZELDA?
Oh, SORRY, MAN! I THOUGHT YOU'D STILL BE DOZING OR I'D BE BACK BY NOW.
BOBBY...? YOU TWO KNOW EACH OTHER?
YEAH, WE'RE BUDS! HEY, THIS SUPERBAD BARISTA IS ZELDA, SHE--
--Oh WAIT, YOU JUST SAID HER NAME. SO HOW DO YOU GUYS KNOW EACH OTHER?

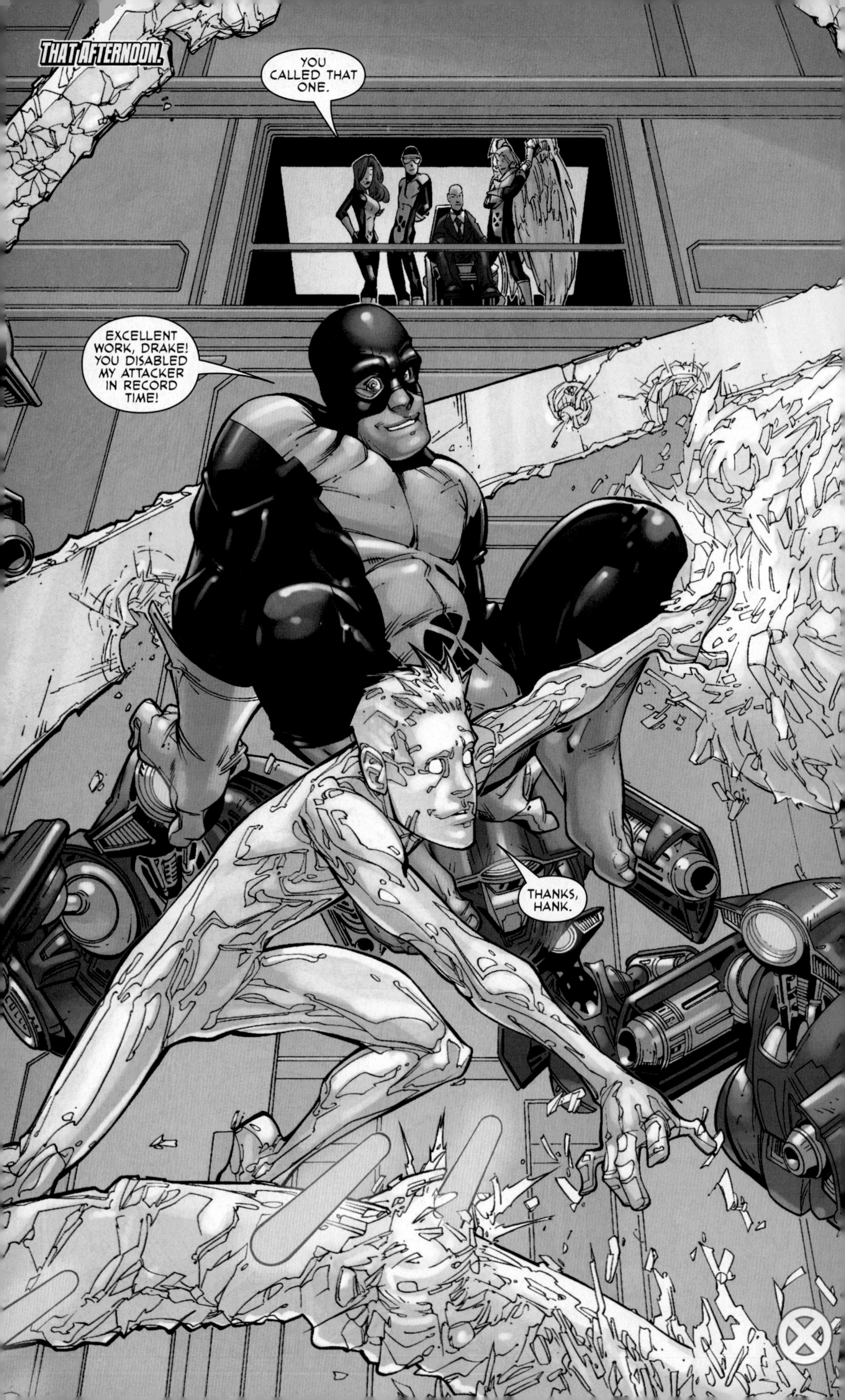
THAT AFTERNOON.
YOU CALLED THAT ONE.
EXCELLENT WORK, DRAKE! YOU DISABLED MY ATTACKER IN RECORD TIME!
THANKS, HANK.

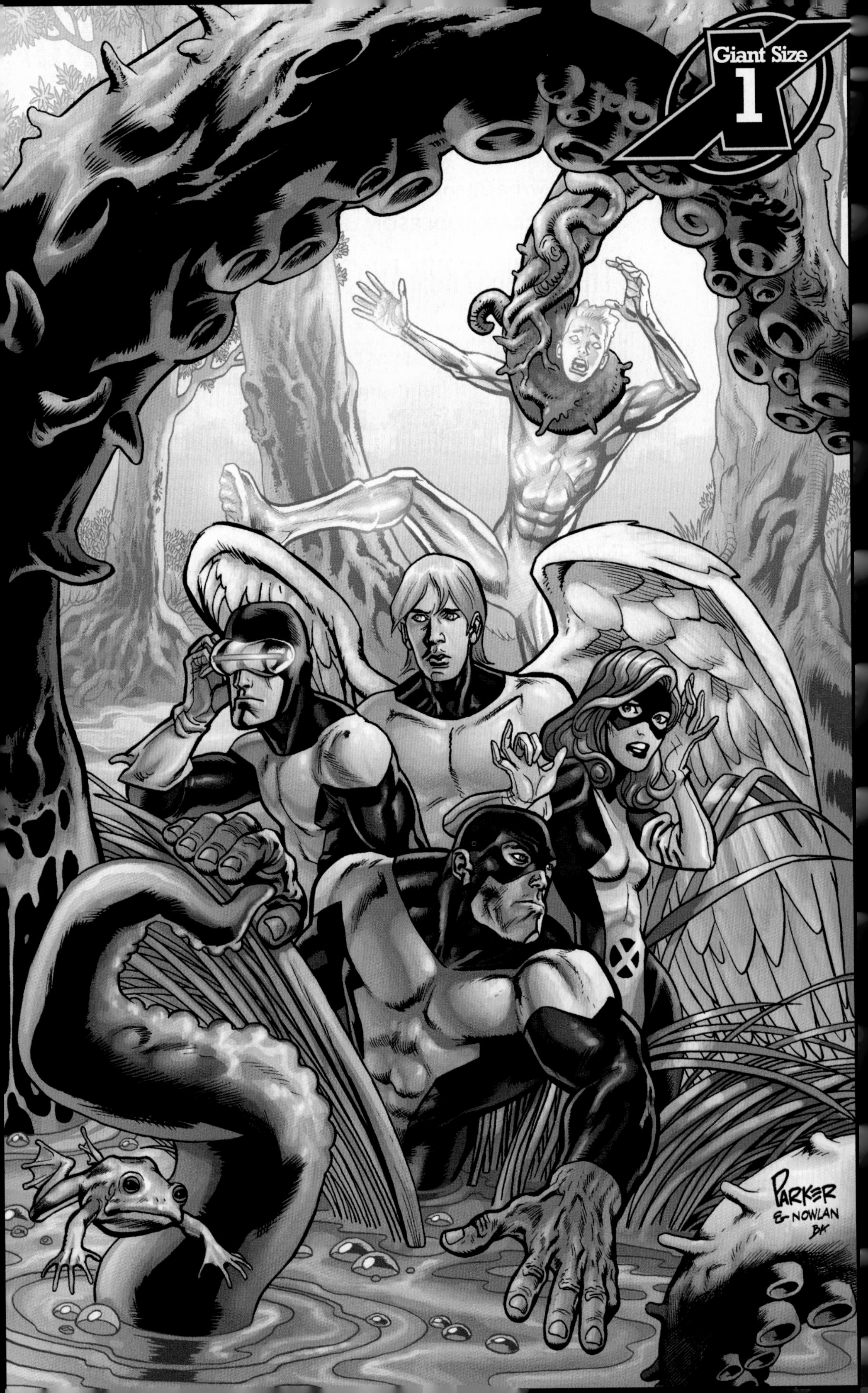
Giant Size
1
PARKER
& NOWLAN

CHILLING FEATURES FROM BEYOND!

COVER/OPENING & CLOSING CREDITS

JEFF PARKER writer/penciler   **KEVIN NOWLAN** inker

BRAD ANDERSON colorist

THE THING (FROM ANOTHER AISLE)

JEFF PARKER writer   **DEAN HASPIEL** artist

MICHAEL CAVALLARO colorist

ALUMNI

DAVID WILLIAMS artist   **TIM TOWNSEND** inker

VAL STAPLES colorist

INVASION OF THE BOBBY SNATCHERS

JEFF PARKER writer   **NICK KILISLIAN** penciler

CHRIS SOTOMAYOR colorist

VIGIL OF THE MAD

ROGER LANGRIDGE writer/artist

THE DAY THE EARTH JUST WOULD NOT STAND STILL

JEFF PARKER writer   **MICHAEL CHO** artist

BLAMBOT'S NATE PIEKOS letterer   **NATHAN COSBY** editor
IRENE LEE production   **JOE QUESADA** editor in chief
MARK PANICCIA & RALPH MACCHIO consulting   **DAN BUCKLEY** publisher

THE MARK OF THE MONSTER – Classic Feature!

ROY THOMAS writer   **DON HECK** penciler
GEORGE TUSKA inker   **ARTIE SIMEK** letterer   **STAN LEE** editor

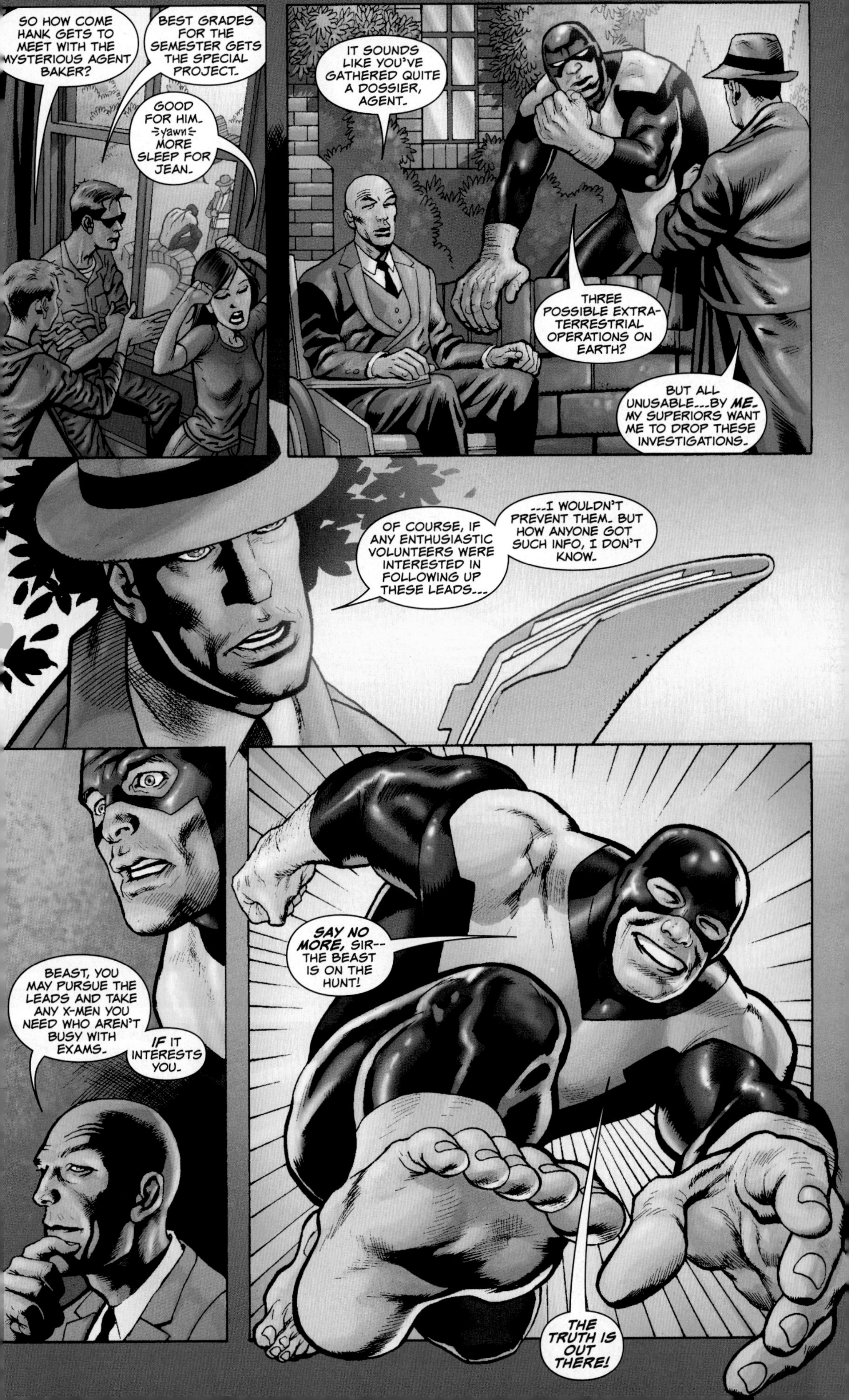
SO HOW COME HANK GETS TO MEET WITH THE MYSTERIOUS AGENT BAKER?
BEST GRADES FOR THE SEMESTER GETS THE SPECIAL PROJECT.
GOOD FOR HIM. *yawn* MORE SLEEP FOR JEAN.
IT SOUNDS LIKE YOU'VE GATHERED QUITE A DOSSIER, AGENT.
THREE POSSIBLE EXTRA-TERRESTRIAL OPERATIONS ON EARTH?
BUT ALL UNUSABLE...BY ***ME***. MY SUPERIORS WANT ME TO DROP THESE INVESTIGATIONS.
OF COURSE, IF ANY ENTHUSIASTIC VOLUNTEERS WERE INTERESTED IN FOLLOWING UP THESE LEADS...
...I WOULDN'T PREVENT THEM. BUT HOW ANYONE GOT SUCH INFO, I DON'T KNOW.
BEAST, YOU MAY PURSUE THE LEADS AND TAKE ANY X-MEN YOU NEED WHO AREN'T BUSY WITH EXAMS.
IF IT INTERESTS YOU.
SAY NO MORE, SIR-- THE BEAST IS ON THE HUNT!
THE TRUTH IS OUT THERE!

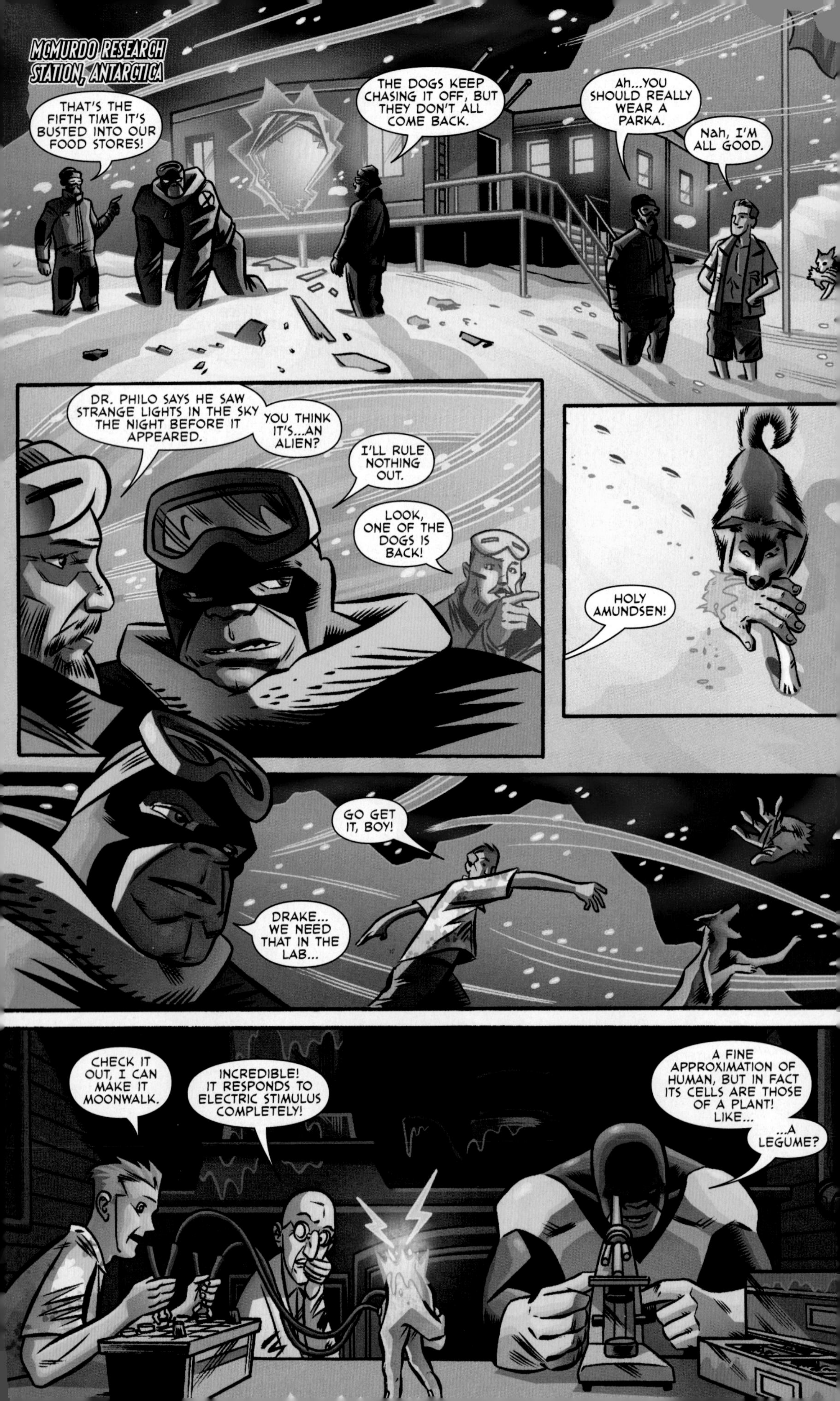

McMURDO RESEARCH STATION, ANTARCTICA
THAT'S THE FIFTH TIME IT'S BUSTED INTO OUR FOOD STORES!
THE DOGS KEEP CHASING IT OFF, BUT THEY DON'T ALL COME BACK.
Ah...YOU SHOULD REALLY WEAR A PARKA.
Nah, I'M ALL GOOD.
DR. PHILO SAYS HE SAW STRANGE LIGHTS IN THE SKY THE NIGHT BEFORE IT APPEARED.
YOU THINK IT'S...AN ALIEN?
I'LL RULE NOTHING OUT.
LOOK, ONE OF THE DOGS IS BACK!
HOLY AMUNDSEN!
GO GET IT, BOY!
DRAKE... WE NEED THAT IN THE LAB...
CHECK IT OUT, I CAN MAKE IT MOONWALK.
INCREDIBLE! IT RESPONDS TO ELECTRIC STIMULUS COMPLETELY!
A FINE APPROXIMATION OF HUMAN, BUT IN FACT ITS CELLS ARE THOSE OF A PLANT! LIKE...
...A LEGUME?

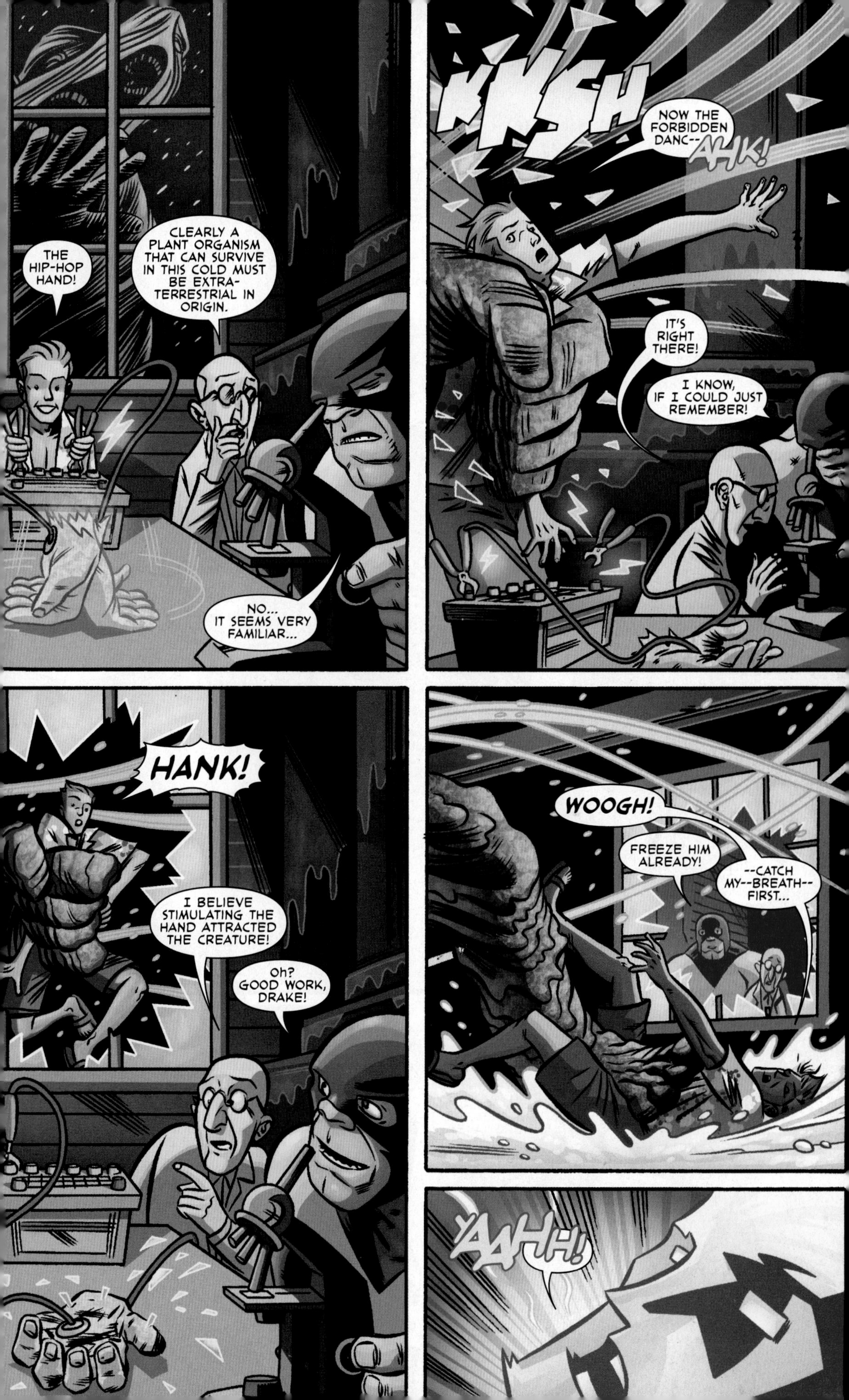
THE HIP-HOP HAND!
CLEARLY A PLANT ORGANISM THAT CAN SURVIVE IN THIS COLD MUST BE EXTRA-TERRESTRIAL IN ORIGIN.
NO... IT SEEMS VERY FAMILIAR...
KRSH
NOW THE FORBIDDEN DANC--AHK!
IT'S RIGHT THERE!
I KNOW, IF I COULD JUST REMEMBER!
HANK!
I BELIEVE STIMULATING THE HAND ATTRACTED THE CREATURE!
Oh? GOOD WORK, DRAKE!
WOOGH!
FREEZE HIM ALREADY!
--CATCH MY--BREATH--FIRST...
YAAHH!

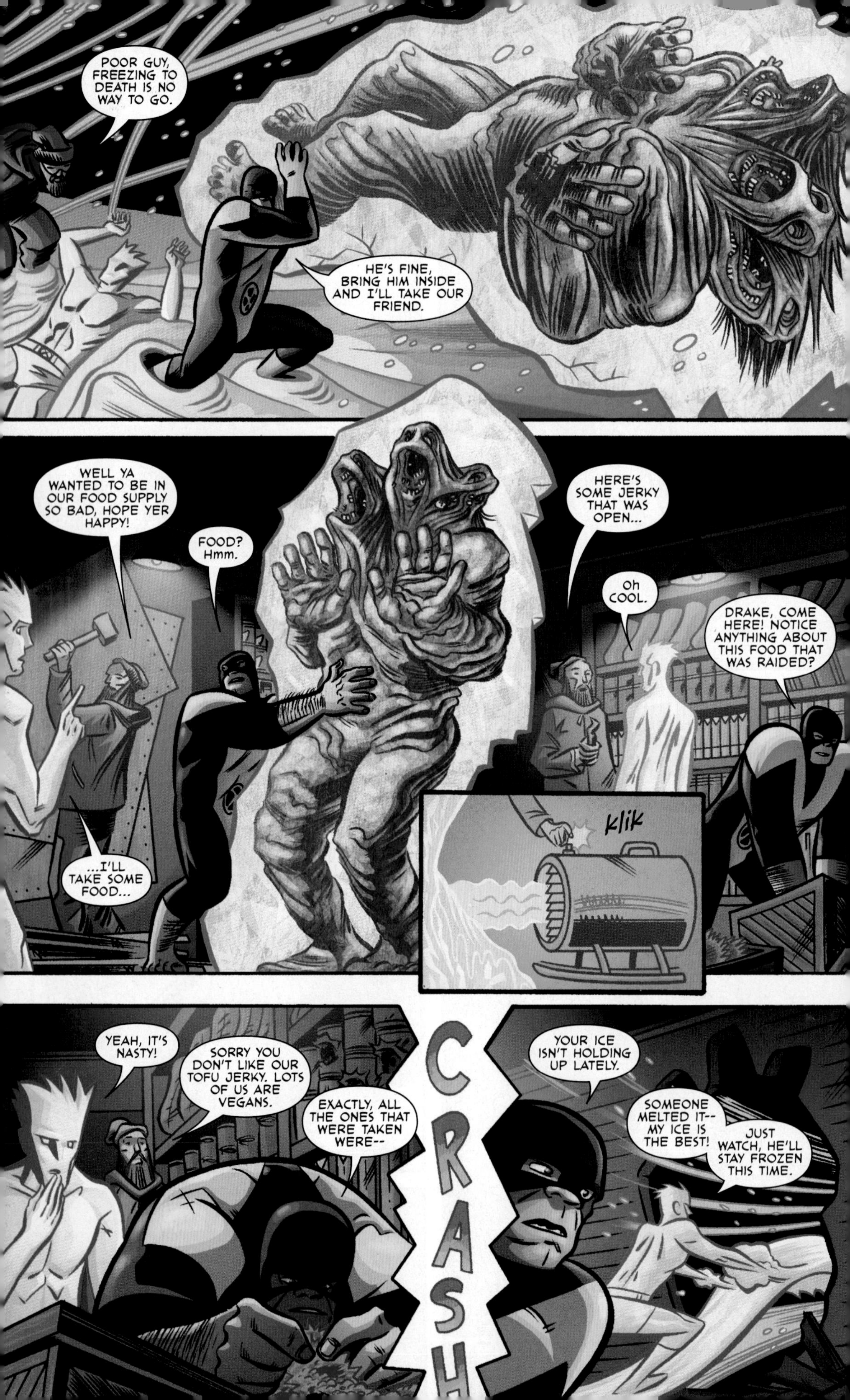
POOR GUY, FREEZING TO DEATH IS NO WAY TO GO.
HE'S FINE, BRING HIM INSIDE AND I'LL TAKE OUR FRIEND.
WELL YA WANTED TO BE IN OUR FOOD SUPPLY SO BAD, HOPE YER HAPPY!
FOOD? Hmm.
...I'LL TAKE SOME FOOD...
HERE'S SOME JERKY THAT WAS OPEN...
Oh COOL.
DRAKE, COME HERE! NOTICE ANYTHING ABOUT THIS FOOD THAT WAS RAIDED?
klik
YEAH, IT'S NASTY!
SORRY YOU DON'T LIKE OUR TOFU JERKY. LOTS OF US ARE VEGANS.
EXACTLY, ALL THE ONES THAT WERE TAKEN WERE--
CRASH
YOUR ICE ISN'T HOLDING UP LATELY.
SOMEONE MELTED IT-- MY ICE IS THE BEST!
JUST WATCH, HE'LL STAY FROZEN THIS TIME.

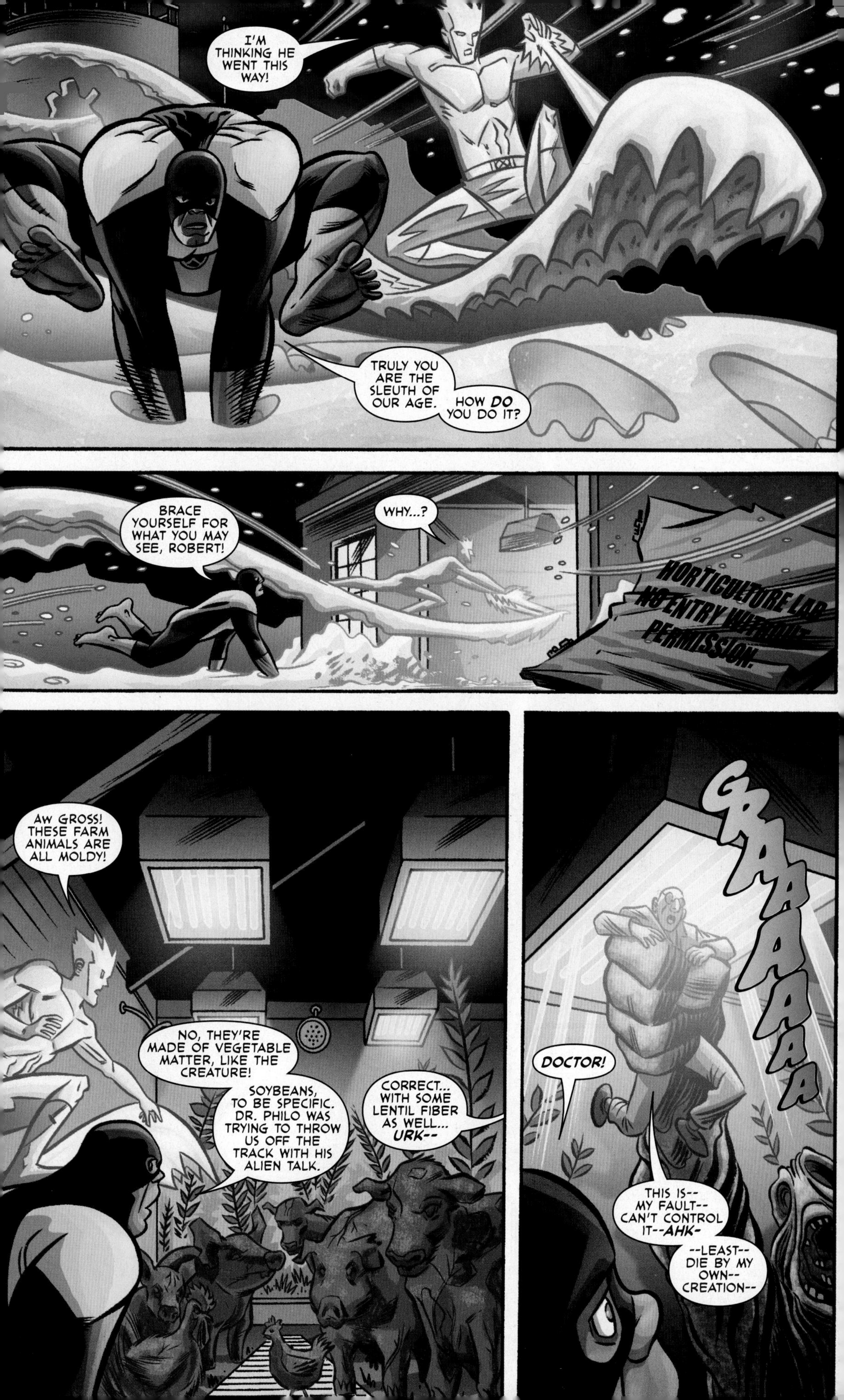
I'M THINKING HE WENT THIS WAY!
TRULY YOU ARE THE SLEUTH OF OUR AGE.
HOW *DO* YOU DO IT?
BRACE YOURSELF FOR WHAT YOU MAY SEE, ROBERT!
WHY...?
HORTICULTURE LAB NO ENTRY WITHOUT PERMISSION.
AW GROSS! THESE FARM ANIMALS ARE ALL MOLDY!
NO, THEY'RE MADE OF VEGETABLE MATTER, LIKE THE CREATURE!
SOYBEANS, TO BE SPECIFIC. DR. PHILO WAS TRYING TO THROW US OFF THE TRACK WITH HIS ALIEN TALK.
CORRECT... WITH SOME LENTIL FIBER AS WELL... *URK--*
GAAAAAAAAA
DOCTOR!
THIS IS-- MY FAULT-- CAN'T CONTROL IT--*AHK-*
--LEAST-- DIE BY MY OWN-- CREATION--

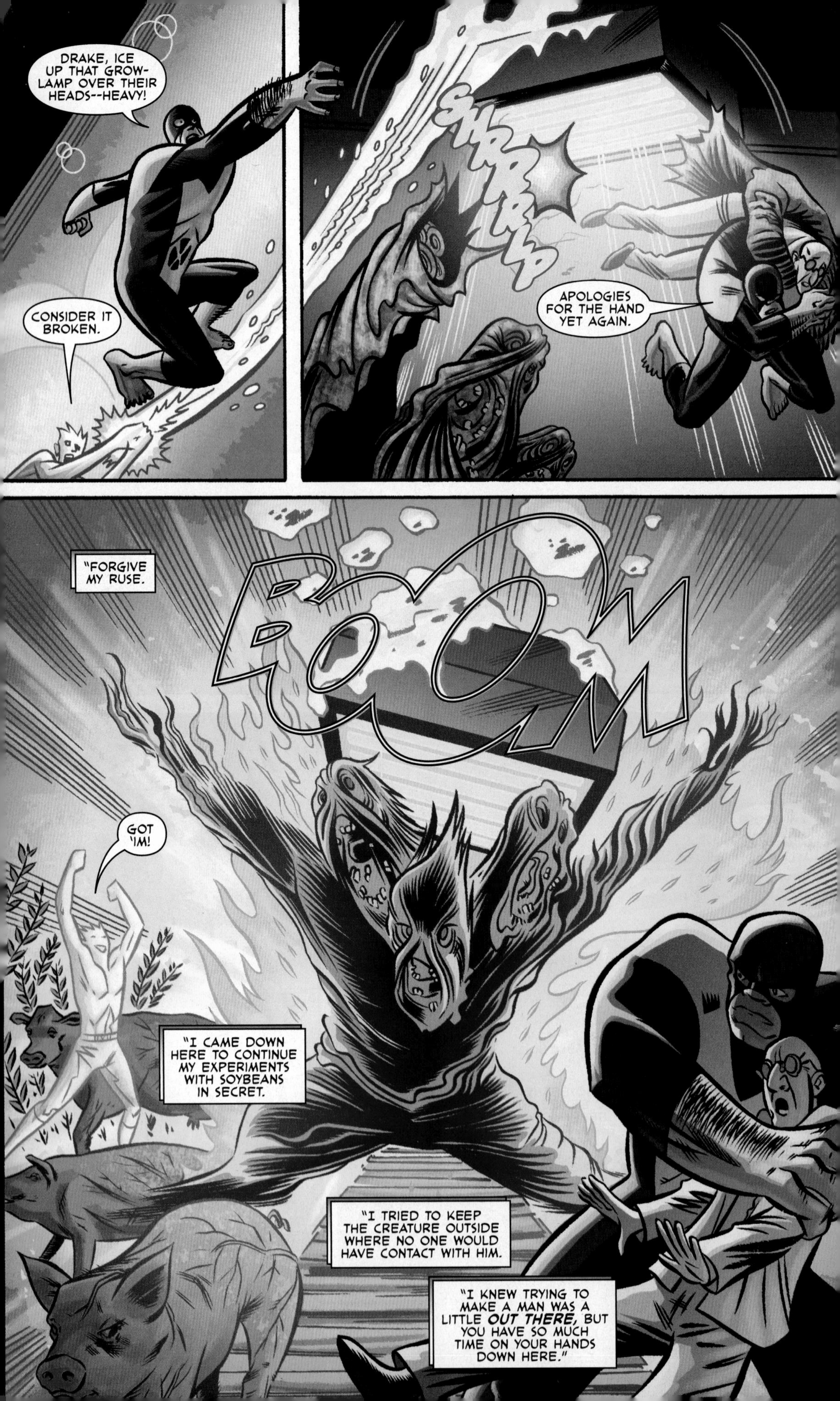

DRAKE, ICE UP THAT GROW-LAMP OVER THEIR HEADS--HEAVY!
CONSIDER IT BROKEN.
SHRRRIP
APOLOGIES FOR THE HAND YET AGAIN.
"FORGIVE MY RUSE.
BOOM
GOT 'IM!
"I CAME DOWN HERE TO CONTINUE MY EXPERIMENTS WITH SOYBEANS IN SECRET.
"I TRIED TO KEEP THE CREATURE OUTSIDE WHERE NO ONE WOULD HAVE CONTACT WITH HIM.
"I KNEW TRYING TO MAKE A MAN WAS A LITTLE ***OUT THERE,*** BUT YOU HAVE SO MUCH TIME ON YOUR HANDS DOWN HERE."

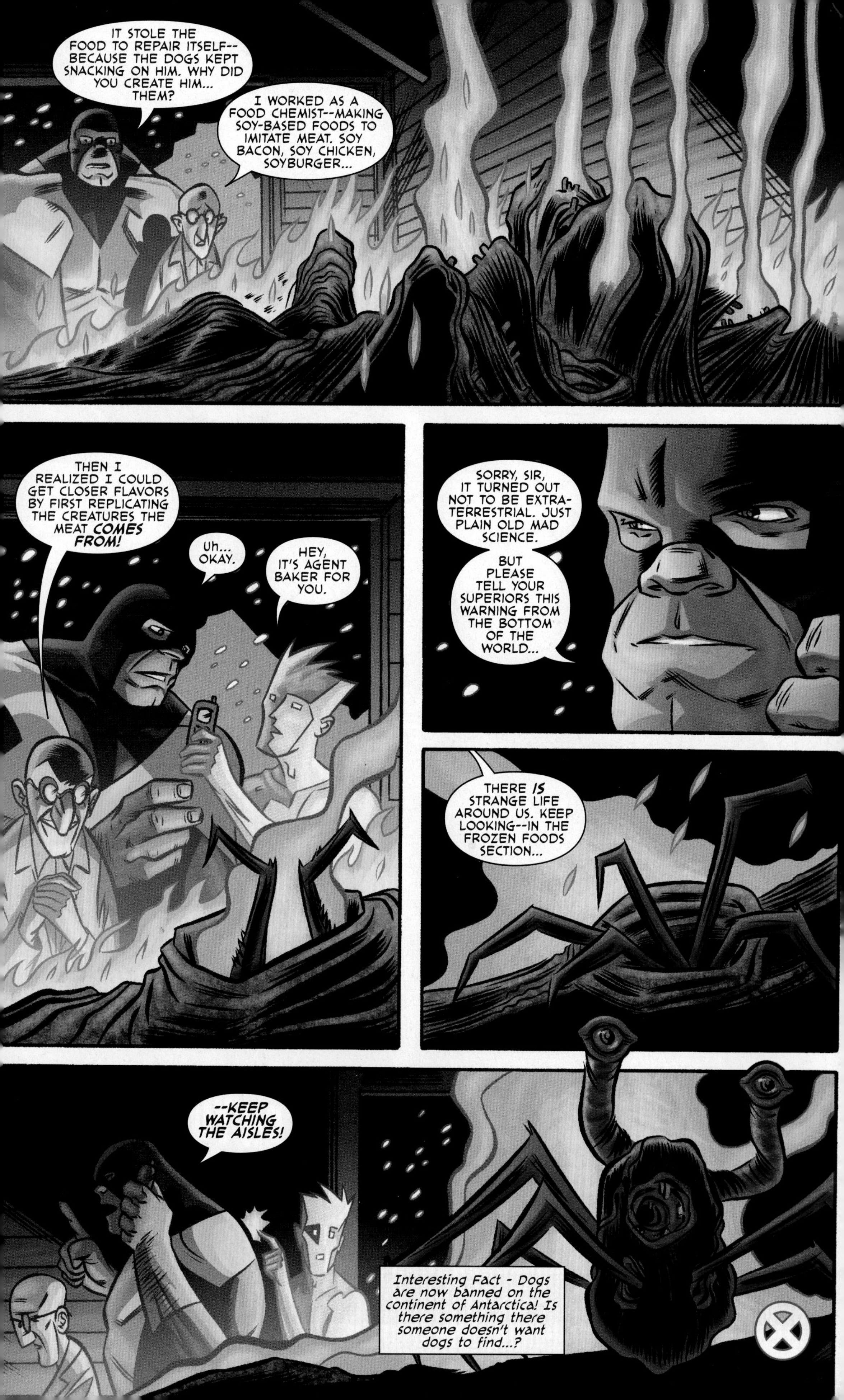
IT STOLE THE FOOD TO REPAIR ITSELF-- BECAUSE THE DOGS KEPT SNACKING ON HIM. WHY DID YOU CREATE HIM... THEM?
I WORKED AS A FOOD CHEMIST--MAKING SOY-BASED FOODS TO IMITATE MEAT. SOY BACON, SOY CHICKEN, SOYBURGER...
THEN I REALIZED I COULD GET CLOSER FLAVORS BY FIRST REPLICATING THE CREATURES THE MEAT COMES FROM!
Uh... OKAY.
HEY, IT'S AGENT BAKER FOR YOU.
SORRY, SIR, IT TURNED OUT NOT TO BE EXTRA-TERRESTRIAL. JUST PLAIN OLD MAD SCIENCE.
BUT PLEASE TELL YOUR SUPERIORS THIS WARNING FROM THE BOTTOM OF THE WORLD...
THERE IS STRANGE LIFE AROUND US. KEEP LOOKING--IN THE FROZEN FOODS SECTION...
--KEEP WATCHING THE AISLES!
Interesting Fact - Dogs are now banned on the continent of Antarctica! Is there something there someone doesn't want dogs to find...?

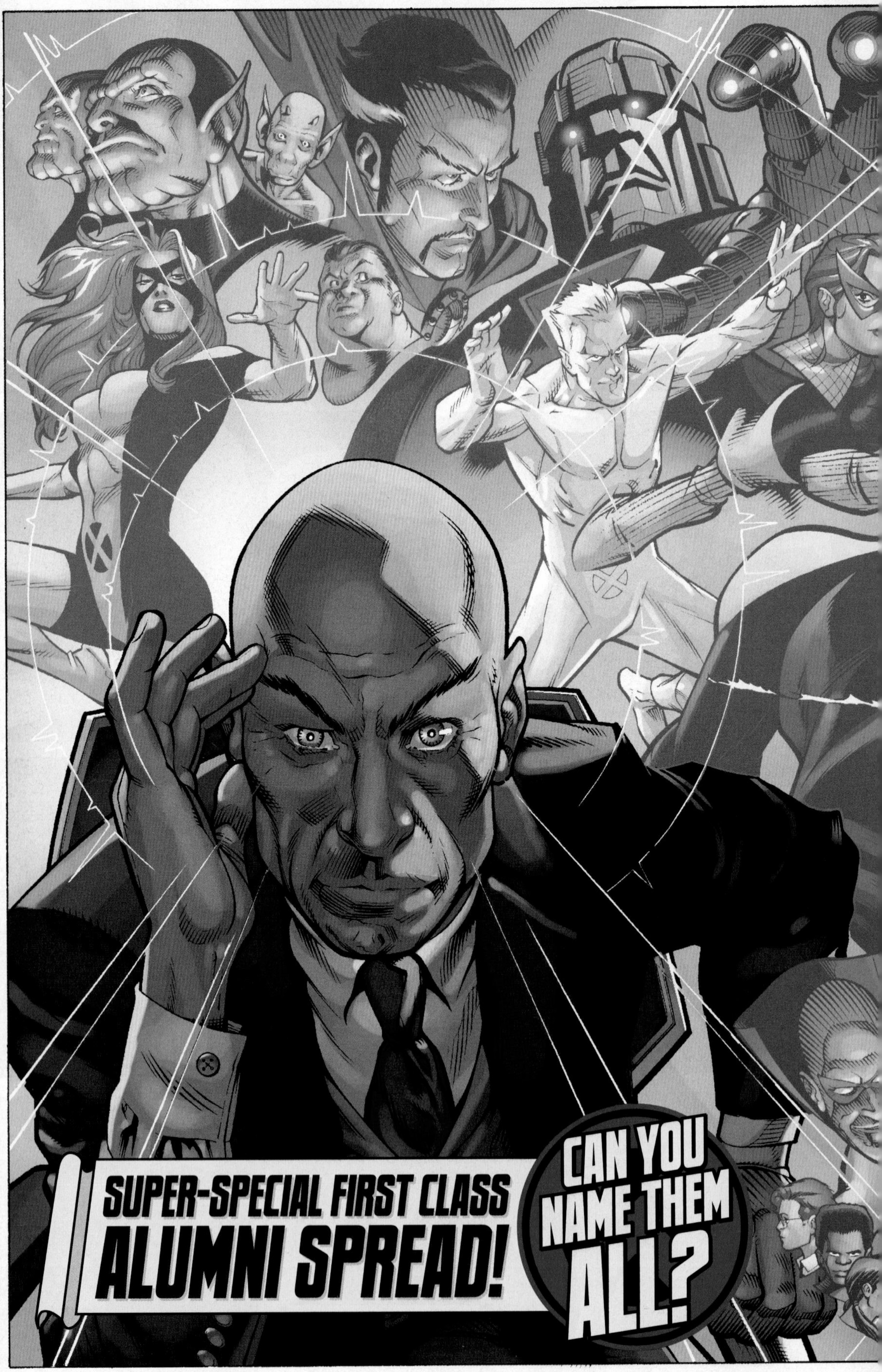

SUPER-SPECIAL FIRST CLASS
ALUMNI SPREAD!
CAN YOU NAME THEM ALL?

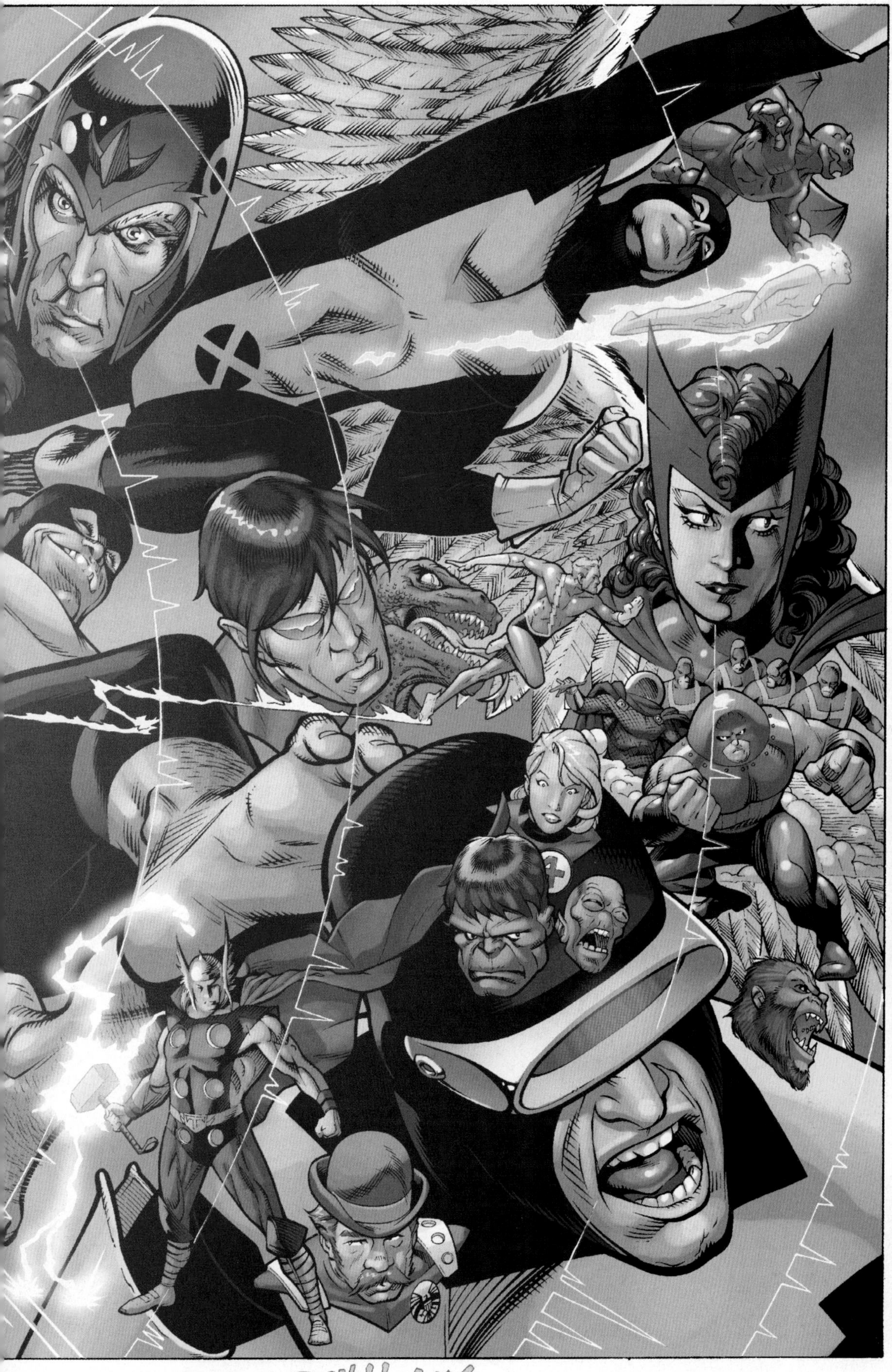

D. WILLIAMS. TOWNSEND

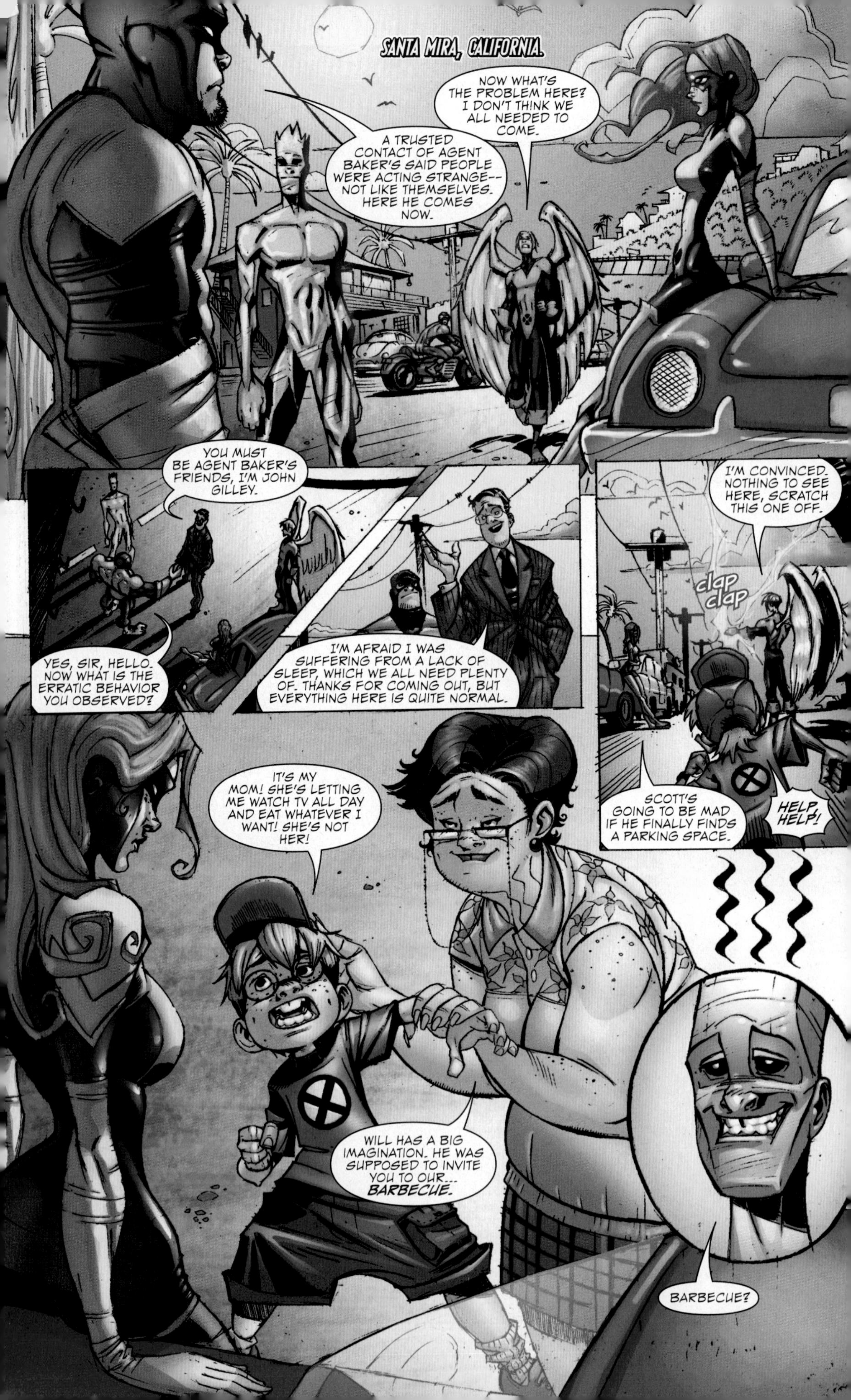
SANTA MIRA, CALIFORNIA.
NOW WHAT'S THE PROBLEM HERE? I DON'T THINK WE ALL NEEDED TO COME.
A TRUSTED CONTACT OF AGENT BAKER'S SAID PEOPLE WERE ACTING STRANGE--NOT LIKE THEMSELVES. HERE HE COMES NOW.
YOU MUST BE AGENT BAKER'S FRIENDS, I'M JOHN GILLEY.
YES, SIR, HELLO. NOW WHAT IS THE ERRATIC BEHAVIOR YOU OBSERVED?
I'M AFRAID I WAS SUFFERING FROM A LACK OF SLEEP, WHICH WE ALL NEED PLENTY OF. THANKS FOR COMING OUT, BUT EVERYTHING HERE IS QUITE NORMAL.
I'M CONVINCED. NOTHING TO SEE HERE, SCRATCH THIS ONE OFF.
clap clap
SCOTT'S GOING TO BE MAD IF HE FINALLY FINDS A PARKING SPACE.
HELP, HELP!
IT'S MY MOM! SHE'S LETTING ME WATCH TV ALL DAY AND EAT WHATEVER I WANT! SHE'S NOT HER!
WILL HAS A BIG IMAGINATION. HE WAS SUPPOSED TO INVITE YOU TO OUR... BARBECUE.
BARBECUE?

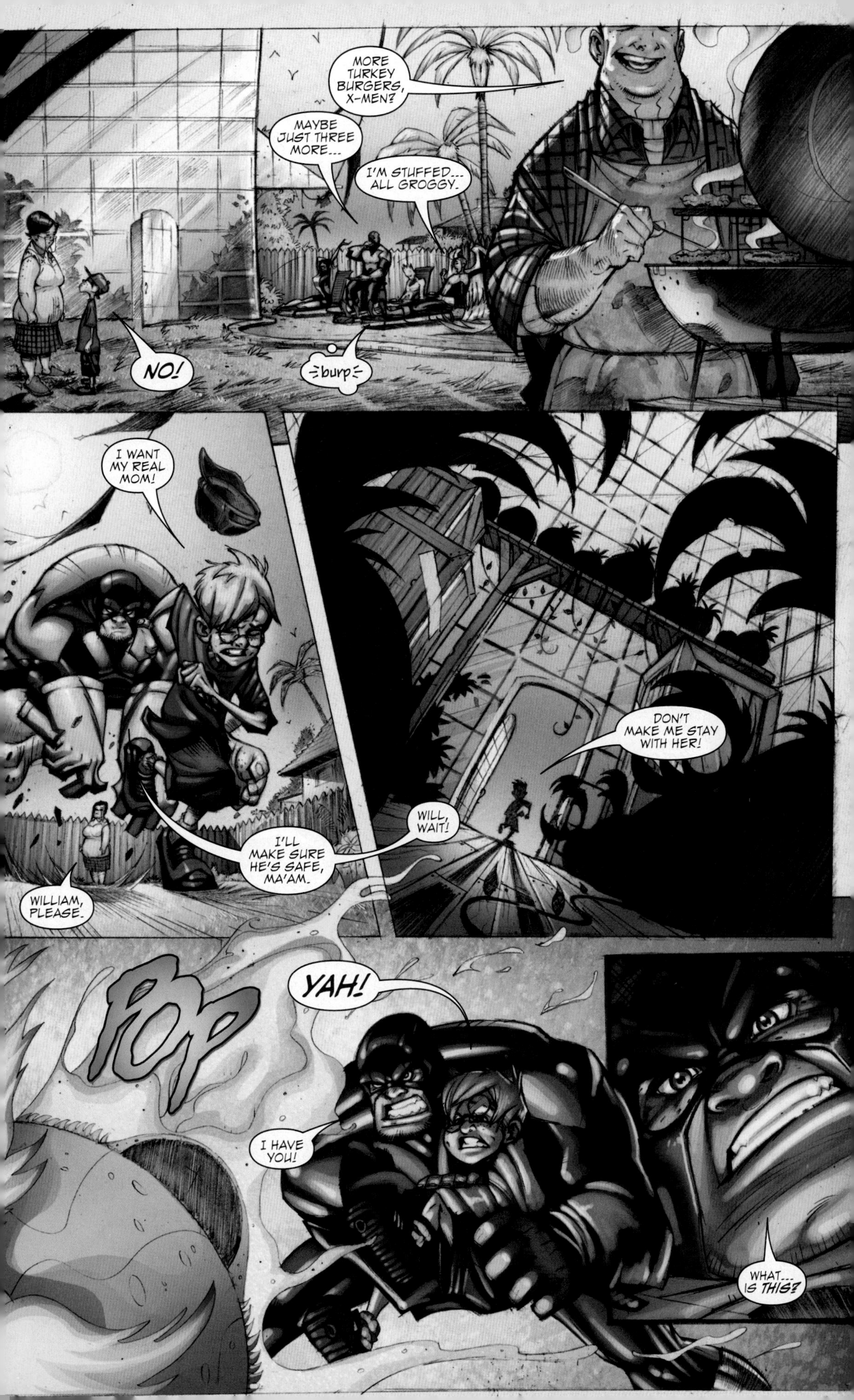
MORE TURKEY BURGERS, X-MEN?
MAYBE JUST THREE MORE...
I'M STUFFED... ALL GROGGY.
NO!
burp
I WANT MY REAL MOM!
DON'T MAKE ME STAY WITH HER!
WILL, WAIT!
I'LL MAKE SURE HE'S SAFE, MA'AM.
WILLIAM, PLEASE.
POP
YAH!
I HAVE YOU!
WHAT... IS THIS?

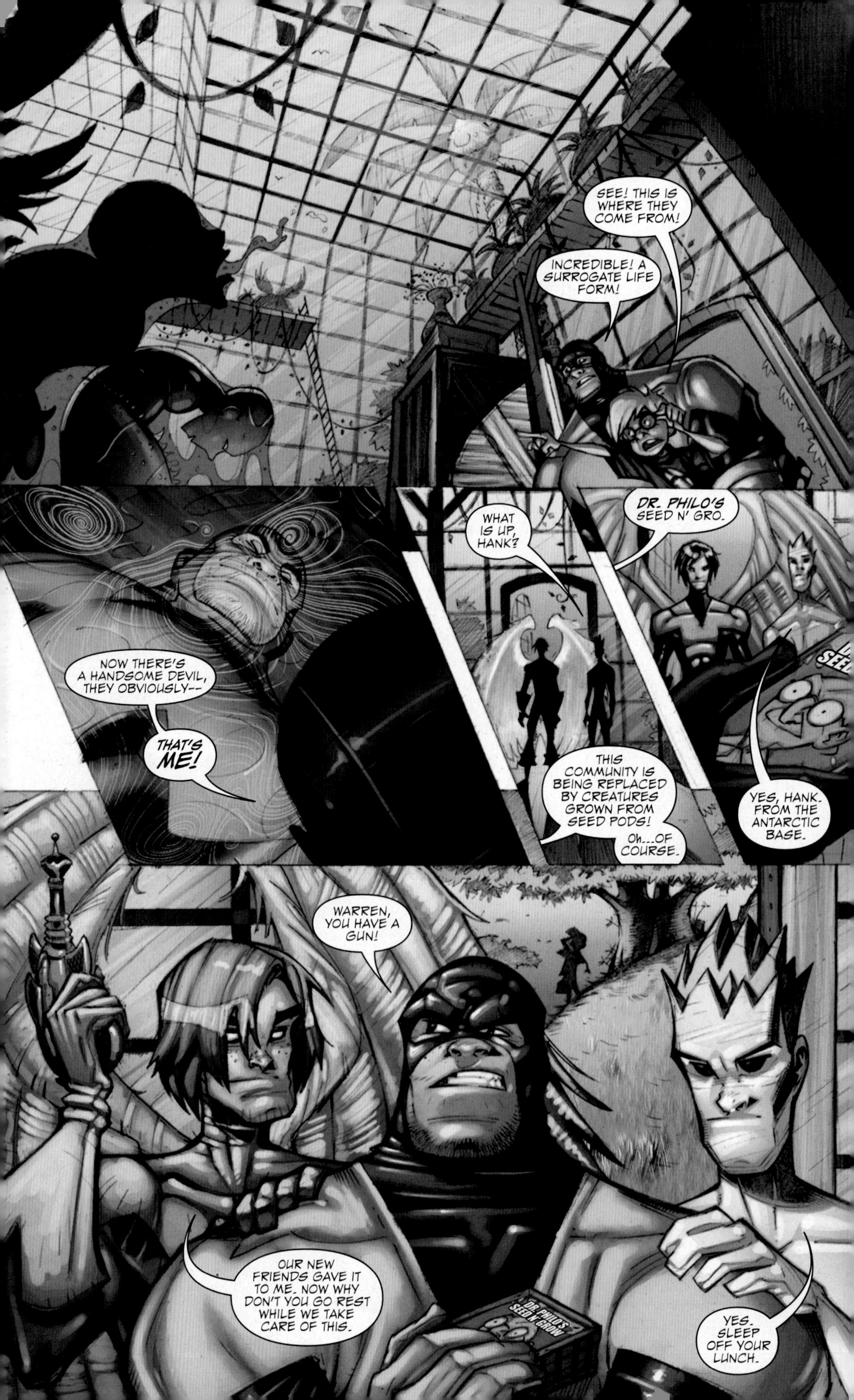
SEE! THIS IS WHERE THEY COME FROM!
INCREDIBLE! A SURROGATE LIFE FORM!
NOW THERE'S A HANDSOME DEVIL, THEY OBVIOUSLY--
THAT'S ME!
WHAT IS UP, HANK?
THIS COMMUNITY IS BEING REPLACED BY CREATURES GROWN FROM SEED PODS!
Oh...OF COURSE.
DR. PHILO'S SEED N' GRO.
YES, HANK. FROM THE ANTARCTIC BASE.
WARREN, YOU HAVE A GUN!
OUR NEW FRIENDS GAVE IT TO ME. NOW WHY DON'T YOU GO REST WHILE WE TAKE CARE OF THIS.
DR. PHILO'S SEED N' GROW
YES. SLEEP OFF YOUR LUNCH.

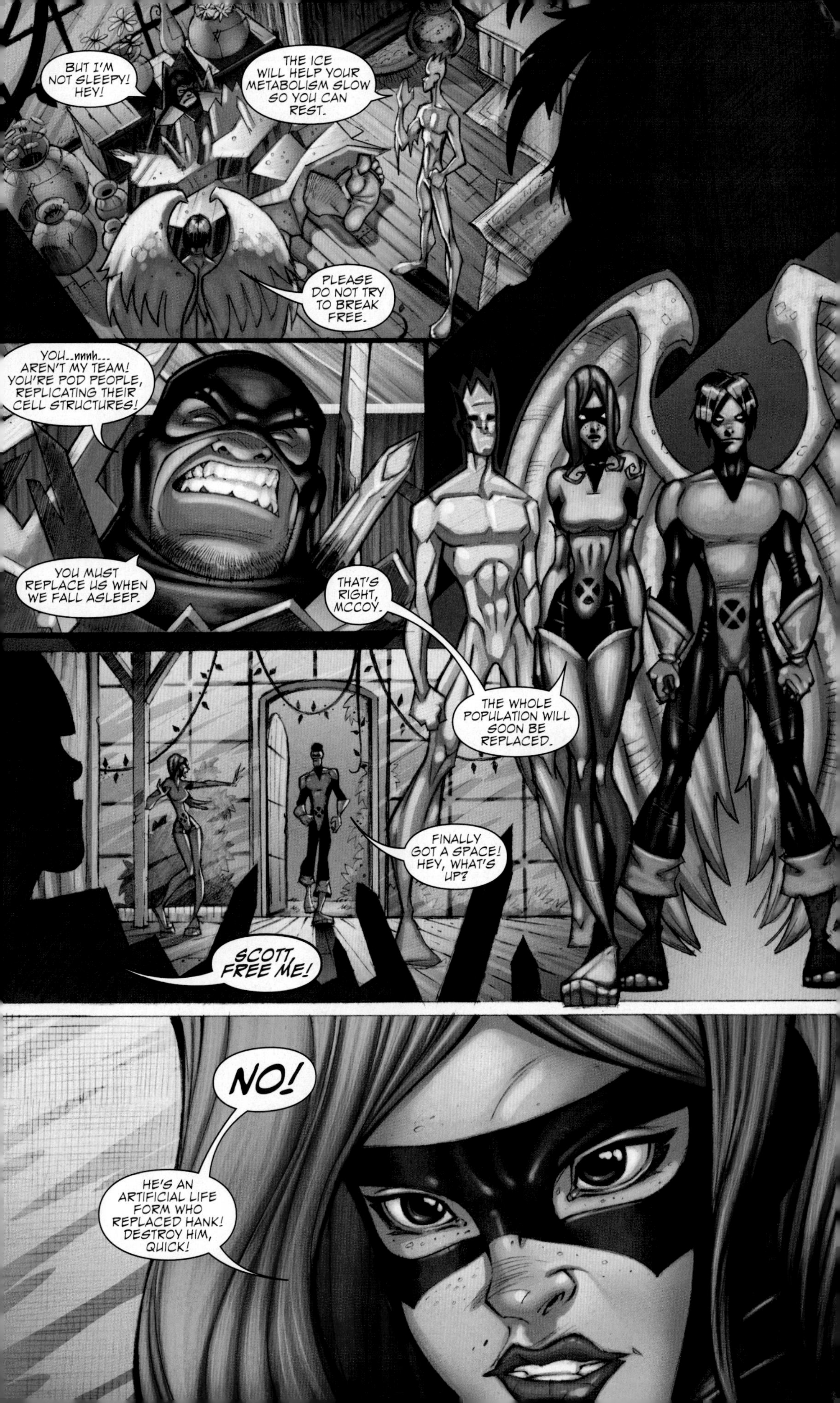
BUT I'M NOT SLEEPY! HEY!
THE ICE WILL HELP YOUR METABOLISM SLOW SO YOU CAN REST.
PLEASE DO NOT TRY TO BREAK FREE.
YOU...nnnh... AREN'T MY TEAM! YOU'RE POD PEOPLE, REPLICATING THEIR CELL STRUCTURES!
YOU MUST REPLACE US WHEN WE FALL ASLEEP.
THAT'S RIGHT, MCCOY.
THE WHOLE POPULATION WILL SOON BE REPLACED.
FINALLY GOT A SPACE! HEY, WHAT'S UP?
SCOTT, FREE ME!
NO!
HE'S AN ARTIFICIAL LIFE FORM WHO REPLACED HANK! DESTROY HIM, QUICK!

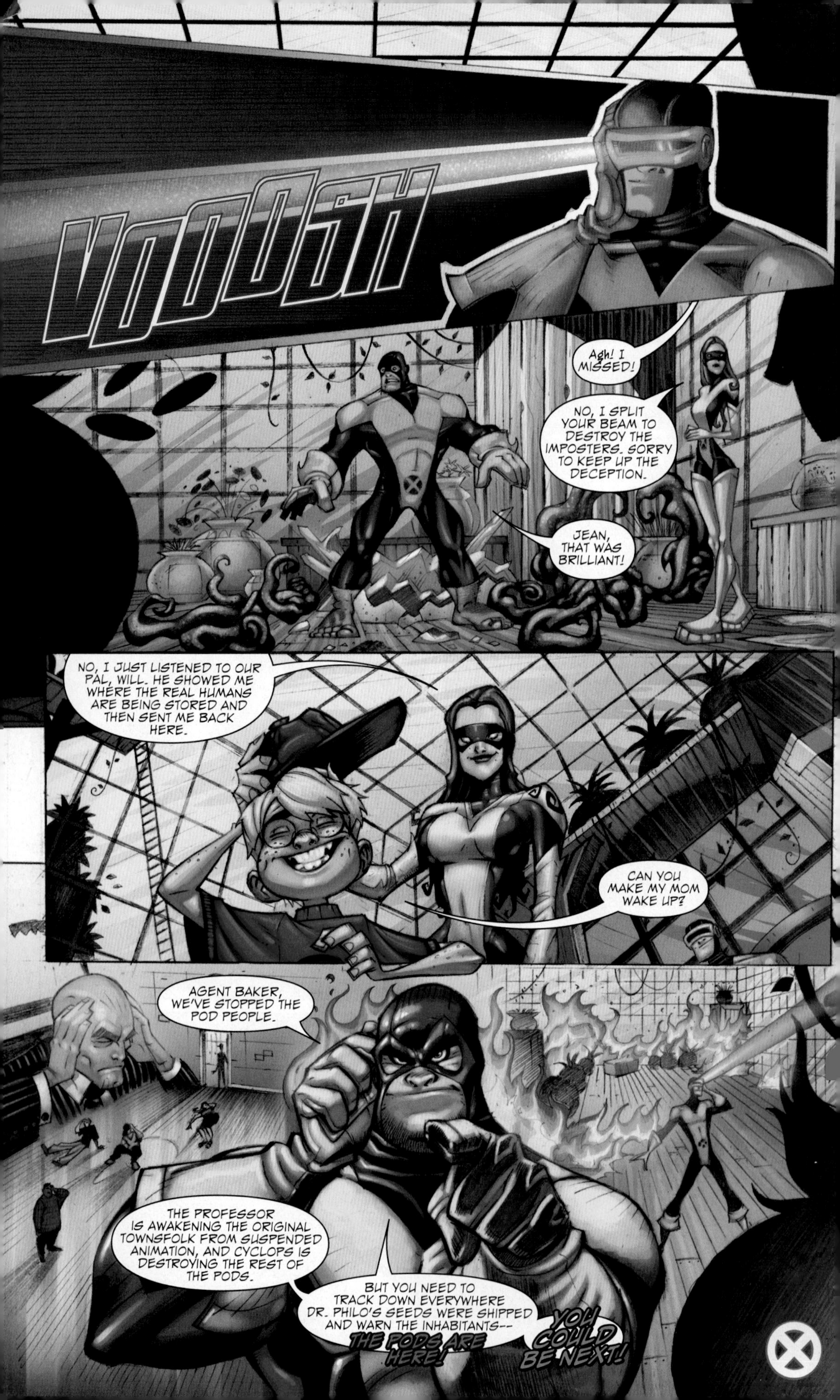
VOOOSH
Agh! I MISSED!
NO, I SPLIT YOUR BEAM TO DESTROY THE IMPOSTERS. SORRY TO KEEP UP THE DECEPTION.
JEAN, THAT WAS BRILLIANT!
NO, I JUST LISTENED TO OUR PAL, WILL. HE SHOWED ME WHERE THE REAL HUMANS ARE BEING STORED AND THEN SENT ME BACK HERE.
CAN YOU MAKE MY MOM WAKE UP?
AGENT BAKER, WE'VE STOPPED THE POD PEOPLE.
THE PROFESSOR IS AWAKENING THE ORIGINAL TOWNSFOLK FROM SUSPENDED ANIMATION, AND CYCLOPS IS DESTROYING THE REST OF THE PODS.
BUT YOU NEED TO TRACK DOWN EVERYWHERE DR. PHILO'S SEEDS WERE SHIPPED AND WARN THE INHABITANTS-- THE PODS ARE HERE!
YOU COULD BE NEXT!

LI'L CHARLIE XAVIER *in*

VIGIL of the MAD

or *The Beastly Child*

by George R. Darling

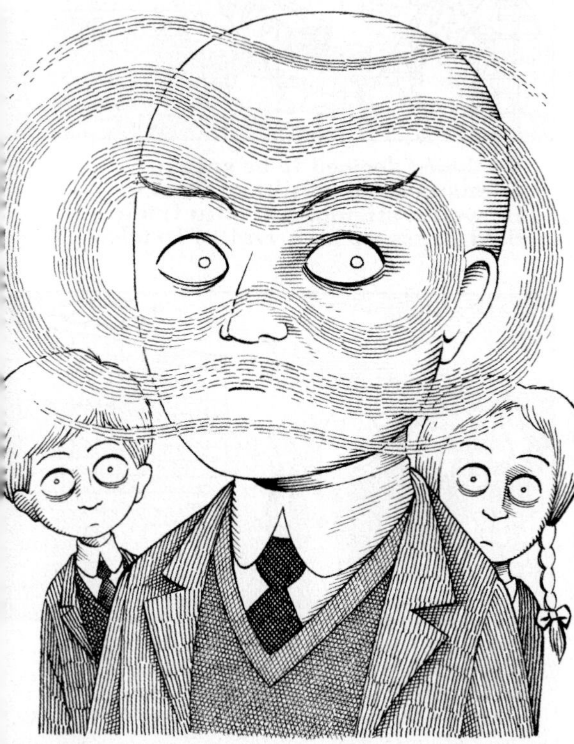

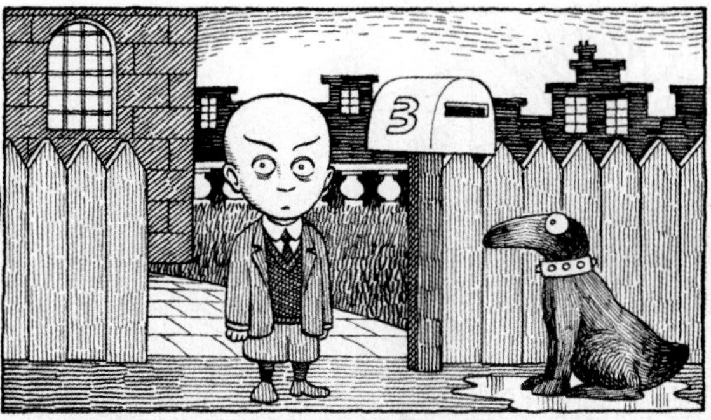
3

In Midwich Street there lived a child
Whose mutant genes made him reviled.
A creepy little boy was he;
Charlie X at Number Three.

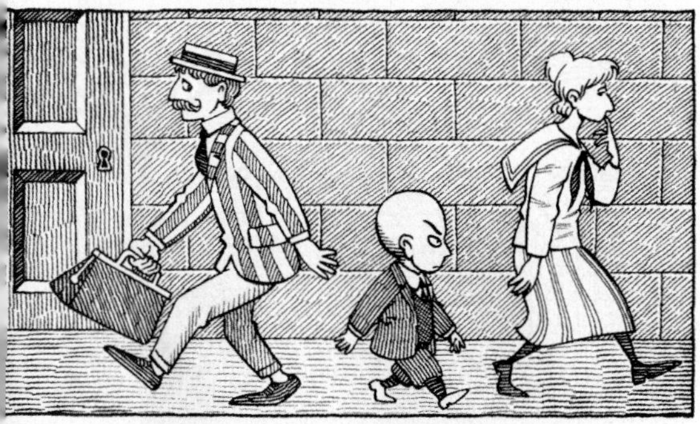

The grown-ups mostly thought him odd
And hurried past with ne'er a nod.
Their presence Xavier seldom missed;
They might as well just not exist.

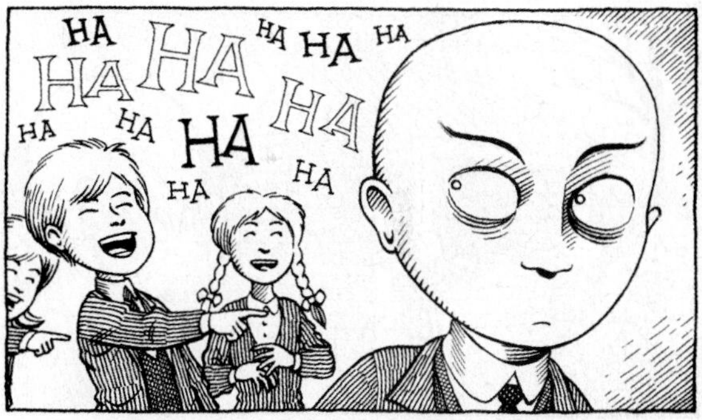
HA
HA HA HA HA HA
HA HA
HA HA HA HA
HA HA

The children, though, were rather worse.
They'd tease and taunt and chant and curse.
His eyebrows caused repellent mirth,
As would his head, for what it's worth.

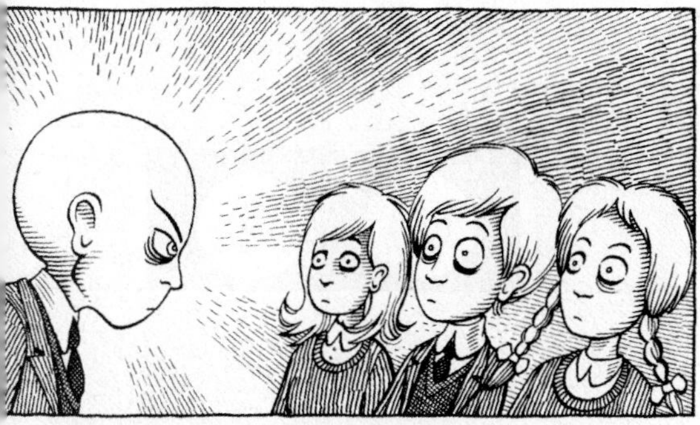

So Charles would use his mighty mind
To punish them for being unkind.
With all his great telepathy
He'd make the others act like he.

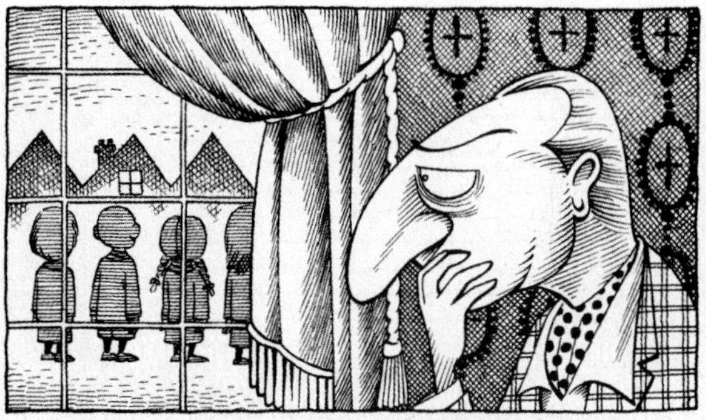

Now, Doctor Jones at Number Four
Had never seen the like before.
Examining this child so bright
Consumed his thoughts both day and night.

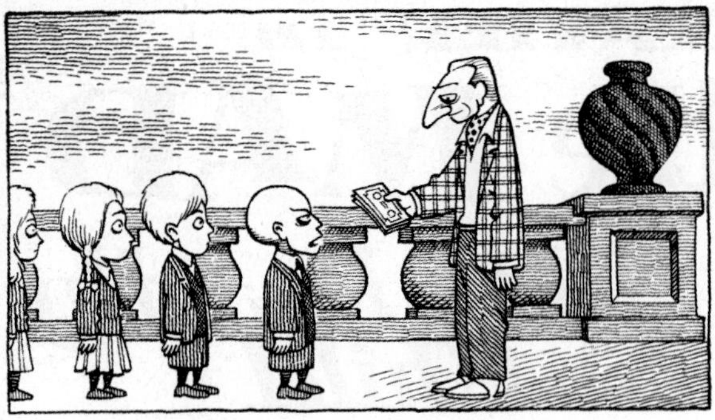

He'd try politeness, try cajoling,
Try delighting, try bankrolling.
Nothing seemed young Charles to sway.
Instead he told him, *"Go away!"*

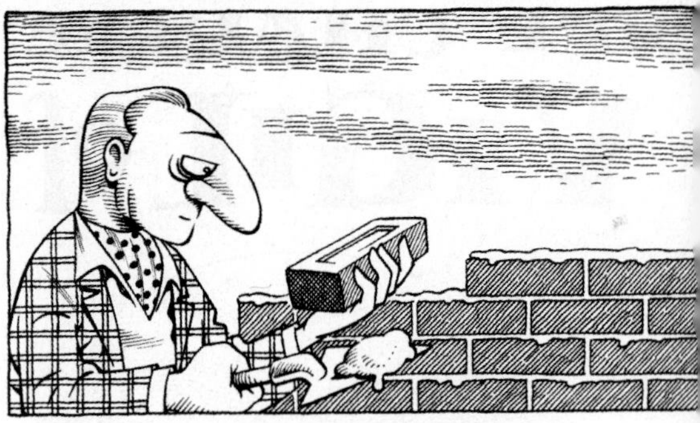

So Jones decided to be sneaky.
To ensnare this child so freaky,
He would attempt a tricky trick—
He'd dress up as a wall of brick.

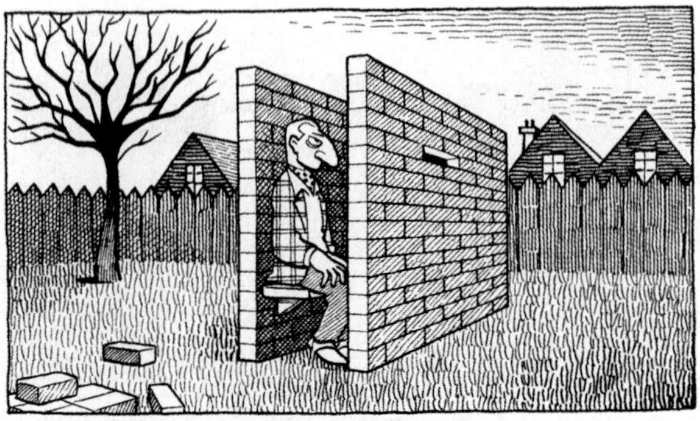

He built it hollow, filled within
With sandwiches and books and gin.
And lastly, on a little shelf,
He filled the wall up with himself.

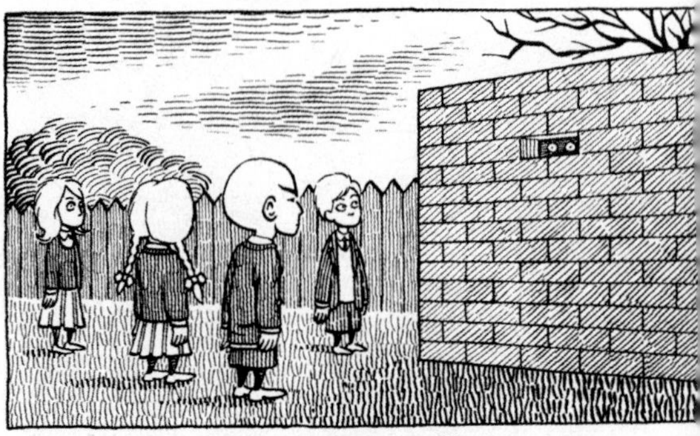

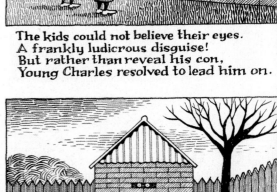

The kids could not believe their eyes.
A frankly ludicrous disguise!
But rather than reveal his con,
Young Charles resolved to lead him on.

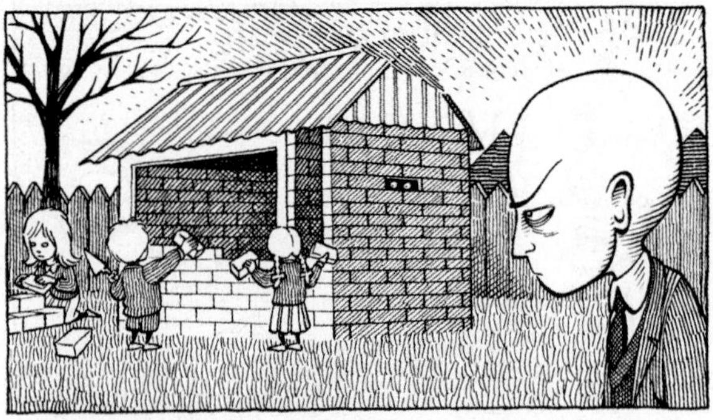

Pretending to believe the ploy,
Charles made each little girl and boy
With mortar, trowel and bricks of red
Convert this wall into a shed.

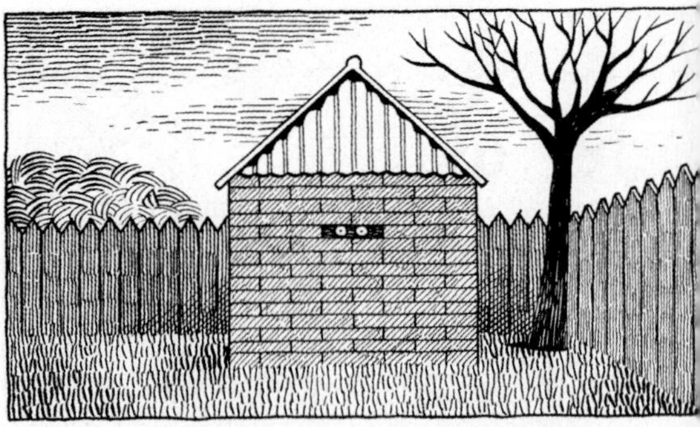

So there stood Jones. He stood until
The cows came home. He stands there still.
Charles quite forgot about the game;
Forgot the wall; forgot Jones' name.

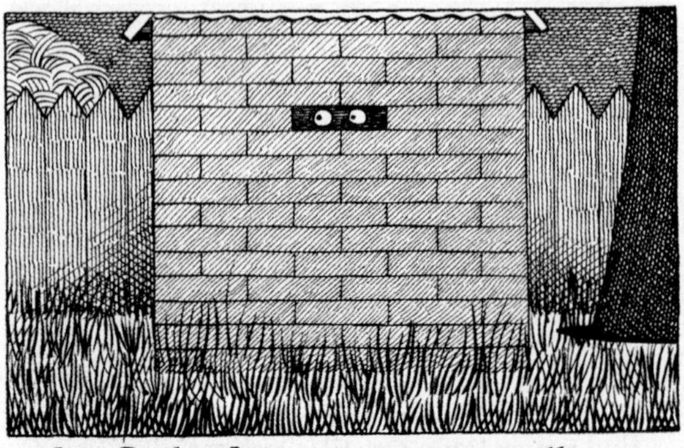

Now Doctor Jones can scarce recall
Of how he once was not a wall.
The grass grows high around his feet.

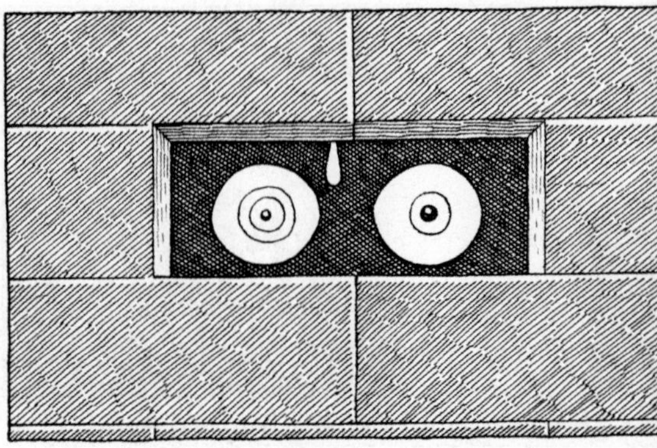

His eyes remain.
Our tale's complete.

END

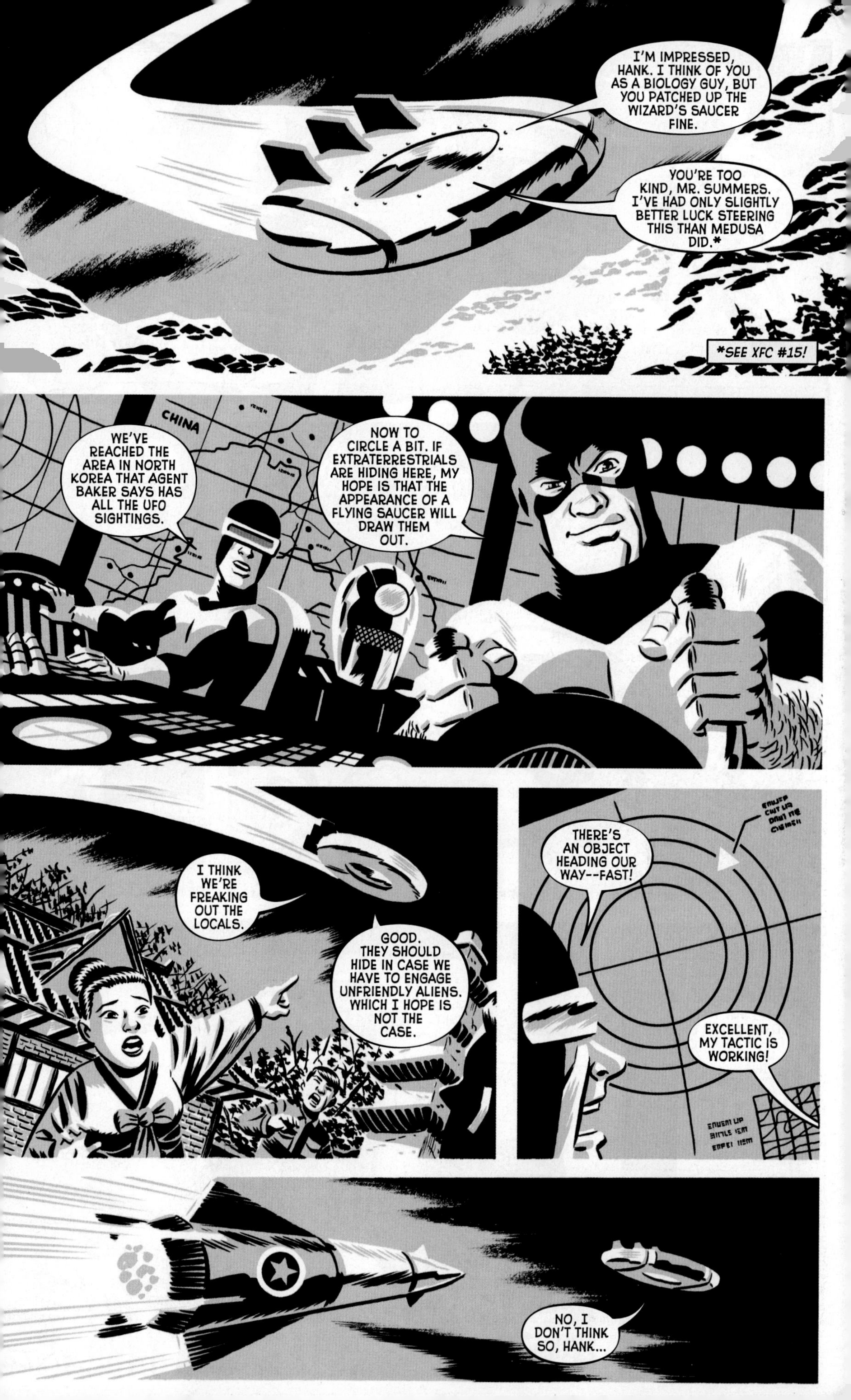
I'M IMPRESSED, HANK. I THINK OF YOU AS A BIOLOGY GUY, BUT YOU PATCHED UP THE WIZARD'S SAUCER FINE.
YOU'RE TOO KIND, MR. SUMMERS. I'VE HAD ONLY SLIGHTLY BETTER LUCK STEERING THIS THAN MEDUSA DID.*
*SEE XFC #15!
CHINA
WE'VE REACHED THE AREA IN NORTH KOREA THAT AGENT BAKER SAYS HAS ALL THE UFO SIGHTINGS.
NOW TO CIRCLE A BIT. IF EXTRATERRESTRIALS ARE HIDING HERE, MY HOPE IS THAT THE APPEARANCE OF A FLYING SAUCER WILL DRAW THEM OUT.
I THINK WE'RE FREAKING OUT THE LOCALS.
GOOD. THEY SHOULD HIDE IN CASE WE HAVE TO ENGAGE UNFRIENDLY ALIENS. WHICH I HOPE IS NOT THE CASE.
THERE'S AN OBJECT HEADING OUR WAY--FAST!
EXCELLENT, MY TACTIC IS WORKING!
NO, I DON'T THINK SO, HANK...

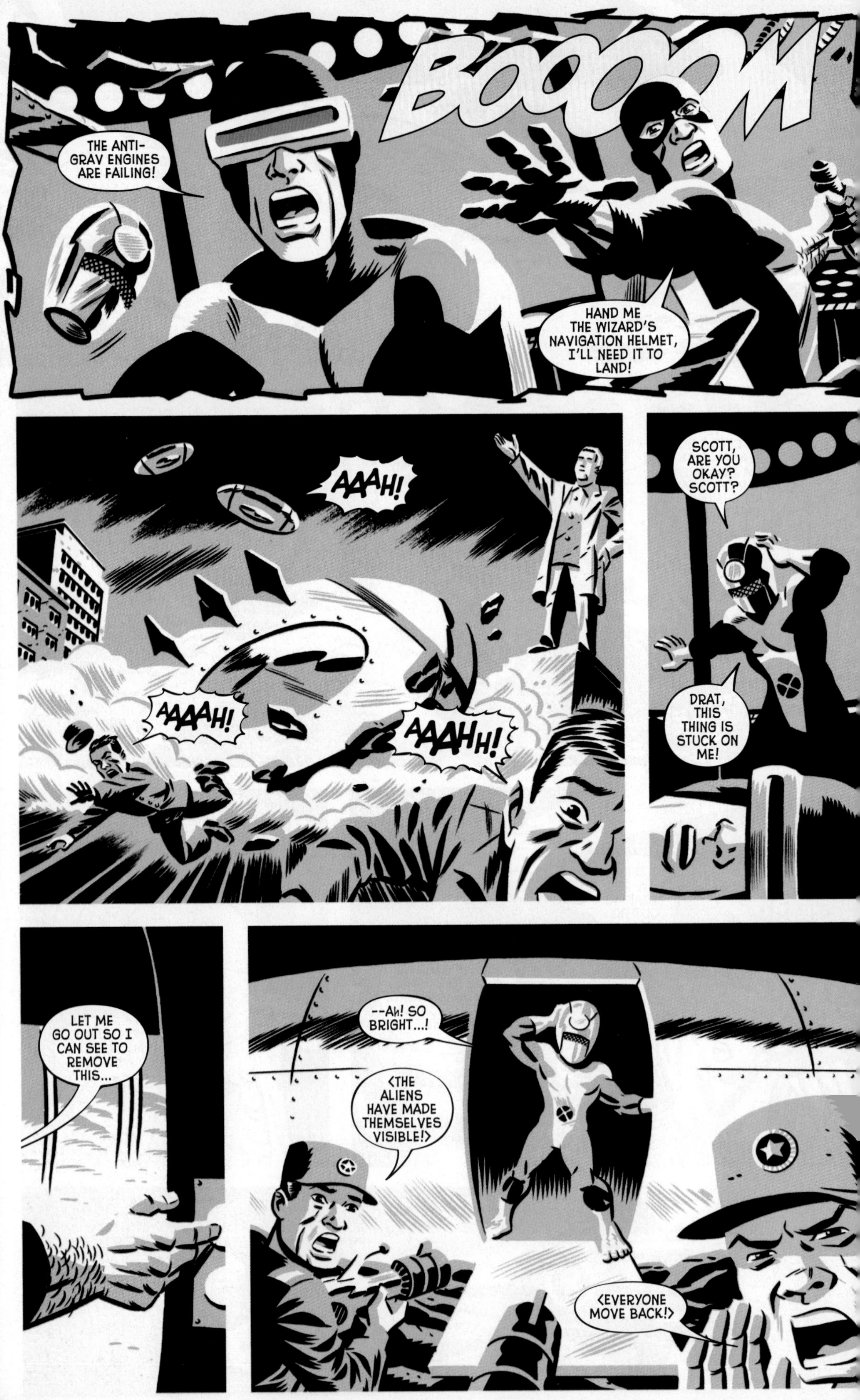
BOOOOM
THE ANTI-GRAV ENGINES ARE FAILING!
HAND ME THE WIZARD'S NAVIGATION HELMET, I'LL NEED IT TO LAND!
AAAH!
AAAAH!
AAAHH!
SCOTT, ARE YOU OKAY? SCOTT?
DRAT, THIS THING IS STUCK ON ME!
LET ME GO OUT SO I CAN SEE TO REMOVE THIS...
--AH! SO BRIGHT...!
<THE ALIENS HAVE MADE THEMSELVES VISIBLE!>
<EVERYONE MOVE BACK!>

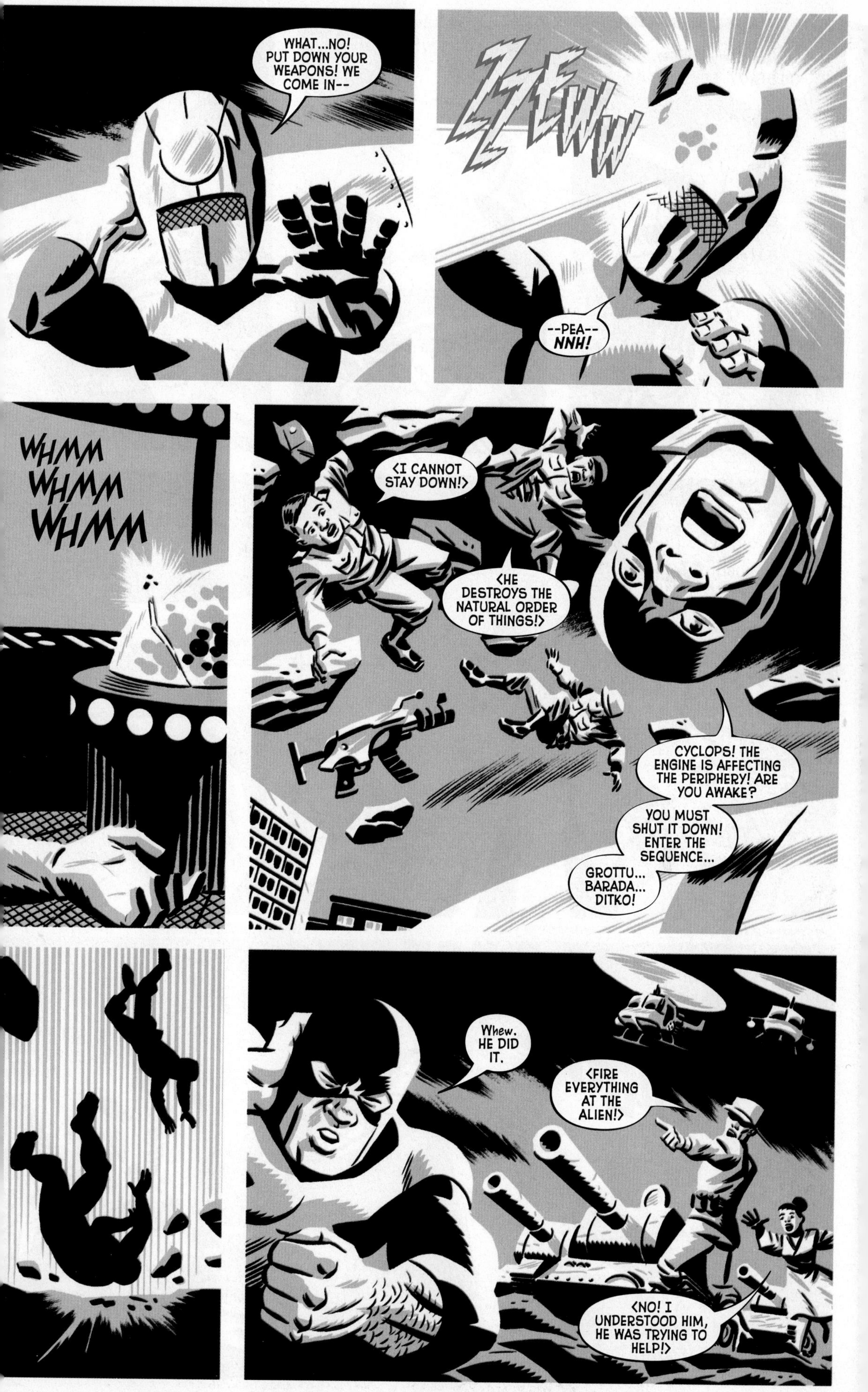
WHAT...NO! PUT DOWN YOUR WEAPONS! WE COME IN--
ZZEWW
--PEA-- NNH!
WHMM WHMM WHMM
<I CANNOT STAY DOWN!>
<HE DESTROYS THE NATURAL ORDER OF THINGS!>
CYCLOPS! THE ENGINE IS AFFECTING THE PERIPHERY! ARE YOU AWAKE?
YOU MUST SHUT IT DOWN! ENTER THE SEQUENCE...
GROTTU... BARADA... DITKO!
Whew. HE DID IT.
<FIRE EVERYTHING AT THE ALIEN!>
<NO! I UNDERSTOOD HIM, HE WAS TRYING TO HELP!>

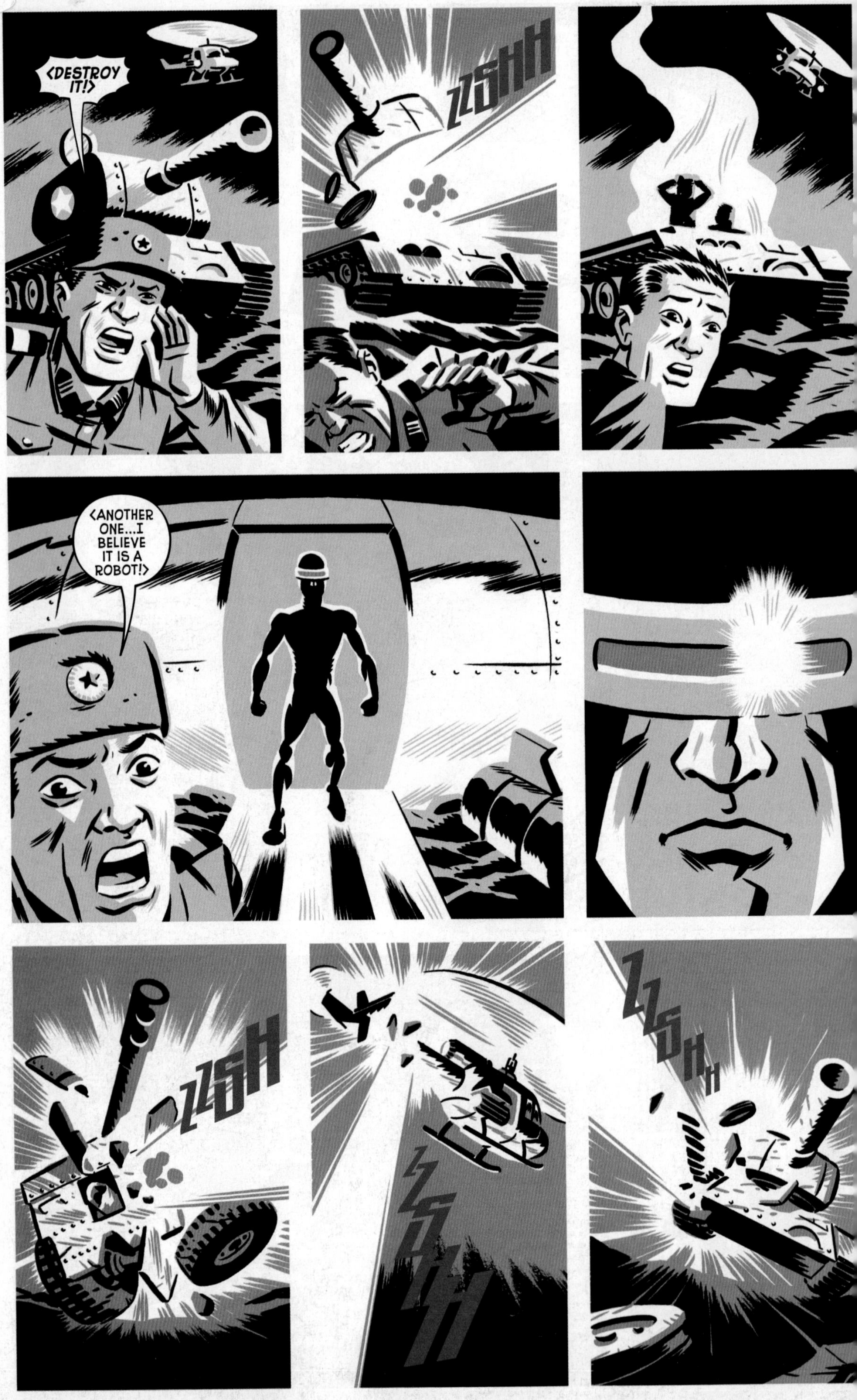
<DESTROY IT!>
ZZSHH
<ANOTHER ONE...I BELIEVE IT IS A ROBOT!>
ZZSH
ZZSHH
ZZSHH

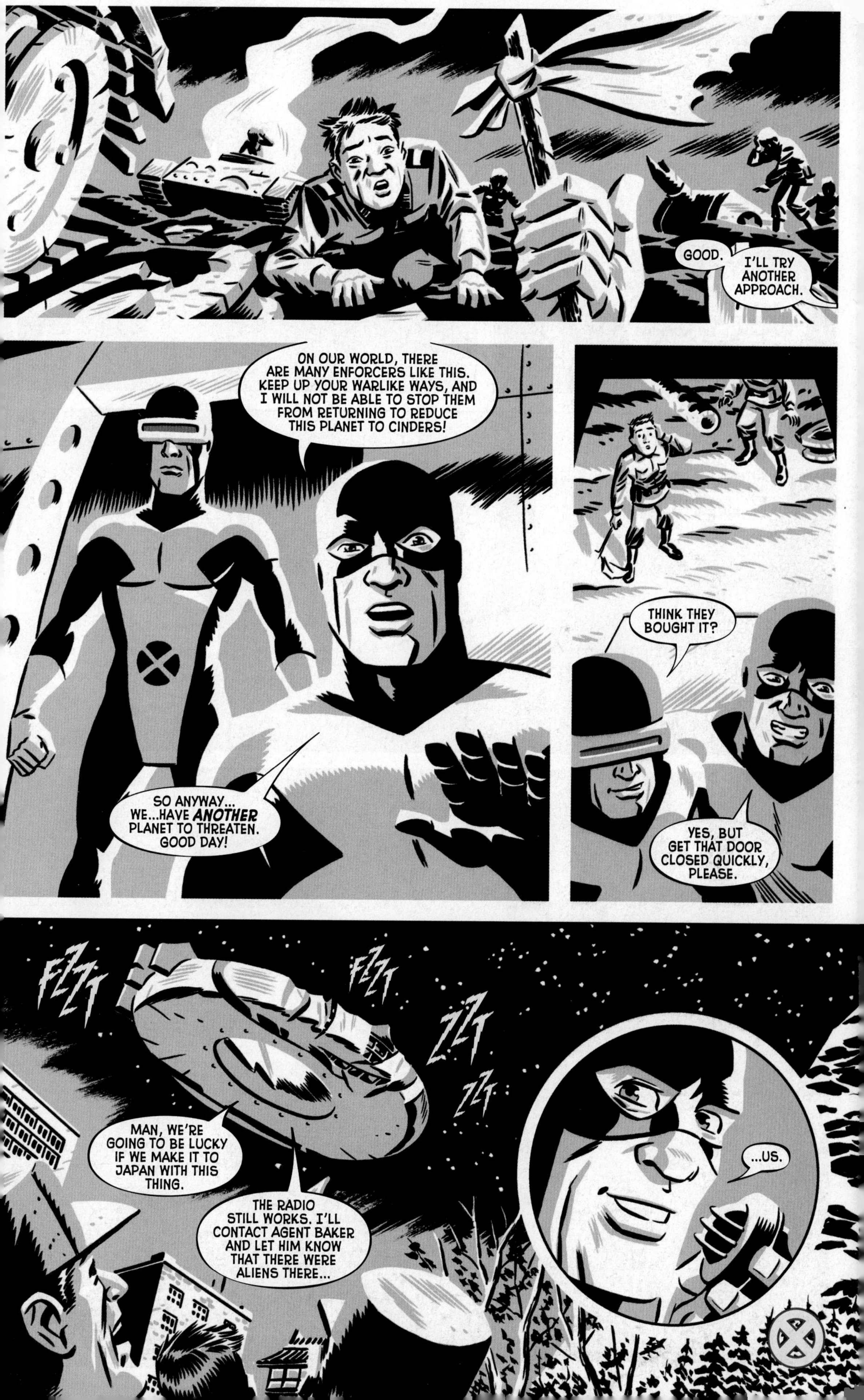
GOOD.
I'LL TRY ANOTHER APPROACH.
ON OUR WORLD, THERE ARE MANY ENFORCERS LIKE THIS. KEEP UP YOUR WARLIKE WAYS, AND I WILL NOT BE ABLE TO STOP THEM FROM RETURNING TO REDUCE THIS PLANET TO CINDERS!
SO ANYWAY... WE...HAVE **ANOTHER** PLANET TO THREATEN. GOOD DAY!
THINK THEY BOUGHT IT?
YES, BUT GET THAT DOOR CLOSED QUICKLY, PLEASE.
FZZT
FZZT
ZZT
ZZT
MAN, WE'RE GOING TO BE LUCKY IF WE MAKE IT TO JAPAN WITH THIS THING.
THE RADIO STILL WORKS. I'LL CONTACT AGENT BAKER AND LET HIM KNOW THAT THERE WERE ALIENS THERE...
...US.

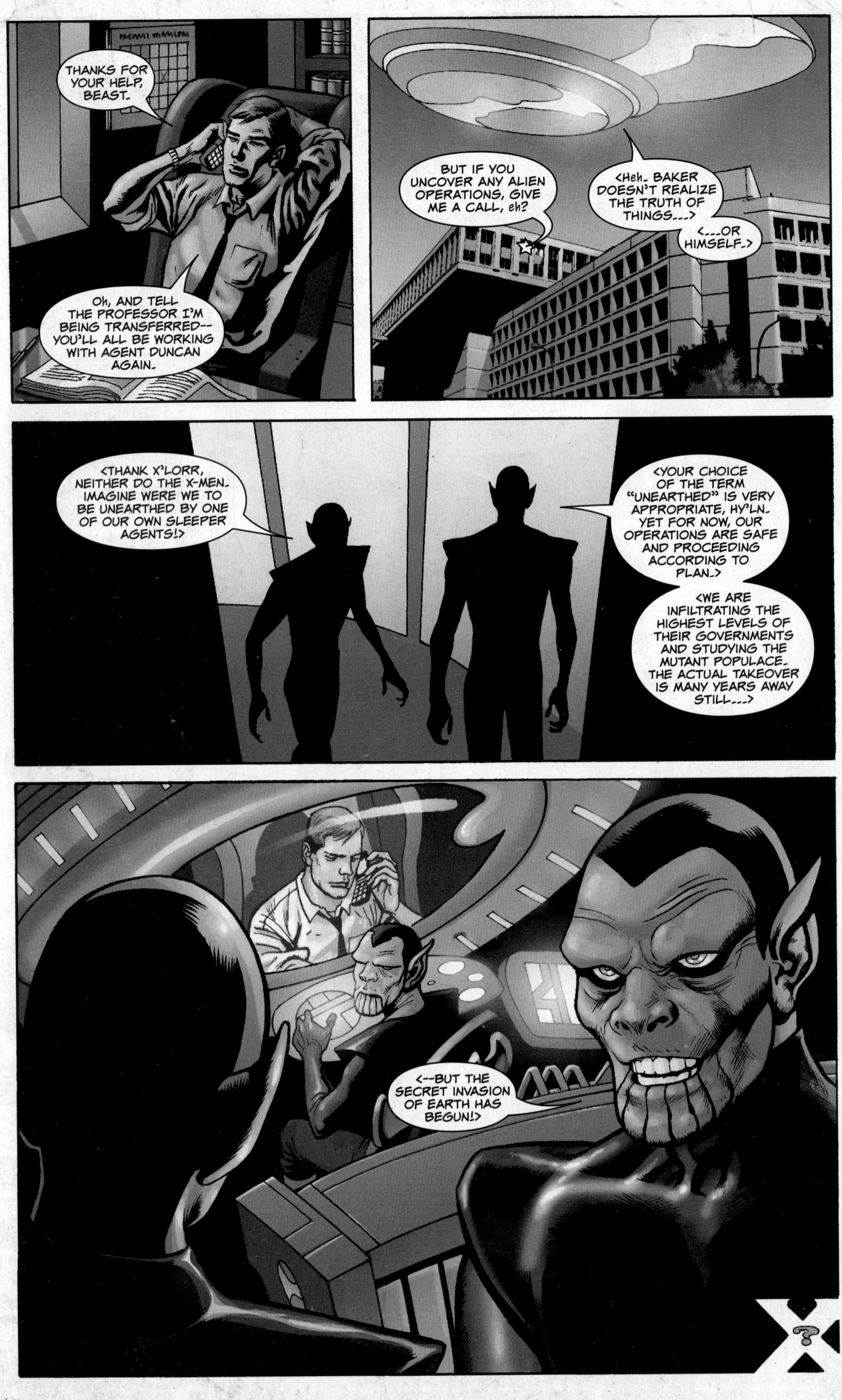

THANKS FOR YOUR HELP, BEAST.
Oh, AND TELL THE PROFESSOR I'M BEING TRANSFERRED-- YOU'LL ALL BE WORKING WITH AGENT DUNCAN AGAIN.
BUT IF YOU UNCOVER ANY ALIEN OPERATIONS, GIVE ME A CALL, eh?
<Heh. BAKER DOESN'T REALIZE THE TRUTH OF THINGS...>
<...OR HIMSELF.>
<THANK X'LORR, NEITHER DO THE X-MEN. IMAGINE WERE WE TO BE UNEARTHED BY ONE OF OUR OWN SLEEPER AGENTS!>
<YOUR CHOICE OF THE TERM "UNEARTHED" IS VERY APPROPRIATE, HY'LN. YET FOR NOW, OUR OPERATIONS ARE SAFE AND PROCEEDING ACCORDING TO PLAN.>
<WE ARE INFILTRATING THE HIGHEST LEVELS OF THEIR GOVERNMENTS AND STUDYING THE MUTANT POPULACE. THE ACTUAL TAKEOVER IS MANY YEARS AWAY STILL...>
<--BUT THE SECRET INVASION OF EARTH HAS BEGUN!>